Second Edition

Comparative
Education Research

Approaches and Methods

CERC Studies in Comparative Education

31. Bob Adamson, Jon Nixon and Feng Su (eds.) (2012): *The Reorientation of Higher Education: Challenging the East-West Dichotomy.* ISBN 978-988-17852-7-5. 314pp. HK$250/US$38.

30. Ruth Hayhoe, Jun Li, Jing Lin & Qiang Zha (2011): *Portraits of 21st Century Chinese Universities: In the Move to Mass Higher Education.* ISBN 978-988-17852-3-7. 483pp. HK$300/US$45.

29. Maria Manzon (2011): *Comparative Education: The Construction of a Field.* ISBN 978-988-17852-6-8. 295pp. HK$200/US$32.

28. Kerry J. Kennedy, Wing On Lee & David L. Grossman (eds.) (2010): *Citizenship Pedagogies in Asia and the Pacific.* ISBN 978-988-17852-2-0. 407pp. HK$250/US$38.

27. David Chapman, William K. Cummings & Gerard A. Postiglione (eds.) (2010): *Crossing Borders in East Asian Higher Education.* ISBN 978-962-8093-98-4. 388pp. HK$250/US$38.

26. Ora Kwo (ed.) (2010): *Teachers as Learners: Critical Discourse on Challenges and Opportunities.* ISBN 978-962-8093-55-7. 349pp. HK$250/US$38.

25. Carol K.K. Chan & Nirmala Rao (eds.) (2009): *Revisiting the Chinese Learner: Changing Contexts, Changing Education.* ISBN 978-962-8093-16-8. 360pp. HK$250/US$38.

24. Donald B. Holsinger & W. James Jacob (eds.) (2008): *Inequality in Education: Comparative and International Perspectives.* ISBN 978-962-8093-14-4. 584pp. HK$300/US$45.

23. Nancy Law, Willem J Pelgrum & Tjeerd Plomp (eds.) (2008): *Pedagogy and ICT Use in Schools around the World: Findings from the IEA SITES 2006 Study.* ISBN 978-962-8093-65-6. 296pp. HK$250/US$38.

22. David L. Grossman, Wing On Lee & Kerry J. Kennedy (eds.) (2008): *Citizenship Curriculum in Asia and the Pacific.* ISBN 978-962-8093-69-4. 268pp. HK$200/US$32.

21. Vandra Masemann, Mark Bray & Maria Manzon (eds.) (2007): *Common Interests, Uncommon Goals: Histories of the World Council of Comparative Education Societies and its Members.* ISBN 978-962-8093-10-6. 384pp. HK$250/US$38.

20. Peter D. Hershock, Mark Mason & John N. Hawkins (eds.) (2007): *Changing Education: Lead-ership, Innovation and Development in a Globalizing Asia Pacific.* ISBN 978-962-8093-54-0. 348pp. HK$200/US$32.

19. Mark Bray, Bob Adamson & Mark Mason (eds.) (2014): *Comparative Education Research: Approaches and Methods.* Second edition. ISBN 978-988-17852-8-2. 453pp. HK$250/US$38.

18. Aaron Benavot & Cecilia Braslavsky (eds.) (2006): *School Knowledge in Comparative and Historical Perspective: Changing Curricula in Primary and Secondary Education.* ISBN 978-962-8093-52-6. 315pp. HK$200/US$32.

17. Ruth Hayhoe (2006): *Portraits of Influential Chinese Educators.* ISBN 978-962-8093-40-3. 398pp. HK$250/US$38.

16. Peter Ninnes & Meeri Hellstén (eds.) (2005): *Internationalizing Higher Education: Critical Explorations of Pedagogy and Policy.* ISBN 978-962-8093-37-3. 231pp. HK$200/US$32.

15. Alan Rogers (2004): *Non-Formal Education: Flexible Schooling or Participatory Education?* ISBN 978-962-8093-30-4. 316pp. HK$200/US$32.

Earlier titles in the series are listed on the back page of the book.

CERC Studies in Comparative Education 19

Second Edition

Comparative Education Research

Approaches and Methods

Edited by Mark Bray, Bob Adamson, Mark Mason

Comparative Education Research Centre
The University of Hong Kong

Springer

SERIES EDITOR
Mark Bray, *Director, Comparative Education Research Centre*
The University of Hong Kong, China

ASSOCIATE EDITOR
Yang Rui, *Comparative Education Research Centre*
The University of Hong Kong, China

INTERNATIONAL EDITORIAL ADVISORY BOARD
Robert Arnove, *Indiana University, USA*
Nina Borevskaya, *Institute of the Far East, Moscow, Russia*
Michael Crossley, *University of Bristol, United Kingdom*
Jiang Kai, *Peking University, Beijing, China*
Cristian Pérez Centeno, *Universidad Nacional de Tres de Febrero, Argentina*
Gita Steiner-Khamsi, *Teachers College, Columbia University, USA*

PRODUCTION EDITOR
Emily Mang, *Comparative Education Research Centre*
The University of Hong Kong, China

Comparative Education Research Centre
Faculty of Education, The University of Hong Kong
Pokfulam Road, Hong Kong, China

Second edition © Comparative Education Research Centre 2014

First edition published 2007
ISBN 978-988-17852-8-2   Paperback

COVER
Detail, "Autumn School", from an impressionist landscape by Vietnamese artist,
Dao Hai Phong, reproduced with the kind permission of the painting's owners,
Richard and Louisa Barton.
    Dao Hai Phong was born in Hanoi in 1965 and graduated from the Hanoi
College of Fine Art in 1987. Village scenes and depictions of Hanoi streets
executed in very bright colours such as blue, yellow, green or red are charac-
teristic of his paintings. Phong's work has been exhibited in Hanoi, Hong Kong,
Italy, Laos, Singapore, Switzerland, the UK and the USA.

Printed and bound by The Central Printing Press Ltd. in Hong Kong, China

Contents

List of Tables

List of Figures

Abbreviations

ACER   Australian Council for Educational Research
ACSA   Australian Curriculum Studies Association
ACTEQ   Advisory Committee on Teacher Education & Qualifications
ANOVA   analysis of variance
ANZCIES   Australian and New Zealand Comparative and International Education Society
APEC   Asia-Pacific Economic Cooperation
ASI   Approaches to Studying Inventory
BAICE   British Association for Comparative and International Education
CERC   Comparative Education Research Centre [HKU]
CES   Comparative Education Society
CIES   Comparative and International Education Society
CIESC   Comparative and International Education Society of Canada
CoREF   Renovating Education of the Future Project
CPD   Continuing Professional Development
DFID   Department for International Development
DSS   Direct Subsidy Scheme
EFA   Education for All
ESCS   economic, social and cultural status
ESF   English Schools Foundation
EU   European Union
GDP   Gross Domestic Product
GEEI   Gender Equality in Education Index
GEI   Gender Equality Index
GPI   Gender Parity Index
GSP   Gross State Product
IAEP   International Assessment of Educational Progress
IALS   International Adult Literacy Survey
IBE   International Bureau of Education

IBRD	International Bank for Reconstruction and Development
ICCS	International Civic and Citizenship Education Study
ICT	Information and Communication Technology
IEA	International Association for the Evaluation of Educational Achievement
IESALC	International Institute for Higher Education in Latin America and the Caribbean
IICBA	International Institute for Capacity-Building in Africa
IIEP	International Institute for Educational Planning
IITE	Institute for Information Technologies in Education
IMF	International Monetary Fund
INES	Indicators of Education Systems programme [OECD]
IRE	*International Review of Education*
ITL	Innovative Teaching and Learning Research
JRC-IPTS	Institute for Prospective Technological Studies of the European Commission's Joint Research Centre
KCES	Korean Comparative Education Society
LAs	learning activities
LASW	Learning Activities and Student Work
LPQ	Learning Process Questionnaire
LPS	Laboratorio di Pedagogia sperimentale
MDGs	Millennium Development Goals
MGIEP	Mahatma Gandhi Institute of Education for Peace and Sustainable Development
MoE	Ministry of Education
NAEP	National Assessment of Educational Progress
NAFTA	North American Free Trade Agreement
NFER	National Foundation for Educational Research
NLPN	National Literacy Programme in Namibia
OECD	Organisation for Economic Co-operation and Development
OFSTED	Office for Standards in Education
PIRLS	Progress in International Reading Literacy Study
PISA	Programme for International Student Assessment
PRC	People's Republic of China
QUEST	Quality in Educational Systems Trans-nationally
SACMEQ	Southern and Eastern Africa Consortium for Monitoring Educational Quality
SAR	Special Administrative Region

SAT	Scholastic Aptitude Test
SCALE CCR	Scalability of Creative Classrooms Study
SES	socioeconomic status
SFSO	Swiss Federal Statistics Office
SITES	Second International Technology in Education Study
SPQ	Study Process Questionnaire
SW	student work
TBL	Task-based Learning
TIMSS	Third [also Trends in] International Mathematics and Science Study
UCES	Ukraine Comparative Education Society
UIL	UNESCO Institute for Lifelong Learning
UIS	UNESCO Institute for Statistics
UK	United Kingdom
UN	United Nations
UNESCO	United Nations Educational, Scientific and Cultural Organization
UNICEF	United Nations Children's Fund
USA	United States of America
USAID	United States Agency for International Development
WCCES	World Council of Comparative Education Societies
WIDE	World Inequality Database on Education

Preface

This is the second edition of a book first published in 2007. The editors, authors and co-publishers were delighted with the reception of the first edition. It has been reviewed very positively in 25 academic journals, and has been adopted as a core text for courses in comparative education in all continents of the world. The book has been translated into Chinese, Farsi, French, Italian, Japanese and Spanish, and presented in multiple conferences of member associations of the World Council of Comparative Education Societies (WCCES). As such, the book has contributed to discourses in a wide range of locations and languages.

This second edition of the book in turn benefits from these discourses. The book has been updated and elaborated, particularly with a new chapter on race, class and gender in comparative education. For reasons of length, some parts of the first edition have been omitted, but they can of course still be located in the original version.

Feedback from students, professors and reviewers in academic journals has indicated that the discussion of different units for comparison has been considered especially valuable. A starting point for the book and for some chapters has been a cube presented by Bray and Thomas (1995) which stressed in three-dimensional form the value of multi-level analyses. Both the first edition and this second edition of the book re-evaluate the cube in the context of developments in the field of comparative education. The discussions show that indeed the cube remains useful, though – as recognised originally by Bray and Thomas – it cannot embrace all types of comparative studies and many alternative approaches are desirable.

One of the most detailed reviews of the book was written by Sultana (2011), who explained that he approached the volume from the perspective of the academic leader of a Masters course in comparative education. He had encountered difficulties in selecting a core book for the course, since many comparative education texts adopt either a thematic approach or are country- or region-focused. The present book, he felt, was "refreshingly different" (p.329). He appreciated the framing chapters in Part

xv

I and the concluding remarks in Part III, and especially valued the Units of Comparison in Part II. This, indeed, has been much welcomed by other readers (e.g. Kubow 2007; Langouët 2011). It has therefore been retained in this second edition.

The contributors both to the original and this second edition of the book are all in some way linked to the Comparative Education Research Centre at the University of Hong Kong. The Centre was established in 1994, and is proud to have established a significant reputation. Partly because of the Centre's geographic and cultural location, many chapters give examples from East Asia. At the same time, the book has a global message that also draws on examples from all other regions of the world. This also was among the features that particularly attracted Sultana (2011, p.330), and we hope will prove equally attractive to other readers.

The field of comparative education is dynamic and is evolving in significant ways. We hope through the second edition of this book both to reflect and to contribute to such dynamism.

The Editors

References

Bray, Mark & Thomas, R. Murray (1995): 'Levels of Comparison in Educational Studies: Different Insights from Different Literatures and the Value of Multilevel Analyses'. *Harvard Educational Review*, Vol.65, No.3, pp.472-490.

Kubow, Patricia K. (2007): Review of *Comparative Education Research: Approaches and Methods*, in *Comparative Education Review*, Vol.51, No.4, pp.534-537.

Langouët, Gabriel (2011): 'Recensions', *La revue française d'éducation comparée*, No.7, pp.145-148.

Sultana, Ronald (2011): 'Review Article - Comparative Education: Initiating Novices into the Field', *International Journal of Educational Development*, Vol.31, No.3, pp.329-332.

Introduction

Mark BRAY, Bob ADAMSON & Mark MASON

Approaches and methods have naturally been a major concern in the field of comparative education since its emergence as a distinct domain of studies. Different decades have witnessed different emphases, and the 21ˢᵗ century has brought new perspectives, tools and forums for scholarly exchange. The new perspectives include those arising from the forces of globalisation and the changing role of the state. The new tools include ever-advancing information and transportation technology; and the new forums for scholarly exchange include the internet and electronic journals.

Setting the scene for this book, this Introduction begins with historical perspectives. It highlights some classic works in the field, and notes dimensions of evolution over time. Although many different categories of people may undertake comparative studies of education, these remarks focus chiefly on the work of academics, since that is the main concern of the book. The Introduction then turns to patterns in the new century, observing emerging dynamics and emphases. Finally, it focuses on the contents of the book, charting some of its features and contributions.

Some Historical Perspectives

At the beginning of his classic book, *Comparative Method in Education*, George Bereday (1964, p.7) asserted that from the viewpoint of method, comparative education was entering the third phase of its history. The first phase, he suggested, spanned the 19ᵗʰ century, "was inaugurated by the first scientifically minded comparative educator, Marc-Antoine Jullien de Paris in 1817", and might be called the period of borrowing. Bereday characterised its emphasis as cataloguing descriptive data, following which comparison of the data was undertaken in order to make available the best practices of one country with the intention of copying them elsewhere.

Bereday's second phase, which occupied the first half of the 20th century, "interposed a preparatory process before permitting any trans-plantation". Its founder, Sir Michael Sadler in the United Kingdom (UK), stressed that education systems are intricately connected with the socie-ties that support them (see especially Sadler 1900). Sadler's successors, among whom Bereday identified Friedrich Schneider and Franz Hilker in Germany, Isaac Kandel and Robert Ulich in the United States of America (USA), Nicholas Hans and Joseph Lauwerys in the UK, and Pedro Ros-selló in Switzerland, all paid much attention to the social causes behind educational phenomena. Bereday named this second phase the period of prediction.

Bereday's third phase was labelled the period of analysis, with emphasis on "the evolving of theory and methods, [and] the clear for-mulation of steps of comparative procedures and devices to aid this en-largement of vision". The new historical period, Bereday added (1964, p.9), was a continuation of the tradition of the period of prediction, but it postulated that "before prediction and eventual borrowing is attempted there must be a systematization of the field in order to expose the whole panorama of national practices of education". Bereday's book itself greatly contributed to this analytical approach. The book remains core reading in many courses on comparative education, and still has much to offer. Indeed one contributor to this volume (Manzon, Chapter 4) com-mences with Bereday's four-step method of comparative analysis.

However, even at that time not all scholars agreed with the catego-risation of periods that Bereday presented. Nor, if they did accept the categorisation, did they necessarily agree that the phases were sequential in which the period of prediction had followed and displaced the period of borrowing, and in turn the period of analysis had followed and dis-placed the period of prediction.

Similar remarks may be made about the set of five stages in the de-velopment of the field presented in 1969 in another classic work entitled *Toward a Science of Comparative Education* (Noah & Eckstein 1969, pp.3-7). The first stage was travellers' tales, in which amateurs presented infor-mation on foreign ways of raising children as part of broader descriptions of institutions and practices abroad. The second stage, which became prominent from the beginning of the 19th century, was of educational borrowing; and was followed by the third stage of encyclopaedic work on foreign countries in the interests of international understanding. From the beginning of the 20th century, Noah and Eckstein suggested (p.4), two more stages occurred, both concerned with seeking explanations for the wide variety of educational and social phenomena observed around the globe. The first attempted to identify the forces and factors shaping national educational systems; and the second was termed the stage of social science explanation, which "uses the empirical, quantitative methods of economics, political science, and sociology to clarify relationships between education and society".

The characterisation was widely agreed to have been useful, but the presentation of stages as sequential, with later ones displacing earlier ones, was less widely affirmed. To be fair, Noah and Eckstein did themselves state (p.4) that the stages were far from being discrete in time, and that "each of these types of work in comparative education has persisted down to the present and may be observed in the contemporary literature". However, their characterisation of different historical periods had greater emphasis than this remark about the co-existence of different stages. With the benefit of a few more decades of hindsight, it is apparent that all five categories remain very evident in the literature. For some individual scholars they might provide roughly distinguishable stages in personal career development, with gradation from simplistic notions to more sophisticated analyses; but the field as a whole remains eclectic and disparate in approaches and degrees of sophistication.

Nevertheless, with this pair of books and related works in the 1960s (e.g. King 1964; Bristow & Holmes 1968), the field of comparative education embarked on a period of considerable debate about methodology. The debate was not conducted evenly in all parts of the world, and patterns in English-speaking countries were very different from ones for example in Arabic-speaking, Russian-speaking or Chinese-speaking countries (Benhamida 1990; Djourinski 1998; Wang 1998). Yet scholarship in English-speaking countries exerted significant leadership, and thus deserves particular comment. Moreover, even in that era – a pattern which has become even more visible during the present century – English was asserting itself as a language of international discourse for scholars from multiple linguistic traditions. Thus, for example, another important work in English emerged from a 1971 meeting of international experts at the UNESCO Institute for Education in Hamburg, Germany. The meeting was convened by Tetsuya Kobayashi, a distinguished Japanese scholar of comparative education who at that time was Director of the Institute, and brought together participants from Germany, France, Israel, Poland, Sweden and Switzerland, as well as from such English-speaking countries as Canada, the UK and the USA.

The resulting book, entitled *Relevant Methods in Comparative Education* (Edwards et al. 1973), both illustrated and contributed to the debates about methodology in comparative education, and can be considered another milestone. For example, Barber (1973, p.57) attacked Noah and Eckstein's notion of a science of comparative education as being too positivist and controlled; Halls (1973, p.119) described comparative educators as having an identity crisis with their multiple labels such as 'inductive', 'problem-solving', and 'quantificatory'; and Noonan (1973, p.199) argued for the alternative paradigm represented by the emerging work of the International Association for the Evaluation of Educational Achievement (IEA).

Similar diversity was evident in the 1977 special issue of the US journal *Comparative Education Review* on 'The State of the Art' (Vol.21, Nos. 2 and 3, 1977); and the parallel special issue of the UK journal *Comparative Education* on 'Comparative Education: Its Present State and Future Prospects' (Vol.13, No.2, 1977). The editors of the UK journal would no doubt have agreed with the introductory statement by their US counterparts (Kazamias & Schwartz 1977, p.151):

> Uncertainties about the nature, scope, and value of comparative education were sounded in the mid-1950's when the foundations were laid for its promotion as a respected field of study. Yet at that time it was still possible to identify individuals who were recognized as authoritative spokesmen for this area and writings (texts) which defined its contours and codified its subject matter. Such was the case, for example, with I.L. Kandel and his books *Comparative Education* (1933) and *The New Era in Education* (1955), and Nicholas Hans with his *Comparative Education: A Study of Educational Factors and Traditions* (1949). Today such identifications are no longer possible. There is no internally consistent body of knowledge, no set of principles or canons of research that are generally agreed upon by people who associate themselves with the field. Instead, one finds various strands of thought, theories, trends or concerns, not necessarily related to each other.

A decade later, a follow-up collection of papers that had been published in *Comparative Education Review* since the 1977 State of the Art issue suggested that the field had broadened yet further. The editors (Altbach & Kelly 1986, p.1) observed that:

> There is no one method of study in the field; rather, the field increasingly is characterized by a number of different research orientations. No longer are there attempts to define a single methodology of comparative education, and none of our contributors argues that one single method be developed as a canon.

For example, within the book Masemann (1986) argued for critical ethnography; Theisen et al. (1986) focused on the underachievement of cross-national studies of educational achievement; and Epstein (1986) discussed ideology in comparative education under the heading 'Currents Left and Right'. The final chapter by the editors of the book (Kelly & Altbach 1986, p.310) asserted that four kinds of challenges to established research traditions had emerged:

- challenges to the nation state or national characteristics as the major parameter in defining comparative study;
- questioning of input-output models and exclusive reliance on quantification in the conduct of comparative research;
- challenges to structural functionalism as the major theoretical premise under-girding scholarship; and
- new subjects of enquiry, such as knowledge generation and utilisation, student flows, gender, and the internal workings of schools.

The editors also asserted (Altbach & Kelly 1986, p.1) that scholars had begun to address intranational comparisons as well as transnational ones. However, the book did not provide strong evidence to support this statement. Certainly the field has moved to embrace much more intranational work, some of which is remarked upon in the pages of this book; but in general this was a feature of the 1990s and after, rather than the 1980s and before.

Perspectives for the New Century

In 2000, the UK journal *Comparative Education* published another special issue entitled 'Comparative Education for the Twenty-First Century' (Vol.36, No.3, 2000). It appraised the development of the field since the

1977 special issue mentioned above, and in that connection the opening paper by Crossley and Jarvis (2000, p.261) observed that:

> The significance of continuity with the past emerges as a core theme in the collective articles and many contributions echo a number of still fundamental issues raised previously in 1977. Most notably these include: the multi-disciplinary and applied strengths of the field; 'the complexities of this kind of study'; the dangers of the 'misapplication of findings'; the importance of theoretical analysis and methodological rigour; the (often unrealised and misunderstood) policy-oriented potential; and the enduring centrality of the concepts of cultural context and educational transfer for the field as a whole.

At the same time, Crossley and Jarvis noted that the world had changed significantly. They noted (p.261) that most contributors to the special issue in 2000 saw the future of the field in a more optimistic but more problematic light than had been the case in 1977. This was attributed to a combination of factors, and in particular to:

> the exponential growth and widening of interest in international comparative research, the impact of computerised communications and information technologies, increased recognition of the cultural dimension of education, and the influence of the intensification of globalisation upon all dimensions of society and social policy world-wide.

Indeed these factors had become of increased importance, and the trajectory has continued into the present decade.

The ever-advancing spread of technology has greatly improved access to materials and, despite concerns about the 'digital divide', has reduced the disadvantages faced by scholars in locations remote from libraries and other sources of data. As observed by Wilson (2003, p.30):

> The advent of web pages at international organisations and national statistical services has revolutionised how basic research is undertaken in our field. The development of Internet search engines … has also transformed our research capabilities.

At the same time, technology has spread the influence of the field, making the findings and insights from comparative educators available to a much larger audience than was previously the case through electronic journals, websites and other media. The internet does, however, bring its own baggage, including an emphasis on English that contributes to the dominance of that language (Mouhoubi 2005; Tietze & Dick 2013).

Also of particular significance are shifts in the global centres of gravity. The main roots of the field are commonly considered to lie in Western Europe, from which they branched to the USA. Subsequently, comparative education became a significant field of enquiry in other parts of the world (Manzon 2011). In contemporary times, patterns in Asia are particularly exciting. Japan and Korea have had national comparative education societies since the 1960s, but younger bodies have emerged in mainland China, Hong Kong, Taiwan and the Philippines; and since 1995 Asia as a whole has been served by a regional society (Mochida 2007). The growth of activity in China, including Hong Kong, has been particularly notable (Bray & Gui 2007; Manzon 2013). These developments are bringing new perspectives based on different scholarly traditions and social priorities.

In the millennial special issue of *Comparative Education*, Crossley and Jarvis (2000, p.263) noted that new directions for the field included "new substantive issues, and the potential of more varied and multilevel units of analysis, including global, intranational and micro-level comparisons". Elaborating in his sole-authored paper in the special issue of the journal, Crossley (2000, p.328) observed that:

> While it is already possible to identify concerted efforts to promote, for example, micro-level qualitative fieldwork … and regional studies …, the nation state remains the dominant framework in published work, and few have explicitly considered the various levels.

Crossley then highlighted a paper by Bray and Thomas (1995) which stressed the value of multilevel analysis and which, Crossley suggested, deserved further attention. At the heart of the Bray and Thomas paper was a cube which presented a set of dimensions and levels for comparison. Several chapters in this book refer explicitly to the Bray and Thomas paper, and indeed in many respects it provides a core theme within the volume. The concluding chapter reassesses the cube in the light of the contributions by the various authors in the book.

A further milestone in the literature came with the publication of the *International Handbook of Comparative Education* (Cowen & Kazamias 2009a). The Handbook comprised two thick volumes with 80 chapters. The editors placed much of the historical material in Volume 1, and focused on emerging themes in Volume 2. Their Editorial Introduction stressed (Cowen & Kazamias 2009b, p.4) that:

> Both volumes argue that what is judged to be 'good' comparative education has changed over time. They analyse the shifting academic agendas, the changing perspectives of attention, and the different academic languages used to construct 'comparative education'. They ask why this happens – why does 'comparative education' change its epistemic concerns, its reading of the world, and its aspirations to act upon it? They show the ways in which comparative education responds to the changing politics and economics of real events in the world as well as to the intellectual currents that are strong in particular times and places.

One major section in Volume 2 was about postcolonialism, and another major section was about cultures, knowledge and pedagogies. The former included chapters on curriculum, human rights and social justice; and the latter included chapters on religions and values. Chapters in the subsequent sections included focus on mapping of comparative education, intercultural studies, the importance of context, and unit ideas in comparative education. Yet, even this two-volume Handbook could not cover the whole field; and in any case, as the editors added in their Conclusion (Cowen & Kazamias 2009c, p.1295):

> A Handbook is not intended to freeze a field, to fix a canon, but to rehearse and then release a field of study.... New comparative educations not imagined in this Handbook can – and will – be created.

Part of the purpose of the present book is to provide tools to new generations of researchers so that indeed they can extend the boundaries and undertake endeavours not previously imagined.

The Bray and Thomas Cube

Figure 0.1 reproduces the cube presented by Bray and Thomas (1995, p.475). It was contained in a paper entitled 'Levels of Comparison in Educational Studies: Different Insights from Different Literatures and the Value of Multilevel Analyses'. The paper commenced by noting that different fields within the wider domain of educational studies have different methodological and conceptual emphases, and that the extent of cross-fertilisation was somewhat limited. The field of comparative education, for example, was dominated by cross-national comparisons and made little use of intranational comparisons. In contrast, many other fields were dominated by local foci and failed to benefit from the perspectives that could be gained from international studies. The paper then pointed out that although the field of comparative education had been dominated by cross-national foci, many other domains lacked such perspectives. The authors argued that stronger relationships between different fields would be to the benefit of all.

Figure 0.1: A Framework for Comparative Education Analyses

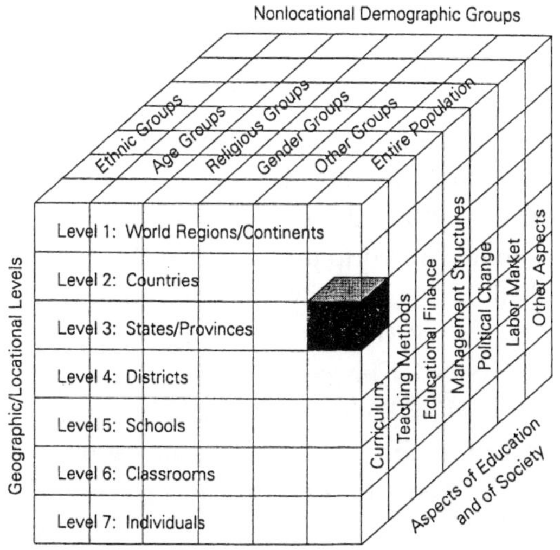

Source: Bray & Thomas (1995), p.475.

On the front face of the cube are seven *geographic/locational* levels for comparison: world regions/continents, countries, states/provinces, districts, schools, classrooms, and individuals. The second dimension contains *nonlocational demographic* groups, including ethnic, age, religious, gender and other groups, and entire populations. The third dimension comprises *aspects of education and of society*, such as curriculum, teaching methods, finance, management structures, political change and labour markets. Many studies that are explicitly comparative engage all three dimensions, and thus can be mapped in the corresponding cells of the diagram. For example, the shaded cell in Figure 0.1 represents a comparative study of curricula for the entire population in two or more provinces.

An overarching point of the Bray and Thomas article was their call for multilevel analyses in comparative studies to achieve multifaceted and holistic analyses of educational phenomena. The authors observed that much research remained at a single level, thereby neglecting recognition of the ways in which patterns at the lower levels in education systems are shaped by patterns at higher levels and vice versa. While researchers can often undertake only single-level studies because of constraints dictated by purpose and availability of resources, Bray and Thomas suggested that researchers should at least recognise the limits of their foci and the mutual influences of other levels on the educational phenomena of interest.

The Bray and Thomas framework has been extensively cited, both in literature that is explicitly associated with the field of comparative education (e.g. Arnove 2001, 2013; Phillips & Schweisfurth 2008; Watson 2012; Brock & Alexiadou 2013) and in broader literature (e.g. Ballantine 2001; Winzer & Mazurek 2012). It has generally been seen as useful, and some authors have endeavoured to take it further by making explicit what was already implicit in the framework. For example, Watson (1998, p.23) highlighted an alternative grouping of countries and societies according to religion and colonial history. Such alternative categories are in fact already represented in the 'nonlocational demographic' dimension of the framework, though rather than being 'nonlocational' they might perhaps be more aptly termed 'pluri-locational' or 'multi-territorial'. The final chapter of this book draws on the other chapters to comment on ways in which the cube could be refined and supplemented to extend conceptualisation in the field.

The Features of this Book

Some features of this book have already been mentioned. They deserve elaboration so that readers can see the context within which the book was prepared and the contributions which it makes.

Beginning with the earlier point about shifting centres of gravity, this book is part of the increased strength of the field in East Asia. All contributors to the book are associated in some way with the Comparative Education Research Centre (CERC) at the University of Hong Kong.

Its three editors have been Directors of that Centre; most of the contributors are or have been academic staff or research students associated with
the Centre; and the other contributors have been visitors for various
lengths of time. Because of this, the book to some extent has an East Asian
orientation. However, all authors also select examples and employ materials from other parts of the world, and the book is global in its messages
and relevance.

A second feature is a mix of dispassionate and of personalised
chapters. Thus, some authors have sought to portray their perspectives in
an objective way, while others have been subjective and even autobio-
graphical. Both genres, it may be suggested, contribute usefully. Perhaps
especially in a field such as comparative education, the backgrounds and
perspectives of the analysts are of major significance. These accounts fit a
tradition in which scholars have recounted their own career histories and
the ways in which personal circumstances have shaped their subsequent
thinking about the field (e.g. Postlethwaite 1999; Jones 2002; Hayhoe 2004;
Klees 2008; Sultana 2009). The approach shows how scholarship can
evolve within the careers of specific individuals, and indicates that
methodological choices adopted by researchers reflect personal circumstances as well as more academic criteria.

In structure, the book has three main sections. First comes a group of
chapters which comment on the nature of the field. Within this group, the
first chapter identifies major purposes for undertaking research in comparative education, and remark on the different perspectives that may be
held by different actors. The second chapter relates the field of comparative education to other domains of enquiry, both within the broad arena
of educational studies and within other disciplinary areas. The third
chapter compares quantitative and qualitative approaches, showing the
strengths and limitations of each and taking studies of literacy as a theme.

The second section turns to specific units for analysis. This section is
the longest in the book, and forms its core. Within the field, examples may
readily be found of comparative study of each of these units for analysis;
but it is less common for academics firmly to consider the strengths and
limitations of their approaches. The various chapters, taken separately,
show multiple facets for viewing their subjects; and together they form a
mosaic which represents a significant proportion of the total field. Eleven
chapters focus on a wide range of units for comparison, commencing with
places and ending with educational achievements.

The concluding section returns to the wider picture. It charts some of the continued diversity in the field and the trends and issues that have become apparent. The discussion then highlights some of the lessons to be learned from comparison of approaches and methods in comparative education research.

Preparation of the first edition of this book was a major exercise of teamwork and coordination, and the experience was echoed in preparation of the second edition. Updates and refinements in analysis have benefited from the inputs of students and of peers around the world. Most chapters have been presented in conferences and/or CERC seminars at the University of Hong Kong. The editors and contributors hope that readers will find the book as stimulating as were the processes of preparation. At the same time, just as the editors and contributors viewed the first edition of the book as a stage in the ongoing development of the field, they have a similar view of the second edition. Indeed the field has many more dimensions to be explored and developed.

References

Altbach, Philip G. & Kelly, Gail P. (1986): 'Introduction: Perspectives on Comparative Education', in Altbach, Philip G. & Kelly, Gail P. (eds.), *New Approaches to Comparative Education*. Chicago: The University of Chicago Press, pp.1-10.

Arnove, Robert F. (2001): 'Comparative and International Education Society (CIES) Facing the Twenty-First Century: Challenges and Contributions'. *Comparative Education Review*, Vol.45, No.4, pp.477-503.

Arnove, Robert F. (2013): 'Introduction: Reframing Comparative Education: The Dialectic of the Global and the Local', in Arnove, Robert F.; Torres, Carlos Alberto & Franz, Stephen (eds.), *Comparative Education: The Dialectic of the Global and the Local*. 4th edition, Lanham: Rowman & Littlefield, pp.1-25.

Ballantine, Jeanne H. (2001): *The Sociology of Education: A Systematic Analysis*. Upper Saddle River, New Jersey: Prentice Hall.

Barber, Benjamin R. (1973): 'Science, Salience and Comparative Education: Some Reflections on Social Scientific Enquiry', in Edwards, Reginald, Holmes, Brian & Van de Graaff, John (eds.), *Relevant Methods in Comparative Education*. Hamburg: UNESCO Institute for Education, pp.57-79.

Benhamida, Khemais (1990): 'The Arab States', in Halls, W.D. (ed.), *Comparative Education: Contemporary Issues and Trends*. Paris: UNESCO, and London: Jessica Kingsley, pp.291-317.

Bereday, George Z.F. (1964): *Comparative Method in Education*. New York: Holt, Rinehart & Winston.

Bray, Mark & Gui, Qin (2007): 'Comparative Education in Greater China: Contexts, Characteristics, Contrasts, and Contributions', in Crossley, Michael; Broadfoot, Patricia & Schweisfurth, Michele (eds.), *Changing Educational Contexts, Issues and Identities: 40 Years of Comparative Education*. London: Routledge, pp.319-349.

Bray, Mark & Thomas, R. Murray (1995): 'Levels of Comparison in Educational Studies: Different Insights from Different Literatures and the Value of Multilevel Analyses'. *Harvard Educational Review*, Vol.65, No.3, pp.472-490.

Bristow, Thelma & Holmes, Brian (1968): *Comparative Education through the Literature: A Bibliographic Guide*. London: Butterworths.

Brock, Colin & Alexiadou, Nafsika (2013): *Education around the World: A Comparative Introduction*. London: Bloomsbury.

Cowen, Robert & Kazamias, Andreas M. (eds.) (2009a): *International Handbook of Comparative Education*. 2 volumes, Dordrecht: Springer.

Cowen, Robert & Kazamias, Andreas M. (2009b): 'Joint Editorial Introduction', in Cowen, Robert & Kazamias, Andreas M. (eds.), *International Handbook of Comparative Education*. Dordrecht: Springer, pp.3-6.

Cowen, Robert & Kazamias, Andreas M. (2009c): 'Conclusion', in Cowen, Robert & Kazamias, Andreas M. (eds.), *International Handbook of Comparative Education*. Dordrecht: Springer, pp.1295-1296.

Crossley, Michael (2000): 'Bridging Cultures and Traditions in the Reconceptualisation of Comparative and International Education'. *Comparative Education*, Vol.36, No.3, pp.319-332.

Crossley, Michael & Jarvis, Peter (2000): 'Introduction: Continuity and Change in Comparative and International Education'. *Comparative Education*, Vol.36, No.3, pp.261-265.

Djourinksi, Alexandre (1998): *Comparative Education*. Moscow: Academia. [in Russian]

Edwards, Reginald; Holmes, Brian & Van de Graaff, John (eds.) (1973): *Relevant Methods in Comparative Education*. Hamburg: UNESCO Institute for Education.

Epstein, Erwin H. (1986): 'Currents Left and Right: Ideology in Comparative Education' in Altbach, Philip G. & Kelly, Gail P. (eds.), *New*

Approaches to Comparative Education. Chicago: The University of Chicago Press, pp.233-259.

Halls, W.D. (1973): 'Culture and Education: The Culturalist Approach to Comparative Studies, in Edwards, Reginald, Holmes, Brian & Van de Graaff, John (eds.), *Relevant Methods in Comparative Education*. Hamburg: UNESCO Institute for Education, pp.119-135.

Hayhoe, Ruth (2004): *Full Circle: A Life with Hong Kong and China*. Hong Kong: Comparative Education Research Centre, The University of Hong Kong.

Jones, Phillip W. (2002): 'Comparative and International Education: A Personal Account'. *Change: Transformations in Education*, Vol.5, No.1, pp.90-105.

Jullien, Marc-Antoine (1817) *Esquisse et Vues Préliminaires d'un Ouvrage sur l'Éducation Comparée*. Paris: Société Établie à Paris pour l'Amélioration de l'Enseignement Élémentaire. Reprinted 1962, Genève: Bureau International d'Éducation.

Kazamias, Andreas M. & Schwartz, Karl A. (1977): 'Introduction'. *Comparative Education Review*, special issue on 'The State of the Art', Vol.21, Nos.2 & 3, pp.151-152.

Kelly, Gail P. & Altbach, Philip G. (1986): 'Comparative Education: Challenge and Response', in Altbach, Philip G. & Kelly, Gail P. (eds.), *New Approaches to Comparative Education*. Chicago: The University of Chicago Press, pp.309-327.

King, Edmund J. (1964): *Other Schools and Ours*. Revised edition, New York: Holt, Rinehart & Winston.

Klees, Steven J. (2008): 'Reflections on Theory, Method, and Practice in Comparative and International Education'. *Comparative Education Review*, Vol.52, No.3, pp.301-328.

Manzon, Maria (2011): *Comparative Education: The Construction of a Field*. Hong Kong: Comparative Education Research Centre, The University of Hong Kong, and Dordrecht: Springer.

Manzon, Maria (2013): 'Teaching Comparative Education in Greater China: Contexts, Characteristics and Challenges', in Wolhuter, Charl; Popov, Nikolay; Leutwyler, Bruno & Skubic Ermenc, Klara (eds.), *Comparative Education at Universities World Wide*. 3rd edition, Sofia: Bulgarian Comparative Education Society, and Ljubljana: University of Ljubljana Faculty of Arts, pp.237-255.

Masemann, Vandra Lea (1986): 'Critical Ethnography in the Study of Comparative Education', in Altbach, Philip G. & Kelly, Gail P. (eds.),

New Approaches to Comparative Education. Chicago: The University of Chicago Press, pp.11-25.

Mochida, Kengo (2007): 'The Comparative Education Society of Asia (CESA)', in Masemann, Vandra; Bray, Mark & Manzon, Maria (eds.), *Common Interests, Uncommon Goals: Histories of the World Council of Comparative Education Societies and its Members*. CERC Studies in Comparative Education 21, Hong Kong: Comparative Education Research Centre, The University of Hong Kong, and Dordrecht: Springer, pp.309-315.

Mouhoubi, Samy (2005): 'Bridging the North South Divide'. *The New Courier* [UNESCO], November, pp.60-62.

Noah, Harold J. & Eckstein, Max A. (1969): *Toward a Science of Comparative Education*. New York: Macmillan.

Noonan, Richard (1973): 'Comparative Education Methodology of the International Association for the Evaluation of Educational Achievement (IEA)', in Edwards, Reginald, Holmes, Brian & Van de Graaff, John (eds.), *Relevant Methods in Comparative Education*. Hamburg: UNESCO Institute for Education, pp.199-207.

Phillips, David & Schweisfurth, Michele (2008): *Comparative and International Education: An Introduction to Theory, Method and Practice*. London: Continuum.

Postlethwaite, T. Neville (1999): *International Studies of Educational Achievement: Methodological Issues*. CERC Studies in Comparative Education 6, Hong Kong: Comparative Education Research Centre, The University of Hong Kong.

Sadler, Sir Michael (1900): 'How Far Can We Learn Anything of Practical Value from the Study of Foreign Systems of Education?' Reprinted 1964 in *Comparative Education Review*, Vol.7, No.3, pp.307-314.

Sultana, Ronald G. (2009): 'Looking Back Before Moving Forward: Building on 15 Years of Comparative Educational Research in the Mediterranean', in Borg, Carmel; Mayo, Peter & Sultana, Ronald G. (eds.), *Mediterranean Studies in Comparative Education*. Malta: Mediterranean Society of Comparative Education (MESCE) and Euro-Mediterranean Centre for Educational Research (EMCER).

Theisen, Gary L.; Achola, Paul P.W. & Boakari, Francis Musa (1986): 'The Underachievement of Cross-National Studies of Achievement', in Altbach, Philip G. & Kelly, Gail P. (eds.), *New Approaches to Comparative Education*. Chicago: The University of Chicago Press, pp.27-49.

Tietze, Susanne & Dick, Penny (2013): 'The Victorious English Language: Hegemonic Practices in the Management Academy'. *Journal of Management Inquiry*, 22 (1), 122-134.

Wang, Chengxu (1998): *The History of Comparative Foreign Education*. Beijing: People's Education Press. [in Chinese]

Watson, Keith (1998): 'Memories, Models and Mapping: The Impact of Geopolitical Changes on Comparative Studies in Education'. *Compare: A Journal of Comparative Education*, Vol.28, No.1, pp.5-31.

Watson, Keith (2012): 'South-East Asia and Comparative Studies'. *Journal of International and Comparative Education*, Vol.1, No.1, pp.31-39.

Wilson, David N. (2003): 'The Future of Comparative and International Education in a Globalised World', in Bray, Mark (ed.) *Comparative Education: Continuing Traditions, New Challenges, and New Paradigms*. Dordrecht: Kluwer, pp.15-33.

Winzer, Margret & Mazurek, Kas (2012): 'Analyzing Inclusive Schooling for Students with Disabilities in International Contexts: Outline of a Model'. *Journal of International Special Needs Education*, Vol.15, No.1, pp.12-23.

I: Directions

1

Actors and Purposes in Comparative Education

Mark BRAY

The nature of any particular comparative study of education depends on the purposes for which it was undertaken and on the identity of the person(s) conducting the enquiry. This first chapter begins by noting different categories of people who undertake comparative studies of education. It then focuses on three of these groups: policy makers, international agencies, and academics. Although this book is chiefly concerned with the last of these groups, it is instructive to note similarities and differences between the purposes and approaches of academics and other groups.

Different Actors, Different Purposes

Among the categories of people who undertake comparative studies of education are the following:

- *parents* commonly compare schools and systems of education in search of the institutions which will serve their children's needs most effectively;
- *practitioners*, including school principals and teachers, make comparisons in order to improve the operation of their institutions;
- *policy makers* in individual countries examine education systems elsewhere in order to identify ways to achieve social, political and other objectives in their own settings;

- *international agencies* compare patterns in different countries in order to improve the advice that they give to national governments and others; and
- *academics* undertake comparisons in order to improve understanding in many domains, including the forces which shape education systems and the roles of education systems in social and economic development.

When parents undertake comparisons, their concern is practical and tied to the evolving needs of their children. If their children are about to reach or have reached kindergarten age, the parents' main focus is on kindergartens; if the children are about to reach or have reached primary school age, the parents' main focus is on primary schools; and so on. Parents may undertake systematic comparisons on carefully-identified criteria; but their purposes and approaches are rather different from those of other groups on the list, and they are not the main focus of this book.

Practitioners such as school principals and teachers are in some respects similar. Their interests are less likely to progress to higher levels of the system in a linear way as the years pass (i.e. from kindergarten to primary to junior secondary, etc.); but they also have practical concerns, and their attention to particular problems is likely to diminish once those problems have been solved.

Related remarks might be made about policy makers. They are given more attention in this book because they are more likely to place their findings in the public domain for external scrutiny; and partly because of the likelihood of such scrutiny, policy makers are more likely to pay attention to methodological issues. Valuable insights may be gained from analysing both the types of comparisons that policy makers commonly undertake, and the types of conclusions that policy makers draw from their comparisons. Sometimes the comparisons are undertaken to inform future decisions, but comparisons are also commonly undertaken to justify decisions that have already been made. Around the world, different cultural and political factors become evident in the ways that policy makers make comparisons.

The comparisons made by international agencies are even more squarely within the focus of this book. Some agencies are explicitly concerned with education, and are mandated to undertake comparison as part of their reason for existence. The United Nations Educational, Scientific and Cultural Organization (UNESCO) is an obvious example. Other important international bodies in education include the World Bank and the Organisation for Economic Co-operation and Development (OECD). These bodies each have their own emphases, but the similarities in the ways that they undertake comparisons are perhaps more obvious than the differences. Like practitioners and policy makers, international agencies undertake most of their comparisons with practical aims in mind, though international agencies may also contribute to broader conceptualisation.

Academics may also be concerned with practical aims, especially when undertaking consultancy assignments and applied research. However, perhaps the main part of academic work is concerned with conceptualisation. Many theories abound within the academic arena. Fashions change over time, and different parts of the world have different emphases. Indeed the field of comparative education itself differs in emphasis in China and Bulgaria, for example. Thus, even with its dominant focus on academic study of education, this book has multiple perspectives.

Policy Makers and Comparative Education

From a practical perspective, much of the field of comparative education has been concerned with copying of educational models. Policy makers in one setting commonly seek information about models elsewhere, following which they may imitate those models with or without adaptation. In some settings this practice has been described as "educational policy borrowing" (see e.g. Steiner-Khamsi 2004; Phillips & Ochs 2007; Steiner-Khamsi & Waldow 2012). However, borrowing is perhaps a misnomer since it implies that the models will be given back after use, which is very rare.

When policy makers seek ideas worth copying, they first have to decide where to look for the ideas. Review of patterns around the world reveals biases in the types of places that policy makers consider worth investigating. One influence arises from language: policy makers who speak and read English are likely to commence with English-speaking countries, their counterparts who speak and read Arabic are likely to commence with Arabic-speaking countries, etc.. Another influence arises from political linkages, for example within the European Union, the Association of Southeast Asian Nations or the Caribbean Community. A third influence arises from perceptions of hierarchy: less developed countries tend to look at more developed countries, and countries that are already economically advanced tend to look at others that are similarly advanced. Policy makers in industrialised countries do not often look for ideas and models in less developed countries, though it is arguable that sometimes they should do so.

Turning to specific examples, clear evidence of importing may be found in the United Kingdom (UK). Beginning with an example from the 1980s and 1990s, some UK reforms were at least partially inspired by experience in the United States of America (USA). They included student loans for higher education, magnet schools, Training & Enterprise Councils, education-business compacts, community colleges, licensed teachers, and Employment Training (Finegold et al. 1992, p.7).

Space constraints preclude detailed analysis of each of these, but some insights may be taken from the first, i.e. student loans. The UK Secretary of Education made three trips to the USA to discuss student aid programmes, and made repeated references in speeches and in print to the benefits of US models (McFarland 1993, p.51). The loan schemes subsequently launched in the UK were part of a package related to the overall government vision for radical reform of education, and the momentum of the political motives caused and permitted policy makers to overlook many details first of how loans had actually worked in the USA and second how they might be expected to work in the UK. Nevertheless, the tools of comparative education were considered useful by these policy makers. The USA was considered an appropriate source for educational models because of personal relationships between the top politicians and because it was perceived to be successful in the global marketplace (Whitty 2012).

Many other countries have also looked to the USA as a source for models. Among them is Switzerland, in which the authorities have not only explicitly referred to models in the USA but also hired US consultants to develop a reform package for schools (Steiner-Khamsi 2002, p.76). As in the UK, the moves were strongly shaped by domestic political forces; and as the domestic political scene changed, so did the strategy for importing models. After a period of heated debate and protest by the teachers' unions, the Ministry of Education publicly distanced itself from US models. Instead, the authorities used references to European reforms, especially in the Netherlands and Denmark. According to Steiner-Khamsi (2002, p.79), this new orientation suited policy makers because the European models were less known in the Swiss education community and were thus less subject to criticism and controversy. In this case, comparative education was being used not only as a source of ideas but also to legitimate the government in actions that it wished to undertake.

During the colonial era, it was standard practice for models of schooling to be imported, albeit usually with some modification, either from the colonising country itself or from other colonies of the same power (Gifford & Weiskel 1971; Altbach & Kelly 1978; Thomas & Postlethwaite 1984). Thus throughout the British empire, for example, many common features in education systems reflected the political frameworks in which the colonies operated, and led to differences from school systems in the French, Portuguese, Spanish and other empires. For instance, whereas secondary schools in UK colonies commonly led to school certificate examinations, in French colonies they lead to the baccalauréat. Other differences ranged from the roles (or lack of roles) for vernacular languages as media of instruction to policies on class size and teachers' pay.

During postcolonial eras, some of the old ties have remained while new ties have developed. This is evident in Hong Kong, which was a UK colony until it reverted to Chinese sovereignty in 1997. The external sources to which policy makers have turned for inspiration may be illustrated by the following four reports published shortly after Hong Kong's political change:

- A 1999 consultation document on the aims of education included an annex on developments elsewhere (Hong Kong 1999, Annex 4). The other locations were China, Japan, Singapore, Taiwan, the UK and the USA.
- Attached to the reform proposals in a 2000 consultation document was an appendix entitled 'Reforms in Other Places' (Hong Kong 2000, Appendix I). The other places were Shanghai, Taipei, Singapore, Japan, the Republic of Korea, Chicago, and the USA.
- A 2002 report on higher education contained an appendix entitled 'International Examples of Institutional Governance and Management' (Sutherland 2002, Appendix D). The examples were the University of Pennsylvania (USA), the University of Wisconsin-Madison (USA), the University of Warwick (UK), the University of Melbourne (Australia), and the Imperial College of Science, Technology & Medicine (UK).
- A 2003 document on teacher competencies by the Advisory Committee on Teacher Education & Qualifications (ACTEQ) contained an appendix focusing on Continuing Professional De-

velopment (CPD) and entitled 'Teachers' CPD Policies and Practices in Selected Regions' (ACTEQ 2003, Appendix C). The selected regions were Scotland, England and mainland China.

These lists contain an interesting mix of locations from which data were collected. The colonial legacies remained evident, with the UK (and two of its component parts – Scotland and England) still very prominent; but the lists also included many other parts of the world. Reflecting the bilingual nature of Hong Kong, in which the two official languages were English and Chinese, the majority of places on the list were either English-speaking or Chinese-speaking societies. The additional societies were advanced industrial countries in Asia – Japan and the Republic of Korea – which were considered to have some cultural affinity and were respected because of their economic successes. Also worth noting is the mix of units for comparison. In some cases comparisons were with countries (Singapore, Japan, Scotland, the USA, etc.); but also on the list were three cities (Shanghai, Taipei and Chicago) which were arguably parallel to Hong Kong in its identity as a city. The report on higher education selected a number of institutions for comparison. In this case, all were from prosperous English-speaking countries – Australia, the UK and the USA.

Instructively, while Hong Kong and its East Asian neighbours looked to such countries as the UK and USA for models, sometimes the UK and USA looked to East Asia for models. An example from England is a report commissioned by the government's Office for Standards in Education (OFSTED) which made a strong case for cross-national study of education, and was taken seriously by a wide audience (Crossley & Watson 2003, pp.2, 6; Alexander 2008, p.9). Particular emphasis in the report was placed on the high achievement scores of pupils in Japan, Hong Kong, Korea and Singapore. In part, the report noted, these scores reflected cultural factors which could not be replicated in the UK; but the report also noted dimensions of systems, schools and classrooms which could be shaped by policy decisions.

Policy makers in the USA have also at times sought to learn from East Asia. In 2009, for example, US President Barack Obama praised the education system of South Korea, telling US educators that "our children spend over a month less in school than children in South Korea every year" (*Korea Times* 2009). He called for Americans "not only to expand effective after-school programs but to rethink the school day to incorporate more time". His remarks surprised Koreans who felt that their school system was too pressurised and would have preferred a more relaxed system along the lines US patterns (e.g. Park 2012). Nevertheless, US educators have also looked carefully at international studies of educational achievement, particularly to see why scores have been higher in parts of Asia and what can be learned (e.g. OECD 2011; Tucker 2011).

While the above paragraphs stress cross-national comparisons, policy makers also learn much from intranational comparisons. This may be especially obvious in federal systems in which major differences exist between states or provinces in the structure and content of education. In India, for example, an Annual Status of Education Report has regularly shown data on enrolments, facilities and children's learning in the majority of the country's 35 states and union territories (e.g. Pratham 2013). It has noted wide variations in available resources for education, and has recommended measures to improve equity and quality. In a rather different economic and social context, Canadian statistics have shown enrolments, expenditures and curriculum variations among the 13 provinces and territories (e.g. Statistics Canada 2013).

In contrast to comparisons across space are comparisons across time. The Canadian report mentioned above (Statistics Canada 2013) made explicit comparisons across time; and this report has many counterparts elsewhere. Policy makers are particularly inclined to make comparisons with the work of their predecessors, usually with the goal of showing how much society has benefited or will benefit from the policies that the contemporary policy makers have devised; but sometimes policy makers also learn from history about obstacles to avoid and the dangers of over-ambition.

Academics are sometimes dismissive of much of the comparative work of policy makers. They may argue that the work of policy makers is excessively governed by ideology, and that it is sometimes weak in design and interpretation. Policy makers may be equally dissatisfied with the work of academics, especially when it fails to lead to clear recommendations that are delivered in a timely manner. However, both groups can learn from each other; and international agencies may be a third group with approaches that are again different and also instructive.

International Agencies and Comparative Education

Because of space constraints, it is necessary to select just a few examples from the huge number of international agencies concerned with education. The three bodies that have been selected are UNESCO, the World

Bank, and the OECD. Each of these bodies has internal variations, and patterns have evolved over time. The variations and evolutions cannot be examined in detail here, but are addressed by such authors as Jones (2006), Rizvi & Lingard (2009), and Singh (2011).

UNESCO

The United Nations Educational, Scientific and Cultural Organization was founded in 1945 in the context of reconstruction following World War II. The authors of its constitution referred to the need to advance mutual knowledge and understanding of peoples, and commenced with the declaration that "since wars begin in the minds of men, it is in the minds of men that the defences of peace must be constructed" (UNESCO 1945). The constitution added that the purpose of the body was:

> To contribute to peace and security by promoting collaboration among the nations through education, science and culture in order to further universal respect for justice, for the rule of law, and for the human rights and fundamental freedoms which are affirmed for the peoples of the world, without distinction of race, sex, language or religion, by the Charter of the United Nations.

Conflict around the world has remained a major problem, and UNESCO has remained strongly committed to this goal.

UNESCO's headquarters are in Paris, France, in addition to which the organisation has a global network of National Offices, Cluster Offices, Regional Bureaus and Liaison Offices. It also has a number of specialist Institutes, among which those having functions specifically concerned with education are the:

- International Institute for Capacity-Building in Africa (IICBA), in Addis Ababa, Ethiopia;
- UNESCO Institute for Lifelong Learning (UIL), in Hamburg, Germany;
- International Institute for Educational Planning (IIEP), in Paris, France and Buenos Aires, Argentina;
- International Institute for Higher Education in Latin America and the Caribbean (IESALC), in Caracas, Venezuela;
- International Bureau of Education (IBE), in Geneva, Switzerland;
- Institute for Information Technologies in Education (IITE), in Moscow, Russia;

- Mahatma Gandhi Institute of Education for Peace and Sustainable Development (MGIEP) in New Delhi, India; and
- UNESCO Institute for Statistics (UIS), in Montreal, Canada.

UNESCO's overarching objectives, and the specific priorities for the education sector, have been set out in its Medium-Term Strategy 2014-2021 (UNESCO 2013). The overarching objectives are "Contributing to lasting peace", and "Contributing to sustainable development and the eradication of poverty". These objectives were set with awareness of the gap between rich and poor and the need for sustained focus on equity and inclusion. The three strategic objectives for the education sector are:

- ◆ Developing education systems to foster quality lifelong learning opportunities for all;
- ◆ Empowering learners to be creative and responsible citizens; and
- ◆ Shaping the future education agenda.

The Medium-Term Strategy stated (UNESCO 2013: 21) that education:

> is both a basic human right and a vector to realize other human rights and achieve international development objectives. Education has a direct impact on poverty reduction, health promotion, gender equality and environmental sustainability. It is at the heart of social inclusion and social transformation and it is widely acknowledged that no country can improve the living conditions of its people without important investments in education.

In order to achieve its goals, UNESCO undertakes comparative study of education to identify practical ways to extend the quantity, improve the quality, and appropriately orient the direction of education around the world. Thus, to some extent the comparative work of UNESCO resembled that of policy makers, commented on above. Indeed UNESCO has a strong policy advisory role, particularly for national governments. The emphasis on the national level reflected the fact that UNESCO is a member of the United Nations in which the nation (country) is by definition the basic building block. UNESCO's membership includes both industrialised and less developed countries, but its main work is focused on the latter.

UNESCO's emphasis on countries as the unit of analysis may be seen in its statistical yearbooks. Table 1.1 illustrates this observation with statistics on lower secondary education. Each country was allocated one line, and in this sense appeared to be equal in status even though the countries displayed vast differences in population and other indicators. Thus China, which had a population of 1,300,000,000 and 3,658,000 lower secondary teachers, was allocated the same amount of space as Maldives, which had a population of 200,000 and 3,000 lower secondary teachers. Countries are also commonly treated as equal units in official meetings convened by UNESCO, with each member state having a single vote.

Table 1.1: Statistics on Lower Secondary Education, Selected Asian Countries

Country	Gross graduation ratio			Teachers		Pupil/
	Total	Male	Female	Number ('000)	% Female	Teacher ratio
Azerbaijan	93	95	91	...	...	...
Bangladesh	...	...	...	205	20	31
Bhutan	67	67	67	2	41	22
Cambodia	35	38	32	25	36	24
China	89	86	93	3,658	49	15
India	...	...	...	1,913	42	31
Indonesia	76	74	77	915	49	13
Kazakhstan	112	113	112	...	...	...
Maldives	...	...	...	3	41	8
Mongolia	103	100	105	...	...	...
Myanmar	47	45	48	60	86	36
Pakistan	35	41	29	...	...	...
Philippines	69	62	77	136	76	39
Republic of Korea	...	...	...	103	68	19
Thailand	76	71	81	129	56	22
Uzbekistan	98	100	96	...	...	...
Vietnam	...	...	...	314	69	17

Notes: (1) The gross graduation ratio is defined as the total number of graduates, regardless of age, from a given level of education (in this case lower secondary) expressed as a percentage of the population at the theoretical graduation age for that level of education. (2) Most data are for 2010, but some are for other years. (3) ... = no data available

Source: UNESCO Institute for Statistics (2012), pp.98-103; 118-120.

However, UNESCO is of course aware of other units for analysis. Thus, although the report from which Table 1.1 was extracted contained no analyses at sub-national level, it did present some supra-national analyses. Figure 1.1 is an example, showing by world region the estimated number of children of primary school age who were out of school. It identifies proportions of children in this age group who had already left school, who were likely to enter school in the future, and who were unlikely to ever enter school. The regions were defined on a combination of geographic and political criteria. Thus, the countries of North Africa were included with the Arab States rather than being grouped with Sub-Saharan Africa; Western Europe was grouped with North America rather than Central and Eastern Europe; and Mexico was grouped with Latin America rather than North America.

Figure 1.1: Children of Primary School Age who were Out of School, by World Region

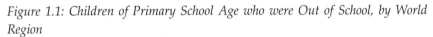

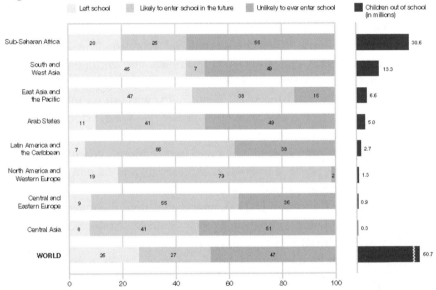

Distribution of primary school-age children out of school (%)

Note: Data are for 2010.

Source: UNESCO Institute for Statistics (2012), p.10.

While much of UNESCO's work is practical, aiming to expand the quantity and improve the quality of education in its member states, the organisation also plays a conceptual role. This is evident in the analytical publications produced not only by the headquarters and regional bureaus (e.g. Ho 2012; UNESCO 2012) but also by its Institutes (e.g. Schiefelbein & McGinn 2009; Bray & Varghese 2011; Nafukho et al. 2011).

In addition, UNESCO contributes to the field of comparative education through two important journals. One is the *International Review of Education (IRE)*, edited at the UNESCO Institute for Lifelong Learning.

This journal has International rather than Comparative in its title, but describes itself (*IRE* 2013) as "the longest-running international periodical on the comparative theory and practice of formal and non-formal education". It was established in 1931, but went through various periods of turbulence before being "reborn" in 1955 under the aegis of what was then called the UNESCO Institute of Education (Roche 2013, p.153). Most articles are in English; but the journal also publishes articles in French, and until a 2013 editorial change (Roche 2013, p.154) was willing to publish articles in German.

The second journal is entitled *Prospects: Quarterly Review of Comparative Education*, and is edited at UNESCO's International Bureau of Education in Switzerland. When the journal was established in 1969, it was edited at the UNESCO headquarters in France, and entitled *Prospects in Education: A Quarterly Bulletin*. In 1972 it was renamed *Prospects: Quarterly Review of Education*, and the word *Comparative* was added to the title in 1995. In contrast to the *International Review of Education*, which can have articles in two languages within a single issue of the journal, *Prospects* may be translated into several languages in its entirety. When the journal was launched, it appeared in English and French; and then in due course other languages were added. The editorial office moved to the International Bureau of Education in 1993, and at that time the journal was appearing in six languages: English, French, Spanish, Arabic, Chinese and Russian. For financial and logistic reasons full publication in all six languages could not be maintained, but the journal always appears in English and sometimes also appears in other languages.

The World Bank

During World War II, financial experts recognised that the post-war world would greatly need international cooperative arrangements to address monetary and financial problems. After several preliminary meetings, representatives of the 44 Allied Nations met in Bretton Woods in the USA in 1944, and established the International Monetary Fund (IMF) and the International Bank for Reconstruction and Development (IBRD). Today, the IBRD is better known as the World Bank. The longer name reflected the institution's original purpose: to lend money to help reconstruct the war-torn countries of Europe. After this reconstruction had been achieved, the Bank turned to the less developed countries of the world. This change of emphasis explains why the full name is no longer so commonly used. The year after the Bretton Woods meeting, 1945, world leaders formed the

United Nations (UN). In 1947 the Bank joined the UN family, and thus is strictly speaking a UN body. However, it operates under a different structure of governance from UNESCO and most other UN bodies.

The World Bank is multisectoral in focus, with projects ranging from agriculture to water supply. The initial decades did not include projects on education, but after the early 1960s the sector gained increasing prominence (Jones 2006, pp.101-131). In 2013, the World Bank described itself as one of the largest external financiers for education in developing countries, adding that it managed a portfolio of US$9 billion and had operations in 71 countries (World Bank 2013). In the decade to 2012, 64 per cent of new projects were devoted to basic education, 17 per cent to upper secondary or vocational education, and 19 per cent to tertiary education (World Bank 2012, p.3). Like UNESCO, particular focus was placed on the Millennium Development Goals (MDGs) and the Education for All (EFA) objectives.

The World Bank headquarters are in Washington DC, USA, and English is the dominant working language. However, multiple languages are used for specific projects, and in 2013 the website (www.worldbank.org) offered some information in 17 languages: Arabic, Bahasa Indonesia, Bulgarian, Chinese, English, French, Khmer, Japanese, Mongolian, Portuguese, Romanian, Russian, Spanish, Thai, Turkish, Ukrainian and Vietnamese. The World Bank has multiple country offices, and employs over 10,000 people worldwide.

Like UNESCO, the World Bank is primarily concerned with the practical application of comparative education, and again much of its analysis has a country focus. Nevertheless, the World Bank presents many analytical studies of education, both in its policy documents (e.g. World Bank 2011) and in research on particular themes (e.g. Patrinos et al. 2009; Majgaard & Mingat 2012; Sondergaard et al. 2012). In line with its mandate, the majority of these studies focus on less developed countries. Eastern and Central Europe has also gained increasing prominence since becoming a focus of World Bank work in the 1990s.

The World Bank does not operate any specialist journals in education, but it does publish articles on education in *The World Bank Research Observer* and *The World Bank Economic Review* (e.g. Dang & Rogers 2008; Cigno 2012; Van de Sijpe 2013). Since the World Bank is a bank, the emphasis in much of its comparative education research is on matters related to economics and financing rather than to such themes as pedagogy and curriculum (Collins & Wiseman 2012; Klees et al. 2012). Again, the country is the dominant unit of analysis.

One membership survey of the US-based Comparative and International Education Society (CIES), which is the largest society of its type in the field, asked respondents to list what they considered to be the most influential governmental and non-governmental organisations impacting on the field of comparative education (Cook et al. 2004, pp.140-141). Among the 188 different organisations listed by the sample, the World Bank was identified as having the most influence and received 19.7 per cent of responses. The other organisations in the top six were UNESCO (15.8%), the United States Agency for International Development (USAID) (7.8%), the United Nations Children's Fund (UNICEF) (5.0%), the United Nations (3.7%), and the OECD (3.5%). The fact that the 69.3% of the 419 respondents were resident in the USA must be taken account, since it implied a bias towards institutions that were prominent in that country and which produced a lot of material in English. Nevertheless, nearly one third of the respondents were resident elsewhere in the world, so the sample was not restricted to US perceptions.

The OECD

The Organisation for Economic Co-operation and Development is younger than UNESCO and the World Bank, having been created in 1961, but owes its origins to the same period of history. It is the successor to the Organisation for European Economic Co-operation (OEEC), which was set up in 1947 with support from the USA and Canada to help rebuild European economies after World War II. The OECD has been described as a "rich man's club" of wealthy nations (Woodward 2009, p.1). The OECD to some extent accepts such a description, though in an official publication (OECD 2008, p.8) has added that:

> The OECD is a group of like-minded countries. Essentially membership is limited only by a country's commitment to a market economy and a pluralistic democracy. It is rich, in that its 30 members [which expanded to 34 in 2010] produce almost 60% of the world's goods and services, but it is by no means exclusive. Non-members are invited to subscribe to OECD agreements and treaties, and the Organisation shares expertise and exchanges views on topics of mutual concern with more than 100 other countries and economies.

The OECD headquarters are in Paris, and its principal working languages are English and French.

Like the World Bank, the OECD has a multisectoral focus. The Economic Department addresses the core business, and is the largest part of the organisation; but other sections focus on the environment, technology, food, communications and employment. The OECD's semi-autonomous bodies include the Nuclear Energy Agency, the International Energy Agency, and the European Conference of Ministers of Transport.

Education also features on this list, and has gained increased prominence. The Directorate for Education (later named the Directorate for Education and Skills) was created in 2002 as a successor to a previous sub-division within the organisation. According to an official statement (OECD 2008, pp.19-20), it "helps member countries achieve high-quality learning for all that contributes to personal development, sustainable economic growth and social cohesion". Specific foci include ways to evaluate and improve outcomes from education, promote quality teaching, and build social cohesion through education.

Particularly well-known among the OECD education publications is the annual *Education at a Glance*. The first edition was published in 1992, and subsequent editions both extended the scope and improved the reliability and comparability of data. This task has not been easy. As observed by Henry et al. (2001, p.94):

> National data can often be incomplete, unreliable and out of phase in terms of timing and methods of data collection …. [F]ederal states like the US, Australia, Canada and Germany provide data in terms of weighted means, a process that cannot be assumed to have been carried out in any uniform fashion. Even aggregations are not always reliable because of changes in definitions and methodology. This is particularly so in collecting data on participation in tertiary education, where reforms in the post-secondary sector often change the ways students are classified for the purposes of allocating grants and benefits.

The OECD has nevertheless persisted with methodological refinements. It has devised techniques of aggregation and approximation to moderate the data supplied, and it has used powers of persuasion to encourage its members to collect data in a common format. The *OECD Handbook for Internationally Comparative Education Statistics* (OECD 2004) charted some of the improvements.

Most parts of *Education at a Glance* take the country as the unit of analysis, with the exception that some tables and charts show Belgium's

Flemish education system separately from its French education system. Figure 1.2 reproduces a chart in which this separation is made. The chart also shows England separately from Scotland, though shows the United States as single entity despite the diversity among its 50 states. Other tables and charts in the same publication (OECD 2013a) showed both the United Kingdom and Belgium as single units, despite their internal diversity.

Figure 1.2: Teachers' Salaries in Lower Secondary Education, in equivalent US$ Converted using Purchasing Power Parities

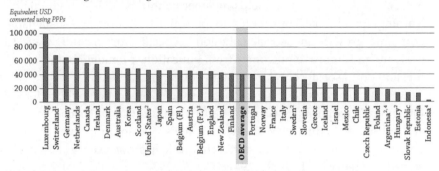

1. Salaries after 11 years of experience; 2. Actual base salaries; 3. Salaries of teachers with typical qualification instead of minimum; 4. Year of reference 2010.

The chart shows annual statutory salaries in 2011 for teachers in public institutions with 15 years of experience and minimum training.

Source: OECD (2013a), p.378.

From a methodological perspective, it is instructive to note that Figure 1.2, needing a common currency, uses US dollars – not in raw form according to prevailing official exchange rates, but according to purchasing powers (i.e. recognising that US$1 may purchase more in some settings than in others). This calculation relies on the accuracy of purchasing-power estimations, and still glosses over variations between different cities and regions within countries; but it is clearly preferable to unmodified exchange rates.

Also worth noting is the way that Figure 1.2 ordered the countries and systems. As noted by Henry et al. (2001, pp.95-96):

> Inevitably, the establishment of a single playing field sets the stage for constructing league tables, whatever the somewhat disingenuous claims to the contrary. Visually, tables or figures of comparative

performance against an OECD or country mean carry normative overtones…. To be above, below or at par with the OECD average invites simplistic or politically motivated comment, despite the pages of methodological and interpretative cautions which abound in the annexes.

Further, the OECD has in some publications expanded its focus considerably beyond its own member states. For example, the 2013 edition of *Education at a Glance* stated (p.21) that coverage included "two non-OECD countries that participate in the OECD Indicators of Education Systems programme (INES), namely Brazil and the Russian Federation, and the other G20 countries that do not participate in INES (Argentina, China, India, Indonesia, Saudi Arabia and South Africa)". Again, such data were mostly presented on a country-by-country basis, despite the internal diversity which might have been especially notable in such countries as China, Indonesia and Russia.

Related observations are applicable to another activity in the education sector, namely the Programme for International Student Assessment (PISA). Under this programme, assessments of the achievements of 15-year-olds in mathematics, science and reading have been undertaken every three years. In the first assessment, the survey was implemented in 43 countries and education systems. The number dropped to 41 in 2003, but grew to 58 in 2006, 65 in 2009, and 67 in 2012.

As explained by the OECD (2013b, p.13):

> The PISA assessment takes a broad approach to measuring knowledge, skills and attitudes that reflect current changes in school priorities… PISA focuses on competencies that 15-year-old students will need in the future and seeks to assess what they can do with what they have learnt – reflecting the ability of students to continue learning throughout their lives by applying what they learn in school to non-school environments, evaluating their choices and making decisions.

The document added (OECD 2013b, p.14) that PISA results "allow national policy makers to compare the performance of their education systems with those of other countries". The results have commonly been presented, especially in newspapers and other media which seek to distil essential messages, in country rankings. The OECD has frequently stressed that interpretations of the data should go beyond simplistic messages of country rankings, but some of its own reports have prioritised this feature. For example, Table 1.2 reproduces the first table in the Executive Summary of the OECD's report on PISA 2009. Countries (and sub-national units, such as Shanghai and Hong Kong) were ranked according to overall scores, which were compared not only with each other but also with the OECD average.

Table 1.2: Rankings on PISA Results in Reading, Mathematics and Science

	Reading	Maths	Science		Reading	Maths	Science
Shanghai-China	556	600	575	Czech Republic	478	493	500
Korea	539	546	538	Slovak Republic	477	497	490
Finland	536	541	554	Croatia	476	460	486
Hong Kong-China	533	555	549	Israel	474	447	455
Singapore	526	562	542	Luxembourg	472	489	484
Canada	524	527	529	Austria	470	496	494
New Zealand	521	519	532	Lithuania	468	477	491
Japan	520	529	539	Turkey	464	445	454
Australia	515	514	527	Dubai (UAE)	459	453	466
Netherlands	508	526	522	Russian Federation	459	468	478
Belgium	506	515	507	Chile	449	421	447
Norway	503	498	500	Serbia	442	442	443
Estonia	501	512	528	Bulgaria	429	428	439
Switzerland	501	534	517	Uruguay	426	427	427
Poland	500	495	508	Mexico	425	419	416
Iceland	500	507	496	Romania	424	427	428
United States	500	487	502	Thailand	421	419	425
Liechtenstein	499	536	520	Trinidad & Tobago	416	414	410
Sweden	497	494	495	Colombia	413	381	402
Germany	497	513	520	Brazil	412	386	405
Ireland	496	487	508	Montenegro	408	403	401
France	496	497	498	Jordan	405	387	415
Chinese Taipei	495	543	520	Tunisia	404	371	401
Denmark	495	503	499	Indonesia	402	371	383
United Kingdom	494	492	514	Argentina	398	388	401
Hungary	494	490	503	Kazakhstan	390	405	400
Portugal	489	487	493	Albania	385	377	391
Macao-China	487	525	511	Qatar	372	368	379
Italy	486	483	489	Panama	371	360	376
Latvia	484	482	494	Peru	370	365	369
Slovenia	483	501	512	Azerbaijan	362	431	373
Greece	483	466	470	Kyrgyzstan	314	331	330
Spain	481	483	488				

☐ Statistically significant *above* the OECD average
▨ Not statistically different from the OECD average
▨ Statistically significant *below* the OECD average

Notes: The data refer to the PISA 2009 assessment. The countries with names in bold were OECD members at the time of the publication of the report.

Source: OECD (2010), p.15.

In addition to country-level rankings, the PISA studies permit analysis of students' motivation to learn, beliefs about themselves, and their learning strategies. The analyses also permit comparisons by gender, socio-economic group and many other units of analysis. PISA has become highly influential among policy-makers (Andere 2008; Pereyra et al. 2011; Breakspear 2012; Meyer & Benavot 2013). In some cases, PISA reports have led to major upheaval, and in other cases they have led to much self-congratulation. Examples of the former include the "PISA shock" in Germany, where policy makers had been complacent about their education systems and were confronted by rankings that were much lower than expected (Waldow 2009). By contrast, Finland has attracted a steady stream of visitors seeking to understand how and why its PISA scores have been consistently at or near the top (Simola & Rinne 2011; Varjo et al. 2013); and since the release of PISA 2009 results, Shanghai has attracted similar attention (Sellar & Lingard 2013).

While PISA is a powerful tool, it also has limitations. Meyer and Benavot (2013, p.21) have pointed out that:

> The fact that this apparatus relies on numbers and statistics does not mean that it is anchored in transparent, objective, uncontestable truth. In fact the 'cloud of data' produced by PISA may easily [permit] anyone [to] find support for any preconceived idea. It creates the opposite of transparency because key assumptions and key decisions about categorization and the construction of measures are *black-boxed* by a complex array of behind-the-scene judgments and decisions.

Defenders of PISA might rightly retort that it provides a great advance on previous tools. Nevertheless, the comparisons in PISA have sometimes lacked the methodological insights that could have been brought by the tools and traditions of the field of comparative education. These include qualitative judgements that emphasise context and history (Pereyra et al. 2011).

Academics and Comparative Education

Less space will be devoted here to the nature of the work of academics in the field of comparative education since Chapter 2 elaborates on this theme – and indeed the whole book is principally devoted to the academic domain. Nevertheless, while again noting that academics commonly undertake consultancies and other practical assignments in which their purposes for comparative study of education may be similar to those of practitioners and policy makers, in general academics are concerned with conceptual and theoretical work. Sometimes they collaborate with policy makers and international agencies in the analysis of data, but an alternative role – evident in some of the critiques of international agencies noted above (Singh 2011; Collins & Wiseman 2012; Klees et al. 2012; Meyer & Benavot 2013) – is to highlight ideological and methodological biases.

Most people see comparative education as an interdisciplinary field which welcomes scholars who are equipped with tools and perspectives from other arenas but who choose to focus on educational issues in a comparative context (Manzon 2011). The questions then are how the field would be defined, where its boundaries lie, and how it is changing over time.

One simple way to define the field is by the membership and work of professional societies. The US-based Comparative and International Education Society (CIES) was mentioned above. With 2,300 individual and institutional members and a history dating from 1956, it is the oldest as well as the largest in the field. Comparable societies exist in other parts of the world, some being national in focus (e.g. serving China, Czech Republic and India), some being sub-national (e.g. serving Hong Kong), some being regional (e.g. serving Europe and Asia), and two being language-based (serving speakers of French and Dutch). Most of these societies are members of the World Council of Comparative Education Societies (WCCES), which was created in 1970 as an umbrella body and which in 2013 had 39 constituent societies (Masemann et al. 2007; WCCES 2013).

In addition, much academic work in the field of comparative education is undertaken by individuals and groups who are not members of these professional societies. Many academics identify more strongly with their parent disciplines, such as psychology, mathematics and sociology, and present their work in the conferences and journals of those disciplines rather than in the conferences and journals of comparative education. Thus, the scale of comparative study of education is much broader than that encompassed by the professional societies which explicitly label themselves as being concerned with the field.

Nevertheless, much can be learned from analysis of the characteristics and inclinations of academics who do choose to identify themselves with the field of comparative education. The survey of CIES members mentioned above (Cook et al. 2004) revealed a diverse and highly eclectic field which was "relatively centerless" (p.136). However, the authors did perceive "a constituency unified around the objectives of understanding better the traditions of understanding one's own system of education by studying those of others' and assessing educational issues from a global perspective" (p.130). Among the themes on which scholars indicated that their work focused, the most frequently-named were globalisation (7.9% of all responses), gender in education (7.6%), education and development (4.6%), equality in education (4.0%), and multiculturalism, race and ethnicity (3.7%); but a huge number of additional themes were named. Diversity was also apparent in methodological approaches and in geographic foci for study.

If patterns in the CIES were to be set aside patterns in other comparative education societies, the picture would show even greater diversity. This observation is elaborated upon in Chapter 2.

Conclusions

This chapter has sketched some of the diversity in actors and purposes in comparative study of education. Parents have very different purposes and therefore approaches from policy makers, and international agencies have very different purposes and approaches from academics. In addition, changes are evident over time.

This book is primarily concerned with the work of academics, and thus with matters of conceptualisation and understanding. Nevertheless, a general point is applicable to all categories, and links to the quotation above from Cook et al. (2004, p.13), namely that people who undertake comparative study of education commonly find not only that they that learn more about other cultures and societies but also that they learn more about their own. This was eloquently expressed by one of the great-grandfathers of the field, Sir Michael Sadler, who wrote in 1900 (reprinted 1964, p.310), that:

> The practical value of studying, in a right spirit and with scholarly accuracy, the working of foreign systems of education is that it will result in our being better fitted to study and understand our own.

The emphasis in this quotation is of an individual looking outwards, identifying another society and then comparing patterns with those in that individual's own society. Sadler suggested (p.312) that the comparison might encourage appreciation of domestic education systems as well as heightening awareness of shortcomings:

> If we study foreign systems of education thoroughly and sympathetically – and sympathy and thoroughness are both necessary for the task – I believe that the result on our minds will be to make us prize, as we have never prized before, the good things which we have at home, and also to make us realise how many things there are in our [own education systems] which need prompt and searching change.

Once the analyst has identified problems, the next logical step is to solutions. Isaac Kandel was a key figure in the generation which followed Sadler's. Kandel's 1933 book (p.xix) listed a set of problems which, he suggested, raised universal questions. Kandel then pointed out that:

> The chief value of a comparative approach to such problems lies in an analysis of the causes which have produced them, in a comparison of the differences between the various systems and the reasons underlying them, and, finally, in a study of the solutions attempted.

The tone of such a statement is more closely allied to theoretical goals; and Kandel's book to some extent established a tradition into which the present book fits. However, the field of comparative education has evolved in very significant ways since Kandel wrote those words. Some ways in which it has evolved, and some valuable ways to promote understanding through the use of different units for comparison, will become evident in the chapters which follow.

References

ACTEQ [Advisory Committee on Teacher Education & Qualifications] (2003): *Towards a Learning Profession: The Teacher Competencies Framework and the Continuing Professional Development of Teachers*. Hong Kong: ACTEQ.

Alexander, Robin (2008): *Essays on Pedagogy*. London: Routledge.

Altbach, Philip G. & Kelly, Gail P. (eds.) (1978): *Education and Colonialism*. New York: Longman.

Andere, Eduardo (2008): *The Lending Power of PISA: League Tables and Best Practice in International Education*. CERC Monographs in Comparative & International Education & Development 6, Hong Kong: Comparative Education Research Centre, The University of Hong Kong.

Bray, Mark & Varghese, N.V. (eds.) (2011): *Directions in Educational Planning: International Experiences and Perspectives*. Paris: UNESCO International Institute for Educational Planning (IIEP).

Breakspear, Simon (2012): *The Policy Impact of PISA: An Exploration of the Normative Effects of International Benchmarking in School System Performance*, OECD Education Working Papers 71, Paris: Organisation for Economic Co-operation and Development (OECD).

Cigno, Alessandro (2012): 'How to Deal with Covert Child Labor and Give Children an Effective Education, in a Poor Developing Country'. *World Bank Economic Review*, Vol.26, No.1, pp.61-77.

Collins, Christopher S. & Wiseman, Alexander W. (eds.) (2012): *Education Strategy in the Developing World: Revising the World Bank's Education Policy*. Bingley: Emerald.

Cook, Bradley J.; Hite, Steven J. & Epstein, Erwin H. (2004): 'Discerning Trends, Contours, and Boundaries in Comparative Education: A Survey of Comparativists and their Literature'. *Comparative Education Review*, Vol.48, No.2, pp.123-149.

Crossley, Michael & Watson, Keith (2003): *Comparative and International Research in Education: Globalisation, Context and Difference*. London: RoutledgeFalmer.

Dang, Hai-Anh & Rogers, F. Halsey (2008): The Growing Phenomenon of Private Tutoring: Does It Deepen Human Capital, Widen Inequalities, or Waste Resources? *World Bank Research Observer*, Vol.23, No.2, pp.161-200.

Finegold, David; McFarland, Laurel & Richardson, William (1992): 'Introduction', in Finegold, David; McFarland, Laurel & Richardson, William (eds.), *Something Borrowed, Something Blue? A Study of the Thatcher Government's Appropriation of American Education and Training Policy. Oxford Studies in Comparative Education*, Vol.2, No.2, pp.7-24.

Gifford, Prosser & Weiskel, Timothy C. (1971): 'African Education in a Colonial Context: French and British Styles', in Gifford, Prosser & Louis, William Roger (eds.), *France and Britain in Africa*. New Haven: Yale University Press, pp.663-711.

Henry, Miriam; Lingard, Bob; Rizvi, Fazal & Taylor, Sandra (2001): *The OECD, Globalisation and Education Policy*. Oxford: Pergamon Press.

Ho, Esther S.C. (2012): *Student Learning Assessment*. Bangkok: UNESCO.

Hong Kong, Education Commission (1999): *Review of Academic System: Aims of Education – Consultation Document*. Hong Kong: Education Commission.

Hong Kong, Education Commission (2000): *Review of Education System: Reform Proposals – Consultation Document*. Hong Kong: Education Commission.

International Review of Education (IRE) (2013): 'Aims and Scope of the Journal', *International Review of Education*, Vol.59, No.2.

Jones, Phillip W. (2006): *Education, Poverty and the World Bank*. Rotterdam: Sense.

Kandel, Isaac L. (1933): *Studies in Comparative Education*. London: George G. Harrap & Company.

Klees, Steven J.; Samoff, Joel & Stromquist, Nelly P. (eds.) (2012): *The World Bank and Education: Critiques and Alternatives*. Rotterdam: Sense.

Korea Times, The (2009): 'Obama Lauds Korea's Education of Children', 11 March. www.koreatimes.co.kr/www/news/nation/2009/03/113_41066.html accessed 5 August 2013.

Majgaard, Kirsten & Mingat, Alain (2012): *Education in Sub-Saharan Africa: A Comparative Analysis*. Washington DC: The World Bank.

Manzon, Maria (2011): *Comparative Education: The Construction of a Field*. CERC Studies in Comparative Education 29, Hong Kong: Comparative Education Research Centre, The University of Hong Kong, and Dordrecht: Springer.

Masemann, Vandra; Bray, Mark & Manzon, Maria (eds.) (2007): *Common Interests, Uncommon Goals: Histories of the World Council of Comparative Education Societies and its Members*. CERC Studies in Comparative Education 21, Hong Kong: Comparative Education Research Centre, The University of Hong Kong, and Dordrecht: Springer.

McFarland, Laurel (1993): 'Top-up Student Loans: American Models of Student Aid and British Public Policy', in Finegold, David; McFarland, Laurel & Richardson, William (eds.), *Something Borrowed, Something Blue? A Study of the Thatcher Government's Appropriation of American Education and Training Policy. Oxford Studies in Comparative Education*, Vol.3, No.1, pp.49-67.

Meyer, Heinz-Dieter & Benavot, Aaron (eds.) (2013): *PISA, Power and Policy: The Emergence of Global Educational Governance*. Oxford: Symposium.

Nafukho, Frederick Muyia; Wawire, Nelson H.W. & Lam, Penina Mungania (2011): *Management of Adult Education Organisations in Af-*

rica. Hamburg: UNESCO Institute for Lifelong Learning (UIL).

OECD (2004): *OECD Handbook for Internationally Comparative Education Statistics: Concepts, Standards, Definitions and Classifications*. Paris: Organisation for Economic Co-operation and Development (OECD).

OECD (2008): 'The OECD'. Paris: Organisation for Economic Co-operation and Development (OECD).

OECD (2010): *PISA 2009 Results – What Students Know and Can Do: Student Performance in Reading, Mathematics and Science*. Paris: Organisation for Economic Co-operation and Development (OECD).

OECD (2011): *Strong Performers and Successful Reformers in Education: Lessons from PISA for the United States*. Paris: Organisation for Economic Co-operation and Development (OECD).

OECD (2013a): *Education at a Glance 2013: OECD Indicators*. Paris: Organisation for Economic Co-operation and Development (OECD).

OECD (2013b): *PISA 2012 Assessment and Analytical Framework: Mathematics, Reading, Science, Problem Solving and Financial Literacy*. Paris: Organisation for Economic Co-operation and Development (OECD).

Park, Se Hoon (2012): 'Why the Korean School System is not Superior'. *New Politics*, Vol.XIII, No.4. http://newpol.org/content/why-korean-school-system-not-superior, accessed 5 August 2013.

Patrinos, Harry Anthony; Barrera-Osorio, Felipe & Guáqueta, Juliana (2009): *The Role and Impact of Public-Private Partnerships in Education*. Washington DC: The World Bank.

Pereyra, Miguel A.; Kotthof, Hans-Georg & Cowen, Robert (eds.) (2011): *PISA Under Examination: Changing Knowledge, Changing Tests, and Changing Schools*. Rotterdam: Sense.

Phillips, David & Ochs, Kimberly (2007): 'Processes of Policy Borrowing in Education: Some Explanatory and Analytical Devices', in Crossley, Michael; Broadfoot, Patricia & Schweisfurth, Michele (eds.), *Changing Educational Contexts, Issues and Identities: 40 Years of Comparative Education*. London: Routledge, pp.370-382.

Pratham (2013): *Annual Status of Education Report (Rural) 2012*. New Delhi: ASER Center. http://www.pratham.org/file/ASER-2012report.pdf, accessed 5 August 2013.

Rizvi, Fazal & Lingard, Bob (2009): 'The OECD and Global Shifts in Education Policy', in Cowen, Robert & Kazamias, Andreas (eds.), *International Handbook of Comparative Education*. Dordrecht: Springer, pp.437-453.

Roche, Stephen (2013): 'Plus ça change: Change and Continuity at the

International Review of Education'. International Review of Education, Vol.59, No.2, pp.153-156.

Sadler, Sir Michael (1900): 'How Far Can We Learn Anything of Practical Value from the Study of Foreign Systems of Education?' Reprinted 1964 in *Comparative Education Review*, Vol.7, No.3, pp.307-314.

Schiefelbein, Ernesto F. & McGinn, Noel F. (2008): *Learning to Educate: Proposals for the Reconstruction of Education in Latin America.* Geneva: UNESCO International Bureau of Education (IBE).

Sellar, Sam & Lingard, Bob (2013): 'Looking East: Shanghai, PISA 2009 and the Reconstituting of Reference Societies in the Global Education Policy Field'. *Comparative Education*, Vol.49, No.4, pp.464-485.

Simola, Hannu & Rinne, Ristu (2011): 'Education Politics and Contingency: Belief, Status and Trust Behind the Finnish PISA Miracle', in Pereyra, Miguel A.; Kotthof, Hans-Georg & Cowen, Robert (eds.), *PISA Under Examination: Changing Knowledge, Changing Tests, and Changing Schools.* Rotterdam: Sense, pp.225-244.

Singh, J.P. (2011): *United Nations Educational, Scientific and Cultural Organization (UNESCO): Creating Norms for a Complex World.* London: Routledge.

Sondergaard, Lars; Murthi, Mamta; Abu-Ghaida, Dina; Bodewig, Christian & Rutkowski, Jan (2012): *Skills, Not Just Diplomas: Managing Education for Results in Eastern Europe and Central Asia.* Washington DC: The World Bank.

Statistics Canada (2013): *Summary Elementary and Secondary School Indicators for Canada, the Provinces and Territories, 2006/2007 to 2010/2011.* Ottawa: Tourism and Centre for Education and Statistics Division, Statistics Canada.

Steiner-Khamsi, Gita (2002): 'Reterritorializing Educational Import: Explorations into the Politics of Educational Borrowing', in Nóvoa, António & Lawn, Martin (eds.), *Fabricating Europe: The Formation of an Education Space.* Dordrecht: Kluwer Academic Publishers, pp.69-86.

Steiner-Khamsi, Gita (ed.) (2004): *The Global Politics of Educational Borrowing and Lending.* New York: Teachers College Press.

Steiner-Khamsi, Gita & Waldow, Florian (eds.) (2012): *Policy Borrowing and Lending in Education: World Yearbook of Education 2012.* London: Routledge.

Sutherland, Stewart R. (Chair) (2002): *Higher Education in Hong Kong: Report of the University Grants Committee.* Hong Kong: University

Grants Committee.

Thomas, R. Murray & Postlethwaite, T. Neville (eds.) (1984): *Schooling in the Pacific Islands: Colonies in Transition*. Oxford: Pergamon Press.

Tucker, Marc S. (2011): *Surpassing Shanghai: An Agenda for American Education Built on the World's Leading Systems*. Cambridge, MA: Harvard University Press.

UNESCO (1945): *Constitution of the United Nations Educational, Scientific and Cultural Organization*. Paris: UNESCO.

UNESCO (2012): *Youth and Skills – Putting Education to Work: Education for All Global Monitoring Report 2012*. Paris: UNESCO.

UNESCO (2013): *Medium-Term Strategy 2014-2021: 37 C/4*. Paris: UNESCO.

UNESCO Institute for Statistics (2012): *Global Education Digest 2012 - Opportunities Lost: The Impact of Grade Repetition and Early School Leaving*. Montreal: UNESCO Institute for Statistics.

Van de Sijpe, Nicolas (2013): 'Is Foreign Aid Fungible? Evidence from the Education and Health Sectors'. *World Bank Economic Review*, Vol.27, No.2, pp.320-356.

Varjo, Janne; Simola, Hannu & Rinne, Risto (2013): 'Finland's PISA Results: An Analysis of Dynamics in Education Politics', in Meyer, Heinz-Dieter & Benavot, Aaron (eds.), *PISA, Power and Policy: The Emergence of Global Educational Governance*. Oxford: Symposium, pp.51-76.

Waldow, Florian (2009): 'What PISA did and did not do: Germany after the 'PISA-shock''. *European Educational Research Journal*, Vol.8, No.3, pp.476-483.

Whitty, Geoff (2012): 'Policy Tourism and Policy Borrowing in Education: A Trans-Atlantic Case Study', in Steiner-Khamsi, Gita & Waldow, Florian (eds.), *Policy Borrowing and Lending in Education: World Yearbook of Education 2012*. London: Routledge, pp.354-370.

Woodward, Richard (2009): *The Organisation for Economic Co-operation and Development (OECD)*. London: Routledge.

World Bank, The (2011): *Learning for All: Investing in People's Knowledge and Skills to Promote Development – World Bank Group Education Strategy 2020*. Washington DC: The World Bank.

World Bank, The (2012): *Education: Year in Review 2012*. Washington DC: The World Bank.

World Bank, The (2013): 'Education: Overview'. http://web.worldbank.org/wbsite/external/topics/exteducation/0,,contentMDK:20575742~menuPK:282393~pagePK:210058~piPK:210062~theSitePK:282386,00.html, accessed 6 August 2013.

World Council of Comparative Education Societies (WCCES) (2013): 'About Us' www.wcces.com accessed 5 August 2013.

2

Scholarly Enquiry and the Field of Comparative Education

Mark BRAY

The previous chapter noted that the field of comparative education is by nature interdisciplinary. This chapter elaborates on this theme, and examines ways in which the field relates to other domains of academic study.

A useful starting point is a 1989 book written by Tony Becher. It was published in second edition in 2001 under the co-authorship of Tony Becher and Paul Trowler, with the title *Academic Tribes and Territories: Intellectual Enquiry and the Culture of Disciplines*. Both editions lucidly analysed dimensions of the academic arena, with the second edition extending analysis and updating it to take account of several powerful influences on the size and shape of higher education. Although both editions were primarily concerned with the United Kingdom (UK) and the United States of America (USA), they also had considerable relevance to other countries. The domain of educational studies was given only passing attention in the books, but patterns and trends in educational studies can be mapped against those in other domains fairly easily. This chapter is chiefly based on the second edition of the book, together with a sequel edited by Trowler et al. (2012a). The chapter also draws on the works of many other scholars, and particularly the conceptual schema presented by Olivera (1988).

Defining Tribes and Mapping Territories

The tribes to which Becher and Trowler referred are academic communities as defined in part by the members of those communities and in part by the institutions which employ them and which locate them in departments, centres or other units. The territories are the academic ideas on which they focus. This includes methodological approaches, subject matter, and modes of discourse.

The subtitle of the book referred to the culture of disciplines. Cultures were defined (Becher & Trowler 2001, p.23) as "sets of taken-for-granted values, attitudes and ways of behaving, which are articulated through and reinforced by recurrent practices among a group of people in a given context". The primary focus of the book was on "practitioners in a dozen disciplines whose livelihood it is to work with ideas … [which] lend themselves to sustained exploration, and which form the subject matter of the disciplines in question".

This statement raises a question about the definition of disciplines. Many authors (e.g. Furlong & Lawn 2011; Manzon 2011; Bridges 2014) have noted that the concept of an academic discipline is not altogether straightforward. Becher and Trowler (2001, p.41) also recognised the point, observing that:

> There may be doubts, for example, whether statistics is now sufficiently separate from its parent discipline, mathematics, to constitute a discipline on its own. The answer will depend on the extent to which leading academic institutions recognize the hiving off in terms of their organizational structures (whether, that is, they number statistics among their fully-fledged departments), and also on the degree to which a freestanding international community has emerged, with its own professional associations and specialist journals.

Nevertheless, Becher and Trowler asserted (p.41) that "people with any interest and involvement in academic affairs seem to have little difficulty in understanding what a discipline is, or in taking a confident part in discussions about borderline or dubious cases".

Within these parameters, various disciplinary groupings have different characteristics. Table 2.1 presents a classification into four categories based on a hard/soft and pure/applied matrix. The boundaries are not sharp, but the classification is nevertheless useful. The table places education in the soft-applied category, describing it as functional and utilitarian, and "concerned with enhancement of [semi-] professional practice". This contrasts with the hard-pure sciences, for example, which are described as cumulative and atomistic, and concerned with universals, quantities and simplification.

Table 2.1: Disciplinary Groupings and the Nature of Knowledge

Disciplinary groupings	Nature of knowledge
Pure sciences (e.g. physics): 'hard-pure'	Cumulative; atomistic (crystalline/tree-like); concerned with universals, quantities, simplification; impersonal, value-free; clear criteria for knowledge verification and obsolescence; consensus over significant questions to address, now and in the future; results in discovery/ explanation.
Humanities (e.g. history) and pure social sciences (e.g. anthropology): 'soft-pure'	Reiterative; holistic (organic/river-like); concerned with particulars, qualities, complication; personal, value-laden; dispute over obsolescence; lack of consensus over significant questions to address; results in under-standing/appreciation.
Technologies (e.g. mechanical engineering, clinical medicine): 'hard-applied'	Purposive; pragmatic (know-how via hard knowledge); concerned with mastery of physical environment; ap-plies heuristic approaches; uses both qualitative and quantitative approaches; criteria for judgement are purposive, functional; results in products/techniques.
Applied social science (e.g. education, law, social administration): 'soft-applied'	Functional; utilitarian (know-how via soft knowledge); concerned with enhancement of [semi-] professional practice; uses case studies and case law to a large extent; results in protocols and procedures.

Source: Becher & Trowler (2001), p.36.

Becher and Trowler also distinguished between emphases in disciplines by framing an analogy between urban and rural ways of life (p.106):

> [We] may liken specialisms which have a high people-to-problem ratio to urban areas, and those with a low one to rural areas. In the first, there is alongside a densely concentrated population a generally busy – occasionally frenetic – pace of life, a high level of collective activity, close competition for space and resources, and a rapid and heavily used information network. By and large, the rural scene, though it may offer frenetic and competitive moments, occasions for communal and involvement and a potential for spreading rumour and gossip like wildfire, displays the opposite characteristics.

In this categorisation, urban and rural specialisms differ not only in the communication patterns but also in the nature and scale of the problems on which their inhabitants are engaged, in the relationships between those inhabitants, and in the opportunities they have for attracting resources. Urban researchers typically select narrow areas of study, containing discrete and separable problems, while their rural counterparts commonly cover a broader stretch of intellectual territory in which the problems are not sharply demarcated or delineated. Competition in urban life can become intense, even cut-throat: an all-out race to find the solution to what is seen as a seminal problem. In rural life it makes more sense to adopt the principle of division of labour – there are plenty of topics, so there is no point in tackling one on which someone else is already engaged. Teamwork is another feature more common in urban than rural settings. Publications in urban fields are typically short and have multiple authors and rapid turn-around times. In rural areas, authors commonly wait over a year, and sometimes considerably longer, for their articles to appear. Books are more important in rural disciplines than in urban ones.

While many of these features are durable, the decades have brought what Becher and Trowler (2001, p.xiii) called "major geomorphic shifts". These shifts have continued significantly during the present century to such an extent that Trowler et al. (2012b, p.257) at least partly agreed with Manathunga and Brew (2012) that the metaphor of tribes and territories might usefully be changed, e.g. to focus on oceans which have tides and in which "spaces 'flow' into each other, merging to form different times of knowledge groupings as problems and needs arise" (Manathunga & Brew 2012, p.51). Yet whatever the metaphor, most analysis would agree that important changes include the increasingly intrusive role of the state, demands for performance, and an increasing need for academics to 'chase the dollar'. The demands of funding bodies have changed the nature of the products produced by academics, and Research Assessment Exercises and similar schemes have extended processes of accountability and heightened anxieties within the academic world. These changes have affected education, including comparative education, alongside other fields.

Education, and Comparative Education, in Relation to Other Domains of Enquiry

Although Table 2.1 explicitly names education as inhabiting a disciplinary territory, its disciplinary basis is not undisputed. The field of education does have departments, degrees and specialist journals, but its intellectual substance tends to draw on other disciplines and rather rarely to assert distinctive characteristics which are unique to the study of education (Furlong & Lawn 2011).

If it is doubtful whether the whole domain of education could be considered a discipline, it is even more doubtful whether comparative education could be considered one. A few people have described comparative education as a discipline (e.g. Youngman 1992; Higginson 2001; Wolhuter & Popov 2007), but most see it as a field which welcomes scholars who are equipped with tools and perspectives from other arenas and who choose to focus on educational issues in a comparative context (Manzon 2011). Such a view has been presented for example by Lê Thành Khôi (1986, p.15), who described comparative education as "a field of study covering all the disciplines which serve to understand and explain education".

Olivera has examined this matter in more detail in a pair of works. The account below draws chiefly on his 1988 foundational paper which he elaborated two decades later in a volume written in Spanish (Olivera 2009). First, he noted (1988, p.174), most knowledge of a scientific level about education consists:

> of a heterogeneous collection of contributions coming from philosophy, psychology, sociology, economics, politics 'of education'. Their authors, usually not personally involved in the education system, naturally bring to these studies the bias of their particular disciplines. The economist worries about the degree of real abilities of the 'human resources' produced by education, and tries to evaluate the cost of their acquisition; the sociologist wants to know whether education prepares people to adapt themselves to their social environment, or perhaps to foster change and revolution; the philosopher, from a wider perspective, inquires into the general meaning and the goals of education, what such goals are and should be in today's world.

Olivera noted that all these contributions of the plural 'sciences of education' are valuable and even indispensable; but he suggested that they remain on the fringes of the specific features of the day-to-day processes of growth and development, the interpersonal relationships between educators and educated, and the corresponding frame of institutional arrangements. Olivera then declared that the domain of education does have a unique disciplinary body of knowledge, and that it deserves a label to reflect that. Existing commonly-used labels, he suggested, are inadequate. Thus Pedagogy is misleading because it does not refer to a knowledge but to an action – that of 'leading' children, first to their teacher and later to learning as such. Olivera also rejected as inadequate the terms Didactics, Sciences of Education (in the plural), and Science of Education (in the singular); and he declared (p.176) that "simply to say 'education' is a semantic nonsense: education is an activity not a knowledge – just as society is not sociology, language is not linguistics, and animals are not zoology".

To overcome this difficulty, Olivera drew on the proposals previously made by Christensen (1984) and Steiner Maccia (1964), and asserted that there was no better word than 'educology'. The word, he declared, "clearly designates all educational knowledge, and nothing but that knowledge, whether scientific or pragmatic, acquired through any discipline". He added that the word might initially look strange, or even pedantic, just as 'sociology' – another Graeco-Latin hybrid – did in its time; but, he claimed, "it brings to educational science such clarity and precision that it should be generally adopted".

Olivera recognised that more important than the name was the basic theoretical structure of the contents of educology, that is, of the whole field of educational knowledge into which every new piece of research could find its place and be tested for congruence with already existing knowledge. Olivera proposed such delineation with the aid of a diagram which separated the human sciences on the one hand from the sciences 'of education' on the other hand, and located educology between them. In turn, these were linked to object-realities as shown in Figure 2.1.

The question then for the present chapter is where comparative education fits into this schema, for it is notably absent from Figure 2.1. To answer this question, Olivera began by noting (p.179) that at the level of common or pre-scientific knowledge, comparison between objects, and therefore the establishment of mental relationships among them, lies at the very origin of concepts and ideas. A refined form of the same mental processes is used at the scientific level for establishing definitions, measuring phenomena, or building models. Thus each component in Figure

2.1 is based on comparison, and the distinctions between the sciences are themselves the results of comparison (between their objects, viewpoints, methods, etc.).

But if comparison as a method is universal, Olivera continued (p.180), a 'comparative' science only deserves this name when it carries comparison to a higher level of abstraction – becoming in effect a 'comparison of comparisons'. Thus, particularly in social disciplines, "the adjective 'comparative' can only be used when the comparison is applied to previously elaborated sets of theoretical statements referring to realities of a similar kind pertaining to discrete social groups". In many comparative fields, including comparative education, one common such social group is a nation or a country; but any case, being 'discrete' these units can always be approached as 'systems'. Since each of those previous sets of knowledge is in itself partially the result of comparison, comparative fields of enquiry in effect present a sort of second-degree use of the comparative method.

In turn, this explains why comparative education was not included in Figure 2.1: it would have required a third dimension to the diagram, since comparative education represents in effect a higher epistemological level. As explained by Olivera (p.181):

> Its approach to truth covers all the particular objects of the disciplines mentioned in the central section of the diagram. But strictly speaking, it does not tackle any of them directly, for it is not interested in any single educational situation, but in two or more at the same time. In order to manage several real objects simultaneously, each of these situations must have been rendered manageable, that is, comparable, through a first level of abstraction.

Thus, commencing with a plurality of these abstract models and using its own theoretical and methodological tools, comparative education produces its own second-degree data and reaches its own conclusions. Such conclusions may be of many kinds, including laws or quasi-laws, provisional theories, confirmations or refutations of previous theories, new hypotheses for future research, and so on. As Olivera concluded (p.181), these products, now of a truly comparative nature, "may of course be used for action on any of the systems originally studied; but above all they enlarge and eventually modify the data and the conclusions of the specific studies, and provide feed-back to individual disciplines".

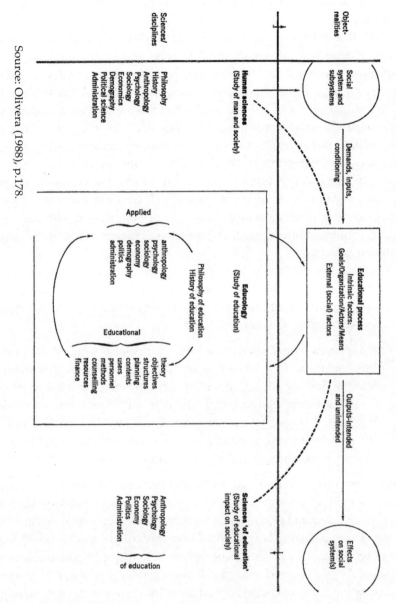

Figure 2.1: Olivera's System-Based Classification of Education-Related Disciplines

Source: Olivera (1988), p.178.

Methodology and Focus in Comparative Education

As explained above, the disciplines which have had the greatest impact on comparative education are clustered in the social sciences. To some extent, therefore, shifts in dominant paradigms within the social sciences have led to shifts in the field of comparative education. This includes the rise of positivism in the 1960s and 1970s, particularly in Europe and North America, the popularity of post-modernism in the 1980s and 1990s, and the ubiquity of globalisation as a lens in the 2000s and 2010s (Epstein 1994; Paulston 2000; Cowen & Kazamias 2009a; Davies 2009; Larsen 2010). However, comparative education scholars have tended to use a fairly limited set of tools from the social sciences. This is partly for the reasons explained above, i.e. that much (or even most) comparative education is in a sense a second-level comparison which relies on units which have already been identified through comparison. Books and journal articles in the field of comparative education contain many commentaries based on literature reviews, but relatively few studies based on survey research, and almost no studies based on experimental methods.

In order to gain a deeper understanding of this phenomenon, Foster et al. (2012) analysed articles published between 2004 and 2008 in four major English-language journals. One was a US journal, namely the *Comparative Education Review*; and the others were UK journals, namely *Comparative Education, Compare: A Journal of Comparative Education,* and the *International Journal of Educational Development*. Foster et al. found (p.712) that the articles "addressed education in society (social context) nearly a third more often than education administration and governance (direct education context), and more than twice as often as direct teaching and learning (education content)." Education policy and planning were the focus of 41 per cent of the articles, followed by education theory (24%), attitudes and values (21%), and globalisation (20%). Information and communication technology, education leadership, examinations, and textbooks each attracted only 2 per cent of the articles. Geographically, 24 per cent of articles focused on Africa, 23 per cent on Asia, 17 per cent on Europe, and 21 per cent on more than one region.

Foster et al. (2012, p.728) also examined the methods. Over half (53%) of the articles employed document review and historical analysis, 35 per cent on survey/quantitative analysis, and 27 per cent on interviews/focus groups. Only 1 per cent used experimental or quasi-experimental methods, and another 1 per cent tracer or longitudinal studies.

This survey to some extent built on an earlier survey by Rust et al. (1999). They had taken a longer time span, namely 1957 to 1995, and focused on *Comparative Education Review, Comparative Education,* and the *International*

Journal of Educational Development. Concerning the 1960s, Rust et al. found (p.100) that 48 per cent were mainly based on literature review and 15 per cent were historical studies. For the 1980s and 1990s, Rust et al. found a marked drop in the two categories – to 26 per cent mainly based on literature review, and 5 per cent historical studies. Reviews of projects had increased, as had participant observation and research based on interviews and questionnaires. In this respect, the field had increased its use of at least some standard social science instruments.

However, dominant themes and methodological approaches have been very different in different parts of the world at particular periods in history. McGrath (2012, p.709), writing an Editorial about the Foster et al. (2012) article was careful to remark that the analysis was conducted on English-medium journals published in a pair of countries that had related research cultures. Such cultures are not necessarily found elsewhere. Along this line, Cowen and Kazamias (2009b, p.4) highlighted the co-existence of multiple comparative educations. Their observation on the one hand applies to different groups within particular countries who have different methodological approaches and domains of enquiry, and who may or may not communicate with each other. It also applies to groups in different countries who operate in different languages with different scholarly traditions, and who also may or may not communicate with counterparts in other countries and language groups.

Beginning with the first of these two groups, it is useful to note the maps of the field produced by Paulston (1997; 2000; see also Weidman & Jacob 2011). Figure 2.2 reproduces one of these maps, showing paradigms and theories in international and comparative education. While it portrays some overlap in the perspectives of humanists and functionalists, it also shows domains in which they operated entirely independently of each other. A similar point could be made from review of bibliographies: many scholars in the field simply ignore others who have different viewpoints, and are nevertheless able to get their work published either because the journals in which they publish are eclectic in focus or because the journals serve different audiences. Epstein (1992, p.23) is among scholars who have pointed out that certain rival epistemological orientations in the field of comparative education are fundamentally incompatible.

Figure 2.2: A Macro-Mapping of Paradigms and Theories in Comparative and International Education

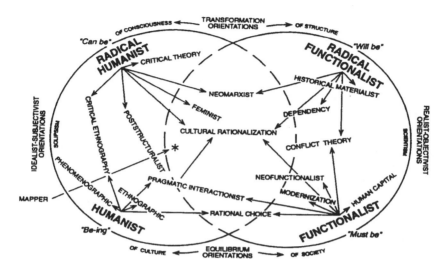

Source: Paulston (1997), p.142.

To the differences which arise between scholars who work in different paradigms within particular countries, and who do not communicate with each other despite being nationals of the same countries and writing in the same languages, may be added the differences between scholars who live in different countries and who write in different languages. Scholars may of course use similar paradigms even though they operate in different languages; but the probability that they will use different paradigms is increased when they do not even share common languages. Concerning this matter, it is instructive to compare the work of Harold Noah and Max Eckstein during the three decades from the mid-1970s with that of Gu Mingyuan. Sets of collected works by these authors have been published by the Comparative Education Research Centre at the University of Hong Kong, and thus may easily be placed side by side (Noah & Eckstein 1998; Gu 2001). Among the major concerns of Noah and Eckstein, who were based in the USA and who operated mainly in the English- speaking arena, were methodological issues in the positivist framework and oriented to First World concerns. Gu, by contrast, operated mainly in the Russian- and Chinese-speaking arenas. His writings, particularly during the early part of his career, were couched within a Marxist-Leninist framework, and he was especially concerned with the lessons that China could learn from industrialised countries. Especially during the 1970s and 1980s, the comparative education world in which Gu lived was a very different environment from that in which Noah and Eckstein lived.

Everywhere, one domain in which the fundamentals of the field of comparative education could be challenged concerned the extent to which the writings in the field were actually comparative. A longstanding complaint by many scholars in the field (e.g. Cummings 1999; Little 2000; Wolhuter 2008) has been that many articles even in journals which explicitly include the word Comparative in their titles, such as *Comparative Education* and *Comparative Education Review*, contain large numbers of single-country studies in which the nature and extent of comparison is open to question. In conferences devoted to the field, in which the screening processes are usually much more lax than for publication in journals, the conceptual looseness is even more pronounced. Thus, as noted by Olivera (1988, pp.166-167), for example:

> The list of papers presented to the last two World Congresses of Comparative Education Societies (Paris, 1984; Rio de Janeiro, 1987: over 350 papers in all) is … very revealing. Only a minority (19 per cent in Paris, 26 per cent in Rio) are genuinely comparative studies, dealing either with worldwide educational problems or with specific issues studies in two or more countries. Another 13-17 per cent attach themselves to problems of theory, epistemology or methodology. On the other hand, about half of the papers (45 per cent in Rio) are case-studies, which do no more than describe and sometimes analyse a system, a historical process, an innovation or a special national situation. Not only is there no comparison here, but they make no attempt to draw any conclusions or at least to suggest some hypothesis which could be useful in other contexts. Then, a sizeable number (7 per cent in Rio) propose some reflections on education or describe some innovation in a general way, without reference to any concrete situation.

Part of the reason for this looseness arises from alliances between the field of comparative education and the field of international education, which Wilson (1994) described as Siamese twins. The term international education means different things to different people. For example, some individuals describe it as the process of training people to see themselves as international in orientation (e.g. Gellar 2002); while others have used the term international education to mean "the various types of educational and cultural relations among nations" (Scanlon & Shields 1968, p.x). The distinction drawn by Rust (2002, p.iii) is that comparative education covers more academic, analytic and scientific aspects of the field, while international education is related to cooperation, understanding, and exchange elements. In the US, the Comparative Education Society (CES), which had been founded in 1956, was renamed the Comparative and International Education Society (CIES) in 1968 (Swing 2007), though the official journal of that society retained its name as the *Comparative Education Review*. Other professional societies in which the twin fields are placed together include the Comparative and International Education Society of Canada (CIESC), the British Association for International and Comparative Education (BAICE), and the Australian and New Zealand Comparative and International Education Society (ANZCIES).

The ambiguities reflected in these names contribute to the ambiguities in the field. The editors of the CIES journal find it difficult to reject articles which could be described as part of international education rather than comparative education, since the former is as much a part of the name of the CIES as is the latter, even though the title of the journal reflects only the comparative side of the society's name. For some time a similar remark applied to the BAICE journal, which was entitled *Compare: A Journal of Comparative Education*, but in 2009 the problem was resolved by making the sub-title *A Journal of Comparative and International Education* (Bray 2010). The CIESC journal has the opposite bias, because it is entitled *Canadian and International Education* and thus does not mention comparison in its title. The ANZCIES journal has a different configuration as the *International Education Journal: Comparative Perspectives*.

The World Council of Comparative Education Societies (WCCES) does not contain the word International in its title, and in that sense is less constrained by the ambiguities that confront the four above-named national societies. However, these four bodies are among the 39 constituent societies of the WCCES, and the world body is thus also influenced by the ambiguities – especially because the US-based Comparative & International Education Society (CIES) has always been the largest and most active of the WCCES constituent societies (Masemann et al. 2007). Thus, when World Congresses of Comparative Education Societies are organised on behalf of the WCCES, loose definitions of the field are always used. In the specific cases of the 1984 Paris Congress and the 1987 Rio de Janeiro

Congress mentioned above, the organisers, as noted by Olivera (1988, p.168), did not feel entitled to refuse any of the papers to which Olivera referred since there seemed to be no accepted criteria to define what was and what was not comparative education. The same issue has recurred in each subsequent Congress.

Geomorphic Shifts

As noted above, Becher and Trowler (2001) observed major changes in the domain of higher education, particularly in the UK and the US. These changes brought what Becher and Trowler called "major geomorphic shifts" in the landscape on which the academic territories lay. Among the causes were the increasingly intrusive role of the state, demands for performance, and an increasing need for academics to 'chase the dollar'. The impact of these changes has been felt in the field of comparative education as well as in other fields. However, the nature of the geomorphic shifts has been different in different parts of the world; and despite the geomorphic shifts, many continuities are evident.

In the UK and the US, one way in which the state has affected the field of comparative education has been through foreign aid policies. Indeed the paper by Foster et al. (2012) originated in work commissioned by the UK government's Department for International Development (DFID), which wished to support planning for research funding within the framework of UK foreign aid. Similarly, Rust et al. (1999) found that during the 1980s and 1990s, reviews of projects were more prominent than in earlier years in the three journals that they surveyed. Many of these projects were conducted under the auspices of DFID or its predecessors, and of the United States Agency for International Development (USAID). The projects commonly employed academics as consultants, and the types of projects on which those government bodies chose to focus in turn influenced the field of comparative education. Insofar as projects focused on primary rather than secondary education or vocational education, for example, academic papers were written about those domains. Also, many papers in UK and US journals have been concerned about the role of external assistance *per se*, including the work not only of bilateral agencies but also of multilateral ones such as the World Bank and UNESCO.

The policies of multilateral agencies and of governments in both rich and poor countries have also influenced the extent to which particular countries have been given prominence in the field. This point may be illustrated by contrasting the visibility in the comparative education conferences and literature of Nigeria and China. During the 1970s and 1980s Nigeria was relatively visible, first because of the foreign aid projects in Nigeria, second because Nigeria used its oil-generated revenues to recruit many foreign nationals for its education system, and third because the Nigerian government funded many Nigerians to go abroad for higher education. By the 1990s, the oil boom had evaporated and external bodies were less interested in Nigeria. Also, conditions for research in Nigeria by non-Nigerians became even more difficult than they had been, in part because of social unrest. By contrast, before the 1990s very few papers on China were presented in the conferences and journals of the UK and US comparative education societies. This was chiefly because the Chinese government operated a relatively closed-door policy, neither letting foreign researchers in nor encouraging Chinese scholars to go out. Related to this, the UK and US governments operated few projects in China. By the 2000s, however, this picture had changed dramatically. Many Chinese scholars were studying in UK and US universities, and had brought their insights and data with them. Foreign nationals found it much easier to visit China through a range of programmes, including aid and international exchange projects financed by foreign governments. A further significant element was the increase in the number of Chinese scholars who learned English and who therefore on the one hand had access to literature in English and on the other hand were able to communicate with outsiders in that language.

Another geomorphic shift of great significance to the field of comparative education was the break up of the Soviet Union. Insofar as countries were a major unit of analysis, the division of the USSR into 15 sovereign states greatly increased the visibility of those states in the field. As in China, moreover, the English language became much more widely spoken than had previously been the case.

Concerning performance, which was another element identified by Becher and Trowler, the UK became well known for its Research Assessment Exercises, which had counterparts in Hong Kong and various other places. These Exercises increased pressure on academics to publish, and in the field of comparative education contributed to the expansion of existing journals and to the launching of new ones. Expansion may be illustrated by the facts that:

- in 1992, the Netherlands-published *International Review of Education* increased from four to six issues a year;
- in 1993 the UK journal *Compare: A Journal of Comparative Education* increased from two to three issues a year, in 2003 it further expanded to four issues, in 2007 to five issues, and in 2009 to six issues.
- in 1998, the UK journal *International Journal of Educational Development* increased from four to six issues a year; and
- in 2002, the Chinese journal *Comparative Education Review* increased from six to 12 issues a year.

New journals appearing since the turn of the century include:

- *Comparative and International Education Review*, launched in Greece in 2003;
- *Research in Comparative and International Education*, which was launched in the UK in 2006; and
- the *Journal of International and Comparative Education*, which was launched by the University of Malaya in 2012.

In addition, of course, many comparative education scholars published in journals which were not specifically dedicated to the field. They also published books and contributed chapters to edited works. The expansion in publication outlets partly reflected general growth in higher education, and thus in the number of academics working in universities, but also the increased pressure on academics to conduct research and publish their findings.

The third element in the geomorphic shift identified by Becher and Trowler (2001) was the increased pressure to generate income. This pressure was chiefly caused by a general tendency of governments to reduce the extent to which they funded higher education institutions, and was coupled with higher education expansion which intensified competition between institutions. Many institutions sought to increase their non-government revenues through recruitment of fee-paying overseas students. This trend was especially evident in Australia, where higher education for overseas students became a major industry (Ninnes & Hellstén 2005; Zipin & Brennan 2012). In the process, the institutions and their staff members became more outward-looking. This internationalisation further contributed to the field of comparative education.

Related to this phenomenon, and forming a further major geomorphic shift, has been the advent and impact of globalisation. Easton

(2007, pp.7-8) has pointed out that globalisation is in many respects an old concept with deep roots, but the scale, nature and impact of globalisation during the 1990s and initial decades of the present century has certainly been new. In some respects, globalisation has revitalised the field of comparative education by emphasising the need for cross national perspectives and by providing new themes for analysis. However, in another sense it has diluted the field because large numbers of academics consider themselves to have international and comparative perspectives but have weak or non-existent grounding in the methodologies and traditions of the field (Crossley & Watson 2003, pp.1-11; Mitter 2009, p.98).

Finally, geomorphic shifts have been brought by technology. One component of this has been increased access to inexpensive air travel, which has facilitated the work of scholars who wish to undertake research outside their own countries. Perhaps even more significant has been the advent of the internet, which has greatly increased access to information. Accompanying the internet, e-mail permits academics dispersed around the globe to communicate with each other almost instantaneously at low cost. New technologies have also brought changes in the publishing industry. Many new journals are solely internet-based; and among the traditional journals, most have moved to electronic publication in parallel to their paper versions.

Partly because several of these geomorphic shifts were global in scope, the geographic differences in the field, highlighted above by contrasting the book written by Noah and Eckstein with that written by Gu, tended to narrow. Enlarging on this example, as China opened up and as English became more widespread, scholars in China paid more attention to the literatures and methodological approaches of Western countries. Academic interchange between the two cultures increased, facilitated by translations of materials and by cross-national visits by both sides.

Nevertheless, despite these geomorphic shifts, some characteristics of the field of comparative education have remained as pronounced in the present century as they were in previous eras. Thus, referring back to Olivera's comments about the lack of disciplinary coherence in the offerings at the Paris (1984) and Rio de Janeiro (1987) World Congresses of Comparative Education Societies, it is unlikely that analysis of offerings at the subsequent World Congresses would have done much to change his perspective.[1] Despite attempts in some quarters to circumscribe the field of comparative education more tightly, it remains very loosely defined in all regions of the world. The journals written in Chinese, German, English, French, Japanese, Korean and Spanish may differ from each other in their methodological emphases and in the themes chosen by their contributors, but are broadly comparable in their eclecticism and in the fact that they are methodologically much less rigorous than most purists in the field of comparative education would desire.

Conclusions

The extent to which education would be considered a discipline could be disputed. Becher and Trowler (2001) did consider it a discipline, albeit in the soft and applied categories. Other observers would consider it to be a field of study which welcomes scholars who have been trained in other domains. The field has developed significantly over the decades and centuries but, as noted by Olivera (1988, p.174), "an educator is not easily accepted as a member of the scientific community, unless he or she has had formal training in some other social discipline". Nevertheless, Olivera made a case for asserting the disciplinary identity of education more strongly, and proposed the more widespread use of the label 'educology'.

If education cannot easily be described as a discipline, the field of comparative education is even further from that status. The academic tribe which operates under the label of comparative education is a fairly loose grouping of individuals. It is related to another tribe which operates under the label of international education and which to some extent inhabits the same territory. There has been considerable inter-marriage between members of these tribes, leading to corresponding mixes in the characteristics of offspring (Wilson 1994, p.450; Turner 2010, pp.268-270).

One merit of an environment in which scholars from a range of disciplines are welcome to converge is that cross-fertilisation between approaches can be permitted and encouraged. This does occur to some extent in comparative education: economists, sociologists, demographers and political scientists meet together and illuminate each other through their varying perspectives on education systems and processes in differ-

---

[1] The subsequent World Congresses were held in in Montreal (1989), Prague (1992), Sydney (1996), Cape Town (1998), Chungbuk, South Korea (2001), Havana (2004), Sarajevo (2007), Istanbul (2010), and Buenos Aires (2013).

ent countries and cultures. However, the extent of cross-fertilisation is in many respects disappointing. As in multi-disciplinary universities where the Faculties of Law, Science, Architecture, Dentistry and Education do not usually have much intellectual interflow, and instead tend to inhabit separate intellectual territories within the same geographic space, the field of comparative education is also compartmentalised. Positivists and neo-Marxists do occasionally clash, and even more occasionally learn from each other, but in general they ignore each other. Similar remarks may be made about psychologists and anthropologists, and, moving to area specialisms, Africanists and Sinologists, for example.

Returning to Becher and Trowler's distinction between 'urban' and 'rural' fields, comparative education is on the whole rural in nature. Researchers typically cover broad stretches of intellectual territory in which the problems are not sharply demarcated or delineated, and the field does not have fierce competition resembling that in microchip technology or research on HIV/AIDS, for example. Team work in comparative education may be considered useful, but even when the teams exist they tend to be loosely organised. Instead it is commonly considered more sensible to opt for division of labour, on the grounds that plenty of topics await exploration and that there is little point in tackling ones on which others are intensively engaged. As in other rural fields of study, comparative education tends to have quite lengthy publication lag times, and book-length works are an important form of scholarly output in addition to journal articles.

Like other domains of enquiry, however, the territory of comparative education has undergone some geomorphic shifts in recent years. These shifts partly arise from the increasing intrusiveness of the state in higher education, from demands for performance, and from financial pressures. Other factors include technological advances, and geopolitical changes. These geomorphic shifts have altered the ways in which groups within the field of comparative education have defined themselves and have related both to each other and to academics in other fields. Certain ways of thinking, such as those associated with Cold War politics, have gone out of fashion, while others, including those related to globalisation, have come into fashion.

However, the field continues to tolerate considerable descriptive work of a low intellectual calibre. This is especially evident in conferences devoted to comparative education, where screening processes are even less rigorous than for publications. Thus, in addition to the extensive disciplinarity and interdisciplinarity is a considerable amount of non-disciplinarity. Alternatively, slightly adjusting the last of these words, the field of comparative education contains considerable undisciplined thinking, in which vague ideas and poorly thought-out methods of analysis are tolerated alongside more rigorous work. Some conference organisers and publishers would defend this situation on the grounds that undisciplined scholars, particularly if they are neophytes in the field, may at least have potential to inform their listeners and to become more rigorous in their own work. Other participants and observers would consider this eclecticism and lack of discipline to be detrimental to the field and to the advance of intellectual enquiry (Wiseman & Anderson 2013).

Among Olivera's (1988) pertinent observations was (p.175) that:

> In principle … only the educator is in a position to develop the science of education (as sociology is developed by sociologists, economics by economists or demography by demographers) with the help of, but not subservient to, other social scientists. But on the other hand, educators are not usually trained scientists, and anyway the time-consuming requirements of their profession would not leave them leisure to elaborate scientifically the data they gather in their work.

This remark presents a strong rationale for thinking not only within but also across disciplines. This process itself requires analysis of the nature of disciplines, and of the factors which contribute to the development of those disciplines.

References

Becher, Tony (1989): *Academic Tribes and Territories: Intellectual Enquiry and the Cultures of Disciplines*. Buckingham: The Society for Research into Higher Education & Open University Press.

Becher, Tony & Trowler, Paul R. (2001): *Academic Tribes and Territories: Intellectual Enquiry and the Culture of Disciplines*. 2nd edition. Buckingham: The Society for Research into Higher Education & Open University Press.

Bray, Mark (2010): 'Comparative Education and International Education in the History of *Compare*: Boundaries, Overlaps and Ambiguities'. *Compare: A Journal of Comparative and International Education*, Vol.40,

No.6, pp.711-725.

Bridges, David (2014): 'The Discipline(s) of Educational Research' in Reid, Alan D.; Hart, E. Paul & Peters, Michael A. (eds.), *A Comparison to Research in Education.* Dordrecht: Springer, pp.31-39.

Christensen, James (1984): 'Comparative Educology: A Bridging Concept for Comparative Educational Enquiry'. Paper presented at the Fifth World Congress of Comparative Education Societies, Paris. [as cited in Olivera 1988]

Cowen, Robert & Kazamias, Andreas M. (eds.) (2009a): *International Handbook of Comparative Education.* Dordrecht: Springer.

Cowen, Robert & Kazamias, Andreas M. (2009b): 'Joint Editorial Introduction', in Cowen, Robert & Kazamias, Andreas M. (eds.), *International Handbook of Comparative Education.* Dordrecht: Springer, pp.3-6.

Crossley, Michael & Watson, Keith (2003): *Comparative and International Research in Education: Globalisation, Context and Difference.* London: RoutledgeFalmer.

Cummings, William K. (1999): 'The InstitutionS of Education: Compare, Compare, Compare!'. *Comparative Education Review,* Vol.43, No.4, pp.413-437.

Davies, Lynn (2009): 'Comparative Education in an Increasingly Globalised World', in Zajda, Joseph & Rust, Val (eds.), *Globalisation, Policy and Comparative Research: Discourses of Globalisation.* Dordrecht: Springer, pp.13-34.

Easton, Brian (2007): *Globalisation and the Wealth of Nations.* Auckland: Auckland University Press.

Epstein, Erwin H. (1992): 'The Problematic Meaning of "Comparison" in Comparative Education', in Schriewer, Jürgen in cooperation with Holmes, Brian (eds.), *Theories and Methods in Comparative Education.* 3rd edition, Frankfurt am Main: Peter Lang, pp.3-23.

Epstein, Erwin H. (1994): 'Comparative and International Education: Overview and Historical Development', in Husén, Torsten & Postlethwaite, T. Neville (eds.), *The International Encyclopedia of Education.* 2nd edition, Oxford: Pergamon Press, pp.918-923.

Foster, Jesse; Addy, Nii Antiaye & Samoff, Joel (2012): 'Crossing Borders: Research in Comparative and International Education'. *International Journal of Educational Development,* Vol.32, No.6, pp.711-732.

Furlong, John & Lawn, Martin (eds.) (2011): *Disciplines of Education: Their Role in the Future of Education Research.* London: Routledge

Gellar, Charles A. (2002): 'International Education: A Commitment to

Universal Values'. in Hayden, Mary; Thompson, Jeff & Walker, George (eds.), *International Education in Practice: Dimensions for National and International Schools*. London: Kogan Page, pp.30-35.

Gu Mingyuan (2001): *Education in China and Abroad: Perspectives from a Lifetime in Comparative Education*. CERC Studies in Comparative Education 9. Hong Kong: Comparative Education Research Centre, The University of Hong Kong.

Higginson, J.H. (2001): 'The Development of a Discipline: Some Reflections on the Development of Comparative Education as Seen through the Pages of the Journal *Compare*', in Watson, Keith (ed.), *Doing Comparative Education Research: Issues and Problems*. Oxford: Symposium, pp.373-388.

Larsen, Marianne A. (2010): *New Thinking in Comparative Education: Honouring Robert Cowen*. Rotterdam: Sense.

Lê Thành Khôi (1986): 'Toward a General Theory of Education', *Comparative Education Review*, Vol.30, No.1, pp.12-29.

Little, Angela (2000): 'Development Studies and Comparative Education: Context, Content, Comparison and Contributors'. *Comparative Education*, Vol.36, No.3, pp.279-296.

Manathunga, Catherine & Brew, Angela (2012): 'Beyond Tribes and Territories: New Metaphors for New Times', in Trowler, Paul; Saunders, Murray & Bamber, Veronica (eds.), *Tribes and Territories in the 21st Century: Rethinking the Significance of Disciplines in Higher Education*. London: Routledge, pp.44-56.

Manzon, Maria (2011): *Comparative Education: The Construction of a Field*. Hong Kong: Comparative Education Research Centre, The University of Hong Kong, and Dordrecht: Springer.

Masemann, Vandra; Bray, Mark & Manzon, Maria (eds.) (2007): *Common Interests, Uncommon Goals: Histories of the World Council of Comparative Education Societies and its Members*. CERC Studies in Comparative Education 21, Hong Kong: Comparative Education Research Centre, The University of Hong Kong, and Dordrecht: Springer.

McGrath, Simon (2012): 'Editorial: Researching International Education and Development'. *International Journal of Educational Development*, Vol.32, No.6, pp.709-710.

Mitter, Wolfgang (2009): 'Comparative Education in Europe', in Cowen, Robert & Kazamias, Andreas M. (eds.), *International Handbook of Comparative Education*. Dordrecht: Springer, pp.87-99.

Ninnes, Peter & Hellstén, Meeri (eds.) (2005): *Internationalizing Higher*

Education: Critical Explorations of Pedagogy and Policy. CERC Studies in Comparative Education 16. Hong Kong: Comparative Education Research Centre, The University of Hong Kong, and Dordrecht: Springer.

Noah, Harold J. & Eckstein, Max A. (1998): *Doing Comparative Education: Three Decades of Collaboration*. CERC Studies in Comparative Education 6. Hong Kong: Comparative Education Research Centre, The University of Hong Kong.

Olivera, Carlos E. (1988): 'Comparative Education: Towards a Basic Theory', *Prospects: Quarterly Review of Education*, Vol.XVIII, No.2, pp. 167-185.

Olivera, Carlos E. (2009): *Introducción a la Educación Comparada*. San José, Costa Rica: Editorial Universidad Estatal a Distancia.

Paulston, Rolland G. (1997): 'Mapping Visual Culture in Comparative Education Discourse'. *Compare: A Journal of Comparative Education*, Vol.27, No.2, pp.117-152.

Paulston, Rolland G. (ed.) (2000): *Social Cartography: Mapping Ways of Seeing Social and Educational Change*. New York: Garland.

Rust, Val D. (2002): 'Editorial: The Place of International Education in the *Comparative Education Review*'. *Comparative Education Review*, Vol.46, No.3, pp.iii-iv.

Rust, Val D.; Soumaré, Aminata; Pescador, Octavio & Shibuya, Megumi (1999): 'Research Strategies in Comparative Education'. *Comparative Education Review*, Vol.43, No.1, pp.86-109.

Scanlon, David G. & Shields, James J. (1968): 'Introduction', in Scanlon, David G. & Shields, James J. (eds.), *Problems and Prospects in International Education*. New York: Teachers College Press, pp.ix-xxii.

Swing, Elizabeth Sherman (2007): 'The Comparative and International Education Society (CIES)', in Masemann, Vandra; Bray, Mark & Manzon, Maria (eds.), *Common Interests, Uncommon Goals: Histories of the World Council of Comparative Education Societies and its Members*. CERC Studies in Comparative Education 21, Hong Kong: Comparative Education Research Centre, The University of Hong Kong, and Dordrecht: Springer, pp.94-115.

Steiner Maccia, Elizabeth (1964): 'Logic of Education and Educatology: Dimensions of Philosophy of Education'. *Proceedings of the Twentieth Annual Conference of the Philosophy of Education*. [as cited in Olivera 1988]

Trowler, Paul; Saunders, Murray & Bamber, Veronica (eds.) (2012a): *Tribes and Territories in the 21st Century: Rethinking the Significance of Disciplines in Higher Education*. London: Routledge.

Trowler, Paul; Saunders, Murray & Bamber, Veronica (2012b): 'Conclusion: Academic Practices and the Disciplines in the 21st Century', in Trowler, Paul; Saunders, Murray & Bamber, Veronica (eds.), *Tribes and Territories in the 21st Century: Rethinking the Significance of Disciplines in Higher Education*. London: Routledge, pp.241-258.

Turner, David A. (2010): 'The Twin Fields of Comparative and International Education', in Masemann, Vandra; Majhanovich, Suzanne; Truong, Nhung & Janigan, Kara (eds.), *A Tribute to David N. Wilson: Clamouring for a Better World*. Rotterdam: Sense, pp.261-270.

Weidman, John C. & Jacob, W. James (eds.) (2011): 'Mapping Comparative, International and Development Education: Celebrating the Work of Rolland G. Paulston', in Weidman, John C. & Jacob, W. James (eds.), *Beyond the Comparative: Advancing Theory and its Application to Practice*. Rotterdam: Sense, pp.1-16.

Wilson, David N. (1994): 'Comparative and International Education: Fraternal of Siamese Twins? A Preliminary Genealogy of Our Twin Fields'. *Comparative Education Review*, Vol.38, No.4, pp.449-486.

Wiseman, Alexander & Anderson, Emily (eds.) (2013): *Annual Review of Comparative and International Education*. Bingley: Emerald.

Wolhuter, C.C. (2008): 'Review of the Review: Constructing the Identity of Comparative Education'. *Research in Comparative and International Education*, Vol.3, No.4, pp.323-344.

Wolhuter, Charl & Popov, Nikolay (eds.) (2007): *Comparative Education as Discipline at Universities World Wide*. Sofia: Bureau for Educational Services.

Youngman, Frank (1992): 'Comparative Education as an Academic Discipline', in Kouwenhoven, G.W.; Weeks, Sheldon G. & Mannathoko, Changu (eds.), *Proceedings of the Comparative Education Seminar*. Gaborone: Botswana Educational Research Association, pp.19-27.

Zipin, Lew & Brennan, Marie (2012): 'Governing the Claim of Global Futures within Australian Higher Education', in Adamson, Bob; Nixon, Jon & Su, Frank (eds.), *The Reorientation of Higher Education: Challenging the East-West Dichotomy*. CERC Studies in Comparative Education 31, Hong Kong: Comparative Education Research Centre, The University of Hong Kong, and Dordrecht: Springer, pp.247-268.

3

Quantitative and Qualitative Approaches to Comparative Education

Gregory P. FAIRBROTHER

Among the many approaches to research, a broad classification distinguishes between the quantitative and the qualitative. Boundaries may be difficult to determine, and the approaches may not be mutually exclusive. Nevertheless, the two approaches deserve focus because they permit different types of insights.

The chapter begins with a description of the characteristics of the approaches and how they differ with regard to purposes, structures and theories. It also addresses questions of objectivity, values, and relationships between researcher and researched. The chapter next turns to quantitative and qualitative approaches to research on one prominent topic within the field of comparative education, that of literacy. It first reviews how researchers on literacy coming from the two traditions present the advantages of their respective approaches. It then argues that among the goals of both quantitative and qualitative research on literacy is to seek answers to the same four fundamental questions while differing in their approaches to doing so. The questions are how literacy can be accurately defined and depicted; where variations in literacy lie; what leads to literacy; and what the consequences of literacy are. Both quantitative and qualitative approaches to answering these questions are compared, using specific examples from published research.

Quantitative and Qualitative Research Methods in Education

In his *Educational Research Primer*, Picciano (2004) provided a simple comparison of quantitative and qualitative research methods in education. He defined quantitative research as relying on "the collection of numerical data which are then subjected to analysis using statistical routines" (p.51). By contrast, he suggested, qualitative research relies on "meanings, concepts, context, descriptions, and settings" (p.32). Quantity refers to amounts, while quality refers to the essence of things.

Among quantitative types of research, Picciano mentions descriptive studies, correlational research, causal comparative research, and experimental studies. Qualitative research methods include ethnography, historical research, and case study research. To explain the differences between these methods, Picciano compared them along the lines of purpose, data sources, methods of data collection, data analysis, and reporting. For example, the purpose of a quantitative correlational study is to use numerical data to describe relationships between variables and to predict consequences following from these relationships, whereas the purpose of a qualitative ethnographic study is to describe and interpret a phenomenon observed in its natural setting. Different purposes are accompanied by specific sources of data. The correlational study relies on quantitative data from school databases, test scores, surveys and questionnaires, while the ethnographic study is based on observations, field notes, and even photographs and videos.

As a preface to his detailed descriptions of the various quantitative and qualitative research methods, Picciano noted (p.32) that "a grand debate has existed for decades on the virtues of one approach over the other. Rather than enter this debate, we note that both approaches are highly respected and, when done well, add equally to the knowledge base". Like Picciano, this chapter does not dwell on the quantitative-qualitative debate. Instead, like others who seek to transcend the divide (Brannen 2005; Onwuegbuzie & Leech 2005; Gorard and Taylor 2004; Greene 2007; Howe 2003), it examines how both broad approaches address similar fundamental questions about social and educational issues, with specific methodological choices meeting the need to answer specific nuanced research questions.

Quantitative Approaches

The overarching purpose of quantitative research methods in education is the identification of laws which contribute to the explanation and prediction of educational phenomena (Ary et al. 2010; Bryman 1988; Hartas 2010). Laws of association claim a functional dependence between objects, while laws of causation imply a fixed succession of events. The adherence of quantitative approaches to a nomothetic mode of reasoning means that researchers consider such laws to be universal, regardless of differences in time or place. Laws accordingly make it possible to explain and predict relationships between phenomena across contexts.

Bryman (1988) noted that establishing causality is one of the primary preoccupations of quantitative research. Explanations, or questions of 'why', imply a search for causes, specifying certain causal factors and ruling out alternatives. A particularly effective method for establishing causal relationships is the experiment; but many researchers rely on correlational studies, with data gathered through surveys, to argue for causation. Bryman noted that to make such an argument, these researchers must demonstrate a relationship between variables, that the relationship is not produced by a third variable, and that the variables are in a logically temporal order.

Because of quantitative researchers' commitment to nomothetic reasoning, their research has the further purpose of generalising findings to larger populations and other research locations. This goal is said to be achieved through the use of random, representative samples in experimental and survey research. The attempt to replicate research findings is a further step engaged in by quantitative researchers in order to strengthen the claim of generalisation. Scholars advocating comparative methods draw the purposes of generalisation and explanation together, claiming that generalisability is enhanced when greater variation is introduced to the explanatory variables of interest (May 2011). The maximisation of variation is said to be made possible at the level of society, justifying the use of cross-national and cross-cultural research (van de Vijver & Leung 1997).

A further purpose of quantitative studies is deduction, theory or hypothesis testing, and verification. This goal leads quantitative research to be characterised as confirmatory, and reflects the typical structure of the quantitative research process. Such a process is said to start with a general theory and move on to the statement of more specific hypotheses, the operationalisation of concepts as variables for the collection of data, and then to statistical analysis of such data.

This structured approach to research is a defining factor of quantitative traditions. Researchers using surveys and experimental methods generally need to decide on the specific issues of focus at the beginning of the research, before data collection instruments such as questionnaires are designed and data are gathered. Because of this, the broad outline of findings can often be determined from the outset. This approach means that the research focuses on and is limited to a relatively narrow range of concepts. In order to study these concepts, they must be operationalised, or transformed into 'variables' which can be observed, measured, and related to one another. As Bryman (1988, p.22) stated, the social world thus "tends to be broken down into manageable packages: social class, racial prejudice, religiosity, leadership style, aggression, and so on". These characteristics of the quantitative method lead it to be associated with precision, rigour, reliability and persuasiveness. 'Hard' data are collected through structured, systematic procedures and are amenable to verification by others.

These claims are strengthened with the supposition in quantitative methodology that the methods and data have not been affected by the researcher. With limited, or even an absence of direct contact between the researcher and the subjects of research, the image of a detached scientific observer is maintained. The researcher takes on an outsider's, 'etic' perspective, with as little involvement with research subjects as possible, leading to the claim that quantitative research is objective and value-free. Standardised questionnaires and concerted efforts at random sampling are designed to reduce or even eliminate human bias.

Qualitative Approaches

The description of the qualitative research perspective on the question of objectivity and values, as well as other questions below, demonstrates the contrasts between the two perspectives in terms of the approach to and purpose of research (Greene 2007; Hartas 2010). In the qualitative tradition, objectivity is challenged, and the process of research and the 'facts' it reveals are seen to be laden with values. Rather than a position of detachment between researcher and subjects, qualitative approaches see researchers themselves as instruments of data collection, often with sustained and intimate contact and relationships with their subjects, further defying claims of a need for objectivity. Guba and Lincoln (1994, p.107) maintain that "the notion that findings are created through the interaction of inquirer and phenomenon (which, in the social sciences, is usually people) is often a more plausible description of the inquiry process than is the notion that findings are discovered through objective observation".

A related point is that a fundamental purpose of qualitative research is to capture the research subject's perspective and views of values, actions, processes, and events. Qualitative research presents the 'emic', insider's perspective, empathising with the subjects of research. Through methods such as detailed participant observation and in-depth unstructured interviews, subjects are given far more latitude to share their own views, with the researcher tending towards surrendering control to the researched in the process of inquiry.

In contrast to the quantitative methodology which seeks general explanatory laws, the qualitative approach sometimes denies that such laws can ever be found. Qualitative researchers therefore take an ideographic rather than a nomothetic approach, meaning that they locate their findings in specific time periods and places (Bryman 1988; Greene 2007). Research conducted in a specific place does not have as its primary aim generalisation to other places; instead the attention is focused on events, processes and behaviours in the immediate context. At the same time, rather than limited to particular variables of interest, the qualitative approach is more holistic and naturalistic, examining entire social entities such as schools or communities at many levels and along many dimensions. The goal of this approach is again an interpretive, empathetic understanding, and an attempt to capture the meanings that research subjects attribute to their own particular, yet whole, situations.

Bryman (1988) noted that qualitative researchers' attention to their informants' perspectives leads to an avoidance of preconceived structure and predetermined notions. Therefore studies are characterised by openness and flexibility. This contrasts with the work of quantitative researchers, who tend towards deciding at the outset upon concepts which can be operationalised and measured. Qualitative researchers may or may not have specific research problems as predetermined targets of investigation. Instead, the decisions on foci may be delayed well into the research process, allowing for unexpected issues to be pursued. Qualitative research can therefore be more easily characterised as inductive and exploratory, rather than deductive and confirmatory.

The same considerations apply to the position of theory in qualitative research. Given their adherence to the insider's perspective and to an inductive, flexible, and unstructured approach, qualitative researchers do not normally start with a theory to be tested or validated. A preconceived theory could be viewed as a constraint in the research process, and could prove to be a poor fit with the revealed perspectives of research subjects. The discovery, formulation, and testing of 'grounded' theoretical explanations instead are conducted simultaneously with the process of data collection and analysis.

Finally, in presenting research findings rather than explicating statistical relationships among carefully delineated and measured concepts, qualitative researchers tend toward providing rich, deep, detailed descriptions. Such detail contributes to explaining participants' perspectives and developing an understanding of the meanings they attach to the phenomena of interest. At the same time, qualitative researchers go beyond pure description to analyse, interpret, and offer explanations of complex situations and phenomena.

Considerations for Comparative Education
Several of the issues associated with the use of quantitative and qualitative methods identified above have special salience in comparative education research. On the one hand, there is a certain pressure within parts of the field for the use of quantitative methods. This goes along with a shift over time within the field of comparative education from historical, explanatory studies towards studies employing statistical information and quantitative data analysis procedures. Some researchers are drawn to the quest for generalisable explanations and universal principles applicable to educational phenomena across societies and cultures. Concomitantly, there is an attraction for some scholars and policy-makers to the transfer of educational theories, practices, and policies across international borders, and a desire to seek global solutions to global problems. Large-scale databases from international studies of educational achievement, and education statistics gathered by international agencies, can attract both experienced and novice researchers because of their availability and influence. Finally, research commissioned by governments or international organisations may carry a preference for particular method and theories.

On the other hand, there is comparable pressure for qualitative studies, sometimes in reaction to the perceived shortcomings of quantitative methods. Qualitative researchers in comparative education share a strong belief in the importance of cultural, political and social contexts, and the position that education cannot be decontextualised from its local culture. Qualitative research is also advocated because of an awareness of the shortcomings and problems associated with large bodies of cross-national statistical data, often uncritically employed without consideration of potential bias, and with units of analysis (usually nation states) compared without considering local contexts and internal variation. With regard to the question of the objectivity or value-ladenness of the research endeavour, qualitative researchers draw attention to the need for sensitivity to the greater potential for bias and unquestioned assumptions when researchers work outside their own cultural contexts. They maintain that effort must be made to become conscious of such biases and to question one's own assumptions while trying to understand the assumptions underlying the societies and cultures which are the targets of research.

Quantitative and Qualitative Research on Literacy

To deepen the discussion and compare quantitative and qualitative methods in comparative education, this chapter turns to a description of a range of studies on a particular theme, literacy. It demonstrates that both types of research can seek answers to fundamentally similar questions. Literacy has been noted as a prominent concern of comparative education researchers, not least because of the influence on research agendas of powerful international agencies such as UNESCO and the World Bank (Crossley & Watson 2003). Studies on literacy abound in journals such as the *Comparative Education Review, International Review of Education*, and *International Journal of Educational Development*. They range from large-scale cross-national quantitative studies of literacy achievement to small-scale, in-depth ethnographies.

While studies of literacy vary widely as to their research methods, contexts and specific questions addressed, they also exhibit fundamental similarities in purpose. Specifically, they seek answers to at least four basic questions:

1. How can literacy be accurately defined and depicted?
2. Where do variations in literacy lie?
3. What leads to literacy?
4. What are the consequences of literacy?

Some of the studies examined below identify themselves as ethnographies or as large-scale quantitative research studies. Others have employed mixed methods. For the purpose of differentiating between quantitative and qualitative methods, simple distinctions have been made according to the nature of the data reported. For the present discussion, studies which mainly report results in the form of numbers and statistics are treated as quantitative, and policy and historical studies are grouped within the broad qualitative tradition.

How can Literacy be Accurately Defined and Depicted?
Both quantitative and qualitative studies seek answers to the fundamental question of how literacy can accurately be defined and depicted, but differ in their approach to and interpretation of the question. Quantitative studies approach this question by seeking an accurate, objective method to measure literacy, often defining literacy from the outset. The cross-national 2011 Progress in International Reading Literacy Study (PIRLS), refining conceptions of literacy from previous International Association for the Evaluation of Educational Achievement (IEA) literacy studies, started with a definition of reading literacy as "the ability to understand and use those written language forms required by society and/or valued by the individual" (Mullis et al. 2009, p.11).

Another cross-societal study, the International Adult Literacy Survey (IALS), started with a set definition of functional literacy as "the ability to understand and employ printed information in daily activities at home, at work and in the community", and directly measured the three associated domains of prose, document and quantitative literacy (Darcovich 2000, p.369). This survey was viewed by the researchers as an innovation because it measured varying degrees of literacy in each of the domains – measures judged more accurate than the dichotomous literate/illiterate used in numerous other studies.

Jennings (2000) similarly claimed that the 97.5 per cent adult literacy rate for Guyana reported by the government to international aid agencies was inflated because it was based on the percentage of enrolment in primary schools rather than on a direct assessment of literacy. On the basis of the results of the Functional Literacy Survey of Out-of-School Youth, which defined functional literacy as "the ability of the individual to apply skills in reading, writing, calculation and basic problem-solving in those activities in which literacy is required for effective functioning in his/her own group and community", Jennings estimated that Guyana's actual literacy rate was more than 20 percentage points lower.

Dealing with a similar problem, Lavy and Spratt (1997) complained that national-level census-based statistics suffered from inaccuracy, incomparability, questionable assumptions, unclear definitions, and mis-interpretation. Solutions to these problems, they argued, were important for moving toward the improvement of policies and programs to battle illiteracy. The Morocco Literacy Study on which they reported directly assessed individuals on a variety of literacy skills, and at the same time asked respondents to make self-judgments of their reading, writing and mathematics abilities. Based on their comparison of these two measures, the researchers found that self-reports rarely underestimated but often overestimated actual literacy skills, leading them to conclude (p.128) that "healthy 'literacy rates' ... may in fact contain a high proportion of persons with very minimal literacy skills". In one more study comparing and finding differences in objective (directly assessed) and subjective (self-reported) literacy rates from samples in Ethiopia and Nicaragua, Schaffner (2005) concluded that measures of literacy employed in household surveys overstated actual literacy rates, especially in countries with low average schooling levels, and that this finding had implications for understanding of the number of years of schooling necessary to develop literacy among most students.

Introducing his qualitative study, Maddox (2005, p.123) wrote: "Processes of assessment have generally focused on narrowly oriented tests of ability, rather than examining how people have applied such learning in their daily lives." This statement describes well the difference between the quantitative and qualitative approaches in addressing the question of how literacy should be most accurately defined and depicted. While quantitative researchers have sought ways to assess and measure literacy skills more accurately and objectively, qualitative researchers have tended to look to their research subjects for insight into what literacy means to literates themselves, judging this to be the most accurate representation. As one example, in contrast to the idea of literacy as a public practice associated with national development, Maddox found in his ethnographic study of Bangladeshi women that literacy activities were often conducted surreptitiously in private, because of the perception among these women of associated risk and vulnerability. Maddox also found that women who could read fluently in Arabic did not consider reading the Quran as a form of literacy, yet that this ability could in fact raise these women's status within the community. Explaining his findings, Maddox relied not on statistics but on descriptive case studies of individual women and their literacy practices.

In her ethnographic study of native Peruvians, Aikman (2001, pp. 106-107) asked the questions: "What do the Harakmbut consider counts as literacy?", and "How, then, do the Harakmbut use literacy for specific development practices?". These questions were again asked in the context of external development discourses surrounding the Harakmbut's own perceptions of literacy and development. Among her findings was that to these people literacy in Spanish meant promoting their own self-development and access to resources for protecting and promoting indigenous rights. Literacy in their own language had several implications within the group she studied, including both a valuation of their culture and oppositely a reinforcement of their otherness and a loss of status and prestige in the wider Peruvian society.

In another attempt to reveal how literacy is experienced and interacts with power relations in everyday lives, in contrast to professional, social science, and government discourses of literacy as power, Rockhill (1993) conducted life history interviews with Spanish-speaking immigrants in California. In response to her women interviewees who expressed a desire to learn to read and write, Rockhill asked: "Is their goal to become empowered? To act in accord with their rights? To resist? If so, who, what and how do they resist?" (p.163). Referring to academic and policy discussions of the importance of literacy for empowerment in economic, political, and cultural spheres of public activity, she answered: "Conceptions of empowerment, resistance and rights do not capture the way the women we interviewed talk about their longing for literacy, how they think about their lives, what is meaningful to them, or the conflicts they live" (pp.164-165).

These examples illustrate the contrasts between academic, political, and economic discourses and literacy as experienced by the subjects of these studies. Other qualitative researchers have drawn more explicit contrasts between the intentions of literacy educators and development practitioners on one hand, and the newly literate on the other. Explaining how new literates in Gapun, Papua New Guinea "seize hold" of those aspects of literacy for which they have the most use, Kulick and Stroud (1993) noted that the concerns of the promoters of literacy, the Church and schools, were largely peripheral to villagers themselves. They wrote (p.55) that:

> The villagers of Gapun have their own ideas about reading and writing, generated from their own cultural concerns. It has been and continues to be these ideas, and not externally generated and cul-

turally foreign ones which they apply to the written word in the village.

Dyer and Choksi (2001) also explained that their own preconceptions of the literacy needs of Rabari nomads in India were contradicted by their subjects' insights into the meaning of literacy in their lives. Coming from a development assistance perspective, the researchers expected the Rabaris to use new literacy skills to help with animal husbandry, and to appreciate a programme of literacy education within pastoralism revolving around their own knowledge and experience. Instead, through ethnographic work the researchers found that literacy was perceived by the Rabaris mainly as a way to reduce their dependence on others and as associated with being sedentary and offering a better future for their children in the non-pastoral economy.

In sum, both quantitative and qualitative researchers of literacy have dealt with the fundamental question of how to define and depict literacy accurately. In the quantitative studies described above, the goal was to identify a more objective and reliable method for measuring literacy skills, in the face of alternatively employed national-level statistics and subjective measures. The definition of literacy itself was normally assumed or defined at the outset based on theoretical literature. In contrast, the qualitative studies of individuals, also concerned with accuracy in the face of external conceptions of literacy, privileged the meanings of research subjects themselves and drew attention to the uses to which literacy was put. Policy studies sought to shed light on the meaning of literacy as employed by national and international actors which hold the power to set education agendas, whether or not their conceptions of literacy were shared by the targets of their policies. In each case, it was clear that there were differences in the measurement and understanding of literacy, between external actors and subjects, and among subjects themselves. Accordingly, a second fundamental question which both quantitative and qualitative research approaches both attempt to answer in their own ways concerns the locations in which variations in literacy lie.

Where do Variations in Literacy Lie?
Papen's (2001) ethnographic study of the National Literacy Programme in Namibia (NLPN) compared the practices and meanings of literacy in the various social and institutional contexts within the programme, such as training sessions for teachers and events associated with National Literacy Day. Based on her analysis of policy documents, evaluation reports,

political speeches, and her own observations, she maintained that certain understandings of literacy were privileged over others and influenced which literacy practices were employed in the programme. Although focused on one geographic entity, Namibia, her study engaged in comparison of different contexts, eliciting variation at several levels encompassed within a broader conception of comparative education (Bray & Thomas 1995).

Other qualitative studies have examined variation in the meanings attached to literacy in different languages and by different institutions and actors. Reder and Wikelund's (1993) ethnographic study of literacy in an Alaskan fishing community in the United States, described the different social meanings attached to, and conflict and competition between, "Village" and "Outside" literacy practices. They found that these two conceptions of literacy were associated with distinct institutions, with "Village" literacy practices tied to the Orthodox Church and the fishing industry, and "Outside" practices coming from the school and government agencies. In a related vein, based on an ethnographic study of literacy among the Mende of Sierra Leone, Bledsoe and Robey (1993) described the different associations and advantages for pursuing social goals attributed to literacy in Arabic and English. They maintained that literacy in the two languages had different meanings and functions, with Arabic associated with religion, ritual, secrecy, and supernatural power, and English tied to government, bureaucracy, technology, and material wealth. Finally, Robinson-Pant (2000) compared the meanings attributed to literacy by men and women in her ethnography of literacy in a remote area of Nepal. She found that the conceptions of literacy of educated men in Arutar corresponded with the aid agency staff who implemented literacy classes, while women learners saw literacy in a separate light, even in opposition to the dominant, agency, male perspective.

Quantitative researchers have also compared men and women with regard to literacy, but rather than examining differing meanings of literacy, they have focused on differences in literacy skills. Several studies have looked at differentials in literacy achievement and rates on the basis of gender by carrying out direct assessments and eliciting self-reports (Fuller et al. 1994; Jennings 2000). Scholars have also used quantitative methods to examine differentials in literacy achievement and rates based on mother-tongue (Ezzaki et al. 1999; Gunawardena 1997); type of (urban/rural) community (Fuller et al. 1999; Lavy and Spratt 1997); education level (Jennings 2000; Lavy and Spratt 1997); and socio-economic status

(Jennings 2000; Lavy and Spratt 1997). Fuller et al. (1999) also compared literacy rates among Mexican states and in different time periods. Finally, the IEA studies of reading literacy compared direct assessments of children's literacy among different nations, as well as comparing groups based on gender, parents' birthplace, parents' occupation, teachers' gender, and a plethora of other factors (Elley 1994; Mullis et al. 2003; Mullis et al. 2009).

In examining variations in literacy, the qualitative studies described above focused on the different meanings of literacy among groups of people and individuals, institutions, and associated with different languages and practices. They presented findings in the form of descriptions and direct quotations. In some cases, they maintained that differences in the meanings attached to literacy by educators and learners had implications for the outcomes of literacy programs. Quantitative researchers have shared similar concerns in their comparisons of the literacy achievement of numerous types of groups: the implication from the finding that certain groups have lower levels of literacy achievement than others is that ways should be sought to raise their achievement. This was the explicit goal in one quantitative, experimental study which compared the achievement of adults participating in a functional literacy programme with those in a "classical" literacy programme, as well as comparing students' reading test scores before and after participation in the programme (Durgunoğlu et al. 2003). In this case, the comparison was made in order to assess the impact of literacy classes. In numerous other quantitative and qualitative studies, researchers have shared a similar interest in assessing the impact of a variety of other factors on literacy, leading to a third fundamental question to which both research traditions seek the answer: What leads to literacy? As will be shown below, each group approaches this question in different ways.

What Leads to Literacy?
Mangubhai (1999) conducted an experimental study to determine whether a particular educational intervention, the Book Flood Project, led to higher levels of reading skill among participating students in Fiji. Other quantitative researchers have also utilised statistical methods to examine the impact of schooling on literacy outcomes. In their study of women, literacy, and health in rural Mexico, Dexter et al. (1998) hypothesised a relationship between the length of women's childhood schooling and their performance on health-related language and literacy tasks, with data

gathered through direct assessments and interviews and analysed through regression analysis. Using another statistical method, Ezzaki et al. (1999, p.184) sought answers to the questions, "Does Quranic pre-schooling experience facilitate literacy acquisition among rural Moroccan children in primary school? Does any initial advantage carry over into later years of public schooling?". With data collected from a direct reading assessment and students, parents, teachers, and school records, they employed analysis of variance (ANOVA) to determine reading skill differences between Arabic- and Berber-speaking children who had or had not attended Quranic preschools.

In studies more focused on the characteristics and practices of schooling, Fuller and his colleagues attempted to determine, through regression analyses, the relative impact of a variety of school-related factors on literacy in English among children in Botswana (Fuller et al. 1994) and early literacy among children in Brazil (Fuller et al. 1999). With data gathered from direct assessments, classroom observations, teacher and principal interviews and questionnaires, they sought insight into the impact of factors such as school size, class size, textbook supplies, teachers' qualifications and job satisfaction, the frequency of active reading and writing exercises in class, and student time engaged in and disengaged from learning tasks.

In dealing with the question of what leads to literacy, these quantitative studies addressed the more specific question of what interventions or inputs contributed most to the acquisition of literacy. In the evaluation study of a Turkish functional adult literacy programme, the focus of attention was on the input of a literacy course (Durgunoğlu et al. 2003). To determine whether the input was effective and gauge the relative success of the programme, the researchers compared the pre- and post-test scores of its participants, and compared test scores of participants with non-participants. Some non-significant differences between pre- and post-test scores were explained as a result of the insufficient duration of the literacy programme.

In a qualitative study which also evaluated four literacy programmes in rural Mali, Puchner (2003) conducted interviews with and observations of individuals who did or did not become literate after participating in the literacy programmes. In this case the focus was partly on the quality of the input. To explain the relative lack of success, Puchner identified the shortsightedness of programme developers, weaknesses and neglect of the programmes for women, and poor classroom conditions. At the same time, in addition to input-related factors, she identified various social factors, including relations between men and women, gender roles, constraints on women's access to classes, and perceptions of limited use for literacy in the local language, which offered insight into participants' reactions to and attitudes toward the programmes and their expected outcomes. Here, the qualitative researcher's approach to the question of what leads to or hinders literacy was to ask how the attitudes of potential literates toward literacy and literacy education affected their relative success in becoming literate.

This approach to the question is shared by researchers conducting other qualitative studies. Betts (2003) reported extensively on and interpreted the views of rural people in El Salvador with regard to their participation in literacy programmes. Moving beyond explanations of low participation rates in terms of barriers to access and lack of motivation, she detailed the "politics of absence", characterised by resistance to and co-optation of dominant discourses of literacy as power. Other qualitative studies privileged the views of informants in offering explanations for participation, or lack thereof, in literacy programmes. Rockhill (1993) learned from her interviews with Mexican immigrants in Los Angeles that women's efforts to become literate were hindered by the power their husbands held over them in the form of allowing or disallowing them to go to school, and that becoming educated and literate may have represented a form of resistance to this power.

Finally, several qualitative policy studies have examined the effects of international-level influences on the relative success of national-level literacy policies. Mpofu and Youngman (2001) maintained that the dominance of a traditional approach to literacy in international discourse which heavily influenced national-level policies in Botswana and Zimbabwe resulted in relatively ineffective literacy programmes. Mundy (1993), in her analysis of literacy policies in southern Africa, argued that literacy efforts and outcomes could not be understood without taking into consideration external determinants, including changes in the world economy and Africa's worsening position within this economy, as well as the influence of the aid and expertise of international agencies on the development of national literacy policies.

What are the Consequences of Literacy?

Qualitative studies dealing with the question of the consequences of literacy have described the uses to which literacy is put, presented the perspectives of new literates themselves, and interpreted outcomes from literacy based on a holistic picture of the contexts surrounding literacy use. Aikman (2001) found that her Harakmbut informants in Peru considered that among the outcomes of literacy in Spanish were an ability to promote their programme for self-development and greater access to resources to promote their indigenous rights. The Nepali women in Robinson-Pant's (2000) study felt that they had gained a new form of public identity as "educated". At the same time they had gained a social space (the classroom) and a private space and individual voice, as represented by their writing for private and public purposes. The Hmong immigrant men observed and interviewed by Weinstein-Shr (1993) in the USA gained from literacy a tool for negotiating with new public institutions, a tool for mediating between Hmong and American cultural groups, a new social status, and a tool for studying Hmong oral tradition. Similarly, Maddox (2005) interpreted that the literacy of his Bangladeshi women informants represented a challenge to patriarchy as it strengthened women's position relative to men and allowed them to establish their rights. At the same time, literacy created for women new forms of risk and vulnerability related to their new ability to engage with public institutions and conduct private correspondence.

Robinson-Pant (2001) attempted to explore, through ethnographic methods, how women's literacy was linked to health outcomes among participants in a literacy programme in Nepal. She reported similar results as Puchner, that despite differences on a test of health knowledge, the health seeking behaviour of participants and non-participants was quite similar. Explaining the results, she wrote (pp.161-192) that:

> Detailed lifeline interviews showed a very complex picture in relation to how health decisions were made. Rather than demonstrating women's lack of awareness, the interviews revealed a catalogue of poor health services, inadequate family planning counselling, husbands' or in-laws' opposition to family planning and the low value attached to the birth of a girl which forced women to keep trying for a son.

In contrast to the holistic picture of literacy and health behaviours gained from Robinson-Pant's interviews, several quantitative studies looking at the consequences of literacy narrowed their focus to a fixed number of objective, operationalised, measured factors. Dexter et al. (1998) took the number of years of schooling of their rural Mexican women subjects as a measure of literacy to examine whether correlations existed with a direct assessment of health-related spoken and written language tasks. Schnell-Anzola et al. (2005) were interested in determining whether literacy skills mediated the relationship between schooling and health. With data from interviews with 161 Venezuelan mothers and direct assessments of their literacy and health-related communication skills, the researchers hypothesised that the path from mother's schooling to child's health outcomes consisted of four steps: years of mothers' schooling would affect literacy and language skills, which in turn would affect health-related skills such as understanding health messages, which in turn would affect mothers' utilisation of health services, which in turn would affect children's health outcomes.

Other quantitative studies sought to investigate the economic consequences of literacy. Data from the International Adult Literacy Survey revealed relationships between the Survey's direct assessment of functional literacy and individual economic success as measured by individuals' earnings. As Darcovich (2000, p.375) wrote:

> Workers with higher literacy skills generally earn more than those with lower literacy skills, although this effect is not consistent across all levels and countries. Where the effect of literacy on income is present, it is evident even when accounting for gender, parental education and respondents' education.

Here the researchers utilised statistical controls to simplify the type of complex situation Robinson-Pant observed in her small-scale but holistic qualitative study.

Conclusions

The studies of literacy presented above exemplify the basic characteristics of their respective methodologies. Among the quantitative studies, in particular those that engage in cross-national comparison, are those that seek generalisable explanations across contexts. Some of them seek to identify relations of association and causation through experiments and statistical models and techniques. Their research questions and hypotheses tend to be clearly stated at the outset, followed by methods carefully described: sampling, sources of data, measurement of variables, and data analysis procedures. Theoretical concepts, including literacy itself, are operationalised as variables which researchers attempt to measure accurately. Data come from direct assessments, reading tests, structured questions, and detached observations. The voices or opinions of the research subjects are rarely heard.

The qualitative studies, on the other hand, tend to be based more fully on the views of the subjects of research, including the meanings they attach to literacy and the reasons and explanations they themselves provide. The qualitative studies focus more on specific, small-scale contexts. Rather than being limited to particular variables, they try to provide a holistic picture of the meanings, uses and practices of literacy. They tend to be exploratory and expository, with reports of the research not following a fixed structure or stating questions or hypotheses at the outset. Descriptions are detailed and infused with interpretation and theorisation.

Despite these differences, both approaches are concerned with at least four basic questions regarding literacy, with their differences contributing to more complete answers. How can we accurately define and depict literacy? Quantitative researchers answer that we need a way to measure literacy skills more accurately. Qualitative researchers answer that we need to find out how people themselves actually use and practice literacy, not relying only on what external actors say about how literacy skills should be used.

Where do variations in literacy lie? Quantitative researchers answer that to address this question we should measure differences in literacy skills among groups and determine whether these differences occur by chance or are significantly different. Qualitative researchers answer that we should examine how the meanings and uses attributed to literacy by one individual or group differ from others.

What leads to literacy? Quantitative researchers answer that we should try to determine what inputs (which may or may not be altered) can improve literacy skills or literacy rates. Qualitative researchers, assuming the input of literacy education, answer that we should find out how the attitudes towards literacy and literacy education of participants may facilitate or hinder their acquisition of literacy. Qualitative policy researchers answer that we need to find out what policy inputs contribute to or hinder effective literacy promotion efforts.

What are the consequences of literacy? Quantitative researchers answer that we need to determine whether and how literacy contributes to the betterment of other aspects of personal and social life. Qualitative researchers answer that we should not neglect the question of whether new literates experience adverse consequences in addition to the benefits of literacy.

From this chapter's focus on one issue and the comparison of studies taking one or the other approach to researching this issue, what can be added to the methodological debate between quantitative and qualitative methods and on the question of whether these methods are compatible? To answer this, a hypothetical question may be posed: What if we only had the insight into literacy of one or the other of these methods? What if, for example, we only knew what literacy meant to literates themselves and how they made use of their perceived literacy skills, but did not have insight into whether based on their own judgment of their skills they could perform the tasks society expects of literates? What if we knew only of what educational inputs contributed to increased literacy, but not of the subjective factors which influence people's decisions about whether or not to attend school or whether they consider the content of literacy education appropriate or relevant and therefore worth retaining? Thought of in this manner, it becomes clear that despite differences, or the strengths and weaknesses of each approach, only with both approaches can scholars come to a more complete understanding of important educational issues.

A final question addressed in this chapter is how both quantitative and qualitative approaches have been used with respect to explicitly comparative educational research. Of the literacy studies surveyed in this chapter, the ones which to a large extent dealt with comparisons across countries were cross-national quantitative studies of literacy achievement. Quantitative approaches were also used to compare literacy rates, skills, and achievement across places below the national level. Even when limited to one place, quantitative studies did engage in explicit comparisons on a variety of types, including ways of measuring literacy skills, innovative and classical teaching methods, schooling experiences, curricula, language groups, and inputs and outputs. The qualitative studies described above, with their attention to context, focused mainly on one place, often down to the district and village level. However, as with quantitative studies, these qualitative studies also dealt with comparisons along various dimensions at the levels of policy, culture, and individuals, including the various meanings of, uses of, values attached to, inputs to, and outcomes of literacy.

References

Aikman, Sheila (2001): 'Literacies, Languages and Developments in Peruvian Amazonia', in Street, Brian V. (ed.), *Literacy and Development: Ethnographic Perspectives*. London: Routledge, pp.103-120.

Ary, Donald; Jacobs, Lucy Cheser & Sorensen, Chris (2010): *Introduction to Research in Education*. 8th edition, Belmont, California: Wadsworth.

Betts, Julia (2003): 'Literacies and Livelihood Strategies: Experience from Usulután, El Salvador'. *International Journal of Educational Development*, Vol.23, No.3, pp.291-298.

Bledsoe, Caroline H. & Robey, Kenneth M. (1993): 'Arabic Literacy and Secrecy among the Mende of Sierra Leone', in Street, Brian (ed.), *Cross-cultural Approaches to Literacy*. Cambridge: Cambridge University Press, pp.110-134.

Brannen, Julia (2005): 'Mixing Methods: The Entry of Qualitative and Quantitative Approaches into the Research Process'. *International Journal of Social Research Methodology*, Vol.8, No.3, pp.173-184.

Bray, Mark & Thomas, R. Murray (1995): 'Levels of Comparison in Educational Studies: Different Insights from Different Literatures and the Value of Multilevel Analyses'. *Harvard Educational Review*, Vol.65, No.3, pp.472-490.

Bryman, Alan (1988): *Quantity and Quality in Social Research*. London: Routledge.

Crossley, Michael & Watson, Keith (2003): *Comparative and International Research in Education: Globalisation, Context and Difference*. London: RoutledgeFalmer.

Darcovich, Nancy (2000): 'The Measurement of Adult Literacy in Theory and in Practice'. *International Review of Education*, Vol.46, No.5, pp. 367-376.

Dexter, Emily R., LeVine, Sarah E. & Velasco, Patricia M. (1998): 'Maternal Schooling and Health-Related Language and Literacy Skills in Rural Mexico'. *Comparative Education Review*, Vol.42, No.2, pp.139-162.

Durgunoğlu, A.Y.; Öney, B. & Kuşcul, H. (2003): 'Development and Evaluation of an Adult Literacy Program in Turkey'. *International Journal of Educational Development*, Vol.23, No.1, pp.17-36.

Dyer, Caroline & Choksi, Archana (2001): 'Literacy, Schooling and Development: Views of Rabari Nomads, India', in Street, Brian V. (ed.), *Literacy and Development: Ethnographic Perspectives*. London: Routledge, pp.27-39.

Elley, Warwick B. (1994): 'Conclusions', in Elley, Warwick B. (ed.), *The IEA Study of Reading Literacy: Achievement and Instruction in Thirty-two School Systems*. Oxford: Pergamon, pp.223-231.

Ezzaki, Abdelkader; Spratt, Jennifer E. & Wagner, Daniel A. (1999): 'Childhood Literacy Acquisition in Rural Morocco: Effects of Language Differences and Quranic Preschooling', in Wagner, Daniel A. (ed.), *The Future of Literacy in a Changing World*. Cresskill, New Jersey: Hampton Press, pp.183-198.

Fuller, Bruce; Edwards, John H.Y. & Gorman, Kathleen (1999): 'Does Rising Literacy Spark Economic Growth? Commercial Expansion in Mexico', in Wagner, Daniel A. (ed.), *The Future of Literacy in a Changing World*. Cresskill, New Jersey: Hampton Press, pp.373-396.

Fuller, Bruce, Hua, Haiyan & Snyder, Conrad W. (1994): 'When Girls Learn More Than Boys: The Influence of Time in School and Pedagogy in Botswana'. *Comparative Education Review*, Vol.38, No.3, pp. 347-376.

Gorard, Stephen & Taylor, Chris (2004): *Combining Methods in Educational and Social Research*. Maidenhead, UK: Open University Press.

Greene, Jennifer C. (2007): *Mixed Methods in Social Inquiry*. San Francisco: John Wiley & Sons.

Guba, Egon G. & Lincoln, Yvonna S. (1994): 'Competing Paradigms in Qualitative Research', in Denzin, Norman K. & Lincoln, Yvonna S. (ed.), *Handbook of Qualitative Research*. Thousand Oaks, California: Sage, pp.105-117.

Gunawardena, Chandra (1997): 'Problems of Illiteracy in a Literate Developing Society: Sri Lanka'. *International Review of Education*, Vol.43, No.5-6, pp.595-609.

Hartas, Dimitra (ed.) (2010): *Educational Research and Inquiry: Qualitative and Quantitative Approaches*. London: Continuum.

Howe, Kenneth R. (2003): *Closing Methodological Divides: Toward Democratic Educational Research*. Dordrecht: Kluwer Academic Publishers.

Jennings, Zellyne (2000): 'Functional Literacy of Young Guyanese Adults'. *International Review of Education*, Vol.46, No.1-2, pp.93-116.

Kulick, Don & Stroud, Christopher (1993): 'Conceptions and Uses of Literacy in a Papua New Guinean Village', in Street, Brian (ed.), *Cross-*

Cultural Approaches to Literacy. Cambridge: Cambridge University Press, pp.30-61.

Lavy, Victor & Spratt, Jennie (1997): 'Patterns of Incidence and Change in Moroccan Literacy'. *Comparative Education Review*, Vol.41, No.2, pp. 120-141.

Maddox, Bryan (2005): 'Assessing the Impact of Women's Literacies in Bangladesh: An Ethnographic Inquiry'. *International Journal of Educational Development*, Vol.25, No.2, pp.123-132.

Mangubhai, Francis (1999): 'Literacy in the South Pacific: Some Multilingual and Multiethnic Issues', in Wagner, Daniel A. (ed.), *The Future of Literacy in a Changing World*. Cresskill, New Jersey: Hampton Press, pp.213-239.

May, Tim (2011): *Social Research: Issues, Methods and Process*. Maidenhead, UK: Open University Press.

Mpofu, Stanley T. & Youngman, Frank (2001): 'The Dominant Tradition in Adult Literacy: A Comparative Study of National Literacy Programmes in Botswana and Zimbabwe'. *International Review of Education*, Vol.47, No.6, pp.573-595.

Mullis, Ina V.S.; Martin, Michael O.; Gonzalez, Eugenio J. & Kennedy, Ann M. (2003): *PIRLS 2001 International Report: IEA's Study of Reading Literacy Achievement in Primary School in 35 Countries*. Chestnut Hill, MA: International Study Center, Boston College.

Mullis, Ina V.S.; Martin, Michael O.; Kennedy, Ann M.; Trong, Kathleen L.; & Sainsbury, Marian (2009): *PIRLS 2011 Assessment Framework*. Chestnut Hill, MA: TIMSS & PIRLS International Study Center, Boston College.

Mundy, Karen (1993): 'Toward a Critical Analysis of Literacy in Southern Africa'. *Comparative Education Review*, Vol.37, No.4, pp.389-411.

Onwuegbuzie, Anthony J. & Leech, Nancy L. (2005): 'On Becoming a Pragmatic Researcher: The Importance of Combining Quantitative and Qualitative Research Methodologies'. *International Journal of Social Research Methodology*, Vol.8, No.5, pp.375-387.

Papen, Uta (2001): '"Literacy – Your Key to a Better Future"? Literacy, Reconciliation and Development in the National Literacy Programme in Namibia', in Street, Brian V. (ed.), *Literacy and Development: Ethnographic Perspectives*. London: Routledge, pp.40-60.

Picciano, Anthony G. (2004): *Educational Research Primer*. London: Continuum.

Puchner, L. (2003): 'Women and Literacy in Rural Mali: A Study of the Socio-economic Impact of Participating in Literacy Programs in Four Villages'. *International Journal of Educational Development*, Vol.23, No.4, pp.439-458.

Reder, Stephen & Wikelund, Karen Reed (1993): 'Literacy Development and Ethnicity: An Alaskan Example', in Street, Brian (ed.), *Cross-Cultural Approaches to Literacy*. Cambridge: Cambridge University Press, pp.176-197.

Robinson-Pant, Anna (2000): 'Women and Literacy: A Nepal Perspective'. *International Journal of Educational Development*, Vol.20, No.4, pp.349-364.

Robinson-Pant, Anna (2001): 'Women's Literacy and Health: Can an Ethnographic Researcher Find the Links?', in Street, Brian V. (ed.), *Literacy and Development: Ethnographic Perspectives*. London: Routledge, pp.152-170.

Rockhill, Kathleen (1993): 'Gender, Language, and the Politics of Literacy', in Street, Brian (ed.), *Cross-Cultural Approaches to Literacy*. Cambridge: Cambridge University Press, pp.156-175.

Schaffner, Julie (2005): 'Subjective and Objective Measures of Literacy: Implications for Current Results-oriented Development Initiatives'. *International Journal of Educational Development*, Vol.25, No.6, pp.652-657.

Schnell-Anzola, Beatrice; Rowe, Meredith L. & LeVine, Robert A. (2005): 'Literacy as a Pathway Between Schooling and Health-related Communication Skills: A Study of Venezuelan Mothers'. *International Journal of Educational Development*, Vol.25, No.1, pp.19-37.

van de Vijver, Fons & Leung, Kwok (1997): *Methods and Data Analysis for Cross-Cultural Research*. Thousand Oaks, CA: Sage Publications.

Weinstein-Shr, Gail (1993): 'Literacy and Social Practice: A Community in Transition', in Street, Brian (ed.), *Cross-cultural Approaches to Literacy*. Cambridge: Cambridge University Press, pp.272-293.

II: Units of Comparison

4

Comparing Places

Maria MANZON

Comparative education analyses have traditionally focused on geographic entities as the unit of comparison. As this book demonstrates, comparisons can be made across many other units of analysis, including cultures, policies, curricula and systems. Nevertheless, even these alternative domains are inextricably bound to one or more places. In this respect, examining geographic entities as foci of comparative inquiry is an essential step for comparative study of education.

Bray and Thomas (1995) designed a cube for classifying comparative studies in education by level and type. They emphasised that the classification was not exhaustive, and that additional units could be identified. This chapter focuses on the geographic/locational dimension of that cube, and explores other units that are not explicitly identified in it. Using the Bray and Thomas article as a benchmark, the author examines literature that has appeared since publication of the article. This exercise has three main objectives: first to trace the discourse about units of analysis since its publication; second to make explicit some of the units that were implicit in the Bray and Thomas model; and third to select examples of the uses of places as units of comparison, at single levels and at multiple levels, in order to identify methodological issues.

The chapter has four sections. The first comments on some general approaches to comparative inquiry in education, and is followed by further remarks on the Bray and Thomas model. The third and longest section focuses on the locational dimension, presenting illustrations of geographic entities as units of analysis. The final section summarises some methodological points for scholars to consider when comparing places.

General Approaches and Tools for Comparative Education Analyses

Firstly, a conceptual observation needs to be made about the term 'unit of analysis'. In social science research, the unit of analysis refers to the major entity that is being studied. It answers the question 'who' or 'what' is being analysed. The most common units of analysis are individuals, groups, organisations, social artefacts, and social interactions. The comparative sociology literature further distinguishes between the two meanings of unit of analysis: observational and explanatory (Ragin 2006). Observational unit refers to the unit used in data collection and data analysis, while explanatory unit refers to the unit that is used to account for the pattern of results obtained. In this chapter, geographic units of analysis are used in both senses. On the one hand, they indicate the level at which data is collected and, on the other hand, the various levels (e.g. individual, institutional, national, regional or multilevel) at which theoretical explanations may be couched.

Comparative studies in education have principally been locational in nature, examining educational phenomena in different places. Traditionally, these studies have taken as their unit of analysis large macrosocial units and in particular the nation-state (e.g. Sadler 1900; Kandel 1933; Bereday 1964; Fafunwa & Aisiku 1982; Gu 1986).

Table 4.1: Comparative Case Study Analyses

	Most similar systems (msS)	Most different systems (mdS)
Most similar outcomes (msO)	msS-msO	mdS-msO
Most different outcomes (mdO)	msS-mdO	mdS-mdO

Source: Berg-Schlosser (2001), p.2430.

Among the various purposes of comparison (see e.g. Phillips & Schweisfurth 2007, pp.7-25), two are noted here because of the ways in which they shape research methods. One is interpretive, and the other is causal-analytic. Interpretive studies seek to understand educational phenomena, while causal-analytic studies seek to elucidate causation and causal complexity and to identify configurations of causal conditions that produce similar/different outcomes. Ragin and Amoroso (2011) noted that comparative methods may be used to explain either commonality or diversity in outcomes. Table 4.1 classifies four types of comparative case studies, distinguishing between systems/cases and outcomes.

Concerning interpretive studies, Bereday's approach deserves comment. Bereday's (1964) classic book, *Comparative Method in Education*, conceived the field in terms of area studies (in one country or region) and comparative studies (i.e. simultaneous comparison of several countries or regions). Of particular interest is his four-step method of comparative analysis (Figure 4.1), consisting of description, interpretation, juxtaposition, and simultaneous comparison. The purpose of juxtaposition, he suggested (pp.9-10), was to establish "the criterion upon which a valid comparison can be made and the hypothesis for which it is to be made".

Figure 4.1: Bereday's Model for Undertaking Comparative Studies

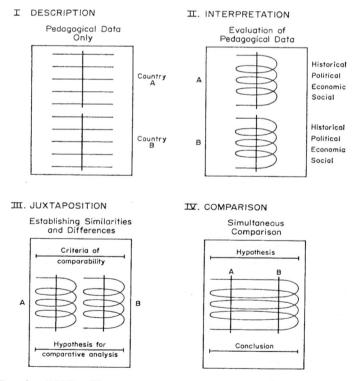

Source: Bereday (1964), p.28.

A prerequisite for any comparative study is to establish the parameters for initial comparability of the chosen units of analysis. In general, instructive analysis can be made when the units for comparison "have sufficient in common to make analysis of their differences meaningful" (Bray 2004, p.248). Thus, establishing a specific dimension of commonality against which two or more cases/contexts can be compared is a prerequisite for a valid comparison (Steiner-Khamsi 2009). Rather than a mechanical identification of similarities and differences between two or more places, attention should be paid to the underlying context of these commonalities and differences and to their causal relevance to the educational phenomenon being examined. In other words, any meaningful comparative study should be able to identify the extent and the reasons for commonalities and differences between the units of comparison, examining the causes at work and the relationships between those causes. Kubow and Fossum (2007) provided a useful tool with 'boxed' juxtapositions of comparisons of featured countries with respect to demographic, geophysical and socio-political factors shaping education (Figure 4.2).

In the case of comparisons which seek to understand the cause-effect relationship in two or more cases, the identification of parameters of comparability is taken a step further, emphasising their causal relevance to the educational issue being examined. Ragin (1987, pp.45, 47-48) identified three basic steps in case-oriented research:

- a search is undertaken for underlying similarities among the units for comparison displaying a common outcome;
- the similarities identified are shown to be causally relevant to the phenomenon of interest; and
- on the basis of similarities identified, a general explanation is formulated.

In some cases, the units for comparison are apparently different but the educational phenomena in both units manifest a common outcome (see 'mdS-msO' in Table 4.1). As Ragin (1987, p.47) explained:

> Investigators must allow for the possibility that characteristics which appear different (such as qualitatively different systems of incentives) have the same consequence. They are causally equivalent at a more abstract level … but not at a directly observable level. Thus, there may be an 'illusory difference' between two objects that is actually an underlying common cause when considered at a more abstract level.

Figure 4.2: Points of Convergence in Different Settings

BRAZIL	Demography and educational implications	SOUTH AFRICA
Attribute: Three main ethnic groups have influenced Brazilian culture: the indigenous peoples or 'Indians', the Portuguese Europeans, and the Africans, owing to Brazil's former use of slaves especially in coastal plantations.		**Attribute:** Around three fourths of the South African population is of African descent, and 10.9% are of European descent (chiefly British or Dutch), 8.9% of mixed descent, and 2.6% are Asian, primarily Indian.
Response: Centuries of intermarriage and racial and cultural mixing have shaped the Brazilian population. A more unified and distinctly Brazilian 'race' has emerged as a result. In spite of the fact that few Brazilians have ancestry strictly of one particular group, over half of the Brazilian population describes itself as white.	How have attributes of the population affected education?	**Response:** The doctrine of racial separation became particularly pronounced beginning with the apartheid-minded Nationalist Party's rise to power in 1948, the 1953 creation of a system of 'Bantu education', and, later, a school system for mixed race or 'coloured people' in 1963 and for Indian people in 1965.
Educational Implication: Though evidence points to limitations in the educational opportunities of less privileged races, since most Brazilians claim the identity of the dominant or high-status race, there has been a general lack of acceptance that racism is a pronounced problem and a lack of recognition for its negative effects in terms of differentiated educational access.		**Educational Implication:** Apartheid's formal system of separation within these four distinct school systems adopted differential access and opportunity into its most fundamental formal structures until dissent, mounting in the 1970s and 1980s, led to the dismantling of the system and Nelson Mandela's election in 1994 as the first South African president from the racial majority.

Source: Kubow & Fossum (2007), p.129.

Ragin also cited cases which appeared very similar, i.e. manifesting an 'illusory commonality' (1987, p.47), but which experienced different outcomes (see msS-mdO in Table 4.1). In these situations, the comparativist should try to identify the causally significant difference that accounts for contradictory outcomes between relatively similar units. In conclusion, Ragin indicated (p.49) that "by examining differences and similarities *in context* it is possible to determine how different combinations of conditions have the same causal significance and how similar causal factors can operate in opposite directions" (see also Ragin & Amoroso 2011). In this respect, Crossley (2009), who has extensively argued for the centrality of context in educational research, hails the Bray and

Thomas (1995) framework as a useful model in enabling the juxtaposition and comparison of different levels of contexts.

These methodological points may find resonance in comparative studies not only of places, but also of other units of analysis discussed in this book. For the purposes of this chapter, the methodological approaches serve as a lens through which the illustrative cases of studies comparing places will be viewed and evaluated. Geographic entities offer a variety of foci for comparative inquiry in education, ranging from the macro level of world regions down to the micro level of classrooms and individuals.

The Bray and Thomas Framework for Comparative Education Analyses

The Bray and Thomas cube presented in the Introduction to this book (Figure 0.1) provides a three-dimensional approach to categorising various foci of comparative studies. The first dimension is *geographic/locational*, within which seven levels are identified. The second dimension corresponds to *nonlocational demographic* groupings; and the third dimension comprises *aspects of education and of society*. These different dimensions address the questions 'where', 'who' and 'what' in comparative analyses.

Scholars have increasingly addressed the notion of space since the 1970s (e.g. Sobe & Fischer 2009; Symaco & Brock 2013), suggesting a 'spatial turn' in scholarship outside of comparative education. For example, Lefebvre (1991) conceptualised space as a social production based on values which affect social practices and perceptions. These scholars view space from a social cultural lens, rather than from a natural and locational perspective. This resonates with the view of those who, recognising the impact of geopolitical shifts on the field of comparative education, have brought to light additional units of analysis and spaces for comparison (e.g. Cowen 2009a; Crossley & Watson 2003; Welch 2008). Aside from the cultural dimension, they have suggested focusing on political and economic dimensions relevant to education when grouping places for comparison. Rappleye (2010, p.74) posited that space "must be understood vis-à-vis the collective international space and the socio-specific space of relations between countries". These varied modalities of spaces, which could be inserted across the locational dimension in the Bray and Thomas cube, include geographic classification based on colonial history, religion, economic alliances, and epistemic culture. With respect to colonial history, for example, territories in Sub-Saharan Africa may be categorised as former British, French or Portuguese colonies, and offer fertile terrain for comparison. As for a shared religious belief and political history, the study by Silova et al. (2007) of six newly independent nations of Central Asia and Azerbaijan is illustrative. Alternatively, regional economic blocks provide instructive units for comparison. As explained by Cowen (2002, p.275):

> These blocks have emerged in West and Central Europe, in North America, in East and Southern Asia, and in South America. They speak to educational equivalencies, mobile professional labour, new links between universities and research and development industries, as well as new forms of hybrid identity for individuals. They may lead to the convergence of some aspects of education, such as curriculum and evaluation, in former national and separated educational systems.

Regional blocks can be incorporated in the cube fairly easily at the level of world regions. Despite these emerging social units of convergence, there is an opposite trend towards divergence manifested in the formation of social groups with a strong sense of sub-national identity, e.g. among the Bretons, Catalans and Scots (Cowen 2000a, p.5). These likewise open up other foci for comparison. Cowen thus concluded that comparative scholars are now invited to "play chess in at least eight or nine dimensions" (2000b, p.340).

Related to the effects of economic globalisation is the contemporary phenomenon of 'knowledge diaspora' (Welch 2008), leading to the formation of new epistemic communities that cut across national and regional boundaries. Another development that poses alternative landscapes for comparative analysis is the growth of 'virtual' universities (e.g. Guri-Rosenblit 2001) and classrooms as a result of developments in information and communications technology. These virtual entities are not located in a physical place, but in 'cyberspace'. While the school/classroom remains the unit of analysis (levels 5 and 6 of the cube), the virtual mode of teaching and learning introduces new elements and forces into the comparative experiment.

The above discussion has brought to light some alternative perspectives on the use of geographic entities as a unit of analysis. Scholars have identified derivative spatial units that have emerged as a result of geopolitical, economic, socio-cultural and technological shifts. These include cultural groupings (by religion, language, ethnicity), political/economic clusters, and epistemic communities. These derivative units are in fact potentially contained in the original Bray and Thomas framework, and are inextricably linked to one or more locations. The following section explores concrete examples of comparative education analyses, taking the different locational levels of the cube as foci of comparison and using both traditional and alternative spatial units of analysis.

Geographic Entities as Units of Analysis

This section focuses on the geographic/locational dimension of the Bray and Thomas cube. The discussion commences with the seven geographic levels represented on the front face, from the highest level of world regions/continents to the lowest level of individuals. Illustrative examples of comparative studies are discussed with a view to identifying their implications and evaluating their methodological effectiveness in elucidating the subjects being compared.

Level 1: World Regions/Continents
Bray and Thomas (1995, p.474) explained the nature of comparisons at the level of world regions and continents, the assumptions that underlie them, and the challenges faced by comparativists when undertaking them:

> A substantial literature focuses on the nature of educational provision in different regions of the world. Typical terms identifying regions are the Balkan States, the European Community, the Caribbean, and the South Pacific. Allied macro-level work takes the continent as the unit of analysis and focuses on such locations as Africa, South America, or Asia.
>
> A key assumption underlying most regional comparisons is that certain shared characteristics differentiate one region from another in educationally important ways. The unifying characteristics of any particular region may include language, political organization, colonial history, economic system, national ambitions, and/or cultural origins. Three particular challenges face authors of cross-regional comparisons. They must convince readers that the characteristics cited as unifying a region are truly shared by the region's members; demonstrate that two or more regions are substantially

similar or different in the nature of their unifying features; and show that such similarities and differences are educationally important.

These observations serve as a guide for the discussion below. The following examples show various ways in which regions may be used as units of comparison. The first example discusses a qualitative comparison of regional economic blocks, while the second involves a quantitative study of 'constructed' world regional groupings.

This first study takes three regional economic groupings as its focus of analysis: the European Union (EU), the North American Free Trade Agreement (NAFTA), and the Asia-Pacific Economic Cooperation (APEC). Dale and Robertson (2002) analysed them as subjects of globalisation, and examined their effects on national education systems. The study crossed three continents and adopted a qualitative approach.

Supranational bodies like the EU, NAFTA and APEC are formed as a result of the deliberate decisions of national governments to grant these entities some autonomy in order to achieve certain common goals. Thus, although they share common geographic bases, albeit constructed ones, the unifying and binding force of each regional entity is the political will of its constituent members, the intensity of which could downplay the importance of intra-regional disparities. In this sense, regional organisations provide a manageable and interesting window through which regions could be viewed.

Dale and Robertson nevertheless noted that regional organisations are nested in a complex web of institutional relations, cultural and political practices, and global developments (2002, p.18). Among the obvious differences are the size and diversity in the member states of each regional organisation. In 2013, NAFTA had three members, the EU had 28 members, and APEC had 21 members including several located outside the Asia-Pacific region. Dale and Robertson further explained (2002, p.29) that:

> The diversity of its membership distinguishes APEC from the other two organisations. The membership covers the whole range of national wealth, from the United States to Papua New Guinea. There are distinct cultural and religious differences among the members, and many of them have education systems that continue to bear (rather different) traces of their colonial histories, so that, overall, there is a correspondingly broad diversity of educational systems and provisions.

Figure 4.3: Mapping the Dynamics of Globalisation through Regional Organisations

Variables to determine external influences on education policy and practice	EU Form and purpose	NAFTA Form and purpose	APEC Form and purpose
Dimensions of power (soft or hard): • **decisions** • **agenda setting** • **rules of the game**			
Nature of effect (direct or indirect) on: • **politics of education** • **education politics**			
Processes/means of influence: • **strategies** • **tactics** • **devices**			
Scope – the extent of influence on different levels of education – **measured through:** • **sovereignty** • **autonomy**			

Source: Dale & Robertson (2002), p.19.

This example is instructive in terms of its comparative method. Its approach reflects to some extent the Bereday method of juxtaposition to establish a basis for comparison. The authors described and examined the purpose and form of the three regional organisations and their impact on education, as determined by key variables such as the strength, scope, and mechanisms employed (Figure 4.3). Simultaneous comparison was done gradually. First, NAFTA was examined as a single case. The EU case that followed was then contrasted with NAFTA, and finally APEC was compared and contrasted with the two preceding bodies. The article deserves emulation in its systematic analysis of issues following its guiding framework in Figure 4.3.

An underlying theme in the comparison of the three organisations is that the greater the diversity among the members forming a regional grouping (in economic wealth, religion, culture, and nature of educational systems), the looser the coupling among them. This is evidenced by the divergent approaches adopted by APEC member states on education policy in contrast to the harmonisation approach of the EU and the rules-based approach of NAFTA. A regional study of this nature and magnitude opens the door for further research examining the contexts of the different member states/economies so as to tease out the factors that account for their divergent or convergent strategies.

The second example considers regional grouping based on geographic proximity, which is a traditional basis for regional groupings. Table 4.2 lists some of the youth literacy rates by major world regions as well as other classifications (World Bank 2013a). The complete table provided by the World Bank included other entries of constructed groupings, such as small states and least developed countries.

Table 4.2: Youth Literacy Rates, by World Regions

	% of total youth population
Arab World	88%
East Asia and Pacific	99%
Europe and Central Asia	99%
Latin America and the Caribbean	97%
Middle East and North Africa	92%
South Asia	80%
Sub-Saharan Africa	70%

Source: Excerpts from World Bank (2013a).

However, each of these regional groupings, whether by geographic proximity or otherwise, requires further analysis. For example, the Middle East and North Africa region comprises 21 countries which, though partly unified by Islam, are quite different in land area, population, economic prosperity and other dimensions. At one extreme is Algeria having 38.5 million people in 919,595 square miles, and at the other extreme is Bahrain with only 1.3 million people in 267 square miles. In terms of economic prosperity, in 2011 the United Arab Emirates had a per capita Gross Domestic Product of US$42,384 in contrast to Yemen's US$2,485 (World Bank 2013b). Thus, without undervaluing the contribution of regional aggregate analyses, this example is taken to make a methodological point. Beneath the apparent homogeneity which 'regions' attempt to convey are demographic differences. The wider these differences, and the more causally significant their relationship to the phenomena being examined, the more cautious should be the interpretation of results.

The above discussion highlights the value of comparisons across world regions. Through the analysis of aggregate data at a supranational level, patterns and trends can be discerned to advance conceptual understanding and contribute to policy improvement. However, regional groupings at the supranational level are not necessarily natural or homogeneous; rather, they embrace (and overshadow) substantial intra-regional diversity.

Classifications by world regions, because of their breadth, can be subject to challenge. The use of the term 'region' may itself be rather indiscriminate. Such is the case with the term 'European' (Fox et al. 2011; Nóvoa 2002), 'Caribbean' (Louisy 2004), 'Mediterranean' (Bray et al. 2013), and 'Latin American' (Beech 2002). These authors underscored the value-laden and constructed nature of supranational regional groupings which are formed not merely on natural, geographical grounds of proximity but also as a result of geopolitical forces. This construction of regional boundaries implies that researchers need to be aware of and sensitive to the plural identities within regions for their analyses to be balanced and meaningful. Groupings by world regions, while useful, inevitably obscure significant divergences at the lower levels. Users of comparative studies of the world-systems genre therefore need to exercise caution when interpreting the data and recommendations derived from them.

Level 2: Countries

Countries have been the dominant unit of analysis in comparative studies since the beginnings of the field (see e.g. Kandel 1933; Hans 1949; Bereday 1964), and remain very prominent.

Before proceeding to the theoretical and methodological issues regarding country-level analysis, some conceptual clarifications are needed. Studies involving cross-national comparisons exhibit some looseness in the use of the term 'country' as synonymous to 'nation'. It is thus worth pausing to clarify some terms. Getis et al. (2011, pp.275-276) made the following distinctions between states, countries, nations, and nation-states:

> A **state** is an independent political unit occupying a defined, permanently populated territory and having full sovereign control over its internal and foreign affairs. A **country** is a synonym for the territorial and political concept of "state". A **nation** is a group of people with a common culture and territory, bound together by a strong sense of unity arising from shared beliefs and customs. A **nation-state** properly refers to a state whose territorial extent coincides with that occupied by a distinct nation or people or, at least, whose pop-

ulation shares a general sense of cohesion and adherence to a set of common values.

This discussion will endeavour to make precise use of these terms.

The first example illustrates Ragin's concept of illusory commonality discussed earlier. The term refers to cases which appear very similar but which experience different outcomes that are in turn traced back to causally significant differences amidst apparent 'illusory' commonalities.

Silova et al. (2007) compared six newly independent states in Eurasia, namely Azerbaijan, Kazakhstan, Kyrgyzstan, Tajikistan, Turkmenistan, and Uzbekistan, examining the role of education in the maintenance of social cohesion. The article described the pre-Soviet and Soviet legacies in education in the pre-1991 independence period, teasing out the complex relations among identity, religion, and education. It then analysed the post-independence systemic crises in state-sponsored secular education systems in these new republics. The study reported variations in the degree of educational deterioration in the different states, owing to their underlying political and economic pathologies. Uzbekistan and Turkmenistan's educational crises exhibited a political 'tipping point', i.e. the point at which institutional and professional capacity drain away so that the educational systems are no longer capable of regenerating themselves. Kyrgyzstan and Tajikistan's educational systems were in the middle tier and were approaching an economic tipping point. Azerbaijan and Kazakhstan, meanwhile, exhibited secular educational systems that had deteriorated but were not yet in crisis.

This study illustrated a methodological point on the careful selection of units that exhibit 'illusory commonality', identifying a shared foundation to make meaningful sense of the resultant differences in the educational phenomena being compared. The next example will explore a case of 'illusory difference', which refers to comparisons which take two or more units that are apparently different but arrive at a similar outcome. An example is the work of Canen (1995).

Canen focused on Brazil and the United Kingdom (UK), and analysed parallels in the roles of teachers' perceptions in the selectivity of education systems. She argued that despite the huge contextual differences between the two places, both faced similar challenges imposed by the multicultural nature of their societies. In this vein, she identified 'multicultural diversity' as the *significant* contextual similarity, amidst the wide differences distinguishing the two countries, which led to a similar resultant feature in both education systems. She concluded (p.235):

Although different in their composition, Brazilian and UK societies are presented with the selectivity of educational systems against specific groups of the population, in which teachers' perceptions and expectations play an important role. In the Brazilian case, the failure of less socially and economically advantaged children through repeating has led some authors to identify at least two sorts of culture in the scope of the school (popular and dominant), stressing the need to prepare teachers to build on pupils' culture to attain effective teaching. In UK, the need for multicultural education both for white and ethnic minority children was stressed, so as to discourage prejudice and racism and to achieve effective equality of opportunity.

Canen could perhaps have recognised more strongly the extent of the dissimilarities between Brazil and UK. Also, substantial intranational diversity exists at the level of sub-regions and states in each country, as evidenced by statistics on demography, racial mix and education. Thus, it might perhaps have been more illuminating to examine the selectivity of the education systems at the lower levels of regions. Brazil has been traditionally divided into five major regions: the Northeast, North, Southeast, South, and Central-West; and in the UK, educational practices are significantly different in England, Wales, Scotland and Northern Ireland. Nevertheless, Canen's article is an instructive example of the value of comparing educational phenomena in apparently dissimilar contexts.

The third example concerns large-scale cross-national comparisons. International comparisons involving large numbers of countries have commonly been undertaken to analyse educational achievement, educational spending and other aspects. Such studies may involve both quantitative and qualitative study. For example, Ferrer et al. (2004) studied patterns of convergence in lower secondary education in 15 EU countries. The work explicitly compared various dimensions of secondary education across the 15 countries: educational administration, curriculum and teacher education.

While these international comparisons are helpful to discern patterns of convergence, the authors acknowledged the complexities of obtaining systematically comparable and equivalent data, owing to cross-national diversity within the EU and further diversity at the sub-national and school levels. In the first place, the structure of lower secondary education differs substantially across the 15 EU countries, with a duration ranging from three to six years, and the typical age of schooling ranging from 10 to 13 years. Moreover, some countries make a clear institutional distinction between primary and secondary schools (mainly in the Nordic countries and Portugal), others offer a 'through-train' between lower and upper secondary education (Austria, Germany, Ireland and the UK), and the rest completely separate the primary, lower secondary, and senior secondary schooling (Naya 2004, pp.45-46).

To the above may be added a further methodological point making reference to the listing of EU 'countries' by Eurydice (2013), e.g. the entry on the Belgium French Community and UK England, respectively. The French community in Belgium is neither a country nor a nation-state.[1] Likewise, England is arguably not a country but a sub-national region of the UK. These underlying differences are obscured in summary tables which allocate equal space to each 'country'. This practice gives the misleading notion that the countries are equivalent or homogeneous units.

The example given here has highlighted some of the complexities in large-scale international comparisons. It has also underscored the fact that substantial differences exist among countries from the same European region. Further challenges are therefore to be expected when comparing a larger sample of countries from different regional contexts. As Bray and Thomas observed (1995, p.478), large-scale international comparisons "gloss over the facts that national boundaries are entirely arbitrary, and that the forces of geography, history, and politics happen to have created units of greatly differing size and content". Thus, without undervaluing the contribution of large-scale international comparisons to a conceptual understanding of educational patterns in various countries, producers and consumers of these studies need to exercise caution in their reporting and interpretation.

Taking the country as a unit of analysis is a legitimate practice considering that each country has a government which is the ultimate political unit exercising sovereignty over its internal and foreign affairs, and countries are thus the traditionally recognised entities of international governance. Moreover, in many countries control of important aspects of education is centralised and shapes national education systems. Thus, data on education are often available on a national aggregate basis.

---

[1] A three-level state structure was created in Belgium in 1993. At the top were the Federal State, the Communities and the Regions, all three of which were equal from the legal viewpoint. There were three communities and three regions: the French, Flemish and German-speaking Communities, and the Flemish Region, the Brussels-Capital Region and the Walloon Region.

Country comparisons, like world-systems comparisons, are thus useful in providing a general framework for understanding and interpretation of relationships between education and society.

However, the use of the country or nation-state as the dominant research framework has been continually challenged (e.g. Cowen 2009b; Carney 2010; Alexiadou & van de Bunt-Kokhuis 2013). Scholars cite world-systems analysis and intranational regional variations as major issues that make the use of the nation-state an inadequate unit of analysis. The main arguments are that national school systems exist within the context of unequal power relations among nations (Kelly & Altbach 1988, p.14), and that regional variations in education within nation-states are often as great if not greater than those between nation-states, which thereby makes intra-national comparisons as significant as inter-national comparisons. Getis et al. (2011) also highlighted the roles of international migration flows, nationalist and separatist movements, and the proliferation of nongovernmental organisations, all of which challenge a state-centric view of social analysis.

Level 3: States/Provinces
The third level of locational comparison is the intranational level of the state or province. Among the factors that make the state/province an appropriate unit of analysis is the high degree of decentralisation in many countries. Strongly decentralised systems exist in both geographically large countries such as Australia, Canada, India and the USA, and in small ones such as Switzerland (Bray 2013). Likewise, countries like the UK offer a locus for meaningful 'home international' research (e.g. Raffe et al. 1999; Taylor et al. 2013). Alternative units at the state level would also include Special Administrative Regions (SARs), such as Hong Kong and Macao which operate with strong autonomy within the People's Republic of China (Bray & Koo 2004).

Taking the state/province as a unit of description is also recommended when significant regional disparities exist within a country. In these cases, intranational comparisons yield more meaningful interpretations than aggregate, cross-national ones. As a corollary, sub-national units may be compared within the same country or between countries or even regions. The following examples illustrate some of these approaches. They elucidate the strengths of state-level comparisons while also pointing out some weaknesses as compared to lower-level studies.

Goldschmidt and Eyermann (1999) provided an interesting example of a quantitative intranational study focusing on US performance on international reading and mathematics achievement tests. The authors presented disaggregated measures to identify relationships between expenditures and outcomes across US states. For educational expenditures, they used the ratio of current public expenditure per pupil relative to the country's Gross Domestic Product (GDP) or the Gross State Product (GSP), its equivalent measure for the state. For student outcomes, the authors used the National Assessment of Educational Progress (NAEP) scores for Grade 8 mathematics in 41 states. They then compared the statistical data of the USA as a whole with 11 other countries, using the 1991 International Assessment of Educational Progress (IAEP) scores for Grade 8 mathematics. Since this analysis did not reveal meaningful results, they finally plotted the 41 US states individually against these 11 countries (Table 4.3).

This innovative approach produced some interesting findings. As commented by the authors (pp.37-38):

> Some states do relatively well, while other states do relatively poorly, based on an international comparison. That is to say that North Dakota, Iowa, Maine, Nebraska, and Wisconsin, are doing as well as Hungary, Switzerland, and Italy. All of these states and nations seem to be 'getting what they pay for'. States such as Alabama, Louisiana, and Mississippi seem to be in the same situation as Jordan. These states seem to lack the investment intensity necessary to generate good test scores.
>
> Of more concern are states such as Florida, West Virginia, and Arkansas, that are spending a great deal on education, given their per capita income, yet are receiving few positive results, in terms of national assessment test score. At the other end of the spectrum, however, Minnesota, New Hampshire, Idaho and Utah, have systems in place that approach the efficiency of top performer Korea.

The authors concluded that this type of analysis provided the USA with models of the best and most cost-efficient educational systems within its national boundaries, which were much easier to emulate than foreign models taken from Switzerland or the Republic of Korea, for example. This did not, however, suggest that the USA or its respective states should be precluded from looking at places and systems outside its national boundaries.

Table 4.3: Comparison of Nations and US States on Percentage Deviation from Expected 1990 Grade 8 Mathematics Scores and Expenditures on Education per Capita

	Percentage deviation in:			Percentage deviation in:	
	NAEP*	Expenditure		NAEP*	Expenditure
Korea, Republic	6.7	-25.4	North Dakota	5.8	17.7
Minnesota	5.0	-1.8	Iowa	5.7	10.8
New Hampshire	3.5	-13.8	**Hungary**	5.1	21.5
Idaho	2.8	-6.8	**Switzerland**	4.1	32.1
Utah	2.7	-20.9	Maine	3.8	12.7
Israel	2.5	-13.4	Nebraska	3.5	2.5
France	2.4	-14.1	Wisconsin	3.5	8.7
Connecticut	1.2	-6.1	**Italy**	2.2	8.1
Massachusetts	1.1	-10.2	Wyoming	1.9	3.2
Missouri	1.0	-11.7	**Ireland**	1.7	3.2
			Colorado	1.6	2.6
			Pennsylvania	1.4	14.5
			Canada	1.1	6.1
			Indiana	0.7	2.8
			New Jersey	0.6	0.9
			Oklahoma	0.2	4.0
Ohio	-0.2	-2.2	Michigan	-0.2	11.5
Virginia	-0.5	-10.5	Rhode Island	-0.9	23.5
Spain	-0.7	-27.6	New York	-1.1	7.3
Arizona	-0.9	-0.5	Texas	-1.2	3.2
Kentucky	-2.3	-17.9	Maryland	-1.5	5.8
Delaware	-2.4	-12.9	South Carolina	-2.5	8.0
Georgia	-3.3	-15.1	New Mexico	-3.0	4.5
California	-3.3	-26.1	Florida	-3.1	11.8
Tennessee	-3.6	-15.3	West Virginia	-3.2	23.1
North Carolina	-3.7	-7.7	**Portugal**	-3.4	19.8
Hawaii	-4.4	-40.9	Arkansas	-4.4	6.1
Alabama	-6.2	-6.8			
Jordan	-6.6	-99.5			
Louisiana	-7.3	-31.3			
Mississippi	-8.2	-4.5			

Note: * For foreign nations 1991 IAEP scores are linked to the 1990 NAEP scores.
Source: Extracted from Goldschmidt & Eyermann (1999), p.40.

While the above analysis is creative and insightful, it deserves some comment from a methodological perspective. Several difficulties arising from international and intranational differences may be noted. As the authors recognised (p.40), intra- and cross-regional disparities exist among their units of analysis:

Depending on the state or country, there may be significant variations in economic wealth within a region of the country and significant differences in educational achievement within social and culture regions.

The first relates to the equivalence in economic purchasing power used in computing 'expenditure on education per capita'. The second relates to the comparability of test scores given that they pertain to students who may belong to different age groups as determined by different education systems. This section refrains from discussing these two issues since they are addressed in other chapters. Instead, it focuses on a third methodological point. The example, while elucidating the value of intranational comparison in view of the highly decentralised system of the USA, overlooked the similarly decentralised structure of some of the countries it included in the league table for comparative purposes. The use of Canada and Switzerland, for example, as places for comparison with states within the USA (e.g. North Dakota and Iowa) glossed over significant subnational differences in those two countries which are as highly decentralised as the USA. It might have been more meaningful to compare Ontario or British Columbia and/or the various Swiss cantons with the respective constituent states of the USA.

In this vein, Switzerland offers an interesting locus for intranational comparisons. Cantonal governments have autonomy in educational matters such as curriculum structure and content, length of the school year, and medium of instruction (German, French, Italian or Romansh). Such a highly decentralised system, characterised by cultural and linguistic diversity (Table 4.4), is a classic case for intranational comparison. Felouzis and Charmillot (2013) conducted multilevel analyses of 12 Swiss cantons to investigate the relationships between school tracking and educational inequality. They observed that the Swiss cantons form a kind of 'school laboratory' since their education systems are similar enough to be comparable, but permit manipulation of some components in order to measure the different impacts on education.

An earlier study by Hega (2001) analysed educational policy making in the 26 cantons of Switzerland. Hega gave an insightful analysis of the politics governing second-language instruction policy across the cantonal boundaries. She highlighted the distinctive educational cultures that had emerged in Switzerland as a result of the interaction between cultural traditions, linguistic heritage and religious beliefs in each canton. This "specific local or regional education culture is reflected, for instance, in the subjects, methods and types of instruction; the organisation of educational institutions and their governance; and the teaching personnel that is trained according to specific methods and develops certain attitudes and techniques" (p.223).

Table 4.4: Demographic and Socio-cultural Characteristics of the Swiss Cantons

Canton	Population in 2011 (in 000s)	German-speakers %	French-speakers %	Italian-speakers %	Romansh-speakers %
Zürich	1,392	85.0	3.5	5.8	0.3
Bern	985	85.7	11.0	3.2	*
Luzern	382	90.7	1.9	3.1	*
Uri	35	94.1	*	*	*
Schwyz	148	90.3	*	3.5	*
Obwalden	36	94.0	*	*	*
Nidwalden	41	95.5	*	*	*
Glarus	39	90.2	*	*	*
Zug	115	86.1	3.1	3.6	*
Fribourg	285	29.4	68.1	2.0	*
Solothurn	257	89.5	2.6	4.8	*
Basel-City	186	80.8	6.1	6.8	*
Basel-Land	275	89.3	4.0	5.6	*
Schaffhausen	77	89.0	*	*	*
Appenzell-Ausserrhoden	53	92.7	*	*	*
Appenzell-Innerrhoden	16	93.8	*	*	*
St. Gallen	483	90.0	1.2	3.5	*
Graubünden	193	76.3	*	12.3	15.6
Aargau	618	89.4	2.3	5.1	*
Thurgau	252	91.0	1.3	4.1	*
Ticino	337	11.1	5.3	87.7	*
Vaud	726	7.1	85.0	5.2	*
Valais	317	28.0	66.5	3.7	*
Neuchatel	173	5.9	88.8	6.1	*
Geneva	460	5.8	80.8	7.3	*
Jura	70	6.7	92.2	3.7	*
Switzerland	**7,956**	**65.6**	**22.8**	**8.4**	**0.6**

Source: Swiss Federal Statistics Office (SFSO), 2013.
* If the coefficient of variation is greater than 10%, the value is not shown by SFSO.

From a methodological viewpoint, this example illustrates the internal complexities and interactions in highly decentralised systems that are also culturally diverse. Sub-national comparisons thus bring into relief the finer yet significant details of educational mosaics which would otherwise not have been captured in generalist country studies and which could have led to reductionist and simplistic interpretations.

As in comparisons at the higher levels, macro level comparison obscures disparities at the micro levels. A final example is provided of an international comparison made taking a pair of sub-national regions. Fry and Kempner (1996) focused on Northeast Brazil and Northeast Thailand, two provincial regions in two different hemispheres. The authors started by comparing the sub-national regions of Brazil, highlighting the regional disparities and identifying Northeast Brazil as the poorest region in the country. This was followed by a multidisciplinary analysis of Northeast Brazil in terms of its geographic and economic conditions, cultures, migration patterns, religions and educational philosophies. A similar exercise was undertaken for Thailand, revealing similar patterns of neglect and underdevelopment in the Northeast region. Finally, a simultaneous comparison of the two north-eastern hinterlands of Brazil and Thailand was made on the basis of their similar economically disadvantaged status relative to the rest of their respective countries. The analysis revealed (p.357) that:

> the neglect of a region and its people may be endemic to the sub-national imperialism or internal colonialism of a country .... Often the most industrialized [region in a country] may exploit the resources and human capital of the less developed region [in its own country]. A critical example of this is Brazil's massive foreign debt. The money borrowed from the International Monetary Fund principally serves the interests of the industrialized South to the detriment and continued neglect of the underdeveloped Northeast and rural areas.

As the authors argued, an overall economic and educational study of Brazil and Thailand might overestimate the aggregate economic performance of each country while overshadowing the 'other Brazil' and the 'other Thailand' (p.335). This example of a cross-cultural comparison of two sub-national regions sharing similar dilemmas identified instructive lessons that would otherwise have passed unnoticed in aggregate cross-national comparisons or in inter-regional comparisons within the same country. In this light, the observation that comparative studies can make "familiar patterns strange and strange patterns familiar" (Bray 2004, p.250) aptly describes the lessons from this example.

The three examples in this section have shown that sub-national comparisons offer rich and deep vistas for understanding educational phenomena which would have been overshadowed at the higher locational levels. While the first example attempted to make a meaningful comparison of the 41 states of a large country with foreign countries, the second example took the small country of Switzerland to examine its mosaic of 26 cantons. The last example showed an alternative approach by taking two similar sub-national regions from two different countries in two different hemispheres as a pair for comparison.

Level 4: Districts

Before discussing some examples of district-level analysis, it would help to unpack the term 'district'. A district is an area of a town or country which has been given official boundaries for administrative purposes. It encompasses places which are below the provincial/state level but are above the school/institutional level. It includes such urban units as towns and cities, as well as rural units of counties and villages.

District-level comparisons are particularly useful when there is significant intra-provincial variation or when aggregate national and/or provincial statistics are not reliable or are misleading due to significant variations across districts and/or technical difficulties in collecting data at higher levels (Bray & Thomas 1995, pp.480-481). These points will be illustrated in the following examples, which take the city, village and sub-district as units of analysis.

Lo (2004) focused on junior secondary history curricula in Hong Kong and Shanghai. The two cities shared features as robust financial centres vying for a share of China's economic market. Shanghai, in contrast to other cities in China, was fast developing as a cosmopolitan city and an attractive home for foreign investment. In this respect, it was more similar to Hong Kong than to other Chinese cities. Nevertheless, Hong Kong and Shanghai differed in their political systems: Hong Kong officially had a capitalist system while Shanghai officially had a socialist one. Recent political changes, however, had created convergence between them. After its decolonisation by the British and return to the Motherland in 1997, Hong Kong's history curriculum had increasingly emphasised national (Chinese) identity. Conversely, China's modernisation drive had boosted global awareness which had impacted on the history curriculum reforms in Shanghai. From this perspective, the two cities served as an illuminating pair for analysing the evolutionary path of their respective history curricula.

From a methodological perspective, a subtle distinction may be made here. Shanghai is clearly a city of China, while Hong Kong is a rather different political entity: it is a Special Administrative Region which operates differently from other cities in China, including Shanghai, despite similarities in economic liberalisation. This is an important factor to consider when analysing the reasons for curricular policy convergence and divergence.

The second example focused on the village as a unit of comparison. Puchner (2003) studied four villages in a district in southern Mali, examining the ways in which power relations shaped women's literacy. The ethnographic study was premised (pp.440-441) on the view that in women's literacy:

> it is especially important to keep in mind that the politics and power structures that characterize the community mediate and in fact dictate the influences that literacy has on the community in general and on women in the community in particular.

Through an in-depth comparison of the practices in the four communities, the study captured the subtle power relations across the villages and made a case for the central policy-makers to take into account the significant factors that determined women's power and position in the community before implementing any structural adjustments to improve literacy (p.457). From a methodological viewpoint, comparative ethnographic studies at this microscopic level show ways to tease out important elements which shape educational phenomena. However, it would have been desirable to see in this study a reference to the socio-political context at the supra-village level, e.g. in the province and country, as well as to the role of culture and religion.

A related example for this category is Dyer's (1996) ethnographic research on the policy innovation in elementary education in India, taking three areas in Baroda District, Gujarat State of India as case study sites. Three groupings of primary schools were selected to reflect a variety of socio-economic settings in that location, mirroring the wider context of India: a tribal area of Chhota Udepur, a rural area of Karjan, and an urban setting of Baroda city. The study demonstrated intra-district diversity within the same state and its implications (p.38):

> Central policy-makers need to recognise the existence of a wide variety of very different educational contexts. As this paper has illustrated even a single District of one State cannot be treated as a homogeneous unit. The implications of heterogeneity for the educational process must be considered in the formulation of any educational innovation in a country of such diversity as India.

The examples given above have elucidated the usefulness of district-level analysis in uncovering dimensions which are causally important in shaping society-education relationships and which are normally obscured in macro level, aggregate studies. A range of units of analysis may be examined taking a city/town on one end of the spectrum, to villages and sub-districts on the other end. Studies at this level reveal meaningful lessons which complement and complete the picture captured in analyses at the upper levels.

Level 5: Schools

When schools are taken as the unit of analysis, the nature of foci changes. As Bray and Thomas noted (1995, p.481), analysis of the higher levels of world regions, countries, provinces, and districts may be concerned with the people who are *not* enrolled in schools as well as with those who are. Research that takes schools as the unit of analysis, by contrast, would focus on the specific communities comprising the schools. Moreover, adoption of the school as the unit of analysis requires a focus on institutional culture, which is rather different from the cultures underlying larger units. The authors added (p.482) that:

> One feature of this level of research is that it can present personalized portraits ... bring[ing] into focus the impact of individual differences among the "ordinary" actors. Another important factor is that schools are sufficiently numerous to permit meaningful random sampling, which would not normally be possible at the world-region, national, or provincial levels, though it could in some contexts be appropriate at the district level.

Most comparative studies taking schools as the unit of analysis focus on entities within the same country, province or district (e.g. Hansen & Woronov 2013), although cross-national studies have also been undertaken (e.g. Vidovich 2004). In fact, cross-national comparisons of schools may actually be undertaken within the same state. Bray and Yamato (2003) demonstrated that international schools within the small territory of Hong Kong represented diverse foreign national systems of education. Two illustrative cases are discussed below.

Benavot and Resh (2001) undertook a comparative study of the implemented curriculum in the Jewish-secular junior high schools of Israel. With a stratified, nationally representative sample of 104 schools, their study demonstrated that despite a relatively centralised educational system, there was significant inter-school diversity in the implementation of national curricular guidelines. This qualitative study is further evidence of the instructive value of analysis at the lower levels as it leads to questioning the taken-for-granted assumption that centralised means homogeneous.

Vidovich (2004) studied two schools in Singapore and Australia which had been internationalising their curricula. The Singapore school was an 'independent', non-religious school, enjoying greater autonomy than government schools but still coming under the control of the Ministry of Education (MoE). By contrast, the Australian school was a mainline Protestant school that had remained 'independent' of the government sector over its long history.

The cross-case analysis of the two schools revealed similarities and differences in the external factors influencing curriculum policy development. While global forces had shaped the internationalisation of both schools' curricula, Singapore was more sensitive to economic globalisation than Australia. Likewise, on the level of national influences, while both schools were labelled 'independent', the Singapore school identified the MoE as most influential while the Australian school considered itself a superior educational institution in the state, setting it apart from the rest (p.449).

These divergent results pointed to deeper contextual differences which significantly influenced school curricular politics. While it is valuable for heuristic purposes to take a pair of schools in two very different places, caution needs to be exercised in determining which of the inherent macro-contextual factors in each place are causally significant to school-level processes. The country's size, political history and culture are significant factors that shape educational politics in Singapore and give different meaning and colour to its concept of an 'independent' school. Given its small size and a history characterised by a determined national effort to establish economic competitiveness and social cohesion among its multicultural groups, Singapore's educational policies would understandably be under the strong control of the Ministry of Education, despite claims and indications of decentralisation. By contrast, Australia's huge territory and tradition of decentralised governance casts its concept of 'independent' schools differently from that of Singapore.

The above examples thus illustrate the usefulness of examining smaller units of analysis such as the school. Such research enriches and deepens conceptual understanding of educational reality. The first example, a nation-wide comparison of schools within a centralised education system, revealed that centralisation may still permit diversity and pluralism. The second example, a comparison of a pair of schools from two very different national contexts, highlighted the need to identify significant contextual differences between the units compared, and examined their relationships with the resulting educational outcomes at the school level.

Level 6: Classrooms

Classrooms as the unit of analysis have not been prominent in the traditional comparative education literature, which has concentrated on the higher levels of educational systems and policies. Alexander (1999, p.109) observed that the increasing importance given to classrooms was due to:

> the growing prominence being given to 'process' variables in input-output studies of the kind conducted for OECD [Organisation for Economic Co-operation & Development]; the rise of school effectiveness research and the extension of its focus from the levels of the system and the school down to that of the classroom; the attempts of educational statisticians, in their turn, to encompass the totality of the educational enterprise, including teaching, in multilevel modelling; the belated discovery by policy-makers caught up in the international league table game that what happens in classrooms is actually rather important; and the equally belated development of pedagogy as a central focus for educational research.

Classrooms offer an interesting space for comparative analyses. They also lend themselves to challenging new domains for investigation such as the emergence of a new space: the virtual classroom. The example below focuses on lessons, a derivative spatial unit related to the classroom.

Anderson-Levitt (2004) compared Grade 1 and 2 reading lessons in three countries: France, Guinea and the USA (Figure 4.4). France and Guinea were chosen on account of their former colonial relationship; the USA was placed as a third case for contrastive purposes to the other two cases, and also because it was competing with France to influence reading instruction in Guinea.

Figure 4.4: Comparison of Lesson Structures

France holistic-analytic	France mainstream	Guinea	US traditional	US process & whole-language
Group discovery or production of a text (*comprehension*)	Group production of a text (*comprehension*)	Proposal of a text (*comprehension*)	Vocabulary preparation (*comprehension*)	
Whole class reading	Whole class reading	Whole class reading	Small group reading	Small group reading Individual reading
Word study	Word study	Word study		
			Comprehension questions (*comprehension*)	Individual production of texts (*comprehension*)
				Teacher reads to or with class (*comprehension*)
Isolation of the sound (*code: analysis*)	Isolation of the sound (*code: analysis*)	Isolation of the sound (*code: analysis*)	Phonics instruction (*code: analysis*)	Phonics instruction (*code: analysis*)
Exercises	Exercises	Exercises	Worksheet, Seatwork	Seatwork, centres
	Dictation (*code: synthesis*)			

Source: Extracted from Anderson-Levitt (2004), p.246.

Anderson-Levitt made a methodological point on the use of the lesson as a unit of analysis (pp.233-234):

> My analysis uses the "lesson" as the unit of comparison, but the meaning of lesson is itself problematic. In the English-language research literature, "lesson" usually refers to a single, continuous session of teaching and learning. However, as we shall see, educators in France and in Guinea define a lesson as a series of sessions that take place over the course of 2 or more days, using the same material and organized around the same goals.... The notion of a lesson is especially complex in U.S. classrooms, where the use of small groups and individual projects means that a language arts session can consist of multiple simultaneous activities.

The study, though starting from a microscopic focus on the lesson, exemplified a multilevel approach to comparison. Its conclusions transcended the four walls of the classroom and teased out similarities and differences across the Guinean, French and US reading lessons.

Level 7: Individuals

Finally, at the lowest level of the Bray and Thomas framework is the individual as a unit of analysis. As the authors explained (p.483):

> Research may also focus on individuals: principals, teachers, parents, pupils, and others. Such studies may have many disciplinary orientations, but are more likely than analyses at other levels to emphasize psychology.

Among the cases they cited are 'personalised reports' focusing for example on students' approaches to learning, or teachers' organisation of lessons, as well as impersonal large-scale surveys of teachers, pupils or other individuals conducted by governments and other bodies. Andrews (2013) investigated four Finnish mathematics teachers who taught in different comprehensive schools, and Pantić et al. (2011) surveyed teachers in five Western Balkan countries.

An example of an effort to transcend the individual level and recognise the influence of higher level factors is the research project Quality in Educational Systems Trans-nationally (QUEST) which examined the influence of national culture on pupil attitudes, classroom practice and learning outcomes in England and France (Broadfoot 1999, p.241). The study was conducted on a sample of 800 children aged 9 to 11 (400 in each country) selected from four schools in each of two contrasting regions in each country (16 schools in total, eight in each country). The study team observed (p.251) that:

> The potential significance for educational outcomes of national cultural differences is well illustrated in this example in the relatively limited spread of scores in France compared to that of the matched sample of English pupils. The indications are that the French tradition of teaching an undifferentiated lesson in which virtually all pupils are expected to be successful results in most pupils indeed being able to master what has been taught. By contrast, the English differentiated approach gives some pupils the possibility of achieving a much more sophisticated level of mastery whilst others are left far behind.

The authors then complemented this investigation with ethnographic 'personalised' reports from the students and noted that English students were more individualistic and freer to express themselves. French students restricted themselves to performing the task required and seemed reluctant to make their personal statements. Finally, the authors concluded (p.254):

> Differences in what two populations of pupils are able to do reflect teachers' different, culturally-based, expectations about children's achievements as well as their different views of the goals of education. These culturally-based differences in teachers' perspectives are further reinforced by similarly culturally-informed differences in the thinking that informs policy-making itself.

This study exemplifies multilevel analysis, relating the findings at the lower level of the student and classroom to the higher level of cross-cultural differences and teaching traditions. It echoes a principle in psychology which conceives the developing person as situated in a nest of ecological environments, "each inside the other like a set of Russian dolls" (Bronfenbrenner 1979, p.3), the relationships of which needed to be analysed for a holistic interpretation of reality. It is also a model of a combined use of qualitative and quantitative research approaches. While studies of this scale require substantial human and financial resources, they contribute substantially to understanding of educational phenomena.

Comparison across Levels

After the above discussion of the seven levels of geographic units for comparison displayed on the front of the Bray and Thomas cube, this section comments on the value of multilevel comparative analysis.

Bray and Thomas (1995, p.484) noted that:

> Various studies use a multilevel design in order to achieve more complete and balanced understandings. While many such studies suffer flaws of various kinds, the fact that they consider their subjects from several different angles facilitates more comprehensive and possibly more accurate presentation of the phenomena they address.
>
> The dominant form of research under the specific label of multilevel analysis has been principally confined to the individual, classroom, and school levels. Such studies have generally omitted careful consideration of the state/province, country, and world region levels, with the result that interpretations have still been arguably unbalanced and incomplete, albeit more informative than before.

Comparative scholars welcomed this appeal to multilevel comparative education analyses, and an increasing number of such studies can be found in the literature (e.g. Hickling-Hudson 2004; Shabaya & Konadu-Agyemang 2004; Alexiadou & van de Bunt-Kokhuis 2013). As Alexander (2001, p.511) explained, multilevel comparisons are crucial for a balanced and holistic understanding of educational phenomena:

> [P]edagogy does not begin and end in the classroom. It can be comprehended only once one locates practice within the concentric circles of local and national, and of classroom, school, system and state, and only if one steers constantly back and forth between these, exploring the way that what teachers and students do in classrooms both reflects and enacts the values of the wider society.

This 'steering back and forth' across the national, provincial, district, school, classroom, and individual levels as well as across national and regional boundaries, enables the researcher to tease out "*spatial* continuities ... differentiating the universal in pedagogy from the culturally specific" (Alexander 2001, p.519).

A final illustration of the process of multilevel analysis is taken from McNess (2004). She investigated teachers' work in England and Denmark, employing an extended case-study approach which linked macro level international and national policy contexts with meso level school and individual case studies. She used the concept of an 'iterative filter' (2004, p.318) to describe the process of multilevel analysis as:

> a process of constant progressive focussing, in which information was filtered through its global and national context in order to illuminate local priorities and individual classroom practice. This recognises Bronfenbrenner's concept of the 'ecological environment' ... (1979, p.3), the relationships of which needed to be explored in order to fully understand the whole. Thus, the analysis moved from the macro policy level to the micro level of personal meaning, through the intermediary mesosystem of the school and classroom structures, while taking account of the ecosystem of the school within its local and regional community. This iteration was not a one-way process but formed part of a recursive loop, so that the data collected at each of these levels both informed and reshaped the research questions and the research findings. This reciprocal movement between the micro and the macro was used to construct

and refine meaning, as well as to check the validity of the data as it was collected.

The iterative process across the macro, meso, and micro levels of societal units and their activity thus illuminated, in this particular case, the contextualised meaning of the 'quality of education'. The study showed that 'quality' was neither universal nor static but individual and situated, and largely determined by custom and practice, current policy and individual teacher experience (p.326). This extended case study shows a path for achieving meaningful, balanced interpretations of reality without requiring substantial investment of human and financial resources.

Conclusions: Methodological Issues in Comparing Places

This chapter has discussed the use of place as a unit of comparative analysis, taking the geographic/locational dimension of the Bray and Thomas (1995) framework for comparative and multilevel analyses as its model and benchmark. It has explored the various levels of places that can be compared, and has identified alternative spaces cited in related literature. These derivative spatial units, partly generated by geopolitical, economic, technological and socio-cultural transformations, are in fact potentially contained in the original framework and can be plotted on the cube. A variety of examples, culled from the specialist literature in comparative education, have been employed to illustrate their mechanics and to evaluate their usefulness. These encompassed both single-level and multilevel comparative analyses. In the process, some comments on methodological issues have been made.

The chapter commenced with an introduction to general approaches to comparative inquiry in education, setting the stage for the introduction of the Bray and Thomas framework in the second section. It argued that comparative studies, whether interpretative or causal-analytic, should pay careful attention to establishing the basis for comparability in order to provide a foundation for meaningful interpretation of results. This implies that when researchers choose the units for comparison, they should diligently identify the parameters for comparability and their causal relevance to the educational phenomena. For this purpose, the similarities and differences of the units being compared should be examined in context, to calibrate whether they are truly educationally important. Researchers should try to be sensitive to the axis of variation, i.e. the axis along which differences may be ranked as to their degree of causal significance on the educational phenomena under study.

As cited in the above discussions, for comparison to be meaningful, the units of analysis should display sufficient commonalities to make their differences significant. There are however cases in which this rule of thumb has not been observed. Canen (1995) seemed to have glossed over the significant intranational diversity in Brazil and the UK; and Vidovich (2004) gave inadequate attention to the obvious inter-national dissimilarities between Australia and Singapore. Both examples took their pair of countries as homogeneous, equivalent units for comparison. This could lead to an imbalanced and misleading interpretation of the data. Moreover, the comparison of curricula in Australia and Singapore (Vidovich 2004) overlooked the difference in magnitude between the two countries, a significant factor which paints an entirely different panorama in terms of educational politics.

These examples warrant an echo of the call for caution made by scholars of comparative education. Such scholars have emphasised the need to establish the terms of comparison – a minimal base of shared commonalities – such terms being causally important to the educational phenomena being researched. In this respect, comparative studies are to some extent like conducting a laboratory experiment. For an experiment to be valid and meaningful, certain variables need to be kept constant. A way to do so is by choosing units of analysis that have sufficient similarities that are educationally relevant. Discrepancies in size and context, as exhibited in the example on Australia and Singapore, and the consequent complexities in their educational governance and autonomy, are significant system-level factors that shape the lower levels of the schools and curricula. For this reason, a comparison between a huge and highly diverse and decentralised place such as Australia with a small, similarly diverse but centralised state such as Singapore deserves reconsideration. Nevertheless, these studies may still reach some meaningful results provided they dispel the 'illusory differences' (Ragin 1987) and prove that such differences are, at an abstract or causal level, not significant. At the least, they can recognise the role of these exogenous factors and the limitations of their findings.

The main part of the chapter elucidated the potentials of the locational dimension of the Bray and Thomas cube, comprising seven levels: world regions, countries, states/provinces, districts, schools, classrooms, and individuals. Alternative spatial units such as regional economic blocks, cities, and virtual (non-physical) classrooms were also discussed. Each locational level captures a different dimension or angle of the educational reality under study and has its strengths and weaknesses. Analyses at the upper levels of the cube (world regions, country, state/ province, district) contribute a broad, general framework of educational and demographic patterns. Studies which limit themselves to the macro levels, however, while useful and meaningful, tend to gloss over significant patterns and distinctive features at the meso and micro levels and their influence on educational events. The example from Dale and Robertson (2002), which analysed the educational strategies and agendas of three regional economic blocks, revealed that significant intra-regional diversity exists among the region's constituencies. Only a further exploration of the micro levels (school, classroom, individuals) and, in the case of highly decentralised and/or diversified countries, of the meso levels (province, district), can render a complete and realistic picture of the determinants of educational phenomena in these entities. In this light, Crossley and Vulliamy (2011) argued in favour of contextualised studies which take into account the dynamic and existential phenomena at the level of the school and the individual, especially in large countries where huge intranational disparities exist.

A corollary to this downward movement from the higher levels of the cube to the lower locational levels is a corresponding upward movement from the lower to the upper layers. Studies conducted at the lower levels of the cube may tend to disengage with the macro level context in which they are embedded. They suffer, on the one hand, from a lack of transferability of conclusions to other contexts, and on the other, from a narrow and incomplete assessment of the determinants of educational phenomena seen at their level. As Sadler (1900, p.310) cautioned: "the things outside the schools matter even more than the things inside schools, and govern and interpret the things inside". This alludes to the need for lower level studies (individual, classroom, and school) to be understood within the broader context of higher levels of the framework (system, state, etc.). Only in this way can studies present a meaningful and comprehensive picture of the relationships between macro and micro levels.

The relative strengths and weaknesses of comparative analyses limited to one level of the geographic hierarchy point to the importance of multilevel research in order to gain a balanced and comprehensive understanding of the complex reality of educational phenomena. Each level is a window on the larger culture (Alexander 2000, p.531). The different levels of geographic units, while distinct, are not disjointed and hermetically sealed spaces. Rather, they are like ecological environments, conceived as a set of nested structures, each inside the next (Bronfenbrenner 1979, p.3). The higher and lower geographic levels mutually influence and shape each other as in a 'dialectic of the global and the local' (Arnove 2013, p.1). A recognition and understanding of the mutual relationships across each of the spatial levels is indispensable for a holistic comprehension of the essence of educational phenomena (see also Schriewer 2006). This fine-grained analysis of educational pathologies is important not only for conceptual understanding but also, and even more, for improvement of policies.

Multilevel analysis need not be undertaken within the confines and limited tools of educational research. Rather, it is highly encouraged that comparative education scholars, as the field's tradition espouses, engage in multidisciplinary collaborative research. Thus, Bray and Thomas (1995, p.488) advocated "cross-fertilization from other fields", wherein micro level quantitative work could be informed by the qualitative contributions from the field of cross-national comparative education. Similarly, macro level comparative researchers would benefit from other fields that investigate the rich diversity at the lower levels of the state, districts, schools, classrooms and individuals, thereby giving their work balance, depth and completeness.

Multilevel comparative analysis is indeed desirable and feasible. While most studies of this kind require large-scale mobilisation of resources within or across countries, this chapter has provided several examples of multilevel comparisons within reach of most comparative researchers who normally focus at the lower levels of the classroom and individuals (e.g. Anderson-Levitt 2004; McNess 2004). At least, researchers who work on a single level of analysis can acknowledge the scope and limitations of their findings by explicitly identifying their location on the knowledge map. One way to do so is through the framework for comparative analyses given here.

Comparative research can help provide tools for understanding and uncovering meaningful relationships from complex educational realities by striving for both conceptual and linguistic equivalence, and emphasising the situatedness in time and space of particular social phenomena (McNess 2004, p.326). This chapter has demonstrated that comparing places provides an exciting locus to examine varied educational phenomena at different levels of the spectrum. It also opens the discussion to exploring other units of analyses which are inextricably linked to place.

References

Alexander, Robin (1999): 'Comparing Classrooms and Schools', in Alexander, Robin; Broadfoot, Patricia & Phillips, David (eds.), *Learning from Comparing: New Directions in Comparative Educational Research, Vol.1: Contexts, Classrooms and Outcomes*. Oxford: Symposium Books, pp.109-111.

Alexander, Robin (2000): *Culture and Pedagogy: International Comparisons in Primary Education*. Oxford: Blackwell.

Alexander, Robin (2001): 'Border Crossings: Towards a Comparative Pedagogy'. *Comparative Education*, Vol.37, No.4, pp.507-523.

Alexiadou, Nafsika & van de Bunt-Kokhuis, Sylvia (2013): 'Policy Space and the Governance of Education: Transnational Influences on Institutions and Identities in the Netherlands and the UK'. *Comparative Education*, Vol.49, No.3, pp.344-360.

Anderson-Levitt, Kathryn M. (2004): 'Reading Lessons in Guinea, France, and the United States: Local Meanings or Global Culture?'. *Comparative Education Review*, Vol.48, No.3, pp.229-252.

Andrews, Paul (2013): 'Finnish Mathematics Teaching from a Reform Perspective: A Video-Based Case-Study Analysis'. *Comparative Education Review*, Vol.57, No.2, pp.189-211.

Arnove, Robert F. (2013): 'Introduction: Reframing Comparative Education: The Dialectic of the Global and the Local', in Arnove, Robert F.; Torres, Carlos Alberto & Franz, Stephen (eds.), *Comparative Education: The Dialectic of the Global and the Local*. 4th edition, Lanham: Rowman & Littlefield, pp.1-25.

Beech, Jason (2002): 'Latin American Education: Perceptions of Linearities and the Construction of Discursive Space'. *Comparative Education*, Vol.38, No.4, pp.415-427.

Benavot, Aaron & Resh, Nura (2001): 'The Social Construction of the Local School Curriculum: Patterns of Diversity and Uniformity in Israeli Junior High Schools'. *Comparative Education Review*, Vol.45, No.4, pp.504-536.

Bereday, George Z.F. (1964): *Comparative Method in Education*. New York: Holt, Rinehart & Winston.

Berg-Schlosser, Dirk (2001): 'Comparative Studies: Method and Design', in Smelser, Neil J. & Baltes, Paul B. (eds.), *International Encyclopedia of the Social and Behavioural Sciences*. Amsterdam: Elsevier, pp.2427-2433.

Bray, Mark (2004): 'Methodology and Focus in Comparative Education', in Bray, Mark & Koo, Ramsey (eds.), *Education and Society in Hong Kong and Macao: Comparative Perspectives on Continuity and Change*. 2nd edition. CERC Studies in Comparative Education 7, Hong Kong: Comparative Education Research Centre, The University of Hong Kong, pp.237-350.

Bray, Mark (2013): 'Control of Education: Issues and Tensions in Centralization and Decentralization', in Arnove, Robert F.; Torres, Carlos Alberto & Franz, Stephen (eds.), *Comparative Education: The Dialectic of the Global and the Local*. 4th edition, Lanham: Rowman & Littlefield, pp.201-222.

Bray, Mark & Koo, Ramsey (eds.) (2004): *Education and Society in Hong Kong and Macao: Comparative Perspectives on Continuity and Change*. 2nd edition. CERC Studies in Comparative Education 7, Hong Kong: Comparative Education Research Centre.

Bray, Mark; Mazawi, André & Sultana, Ronald (eds.) (2013): *Private Tutoring across the Mediterranean: Power Dynamics, and Implications for Learning and Equity*. Rotterdam: Sense.

Bray, Mark & Thomas, R. Murray (1995): 'Levels of Comparison in Educational Studies: Different Insights from Different Literatures and the Value of Multilevel Analyses'. *Harvard Educational Review*, Vol.65, No.3, pp.472-490.

Bray, Mark & Yamato, Yoko (2003): 'Comparative Education in a Microcosm: Methodological Insights from the International Schools Sector in Hong Kong', *International Review of Education*, Vol.49, Nos. 1 & 2, pp.49-71.

Broadfoot, Patricia (1999): 'Comparative Research on Pupil Achievement: In Search of Validity, Reliability and Utility', in Alexander, Robin; Broadfoot, Patricia & Phillips, David (eds.), *Learning from Comparing: New Directions in Comparative Educational Research, Vol.1: Contexts, Classrooms and Outcomes*. Oxford: Symposium Books, pp.237-259.

Bronfenbrenner, Urie (1979): *The Ecology of Human Development: Experiments by Nature and Design*. Cambridge: Harvard University Press.

Canen, Ana (1995): 'Teacher Education in an Intercultural Perspective: A Parallel between Brazil and the UK'. *Compare: A Journal of Comparative Education*, Vol.25, No.3, pp.227-238.

Carney, Stephen (2010): 'Reading the Global: Comparative Education at the End of an Era', in Larsen, Marianne A. (ed.), *New Thinking in Comparative Education: Honouring Robert Cowen*. Rotterdam: Sense, pp.125-142.

Cowen, Robert (2000a): 'Educación Comparada'. *Propuesta Educativa*, Vol.10, No.23, pp.4-6.

Cowen, Robert (2000b): 'Comparing Futures or Comparing Pasts?'. *Comparative Education*, Vol.36, No.3, pp.333-342.

Cowen, Robert (2002): 'Sketches of a Future: Renegotiating the Unit Ideas of Comparative Education', in Caruso, Marcelo & Tenorth, Heinz-Elmar (eds.), *Internationalisierung/Internationalisation. Semantik und Bildungssystem in vergleichender Perspektive/Comparing Educational Systems and Semantics*. Frankfurt am Main: Peter Lang, pp.271-283.

Cowen, Robert (2009a): 'Then and Now': Unit Ideas and Comparative Education', in Cowen, Robert & Kazamias, Andreas M. (eds.), *International Handbook of Comparative Education*. Dordrecht: Springer, pp.1277-1294.

Cowen, Robert (2009b): 'The National, the International, and the Global', in Cowen, Robert & Kazamias, Andreas M. (eds.), *International Handbook of Comparative Education*. Dordrecht: Springer, pp.337-340.

Crossley, Michael (2009): 'Rethinking Context in Comparative Education', in Cowen, Robert & Kazamias, Andreas M. (eds.), *International Handbook of Comparative Education*. Dordrecht: Springer, pp.1173-1187.

Crossley, Michael & Vulliamy, Graham (2011): *Qualitative Educational Research in Developing Countries: Current Perspectives*. New York: Garland Press.

Crossley, Michael & Watson, Keith (2003): *Comparative and International Research in Education: Globalisation, Context and Difference*. London: RoutledgeFalmer.

Dale, Roger & Robertson, Susan, L. (2002): 'The Varying Effects of Regional Organizations as Subjects of Globalization of Education'. *Comparative Education Review*, Vol.46, No.1, pp.10-36.

Dyer, Caroline (1996): 'Primary Teachers and Policy Innovation in India: Some Neglected Issues'. *International Journal of Educational Development*, Vol.16, No.1, pp.27-40.

Eurydice (2013). *Recommended Annual Taught Time in Full-time Compulsory Education in Europe 2012/13. Eurydice Facts and Figures.* Eurydice taught_time_EN.pdf. Accessed 24 September 2013.

Fafunwa, A. Babs & Aisiku, J.U. (eds.) (1982): *Education in Africa: A Comparative Survey.* London: George Allen & Unwin.

Felouzis, Georges & Charmillot, Samuel (2013): 'School Tracking and Educational Inequality: A Comparison of 12 Education Systems in Switzerland'. *Comparative Education,* Vol.49, No.2, pp.181-205.

Ferrer, Ferran; Naya, Luis & Valle, Javier (eds.) (2004): *Convergencias de la Educación Secundaria Inferior en la Unión Europea.* Madrid: Secretaria General de Educación, Centro de Investigación y Documentación Educativa [CIDE], Ministerio de Educación y Ciencia.

Fox, Christine; Majhanovich, Suzanne & Gök, Fatma (2011): 'Bordering and Re-bordering in Education: Introduction'. *International Review of Education,* Vol.57, Nos.3-4, pp.247-260.

Fry, Gerald & Kempner, Ken (1996): 'A Subnational Perspective for Comparative Research: Education and Development in Northeast Brazil and Northeast Thailand'. *Comparative Education,* Vol.32, No.3, pp.333-360.

Getis, Arthur; Getis, Judith; Bjelland, Mark D. & Fellmann, Jerome D. (2011): *Introduction to Geography.* 13th edition. New York: McGraw-Hill Higher Education.

Goldschmidt, Pete & Eyermann, Therese S. (1999): 'International Educational Performance of the United States: Is There a Problem that Money can Fix?' *Comparative Education,* Vol.35, No.1, pp.27-43.

Gu, Mingyuan (1986 [translated to English and printed in 2001]): 'Issues in the Development of Comparative Education in China', in Gu, Mingyuan, *Education in China and Abroad: Perspectives from a Lifetime in Comparative Education.* CERC Studies in Comparative Education 9, Hong Kong: Comparative Education Research Centre, The University of Hong Kong, pp.219-226.

Guri-Rosenblit, Sarah (2001): Virtual Universities: Current Models and Future Trends. *Higher Education in Europe,* Vol.26, No.4, pp.487-499.

Hans, Nicholas (1949): *Comparative Education: A Study of Educational Factors and Traditions.* London: Routledge & Kegan Paul.

Hansen, Mette Halskov & Woronov, T.E. (2013): 'Demanding and Resisting Vocational Education: A Comparative Study of Schools in Rural and Urban China'. *Comparative Education,* Vol.49, No.2, pp. 242-259.

Hega, Gunther M. (2001): 'Regional Identity, Language and Education Policy in Switzerland'. *Compare: A Journal of Comparative Education*, Vol.31, No.2, pp.205-223.

Hickling-Hudson, Anne (2004): 'South-South Collaboration: Cuban Teachers in Jamaica and Namibia'. *Comparative Education*, Vol.40, No.2, pp.289-311.

Kandel, Isaac L. (1933): *Studies in Comparative Education*. London: George G. Harrap & Company.

Kelly, Gail P. & Altbach, Philip G. (1988): 'Alternative Approaches in Comparative Education', in Postlethwaite, T. Neville (ed.), *The Encyclopedia of Comparative Education and National Systems of Education*. Oxford: Pergamon Press, pp.13-19.

Kubow, Patricia K. & Fossum, Paul R. (2007): *Comparative Education: Exploring Issues in International Context*. 2nd edition, Upper Saddle River: Pearson Merrill Prentice Hall.

Lefebvre, Henri (1991): *The Production of Space*. Oxford: Blackwell.

Lo, Tin-Yau Joe (2004): 'The Junior Secondary History Curricula in Hong Kong and Shanghai: A Comparative Study'. *Comparative Education*, Vol.40, No.3, pp.343-361.

Louisy, Pearlette (2004): 'Whose Context for What Quality? Informing Education Strategies for the Caribbean'. *Compare: A Journal of Comparative Education*, Vol.34, No.3, pp.285-293.

McNess, Elizabeth (2004): 'Culture, Context and the Quality of Education: Evidence from a Small-Scale Extended Case Study in England and Denmark'. *Compare: A Journal of Comparative Education*, Vol.34, No.3, pp.315-327.

Naya, Luis (2004): 'Administración Educativa y Gestión de Centros', in Ferrer, Ferran, Naya, Luis & Valle, Javier (eds.), *Convergencias de la Educación Secundaria Inferior en la Unión Europea*. Madrid: Secretaria General de Educación, Centro de Investigación y Documentación Educativa [CIDE], Ministerio de Educación y Ciencia, pp.17-48.

Nóvoa, Antonio (2002): 'Fabricating Europe: The Formation of an Education Space', in Nóvoa, Antonio & Lawn, Martin (eds.), *Fabricating Europe*. Dordrecht: Kluwer Academic Publishers, pp.1-13.

Pantić, Nataša; Wubbels, Theo & Mainhard, Tim (2011): 'Teacher Competence as a Basis for Teacher Education: Comparing Views of Teachers and Teacher Educators in Five Western Balkan Countries'. *Comparative Education Review*, Vol.55, No.2, pp.165-188.

Phillips, David & Schweisfurth, Michele (2007): *Comparative and International Education: An Introduction to Theory, Method and Practice*. London: Continuum.

Puchner, L. (2003): 'Women and Literacy in Rural Mali: A Study of the Socio-Economic Impact of Participating in Literacy Programs in Four Villages'. *International Journal of Educational Development*, Vol.23, No.4, pp.439-458.

Raffe, David; Brannen, Karen; Croxford, Linda & Martin, Chris (1999): 'Comparing England, Scotland, Wales and Northern Ireland: The Case for 'Home Internationals' in Comparative Research'. *Comparative Education*, Vol.35, No.1, pp.9-25.

Ragin, Charles C. (1987): *The Comparative Method: Moving beyond Qualitative and Quantitative Strategies*. Berkeley: University of California Press.

Ragin, Charles C. (2006): 'Comparative Sociology and the Comparative Method', in Sica, Alan (ed.), *Comparative Methods in the Social Sciences*. London: SAGE, pp.159-178.

Ragin, Charles C. & Amoroso, Lisa M. (2011): *Constructing Social Research: The Unity and Diversity of Method*. 2nd edition. London: SAGE.

Rappleye, Jeremy (2010): 'Compasses, Maps, and Mirrors: Relocating Episteme(s) of Transfer, Reorienting the Comparative Kosmos', in Larsen, Marianne A. (ed.), *New Thinking in Comparative Education: Honouring Robert Cowen*. Rotterdam: Sense, pp.57-79.

Sadler, Sir Michael (1900): 'How Can We Learn Anything of Practical Value from the Study of Foreign Systems of Education?'. Reprinted 1964 in *Comparative Education Review*, Vol.7, No.3, pp.307-314.

Schriewer, Jürgen (2006): 'Comparative Social Science: Characteristic Problems and Changing Problem Solutions'. *Comparative Education*. Vol.42, No.3, pp.299-336.

Shabaya, Judith & Konadu-Agyemang, Kwadwo (2004): 'Unequal Access, Unequal Participation: Some Spatial and Socio-Economic Dimensions of the Gender Gap in Education in Africa with Special Reference to Ghana, Zimbabwe and Kenya'. *Compare: A Journal of Comparative Education*, Vol.34, No.4, pp.395-424.

Silova, Iveta; Johnson, Mark S. & Heyneman, Stephen P. (2007): 'Education and the Crisis of Social Cohesion in Azerbaijan and Central Asia'. *Comparative Education Review*, Vol.51, No.2, pp.159-180.

Sobe, Noah & Fischer, Melissa (2009): 'Mobility, Migration and Minorities in Education', in Cowen, Robert & Kazamias, Andreas M. (eds.), *In-*

ternational Handbook of Comparative Education. Dordrecht: Springer, pp.359-371.

Steiner-Khamsi, Gita (2009): 'Comparison: *Quo Vadis?*', in Cowen, Robert & Kazamias, Andreas M. (eds.), *International Handbook of Comparative Education*. Dordrecht: Springer, pp.1143-1158.

Swiss Federal Statistical Office (2013): Regional Portraits: Cantons (2008-2012). http://www.bfs.admin.ch/bfs/portal/en/index/regionen/kantone/daten.html, Accessed 24 September 2013.

Symaco, Lorraine Pe & Brock, Colin (2013): 'Editorial: Educational Space'. *Comparative Education*, Vol.49, No.3, pp.269–274.

Taylor, Chris; Rees, Gareth & Davies, Rhys (2013): 'Devolution and Geographies of Education: The Use of the Millennium Cohort Study for 'Home International' Comparisons across the UK'. *Comparative Education*, Vol.49, No.3, pp.290-316.

Vidovich, Lesley (2004): 'Towards Internationalizing the Curriculum in a Context of Globalization: Comparing Policy Processes in Two Settings'. *Compare: A Journal of Comparative Education*, Vol.34, No.4, pp. 443-461.

Welch, Anthony R. (2008): 'Nation State, Diaspora and Comparative Education', Joseph Lauwerys Lecture, Comparative Education Society in Europe Biennial Conference, July; University of Athens.

World Bank (2013a): Data by Topic. World Bank Indicators. http://data.worldbank.org/topic/education. Accessed 20 September 2013.

World Bank (2013b): Data by Country. World Bank Indicators. http://data.worldbank.org/country. Accessed 30 August 2013.

5

Comparing Systems

Mark BRAY & Kai JIANG

A great deal of comparative education research has focused on systems of education. Sometimes, however, this focus has been implicit rather than explicit, and the units of analysis have not always been clearly defined. This chapter begins by noting some prominent examples in which scholars have focused – or claimed to have focused – on systems of education. It then discusses methodological issues relating to the use of education systems as a unit of analysis in comparative research. It notes that some countries have multiple systems of education, and thus that research which focuses on systems can be intra-national as well as cross-national.

Familiar Approaches but Loose Usages

The focus on systems has a long history in the field of comparative education. For example, the title of Sadler's (1900) oft-cited address was: 'How far can we learn anything of practical value from the study of foreign systems of education?'. Kandel (1933, pp.83-206) focused on the organisation of national systems of education in six countries; the book by Cramer and Browne (1956) was entitled *Contemporary Education: A Comparative Study of National Systems*; and the following decade brought Moehlman's (1963) book entitled *Comparative Educational Systems*.

This focus was maintained during subsequent decades. Books appearing during the 1980s included Ignas and Corsini's (1981) *Comparative Educational Systems* and the set of three volumes co-edited by Cameron et al. (1983) entitled *International Handbook of Education Systems*. These were followed by the *Encyclopedia of Comparative Education and National Systems of Education*, which was edited by Postlethwaite and appeared in first edition in 1988 and second edition in 1995. More recent books include Marlow-Ferguson's (2002) *Survey of Educational Systems Worldwide*, and Greger and Walterová's (2012) volume on *The Transformation of Educational Systems in Post-Communist Countries*.

However, some of these works were remiss in the clarity of definition. As noted by the previous chapter in the present book, the field of comparative education has been dominated by locational comparisons which have given particular prominence to the country or nation-state. Many of the works cited above in practice took countries as their principal unit of analysis. Their authors may have felt justified to use the word 'system' insofar as they referred to national education systems; but few explored the conceptual boundaries of those national education systems or investigated the extent to which other systems co-existed within and across national boundaries. Many of the authors presented national education systems as if the nations in question had only single systems.

This point may be explained further by looking at a pair of examples written four decades apart. The book by Moehlman (1963) took it as self-evident that readers knew what systems were, and proceeded to a set of 11 country chapters which implied that national boundaries and system boundaries were basically coterminous. It was particularly inappropriate to imply that the United States of America (USA) had a unified education system. The section on the USA did note (p.79) that each of the 50 states "controls its own system of education", but this observation was not followed up to note the differences between these systems, and the bulk of the discussion in that chapter (pp.75-81) was an overview of the country as a whole. More recently, Marlow-Ferguson's (2002) encyclopaedia was organised country by country, commencing with Afghanistan and ending with Zimbabwe, and mostly describing education in those countries as if it were in each case a unified entity. Even such countries as Belgium, Canada and Vanuatu, which each internally have strikingly different systems operating in different languages and with different structures, were presented in generalities as if they had unified national education systems. This was not only misleading but was also a missed opportunity for conceptual understanding. Comparison of systems within countries would have permitted identification of instructive similarities and differences, and would have promoted understanding of the forces which had contributed to those patterns.

Further, the tendency to focus on education systems by country obscures the fact that some systems operate across national boundaries. Schools run for example by religious bodies, such as the Roman Catholic Church, may have commonalities across national boundaries (Daun & Arjmand 2005; Griffin 2006; Brock 2010). In a rather different domain, since 1999 universities in 29 European countries have increasingly been harmonised under the 'Bologna Process' – named after the city in Italy in which representatives from 29 European countries agreed on guidelines "to promote the European system of higher education" (Bologna 2013). And considering yet another domain, many cities with substantial international communities host schools following the education systems of other countries and being supervised and/or accredited by authorities in those countries (Hayden & Thomson 2008; Bates 2011).

Defining and Identifying Education Systems

It must be admitted that scholars who are conscientious and careful in their use of terms encounter major difficulties when defining education systems. Among the classic scholars cited above, Kandel (1933, p.83) was concerned with national systems and observed that: "To define a national system of education is not simple, despite the frequent use of the term." The difficulty of finding an adequate definition, he added:

> is not due primarily to the vast range of influences, formal and informal, which enter into the formation of the attitudes and outlook of the members of a nation, but to the absence of a single criterion by which the existence of a national system may be tested.

This problem has not been resolved. For scholars of comparative education, problems are compounded by the fact that some languages have several different words which can each be translated as system but which each have different nuances and implications. In Chinese, for example:

- *jiaoyu zhidu* [教育制度] covers all kinds of educational institutions, including both schools and the government institutions that administer them, and stresses the institutional aspect;
- *jiaoyu tizhi* [教育体制] means the system through which educational institutions are organised and controlled;
- *jiaoyu xitong* [教育系统] means an arrangement in which various component parts are linked together; and

- *jiaoyu tixi* [教育体系] is similar to *jiaoyu xitong* [教育系统], but stresses the structural rather than the institutional aspect.

For the purposes of this chapter, a system can be understood as a group of interacting, interrelated, or interdependent components forming a complex whole. The generic definition presented by Allport (1955, p.469) was:

> any recognizably delimited aggregate of dynamic elements that are in some way interconnected and interdependent and that continue to operate … in such a way as to produce some characteristic total effect. A system, in other words, is something that is concerned with some kind of activity and preserves a kind of integration and unity; and a particular system can be recognized as distinct from other systems to which, however, it may be dynamically related.

This definition is closest to what in Chinese would be called *jiaoyu xitong* [教育系统], and also fits the conceptions of educational planners working at international levels (see e.g. Göttelmann & Bahr 2012). Further, the definition may also apply to sub-national systems as well as to national ones. The most obvious component parts of education systems would be the institutions that operate together within a common legal and administrative framework, often influenced by orientation towards particular examinations, conditions of service for teachers, admissions regulations for students, etc..

It is useful also to refer to Archer's (1979) book, *Social Origins of Educational Systems*, which is widely regarded as a seminal contribution. Like many of her predecessors, Archer was particularly concerned with national education systems overseen by governments. She defined a state education system (p.54) as:

> a nationwide and differentiated collection of institutions devoted to formal education, whose overall control and supervision is at least partly governmental, and whose component parts and processes are related to one another.

She added that education systems are created when the component parts cease to be disparate and unrelated sets of establishments or independent networks, and instead become interrelated to form a unified whole. In geographic terms, much of Archer's analysis was based on Denmark, England, France, Japan and Russia. She noted that in all these countries the state possessed formative, regulative and controlling responsibility for education systems.

However, systems can of course be operated by other bodies as well as by the state. This chapter will include examples of systems operated by religious and other non-government bodies. Moreover, even the state can operate multiple systems and sub-systems. One methodological question might concern classifications and whether particular arrangements are indeed systems or sub-systems. The answer is often to some extent subjective – a fact that illustrates further the methodological challenges and attractions of this domain of enquiry.

Why Compare Systems?

In many cases the rationales for comparing systems are similar to those for undertaking comparisons of other units, particularly locational ones. Especially when the comparisons are of national education systems, then justifications may resemble those set out by Manzon in the previous chapter. Manzon noted interpretive and causal analytical reasons for undertaking comparisons, and highlighted the work of some of the classic scholars. Bereday, who was one of these scholars, was to some extent typical in focusing on systems but in practice making broader statements. Thus, when he wrote (1964, p.5) that "Men [sic] study foreign educational systems simply because they want to know, because men must forever stir in quest of enlightenment", he was in effect presenting a justification for the whole field of comparative education rather than focusing on systems *per se*.

However, the question remains why education systems, and particularly national education systems, have received so much attention. Part of the answer is that the nation-state from the 19th century onwards became a primary unit to organise and govern social, political and economic life. National governments assumed increasingly significant roles in education, and consequently contributed to differences between national education systems. From the beginning of the 19th century, education was increasingly regarded as a tool to reinforce national strength. This tradition perhaps reached its peak during the second half of the 20th century. In more recent times, the forces of globalisation have eroded these views (see e.g. Mitter 2004; Spring 2009; Maringe et al. 2013). However, many international agencies still base their work on the nation state and both maintain and promote the notion of national education systems (see e.g.

UNESCO International Bureau of Education 2000; Asian Development Bank 2001; UNESCO 2011; Commonwealth Secretariat 2012). Much scholarly work also either explicitly or implicitly promotes the concept of nation states with national education systems (e.g. Adams 2004; Wolhuter et al. 2007; Thieme et al. 2012).

Nevertheless, one major reason for studying systems might be to *avoid* the notion of "one country, one system". This goal is achieved when, for example, French-speaking Belgium is treated separately from Flemish-speaking Belgium, Zanzibar is treated separately from mainland Tanzania, and the Canadian Province of Quebec is treated separately from Ontario. The goal can also be achieved when private schools are compared with public schools, when Catholic schools are compared with Protestant schools, and when technical-vocational schools are compared with academic-grammar schools. Further, equation of countries with education systems raises the risk of perspectives which are rather static because national boundaries change infrequently. Analyses of systems that are not defined by geography are more likely to note the flexibility of boundaries and shapes. Thus, focus on systems may in some circumstances reduce the dangers of over-generalisation and oversimplification, and help to show dynamic patterns of change.

A Set of Examples: China

Some of the above points can be illustrated through examples. The focus in this section is on three component parts of the People's Republic of China (PRC), namely mainland China, Hong Kong and Macao.[1] The education systems in each of these places have very different characteristics; but the differences are not only between but also within each location. Thus consideration of the PRC shows the potential for multiple instructive comparisons within a single country.

The Education Systems of Mainland China
Mainland China has a population of 1.3 billion, of which over 220 million

---

[1] The name of this territory is also commonly spelled Macau. That spelling has a long history of usage, and is still the official form in Portuguese. However, in 2000 the government decreed that official spelling in English would be Macao, which has long been an alternative form. This chapter uses the spelling Macao except where making quotations or referring to publications which use the spelling Macau.

are attending schools and universities. It has 289 cities, of which 48 have populations over 500,000; and the total area is 9.6 million square kilometres.

Particularly since a reform launched in the mid-1980s (China 1985), mainland China has undergone major changes in education. Cheng (1991, p.3) observed that "China's education system is amazingly uniform when viewed in the context of its vast geographic area and huge population". This feature was chiefly the result of a highly centralised mode of administration. However, subsequent reforms brought increased diversity not only between but also within different locations (Mok 2003; Gong & Tsang 2011; Qi 2011).

Beginning with the structure of education, many parts of the country have for several decades operated a 6+3+3+4 system (i.e. six years of primary education, three years of junior secondary, three years of senior secondary, and four years of tertiary education). However, particularly until the 1990s other parts operated a 5+4 system at primary/junior secondary, a 5+3 system, 5+1+3 system, nine-year integrated system, or various other combinations. By 2010, children in the majority of provinces were in six-year primary schools, but some variation still existed (Table 5.1). The different structures required different curricula, and led to different outcomes. Central government policies had promoted a move towards uniformity; but diversity remained in part because the overall advocacy of the government favoured decentralisation.

Table 5.1: Proportions of Pupils in a Six-Year Primary School System in Selected Provinces and Municipalities, Mainland China, 2010

Province/ Municipality	Total No. of Primary Pupils	% of Pupils in a 6-year System	Province/ Municipality	Total No. of Primary Pupils	% of Pupils in a 6-year System
Beijing	653,225	99.99	Qinghai	518,992	98.06
Fujian	2,388,917	100.00	Shandong	6,292,476	86.77
Guizhou	4,334,971	100.00	Shanghai	701,578	12.25
Heilongjiang	1,879,609	69.69	Tianjin	505,895	88.63
Henan	10,705,303	99.99	Yunnan	4,352,084	99.99
Hubei	3,655,512	99.99	Xinjiang	1,935,789	99.99
Hunan	4,791,601	100.00	*Mainland China*	99,407,043	99.78

Source: China (2011), pp.526, 534.

Variations also exist within the sub-systems. In earlier decades, the authorities designated some institutions as key schools, most of which were located in cities and county towns (Guo 2005, p.151). These institutions were allocated the best pupils, teachers and other resources within their catchment areas. The rationale was that resources should be focused on the more capable pupils so that they could be prepared for higher education. The key schools were also used as centres of in-service teacher training, and for conducting experiments in curriculum innovation. Key schools comprised only about 5 per cent of the total, but they generated the majority of university candidates in the highly competitive national College Entrance Examination. The central government aims to promote equity of compulsory education. The *Outline of China's National Plan for Medium and Long-Term Education Reform and Development (2010-2020)* discourages differentiation (China 2010, p.22). However, the Ministry of Education admits that it will require a long process to abolish key schools in primary and secondary education.

Further variation exists in provision for China's minority nationalities (Zhao 2010; Postiglione 2012). In 2010, the population of the 55 minority nationalities was estimated at 105 million, i.e. 8.6 per cent of the total population (China, National Bureau of Statistics 2012). National policy advocates bilingual education, supporting use of both minority languages and standardised Chinese in education. This is not implemented with equal enthusiasm in all areas, but the languages of most minorities are taught at least at the primary level.

Diversity has also been brought by the proliferation of private schools. In 2010 private (*minban* 民办) primary schools enrolled 5.38 million pupils representing 5.4 per cent of the total; and private secondary schools enrolled 9.79 million pupils representing 9.8 per cent of the total (China 2011, pp.3-4). These were not large proportions; but in mainland China they were especially significant since 30 years previously there had been no private schools at all. Moreover, at the secondary vocational level, private schools enrolled 9.1 per cent of the total (Hu & Xie 2003, p.179). Many of these institutions had been established in urban centres to serve the children of the newly-prosperous elite, but some were in rural areas and served families seeking different curricular emphases.

Further, especially in the major cities a number of international schools had developed with links to foreign education systems. Again the total numbers were small, but the trends were significant. For example, in 2012 Beijing had 19 international divisions in 16 public high schools, five Sino-foreign cooperative international high schools, and several international high school divisions in private schools (Liu 2012). Similar developments were evident in Shanghai and other parts of the country (Yamato & Bray 2006; Robinson & Guan 2012). Some of these schools followed

English-language curricula, while others stressed the national languages of such countries as Japan and Korea. The diversification is likely to expand significantly during the coming years.

The Education Systems of Hong Kong

Hong Kong is very small compared with mainland China. It has a population of only seven million, and a land area of just 1,071 square kilometres. The island of Hong Kong became a British colony in 1842, and the territory was subsequently enlarged by addition of sections of the mainland and neighbouring islands. In 1997, sovereignty returned to China. However, Hong Kong retains much autonomy as a Special Administrative Region with its own currency and legal system, and with local control over education. Hong Kong does have a rural periphery, but is basically an urban society. As such, a more productive focus for internal comparative education would be different types of school systems within the urban society, rather than systems which serve particular geographic areas.

As in mainland China, the majority of Hong Kong's schools may be described as part of a single territory-wide education system. However, some schools are outside the system; and even within the system there are various sub-systems. Table 5.2 indicates that in 2012/13 only 6.1 per cent of schools were operated directly by the government, though the 72.2 per cent in the aided sector were subject to extensive controls and were also considered part of the public sector. Yet within the aided sector were "systems within systems" of schools operated for example by the Roman Catholic Church and by other religious and philanthropic bodies. The three caput schools were allied to the aided sector, receiving government grants on a head-count (per capita, or caput) basis on a formula developed several decades previously.

Table 5.2: Providers of Primary and Secondary Schooling in Hong Kong, 2012/13

	Primary	Secondary	Total
Government	34	32	66
Aided	423	362	785
Caput	0	3	3
Direct Subsidy Scheme	21	61	82
Private	50	32	82
International	41	29	70
Total	**569**	**519**	**1,088**

Source: Hong Kong, Education Bureau: www.edb.gov.hk

Alongside the government, aided and caput schools were two categories of private schools. The Direct Subsidy Scheme (DSS) had been created in 1991, and allowed aided schools to become private institutions while still receiving government grants. It also allowed private schools to receive grants if they met certain standards and followed certain regulations. The DSS financial and regulatory system differed from that of the mainstream, and therefore created another system within the system (Hong Kong, Education Bureau 2013). Schools which in Table 5.2 are described as private did not receive recurrent grants from the government, though some received allocations of land and other assistance. These schools were permitted greater flexibility in curriculum and other domains.

The last category, of international schools, contains further diversity. In 2011/12 it included 15 schools operated by the English Schools Foundation (ESF) and operated as a group mostly aiming at the International Baccalaureate curriculum. Other schools followed curricula from Australia, Canada, France, Germany, Japan, Korea, Norway and Singapore (Hong Kong, Education Bureau 2012). Thus, some international schools were in effect parts of foreign systems that were operating in Hong Kong (Bray & Yamato 2003, pp.58-59; Ng 2012, p.124).

Perhaps even more interesting from a methodological perspective were individual institutions which operated more than one system. For example, the German-Swiss International School had a section which followed the German curriculum and another section following the curriculum of England. Likewise, the French International School had a section which followed the French curriculum and another section following the International Baccalaureate curriculum; and the Korean International School had a section which followed the Korean curriculum and another section following the curriculum of England. In these schools, the teachers in the different streams were subject to different expectations; and in the French and Korean International Schools the pupils in the different streams paid different fees. Thus comparative analysis of education systems could be undertaken not only within the broad territory of Hong Kong but even within individual institutions.

Within the mainstream education system, another distinguishing characteristic of institutions was their medium of instruction. In this respect, it is instructive to note other aspects of historical evolution. Table 5.3 shows the official classification in the mid-1990s, which at the secondary level distinguished between Anglo-Chinese and Chinese-middle schools. The former were expected to teach in English except for the subjects of Chinese

and Chinese History; and the latter were expected to teach in Chinese except for the subject of English. The Anglo-Chinese schools operated a 5+2
curriculum, while the Chinese-middle schools had until the early 1990s
followed a 5+1 system. The Chinese University of Hong Kong was founded
in 1963 to be the apex of the Chinese-middle school system, and offered a
basic four-year degree programme, while the University of Hong Kong was
at that time the principal apex to the Anglo-Chinese system, and offered a
basic three-year degree programme.

Table 5.3: Secondary Schools in Hong Kong, by Medium of Instruction, 1993/94

	Government	Aided	Private	Total
Anglo-Chinese	33	299	56	388
Chinese	2	14	7	23
Anglo-Chinese & Chinese	3	5	4	12
English	1	5	15	21
Others	-	-	2	2
English & Others	-	-	2	2
Total	**39**	**323**	**86**	**448**

Note: These figures refer to day schools only.
Source: Hong Kong, Education Department (1993), p.55.

Over time, the distinction between the language streams became
blurred. Increasing numbers of Anglo-Chinese schools claimed to be
English-medium in order to attract students, but for reasons of practical
pedagogy actually taught many classes in Chinese. Also, the Chinese University of Hong Kong increasingly selected pupils from the Anglo-Chinese
schools as well as from the Chinese-middle schools (Lee 1993). In 1988 the
government decided first that three years should be the basic length of degree courses in all institutions including the Chinese University of Hong
Kong, and second that all secondary schools in the mainstream should follow a 5+2 system. As a focus for internal comparative education, therefore,
the sub-systems represented by these two language streams ceased to be so
distinct.

In the late 1990s, a further policy change forced a sharper distinction
between schools operating in different media of instruction. Following
stringent screening, only 114 public secondary schools – about one quarter
of the total – were permitted to use English as the medium of instruction for
their 1998 and future intakes. Implementation of this policy again created
two groups of schools that were clearly-defined by medium of instruction
and that could be compared with each other (Standing Committee on
Language Education & Research 2003; Education Commission 2005).

In 2009 the Hong Kong government launched a further reform (Hong Kong 2011), changing from a 6+5+2+3 system (i.e. six years of primary schooling, five years of secondary schooling leading to the School Certificate examinations, two years of senior secondary schooling leading to Advanced Level examinations, and three years for a basic university degree). The new system was 6+3+3+4 (i.e. six years of primary, three years of lower secondary, three years of senior secondary, and four years for a basic university degree). These changes gave scholars and practitioners opportunities for instructive comparison over time, i.e. comparing the old system with the new one.

In parallel, the language domain became more blurred. After a period of "firm guidance" (1997-2008) on the medium of instruction in which schools were required to operate according to clear choices and distinct categories, the government permitted "fine-tuning" with much more blurred categories (Morris & Adamson 2010, pp.152-154).

In summary, while it is possible (and common) to refer to the Hong Kong education system as a distinct entity, close examination reveals considerable diversity in modes of school management and in curricula. As such, Hong Kong has many systems within systems; and structures have changed significantly over time.

The Education Systems of Macao

While Hong Kong may be small compared to mainland China, Macao is smaller still. It has a population of just 560,000 and an area of only 28 square kilometres. Particularly since the mid-1990s, the government has devoted effort to building a Macao education system (Leung 2011; Wang 2011; Macao 2012a). However, considerable internal diversity remains.

As a distinct entity Macao dates its history from 1557, when Portuguese traders secured rights of settlement from the Chinese authorities. The territory remained under Portuguese administration until 1999 when sovereignty reverted to China. The model for the transition resembled that for Hong Kong, and Macao is also a Special Administrative Region which retains its own currency, legal system and control over education (Bray & Koo 2004).

Until the 1990s, Macao's colonial government took little interest in education. It operated a small number of schools with a Portuguese curriculum which catered mainly for the children of expatriate civil servants and of locals with close ties to Portugal. These schools served below 10 per cent of the population. Other children either went to private schools or did not go to school at all. The private schools were not supported, controlled or even monitored by the government. Many schools were operated by religious bodies, but others were run by social service organisations and commercial enterprises (Lau 2009).

One way to classify Macao's schools was set out in an official document (Macau 1989, p.178), which identified four systems of education as shown in Figure 5.1. The models were labelled Portuguese, Anglo-Saxon, Chinese Traditional, and People's Republic of China; but these labels were based on partial misunderstanding of the systems in the places from which the models were presumed to have been imported. This in itself was an example of the need for dissemination of clearer information on the diversity of systems within countries. Anglo-Saxon was a misnomer because the model was imported from Hong Kong rather than the United Kingdom (UK), and in any case the dominant model in Hong Kong was the Anglo-Chinese 5+2 rather than the Chinese-middle 5+1 system. The description of the 6+5 model as PRC was also inappropriate, since the dominant model there was 6+3+3 and none of the other models was 6+5. 'Chinese Traditional' described a model imported from Taiwan, though it was unclear why that label had been chosen.

Figure 5.1: Systems of Education in Macao as Portrayed in a 1989 Official Document

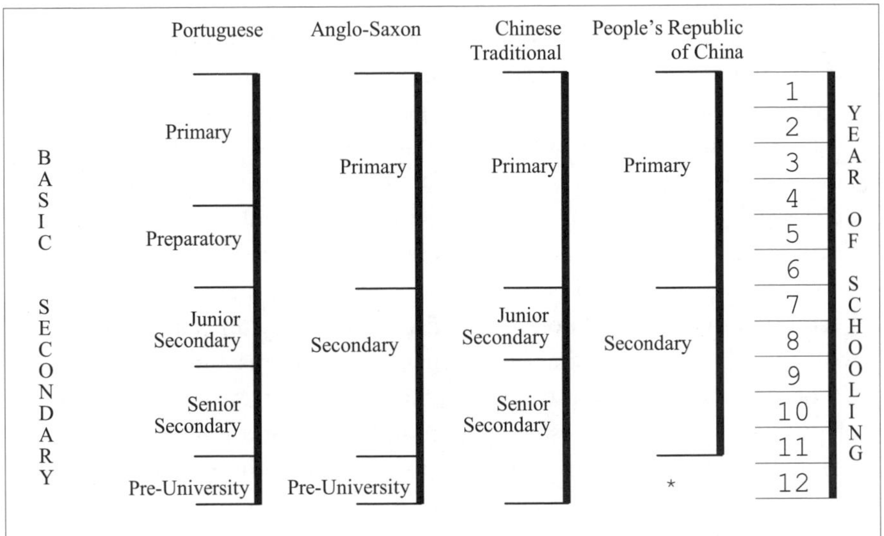

* Some institutions in this system had a 12th grade. This could be considered a pre-university year.

Source: Macau (1989, p.178).

Figure 5.2: Systems of Education in Macao as Portrayed in a 1993 Official Document

In Chinese		In English	In Portuguese	Luso-Chinese	
P R I M A R Y	1	P.1	1	1	1
	2	P.2	2	2	2
	3	P.3	3	3	3
	4	P.4	4	4	4
	5	P.5 Preparatory 5	5	5	5
	6	P.6	6	6	6
S E C O N D A R Y	7	F.I/J.I	7	7	7
	8	F.II/J.II	8	8	8
	9	F.III/J.III	9	9	9
	10	F.IV/S.I	10	10	10
	11	F.V/S.II	11	11	11
	12	*F.VI/S.III	12		12

Y E A R   O F   S C H O O L I N G

Some schools adopt a junior and senior secondary system (3 + 3 years) while others adopt a five years secondary system. Among those schools that adopt the five years secondary system, some provide a further year of Form VI for those students seeking higher education.

Source: Macau (1993a), p.205.

Perhaps following recognition of these questionable aspects, later official publications (e.g. Macau 1993a) classified three of the education systems more simply by their language of instruction (Figure 5.2). However, this classification was not totally by language, for it showed Luso-Chinese schools as a separate category. Luso-Chinese schools were operated by the government mainly in Chinese but with emphasis on Portuguese as a second language. The structure of the Luso-Chinese system differed from that of both the other Chinese-medium schools and the Portuguese-medium schools. Table 5.4 shows the number of schools at that time by their media of instruction. Most private schools were Chinese-medium, though two secondary schools (catering for 2 per cent of pupils) were Portuguese-medium, and seven secondary schools (catering for 19 per cent of pupils) were English-medium. The table also shows shifts over the decades, first in reduction of the number of small primary schools and second in reduction of emphasis on Portuguese in favour of the other two languages.

Table 5.4: Schools in Macao, by Ownership and Medium of Instruction

	Primary		Secondary	
	1992/93	2010/11	1992/93	2010/11
Government				
Chinese	6	1	1	4
Portuguese	2	0	1	1
Private				
Chinese	55	18	24	24
Portuguese	4	1	2	1
English	6	6	7	8
Total	**73**	**26**	**35**	**38**

Note: Schools which had both primary and secondary sections are counted as two institutions.

Sources: Macau (1993b), p.2; Macao (2012b), p.70.

In terms of ownership and management, Table 5.4 simply distinguishes between government and private schools; but within the latter were various sub-groups. One of the largest groups, comprising nearly half the private schools in the early 1990s but slightly less in the early 2010s, was the Union of Catholic Schools. These institutions were accountable to the Bishop, and could in some respects be considered a system. An even larger group in the early 2010s was of schools affiliated to the Chinese Educators' Association. This body had a strong relationship with the government in mainland China and was influenced by policies there (Leung 2011, p.173).

A further way to group the schools in the 2010s was according to whether they had joined the government's free-education scheme. This scheme provided subsidies to allow the schools to provide education free of charge, and also brought regulations on maximum class size (Leung 2011, p.173; Macao 2012a, p.316). In 2010/11, 82.8 per cent of the private schools were part of the free-education scheme.

Nevertheless, even with the much increased government funding and associated regulations, the Macao authorities faced limits in forming a unified Macao education system. Political forces had prevented the introduction of a territory-wide education examination system, and, as observed by Leung (2011, p.181), "when the state attempted to move deeper with its reform measures, such as the school curriculum reform, its capacity for action became constrained". Many teachers had been educated and trained in mainland China, Taiwan and Hong Kong rather than in Macau, and most schools adopted school-based curricula modified from teaching materials imported from those places. Thus, while the government had developed what could be described as a Macao education system which could be compared with the mainstream education systems in Hong Kong and mainland China within the boundaries of China as a whole, the sub-systems of Macao schools in the 2010s still displayed considerable diversity.

Another Set of Examples: United Kingdom

The diversity of education systems within the UK has rather different historical roots and contemporary shape, and thus is worth comparing with the diversity within China. The first important point is that there has never been a single education system in the UK. Thus, for example, the title of Booth's (1985) article 'United Kingdom: System of Education' was misleading and wrong. England, Northern Ireland, Scotland and Wales each have their own systems of education. Within each of these locations is further diversity of systems serving different religious, socio-economic and other groups, though the commentary which follows chiefly focuses on the different systems of each country within the UK.

Raffe et al. (1999) presented a very useful paper on this subject, which set a framework used by scholars such as Brisard et al. (2007) and Menter et al. (2009). Raffe et al. used a metaphor from football to facilitate analysis of education (p.9):

> The UK is represented by four 'national' football teams, those of England, Scotland, Wales and Northern Ireland. Matches between these teams were once called 'home internationals'. Each home country of the UK has its own education and training system; this paper presents the case for 'home international' comparisons of these systems.

The authors proceeded by noting that many people do not understand the differences among the four systems and/or consider such differences to be a nuisance not deserving detailed attention. They added (p.10) that:

> Many researchers shift their focus between England, Great Britain and the UK depending on the institutional context or the availability of data; others purport to cover the UK but in fact describe England, typically dismissing Scotland, Wales and Northern Ireland in the ritual footnote; others simply ignore the differences and treat England, Great Britain and the UK as synonymous.

Yet these differences between the UK systems might be considered not so much a problem as an opportunity for research, an arena for empirical and theoretical challenges, and a source of lessons for policy and practice.

The political contexts have deep roots but also recent developments (Bell & Grant 1977; Gunning & Raffe 2011; Richardson 2011). Wales was politically incorporated with England during the 19th century when its education system developed, and as a result the differences between Welsh and English education have historically been small. However, the systems diverged at the end of the 20th century. The National Curriculum for Wales specified that the Welsh language was compulsory in all state-funded schools, and other differences in curriculum emphases were underpinned by the existence of separate bodies for public examinations and for overall governance (Gorard 2000; Brisard et al. 2007).

The education system in Scotland, by contrast, had long had completely separate identity (Matheson 2000; Richardson 2011). Compulsory education was first promoted by an Act in the 15th century, and Scottish education began to develop as a distinct national system before the union of Scotland and England in 1707. In contemporary times, among the most obvious structural differences is that senior secondary education in Scotland leads to Higher examinations which are followed by a four-year basic degree structure in universities, whereas in England senior secondary education leads to Advanced (A) Level examinations which are followed by a three year basic degree structure in universities. Unlike Wales and England, Scotland does not have a National Curriculum: the authorities have only issued guidelines and never prescriptions on the curriculum. Scotland also has differences in the duration of primary schooling, the system of school inspection, regulations on maximum class size, and the nature of school governance. Differences between education in Scotland and in other parts of the United Kingdom increased during the initial years of the present century following further political processes of devolution (Andrews & Martin 2010; Arnott & Ozka 2010).

Ireland in turn developed a national system of elementary education in the 1830s, earlier than such a system became effective elsewhere, but it was divided along religious lines (Bell & Grant 1977, pp.47-51). In 1920, the main part of Ireland separated from the UK and became an independent republic. The education system of Northern Ireland, which remained part of the UK, diverged from that in the republic and moved closer to the systems of England and Wales. Nevertheless, Northern Ireland retains important differences. For example, the secondary school system in Northern Ireland is selective, with pupils going to grammar schools or secondary intermediate schools according to academic ability. In Scotland and Wales, by contrast, almost all state schools are comprehensive. In England, the pattern is more diverse, with most schools being nominally comprehensive but some areas retaining selective grammar schools. Northern Ireland also has different regulations on school governance, many of which have been shaped by the territory's political and religious history (Dunn 2000; McGuinness 2012).

Further differences have arisen from ways in which policy makers have interacted both with counterparts elsewhere in the UK and with bodies elsewhere in the world. Gunning and Raffe (2011, p.254) observed that unlike federal and quasi-federal systems, the UK "has few formal mechanisms to promote consistency, or even mutual awareness among those making policy for each of its territories". Frequent changes of government structures and rapid turnover of officials have reduced the extent to which even informal and personal links have promoted coordination. Grek and Ozka (2010) have added that compared with their counterparts in England, policy makers in Scotland have been more interested in, and influenced by, developments in the European Union.

Updating the observations of Raffe et al. (1999, pp.17-18), the following summary may be made:

1. *The systems have always been interdependent* to a greater extent than is the case for most separate nation states. The interdependencies have been complex; but the four territories still belong to the same political system, and each remains constrained by such factors as UK fiscal policy and labour market institutions.
2. *The similarities are more important than the differences.* All four systems had common features in the broad institutional structure of schools and colleges; the structure, function and timing of certification; and the scale, structure and functions of higher education.
3. *The differences vary* according to the territories concerned. Despite divergence, England and Wales retain notable similarities while Scotland is the most different.
4. In a much larger number of respects *the differences among the systems represent 'variations upon common themes'.* Similar functions have been performed in slightly different ways, and similar institutions and structures have performed slightly different functions. For example, schools and further education colleges had

broadly similar functions across the four territories, but the differences are still significant.

5. *The social relations and societal contents of education and training vary less* across the four home countries than they typically do across nation states. The most significant cultural differences concern the politics of education and national identity, rather than individual behaviour.

6. Political structures allow for *the relations between the four systems to change rapidly*. There is potential for common ground, but also potential for further divergence in priorities and structures.

Conclusions

At least on the surface, systems have long been a prominent unit of analysis in the field of comparative education. However, detailed scrutiny shows that scholars rarely define what they mean by systems. The field has had a tendency to equate systems with countries, and relatively few studies have explored sub-national and cross-national systems. One challenge arises from definitions, since education systems are not easy to conceptualise or delineate. However, a challenge may be turned into an opportunity: scholars can explore the implications of different definitions and boundaries, and can identify the ways in which different ways of conceptualising education systems can lead to different insights and understandings.

The chapter has remarked that systems may be of multiple types, and can be identified by both spatial and functional criteria. The spatial criteria basically refer to systems defined by geography, such as mainland China, Hong Kong and Macao, or England, Northern Ireland, Scotland and Wales. Functional criteria embrace systems with particular curricula and with administrative frameworks such as mainland China's key schools and Hong Kong's Direct Subsidy Scheme. Systems may also be defined by public or private ownership, and by administrative authority such as churches or other sponsoring bodies. Some scholars might argue that these categories describe sub-systems of larger entities rather than separate systems that operate in parallel. Such matters are themselves worthy of debate and exploration, to examine the nature of boundaries in particular circumstances and at particular points in time.

Through comparison of variations within countries, analysts are able to identify elements which converge and diverge despite common overarching frameworks. This provides an angle for understanding which would differ from that achieved with cross-national comparison. This chapter has particularly highlighted the "home internationals" studies of Raffe et al. (1999), Brisard et al. (2007) and Gunning and Raffe (2011). The principles of such studies could also be relevant to mainland China, Hong Kong and Macao, and to many other countries.

A further observation by Raffe et al. (1999, p.22) concerned the practicalities of undertaking comparative research within countries. In the UK, they suggested, such research may be undertaken more easily and more cheaply because the work is:

> facilitated by a common language, cultural affinities, a common administrative environment and geographical proximity. Costs of travel and communication are lower. Collaboration among UK universities or research institutes, where research is organised and funded along similar lines, is likely to be easier than among institutions in different nation states where these things are organised differently.

This observation could equally apply in Tanzania, the USA, and many other countries. However, Raffe et al. themselves stressed that the argument should not be exaggerated. They found that reconciling the differences in design and definition across the youth cohort surveys of England and Wales, Scotland and Northern Ireland, respectively, was just as difficult and challenging as the construction of a cross-national data set for Ireland, The Netherlands and Scotland. Moreover, intranational comparisons within large countries such as the USA do not necessarily incur lower travel and communication costs than international comparisons between, say, Hungary and Poland. And while in the UK it is possible for researchers to conduct all their work in a single language, that would not be possible if comparing the education systems of Flemish-speaking and French-speaking Belgium or the Canadian provinces of French-speaking Quebec and English-speaking Ontario. This observation raises an instructive comparative question about the ease or difficulty of undertaking similar types of research in different settings.

Taking this further, one might envisage a matrix of internal and cross-national studies. For example, since Canada, Cameroon and Vanuatu all have both Anglophone and Francophone education systems, scholars could conduct not only three separate studies of each country, but also a single study in which the three cases are placed together. Alternatively, holding language as a constant, the diversity within Anglophone Canada has parallels with the USA and with Australia. As in the earlier example, in addition to single-country studies the three cases could be put together.

Other questions are applicable to supranational studies of education systems. Much work remains to be conducted on a wide range of themes, some of which are emerging as the forces of regionalisation and globalisation penetrate more deeply. The Bologna Process in European higher education was mentioned above. It is one domain which has already stimulated much comparative work that has branched into new conceptual avenues (e.g. Curaj et al. 2012; Crosier & Parveva 2013). Other work can usefully focus on such topics as the impact of supranational examinations such as the International Baccalaureate, which to some extent create cross-national school systems based on curriculum (see e.g. Bunnell 2008; Hayden & Thompson 2008); and on the ways in which the agreements of the World Trade Organisation facilitate operation of the education systems of dominant countries across national borders (see e.g. Tilak 2011; Verger & Robertson 2012).

The study of systems can thus itself be multifaceted. On the one hand, it can embrace the focus on national education systems, which has long been a traditional focus in the field; and on the other hand it can embrace a focus on intra-national and cross-national systems. Even small territories, such as Macao, may provide fertile soil for analytical studies; and as illustrated by some international schools in Hong Kong, comparison of systems may even be undertaken at the institutional level. Themes for investigation can include the role and impact of regulatory mechanisms, power distribution, roles of external examinations, language policies, and ideologies. Work which focuses on systems as the unit of analysis is rarely simple, but can indeed be rewarding and instructive.

References

Adams, Don (2004): *Education and National Development: Priorities, Policies, and Planning*. Hong Kong: Comparative Education Research Centre, The University of Hong Kong, and Manila: Asian Development Bank.

Allport, F.H. (1955): *Theoriess of Perception and the Concept of Structure*. New York: Wiley.

Andrews, Rhys & Martin, Steve (2010): 'Regional Variations in Public Service Outcomes: The Impact of Policy Divergence in England, Scotland and Wales'. *Regional Studies*, Vol.44, No.8, pp.919-934.

Archer, Margaret S. (1979): *Social Origins of Educational Systems*. London: SAGE.

Arnott, Margaret & Ozga, Jenny (2010): 'Education and Nationalism: The Discourse of Education Policy in Scotland'. *Discourse: Studies in the Cultural Politics of Education*, Vol.31, No.3, pp.335-350.

Asian Development Bank (2001): *Education and National Development in Asia: Trends, Issues, Policies, and Strategies*. Manila: Asian Development Bank.

Bates, Richard (ed.) (2011): *Schooling Internationally: Globalisation, Internationalisation and the Future for International Schools*. New York: Routledge.

Bell, Robert & Grant, Nigel (1977): *Patterns of Education in the British Isles*. London: George Allen & Unwin.

Bereday, George Z.F. (1964): *Comparative Method in Education*. New York: Holt, Rinehart and Winston.

Bologna (2013): *Bologna Declaration*. http://www.wg.aegee.org/ewg/bolognadeclaration.htm accessed 10 February 2013.

Booth, C. (1985): 'United Kingdom: System of Education', in Husén, Torsten & Postlethwaite, T. Neville (eds.), *The International Encyclopedia of Education*. Oxford: Pergamon Press, pp.5251-5359.

Bray, Mark & Koo, Ramsey (eds.) (2004): *Education and Society in Hong Kong and Macao: Comparative Perspectives on Continuity and Change*. CERC Studies in Comparative Education 7, 2nd edition, Hong Kong: Comparative Education Research Centre, The University of Hong Kong.

Bray, Mark & Yamato, Yoko (2003): 'Comparative Education in a Microcosm: Methodological Insights from the International Schools Sector in Hong Kong'. *International Review of Education*, Vol.49, Nos.1-2. reprinted in Bray, Mark (ed.) (2003): *Comparative Education: Continuing Traditions, New Challenges, and New Paradigms*. Dordrecht: Kluwer Academic Publishers, pp.51-73.

Brisard, Estelle; Menter, Ian & Smith, Ian (2007): 'Researching Trends in Initial Teacher Education Policy and Practice in an Era of Globalization and Devolution: A Rationale and a Methodology for an Anglo-Scottish 'Home International' Study'. *Comparative Education*, Vol.43, No.2, pp.207-229.

Brock, Colin (2010): 'Spatial Dimensions of Christianity and Education in Western European History, with Legacies for the Present'. *Comparative Education*, Vol.46, No.3, pp.289-306.

Bunnell, Tristan (2008): 'The Global Growth of the International Baccalaureate Diploma Programme over the First 40 Years: A Critical Assessment'. *Comparative Education*, Vol.44, No.4, pp.409-424.

Cameron, John; Cowen, Robert; Holmes, Brian; Hurst, Paul & McLean, Martin (eds.) (1983): *International Handbook of Education Systems*. 3 volumes, Chichester: John Wiley & Sons.

Cheng, Kai Ming (1991): *Planning of Basic Education in China: A Case Study of Two Counties in the Province of Liaoning*. Paris: UNESCO International Institute for Educational Planning.

China, People's Republic of (1985): *Reform of China's Educational Structure: Decision of the CPC [Communist Party of China] Central Committee*. Beijing: Foreign Languages Press.

China, People's Republic of (2010): *Outline of China's National Plan for Medium and Long-Term Education Reform and Development (2010-2020)*. Beijing: People's Publishing House. [in Chinese]

China, People's Republic of (2011): *Educational Statistics Yearbook of China 2010*. Beijing: People's Education Press. [in Chinese]

China, National Bureau of Statistics (2012): *Sixth National Population Census of the People's Republic of China*. Beijing: National Bureau of Statistics.

Commonwealth Secretariat (2012): *Commonwealth Education Partnerships 2012/13*. London: Nexus for the Commonwealth Secretariat.

Cramer, John Francis & Browne, George Stephenson (1956): *Contemporary Education: A Comparative Study of National Systems*. New York: Harcourt, Brace & World.

Crosier, David & Parveva, Teodora (2013): *The Bologna Process: Its Impact in Europe and Beyond*. Fundamentals of Educational Planning 97, Paris: UNESCO International Institute for Educational Planning (IIEP).

Curaj, Adrian; Scott, Peter; Vlasceanu, Lazăr & Wilson, Lesley (eds.) (2012): *European Higher Education at the Crossroads: Between the Bologna Process and National Reforms*. Dordrecht: Springer.

Daun, Holger & Arjmand, Reza (2005): 'Islamic Education', in Zajda, Joseph (ed.), *International Handbook on Globalisation, Education and Policy Research: Global Pedagogies and Policies*. Dordrecht: Springer, pp. 377-388.

Dunn, Seamus (2000): 'Northern Ireland: Education in a Divided Society', in Phillips, David (ed.), *The Education Systems of the United Kingdom*.

Oxford: Symposium Books, pp.85-96.

Education Commission (2005): *Report on Review of Medium of Instruction for Secondary Schools and Secondary School Places Allocation*. Hong Kong: Education Commission, Hong Kong Special Administrative Region.

Gong, Xin & Tsang, Mun C. (2011): 'Interprovincial and Regional Inequity in the Financing of Compulsory Education in China', in Huang, Tiedan & Wiseman, Alexander W. (eds.), *The Impact and Transformation of Education Policy in China*. Bingley: Emerald, pp.43-78.

Gorard, Stephen (2000): 'For England, See Wales', in Phillips, David (ed.), *The Education Systems of the United Kingdom*. Oxford: Symposium Books, pp.29-43.

Göttelmann, Gabriele & Bahr, Klaus (2012): *Strengthening of Education Systems*. Paris: UNESCO International Institute for Educational Planning (IIEP).

Greger, David & Walterová, Eliska (eds.) (2012): *Towards Educational Change: The Transformation of Educational Systems in Post-Communist Countries*. London: Routledge.

Grek, Sotiria & Ozka, Jenny (2010): 'Governing Education through Data: Scotland, England and the European Education Policy Space'. *British Educational Research Journal*, Vol.36, No.6, pp.937-952.

Griffin, Rosarii (ed.) (2006): *Education in the Muslim World: Different Perspectives*. Oxford: Symposium Books.

Gunning, Dennis & Raffe, David (2011): '14-19 Education across Great Britain: Convergence or Divergence?'. *London Review of Education*, Vol.9, No.2, pp.245-257.

Guo, Yugui (2005): *Asia's Educational Edge: Current Achievements in Japan, Korea, Taiwan, China, and India*. Lanham, Maryland: Lexington Books.

Hayden, Mary & Thompson, Jeff (2008): *International Schools: Growth and Influence*. Fundamentals of Educational Planning 92, Paris: UNESCO International Institute for Educational Planning (IIEP).

Hong Kong, Education Bureau (2011): 'Education reform highlights'. Hong Kong: Education Bureau.

Hong Kong, Education Bureau (2012): *Prospectus of the Schools Operated by the English Schools Foundation and International Schools in Hong Kong*. Hong Kong: Education Bureau.

Hong Kong, Education Bureau (2013): 'General Information on DSS'. http://www.edb.gov.hk/index.aspx?nodeID=1475&langno=1 accessed 12 February 2013.

Hong Kong, Education Department (1993): *Enrolment Survey 1993*. Hong

Kong: Education Department.

Hu, Wei & Xie, Xiemei (2003): 'System Environment for the Development of China's Private Education', in Yang, Dongping (ed.), *China's Education Blue Book (2003)*. Beijing: Higher Education Press, pp. 176-197.

Ignas, Edward & Corsini, Raymond J. (eds.) (1981): *Comparative Educational Systems*. Itasca: F.E. Peacock Publishers.

Kandel, Isaac L. (1933): *Studies in Comparative Education*. London: George G. Harrap & Company.

Lau, Sin Peng (2009): *A History Education in Macao*. Macao: Faculty of Education, University of Macau.

Lee, W.O. (1993): 'Social Reactions towards Education Proposals: Opting against the Mother Tongue as the Medium of Instruction in Hong Kong'. *Journal of Multilingual and Multicultural Development*, Vol.14, No.3, pp.203-216.

Leung, Joan H. (2011): 'Education Governance and Reform: Bringing the State Back In', in Lam, Newman M.K. & Scott, Ian (eds.), *Gaming, Governance and Public Policy in Macao*. Hong Kong: Hong Kong University Press, pp.163-181.

Liu, Junyan (2012): personal information, Beijing Academy of Education Sciences.

Macao, Government of (2012a): 'Education', in *Macao Yearbook*. Macao: Government of the Macau Special Administrative Region, pp. 315-329.

Macao, Government of (2012b): *Education Survey 2010/2011*. Macao: Documentation and Information Centre of the Statistics and Census Service.

Macau, Governo de (1989): *Inquérito ao Ensino 1987/1988*. Macau: Direcção dos Serviços de Estatística e Censos.

Macau, Governo de (1993a): *Inquérito ao Ensino 1991/1992*. Macau: Direcção dos Serviços de Estatística e Censos.

Macau, Governo de (1993b): *Educação em Números*. Macau: Direcção dos Serviços de Educação e Juventude.

Maringe, F.; Foskett, N. & Woodfield, S. (2013): 'Emerging International-isation Models in an Uneven Global Terrain: Findings from a Global Survey'. *Compare: A Journal of Comparative and International Education*, Vol.42, No.1, pp.9-36.

Marlow-Ferguson, Rebecca (2002): *World Education Encyclopedia: A Survey of Educational Systems*. Detroit: Gale Group.

Matheson, David (2000): 'Scottish Education: Myths and Mists', in Phillips, David (ed.), *The Education Systems of the United Kingdom*. Oxford: Symposium Books, pp.63-84.

McGuinness, Samuel J. (2012): 'Education Policy in Northern Ireland: A Review', *Italian Journal of Sociology of Education*, Vol.1, No.4, pp. 205-237.

Menter, Ian; Hulme, Moira; Jephcote, Martin; Mahony, Pat A. & Moran, Anne (2009): 'Teacher Education in the United Kingdom: A "Home International" Study'. Paper presented to the annual conference of the American Educational Research Association, 13-17 April, San Diego, USA.

Mitter, Wolfgang (2004): 'Rise and Decline of Education Systems: A Contribution to the History of the Modern State'. *Compare: A Journal of Comparative Education*, Vol.34, No.4, pp.351-369.

Moehlman, Arthur H. (1963): *Comparative Educational Systems*. Washington DC: The Center for Applied Research in Education.

Mok, Ka-ho (ed.) (2003): *Centralization and Decentralization: Educational Reforms and Changing Governance in Chinese Societies*. CERC Studies in Comparative Education 13, Hong Kong: Comparative Education Research Centre, The University of Hong Kong, and Dordrecht: Kluwer Academic Publishers.

Morris, Paul & Adamson, Bob (2010): *Curriculum, Schooling and Society in Hong Kong*. Hong Kong: Hong Kong University Press.

Ng, Vinci (2012): 'The Decision to Send Local Children to International Schools in Hong Kong: Local Parents' Perspectives'. *Asia Pacific Education Review*, Vol.13, No.1, pp.121-136.

Postiglione, Gerard A. (2012): 'China, Ethnic Autonomous Regions', in Banks, James A. (ed.), *Encyclopedia of Diversity in Education*. Los Angeles: SAGE, pp.339-340.

Postlethwaite, T. Neville (ed.) (1988): *The Encyclopedia of Comparative Education and National Systems of Education*. Oxford: Pergamon Press.

Postlethwaite, T. Neville (ed.) (1995): *The International Encyclopedia of National Systems of Education*. 2nd edition, Oxford: Pergamon Press.

Qi, Tingting (2011): 'Moving Toward Decentralization? Changing Education Governance in China after 1985', in Huang, Tiedan & Wiseman, Alexander W. (eds.), *The Impact and Transformation of Education Policy in China*. Bingley: Emerald, pp.19-41.

Raffe David; Brannen, Karen; Croxford, Linda & Martin, Chris (1999): 'Comparing England, Scotland, Wales and Northern Ireland: The

Case for "Home Internationals" in Comparative Research'. *Comparative Education*, Vol.35, No.1, pp.9-25.

Richardson, William (2011): 'The Weight of History: Structures, Patterns and Legacies of Secondary Education in the British Isles, c.1200 - c.1980'. *London Review of Education*, Vol.9, No.2, pp.153-173.

Robinson, Jason & Guan, Xuan (2012): 'The Changing Face of International Education in China'. *On the Horizon*, Vol.20, No.2, pp.305-212.

Sadler, Sir Michael (1900): 'How Far Can We Learn Anything of Practical Value from the Study of Foreign Systems of Education?'. Reprinted 1964 in *Comparative Education Review*, Vol.7, No.3, pp.307-314.

Spring, Joel (2009): *Globalization of Education: An Introduction*. New York: Routledge.

Standing Committee on Language Education & Research (2003): *Action Plan to Raise Language Standards in Hong Kong: Final Report of Language Education Review*. Hong Kong: Standing Committee on Language Education & Research.

Tilak, Jandhyala B.G. (2011): *Trade in Higher Education: The Role of the General Agreement on Trade in Services (GATS)*. Fundamentals of Educational Planning 95, Paris: UNESCO International Institute for Educational Planning (IIEP).

Thieme, Claudio; Giménez, Víctor & Prior, Diego (2012): 'A Comparative Analysis of the Efficiency of National Education Systems'. *Asia Pacific Education Review*, Vol.13, No.1, pp.1-15.

UNESCO (2011): *National Journeys towards Education for Sustainable Development*. Paris: UNESCO.

UNESCO International Bureau of Education (2000): *World Data on Education: A Guide to the Structure of National Systems*. Geneva: UNESCO International Bureau of Education.

Verger, Antoni L. & Robertson, Susan (2012): 'The GATS Game-Changer: International Trade Regulation and the Constitution of a Global Education Marketplace', in Robertson, Susan L.; Mundy, Karen; Verger, Antoni & Menashy, Francine (eds.), *Public Private Partnerships in Education: New Actors and Modes of Governance in a Globalizing World*. Cheltenham: Edward Elgar, pp.104-127.

Wang, Zhisheng (2011): 'Diversity or Unification: The Post-colonial Education in Current Situation of Macau'. *Journal of Qinghai Normal University*, Vol.33, No.2, pp.123-126. [in Chinese]

Wolhuter, C.C.; Lemmer, E.M. & de Wet, N.C. (eds.) (2007): *Comparative Education: Education Systems and Contemporary Issues*. Pretoria: Van

Schaik.

Yamato, Yoko & Bray, Mark (2006): 'Economic Development and the Market Place for Education: Dynamics of the International Schools Sector in Shanghai, China'. *Journal of Research in International Education*, Vol.5, No.1, pp.71-96.

Zhao, Zhenzhou (2010): 'China's Ethnic Dilemma: Ethnic Minority Education'. *Chinese Education and Society*, Vol.43, No.1, pp.3-11.

6

Comparing Times

Anthony SWEETING

How may one provide an introduction to comparing times within the field of comparative education that is more than a brief handshake? A prerequisite is to consider the fundamental concepts involved, specifically in respect of 'time' and its application in the field as a unit of comparison.

Time

It is simplistic and improper to confine the meaning of Time to its role in physics as one of the key factors in the calculation of velocity. Instead, one may recognise that its components include ordinal sequencing and duration. And although the ordinal nature or sequence of events may *seem* to be immutable (and therefore absolute), further consideration reveals that, because of such real possibilities as temporal coincidences, simultaneity, or instantaneity and subjective experiences by different individuals, the recognition of sequence may vary. Similarly, via the hazards of memory or the rigours of careful retrospection, it is common for either different people or even a single individual to construct more than one temporal series from the same aggregation of events. Further, as is almost universally recognised, duration, even if measured by the most accurate clock, may be experienced in very different ways depending on interest, engagement, happiness, etc.. Thus, for reasons rather different from those advanced by Einstein or Hawking, one may sensibly conclude that time is in many respects relative, and that it is not a simple, linear, autonomous entity discrete from space, but may properly be considered, existentially as well as physically, an aspect of space-time. Especially in the context of globalisation, with its possibilities of more or less instant communications, a bewilderment of time-zones for individuals, groups, and institutions becomes a (post-modern) reality. For all these (and no doubt other) reasons, time seems particularly suited to the mental application of comparison.

In using time as a unit of comparison, it becomes immediately obvious that there are several 'types' to consider. These include (but are not confined to) astronomical time, biological time, geological time, and the two most significant types for the purposes of this chapter: personal time and historical time. Despite the increasing intrusiveness of clocks and watches, personal time is, in important ways, subjective and relative, whether one is considering it as a whole and in relation to a sense of maturation/ageing or in a more partial way, related to appointments, punctuality, the duration and sequence of lessons, a whole range of different 'calendars' (social, professional, family, recreational, etc.), and a sense of busy-ness or stagnation.

Further, although it is tempting to designate historical time as society's or the state's equivalent of an individual's personal time, more educational importance derives from recognising the interconnections between personal and historical time. Thus, the development of 'historical consciousness' derives from an individual's recognition of the interface of personal with historical time (Rusen 1987; von Borries 1994). With regard to comparing time in comparative education research, one should note that the achievement of historical consciousness involves linkages. In particular, especially in connection with an individual's perception, it is built upon the awareness of one's own place within the context of historical time, as well as the continuing refinement of one's own skills of 'synchronism' (the positive and creative aspects of an ability to detect anachronisms). As far as macro-level comparisons are concerned, however, Cowen's (2002, p.416) reminder about the significance of differences in 'developmental time' is, like the emphasis on different 'presents' by Nóvoa and Yariv-Mashal (2003), particularly valuable. The recognition of the possibility of this type of cultural and contextual difference is crucial to the formation of valid comparisons.

As has already been intimated several 'times' in this chapter, it is also worthwhile to compare and in this way discover the differences between the abstract and complex concept of 'time' itself, in all its numerous usages, and the more familiar notion of '(the) times', as quite commonly illuminated in such expressions as "the life and times of so-and-so". Songwriter Bob Dylan was much closer to the latter sense when he averred that "The times they are a-changing". According to Dylan, people in general, writers and critics, senators, congressmen, mothers and fathers, all need to recognise and all have grounds for recognising the volatility of the times. His list could also include researchers in the field of comparative education. Many of these may wish to compare two or more distinctive times (or phases) in educational development in one or more places, and thereby reach tentative conclusions about the nature of these 'periods'. A few may be confident enough to attempt to identify a *zeitgeist* – a spirit of the times – for each of the periods or ages. Less ambitiously, by comparing events, ideas and attitudes within one period or between more than one, a researcher is able to reach reasoned conclusions about such matters as continuity, change and development.

Cowen (2002), at least in his titular focus on the *moments* of time (and, thus, on temporal units, metaphorically in freeze-frame) appears unnecessarily hampered for the appreciation of the *movement* and *passage* of time, the sense of pace or stagnation. Possibly, part of the obstruction derives from his continuing insistence that comparative education is necessarily confined to the study of more than one education system, normally identified with more than one nation-state (e.g. Cowen 2000, p.335). Moreover, different perceptions of present educational situations and/or future educational prospects are open to comparison, as well as past educational achievements. Therefore, in addition to the somewhat atomistic-sounding 'moments of time', it may be helpful to employ the broader notion of 'comparing times' in delineating the historical dimension.

Historical Approaches to Comparative Education

Periodically, workers in the field of comparative education take time off from their regular labours to ponder the point of it all. Unsurprisingly, such reflections frequently occur at times perceived to be significant anniversaries: the pair of millennial special numbers of *Comparative Education* (Vol.36, No.3, 2000; Vol.37, No.4, 2001), and the special issue of *Compare: A Journal of Comparative and International Education* to note its fourth decade (Vol.40, No.6, 2010), are among the examples of this pattern. Collections such as these, together with more discrete publications about theories and methods related to comparative education research (e.g.

Bereday 1964; Altbach & Kelly 1986; Cummings 1999; Watson 2001; Bray 2003), make extended discussion here unnecessary.

Suffice it to note that the present writer shares the view that comparative education may appear to be both "promiscuous" (Broadfoot 2003, p.275) and "characterised by eclecticism" (Ninnes & Burnett 2003, p.279); that, ostensibly at least, it accommodates area studies, social science-based studies, and development/planning studies, together with numerous hybrids; but that some of its practitioners tend to be more (puritanically?) exclusionary than others – see, for example, Epstein's (1987) criticisms of Farrell's work on Chile. The present writer also accepts the notion that comparative education has, and should value, multidisciplinary traditions. Following several luminaries (e.g. Noah & Eckstein 1998; Broadfoot 2000; Hawkins & Rust 2001; Wilson 2003), he notes that recognition of the value of historical insights by workers/theorists in the field of comparative education itself has a venerable history.

As far as significant research output is concerned, however, there was something approaching a hiatus in historically-oriented comparative education studies in the period from the late 1950s to the 1990s (Rust et al. 1999). This is open to explanations that focus narrowly on changing intellectual fashions, especially the academic popularity of positivist social science approaches from the late 1950s onwards, the attractions of neo-Marxist approaches from the mid-1970s, and the appeal of neo-liberal and post-modernist viewpoints from the 1980s. It is also open to explanations that seek to identify broader (non-intra-field-specific) influences, such as the impact of Sputnik, the end of the Cold War, postcolonial realities and rhetoric, the revolution in micro technology, and so on.

Around the turn of the century, calls for a re-finding, re-invention, and/or re-conceptualisation of historical approaches to comparative education reverberated. Thus, Watson (1998, p.28) declared that "instead of anguishing over the value and justification for comparative education we need to re-find its roots in historical and cultural analysis". Kazamias (2001, p.447) argued for "the reclamation of the disappearing historical legacy in comparative education", but for re-invented historical approaches that make "use of *concepts, abstractions,* or even *theories,* which to a degree more or less, provide lenses or frameworks to compare, explain and interpret historical phenomena" (p.446). And while some comparativists and historians may balk at the frequent recourse to categorical imperatives in Nóvoa and Yariv-Mashal's (2003) polemical essay, many (including the present writer) would accept its finding (p.435) that:

we are facing an important role for historical research within the comparative discipline, one that would enable comparative work to trace the conceptualization of ideas and the formation of knowledge over time and space. One could picture such a theoretical framework for comparative studies as a multidimensional process in which research is grounded in 'local histories', but is based and embedded in different forces, connections, times and places. The reception of each of these histories in different 'presents' will produce an individually, historically contingent social, cultural and educational discourse.

Less dogmatically, Cowen (2000, p.333) argued that "there should be no 'conclusion' if one is discussing comparative educations of the past, and potential comparative educations of the future". "At best", he suggested, "and also at least, there is a continuing conversation". For this reason, he advocated the use of the plural expression 'comparative educations' rather than the singular (and possibly exclusive) 'comparative education'. One can have no serious objection to this suggestion, even though usage of 'comparative education' as a collective, 'catholic' concept may serve to encourage an ecumenical approach, as is commonly alleged to be an outcome of comparative religion. As a modest contribution to Cowen's continuing conversation, one could characterise comparative education as all efforts to detect and comment on similarities and differences between forms of education, whether these forms are expressed in locational or in temporal terms (Sweeting 2001). And, at the risk of provoking the exclusionists, one could also show tolerance (welcome?) for "work done in cognate fields, as well as ... [for] important international work carried out by people who do not identify themselves as 'comparativists'" (Evans 2003, p.418). Presumably, this would include at least some of the work of cross-cultural psychologists, economists of education, educational sociologists, and even historians of education (Green 2002).

Significantly, in an even more germane article, Cowen (2002) chose the journal *History of Education* as an appropriate vehicle for comments on the 'unit ideas' of comparative education, focusing particularly on concepts of time. He argued, at least implicitly, that the two fields (History of Education and Comparative Education) were affiliated and overlapping. More explicitly, he asserted (p.413) that both fields under-theorised time, but speculated that in practice they "are differently sensitive to time and use different concepts of it". Following Cowen's lead, the present chapter, part of a book on approaches and methods in comparative education research, necessarily comments on issues affecting the study and writing of histories of education as well as the more historically aware works within the commonly acknowledged field of comparative education. It seeks to investigate further the concepts of time actually used, and remains open to the possibility that the two fields differ not primarily in the concepts of time to which each appeals, but in the emphasis on it that each presents.

Histories of Education

In one sense, all histories are comparative. Their necessary involvement with time and chronology, continuity and change depends upon a degree of comparison. However, some histories are more comparative than others, in the same way as some 'periods' or 'ages' are more transitional than others.

Prevailing Forms of Histories of Education

Histories of education have their own history, of course (Aldrich 1982; Gordon & Szreter 1989; Lowe 2000; Popkewitz et al. 2001; Gaither 2003). Without the space, time or justification to make a significant addition to this literature, here the present writer is content to construct a (no doubt, incomplete) taxonomy. He considers seven rather different kinds of histories of education in order to assess their role and value in comparative education.

1. *Doctrines of the Great Educators.* This category echoes the title of a once widely-read book (Rusk 1969). While bestriding the academic disciplines of philosophy and history, the approach focuses on a summary of 'doctrines' considered to be seminal in education, commonly including ideas associated with Plato, Aristotle, Comenius, Rousseau and Dewey. Inevitably, works in this category tend to be narrowly text-based (or, more often, derived from paraphrases of the relevant texts). They rarely include a consideration of broader socio-cultural, economic, and/or political aspects, although some contain brief, usually uncritical, biographical data. They have not played a conspicuous part in the modern research literature of comparative education, but one can detect something of a resurgence of their influence with the increasing popularity among academics of dicta emerging from poststructuralists.

2. *Institutional Pieties.* Like the former category, such publications are commonly uncritical and narrow (even parochial). A large sub-category of this type celebrates anniversaries, centenaries, etc. Apart from serving as a repository for what might be expected to be accurate dates, place names, personal names, attendance statistics, and, perhaps, formal curricula, they do not contribute significantly to the process or product of research in the field of comparative education. This does not, of course, mean that all histories of single institutions or even all anniversary publications are of this type. Among honourable exceptions are a publication to celebrate the centenary of the University of London Institute of Education (Aldrich 2002) and another to commemorate the centenary of the University of Hong Kong (Cunich 2012).

3. *Polemical Broadsides.* In one respect very different from the former categories, these types are highly critical. Almost by definition, however, many of them retain a narrow focus, especially those whose main purpose is to affirm a particular political or philosophical position. At least some of the work influenced by critical theory and postcolonialism suffers from this sort of narrowness and partiality. At worst, it abuses historical approaches by subordinating existing evidence to the exigencies of the argument, thereby using evidence in a cavalier and selective way (Carnoy 1974; Meyer et al. 1992; Pennycook 1998). At best, it stimulates both discussion and a search for confirmatory or refutative evidence (Green 1997; Apple 1999, 2000). Thanks to the influence of, among others, critical theorists, dependency and world systems theorists, postcolonialists, postmodernists, and poststructuralists, there can be little doubt that historical perspectives derived from polemics have had and continue to have significant influence on comparative education research.

4. *Policy Studies.* Almost inevitably overlapping with polemical broadsides, a more rigorously research-oriented form of publications that frequently offers historical perspectives and insights comprises those that are most closely related to specific policies. Several such works focused on centralisation and/or decentralisation (e.g. Mok 2003; Bray 2013), other aspects of administration (Watts 1998a; Lau 2002), the apparent paradox between professionalisation and the de-skilling of teachers (Ginsburg 1995; Kwo 2010; Robertson 2012), curriculum policy (Morris et al. 2001; Bol-

ton 2002; Grossman et al. 2008), and perceived effects of globalisation (Mok & Welch 2003; Beech 2009; Maringe et al. 2013). It is not only true that works such as these are useful for researchers in comparative education, it is also the case that the majority of the authors cited above would actually admit to working in this field.

5. *Archival Anthologies/Substitutes.* Among education-focused archival anthologies are works on England and Wales (Maclure 1986), China (Fraser 1965, 1971), and Hong Kong (Sweeting 1990, 2004), although some of these publications also incorporate much non-archival material. Their main value to researchers in comparative education is as a convenient short cut to historical evidence. At their worst, however, in books of this kind obtrusive editorial comment that is predominantly text-centred and even text-modifying (e.g. Bickley 2002) distracts the researcher without adding important historical insights. Archival substitutes include books that are based upon particular legislation (e.g. McCulloch 1994; Jennings 1995). In a more general sense, they are also represented by earlier, largely top-down accounts of historical development (e.g. Curtis 1967; Dent 1970). Their role in comparative education research rarely transcends that of 'crib-book'.

6. *Boiler-plate Accessories.* Of even humbler use are the brief and often bald statements included in publications by some comparativists in a type of passing courtesy to the 'historical dimension'. These often read as if they have been extracted from a much-used, but possibly second-hand, set of boiler-plate expressions (e.g. "Hong Kong was founded as a British colony in 1842 and returned to Chinese sovereignty in 1997"). They are almost invariably confined to macro-political matters and/or top-down, narrowly education-related data (e.g. the dates of Education Acts, and official reports). In comparative education publications, these are better than nothing – but only just. They advance the understanding only of readers who would, otherwise, be completely ignorant of the topic/place/time being discussed, but such readers gain little in terms of profundity or scope.

7. *Social Histories.* On the other hand, increasing numbers of social histories of education have been published (e.g. Silver 1977; Archer 1979; Lowe 1988; Urban 1999; Kallaway 2002; Wegner 2002). These are the sorts of works from which researchers in comparative education are likely to benefit most, especially from

the ways in which they illuminate cultural and other contextual matters and especially in the planning and processing of their research.

Prevailing Theoretical Perspectives

Many historians would agree with Kazamias (2001, p.446) that, if asked to explain themselves, they (or, at least, the majority of their colleagues) typically adopt an a-theoretical position. Others would prefer to describe themselves as eclectic, ready to use the theoretical stances they deem appropriate to the topic they are investigating. It is, however, also the case that both a-theoreticism (mainly as revealed by a disdain for discourse about theory) and eclecticism are, themselves, theoretical standpoints. Moreover, as Kazamias emphasised:

> Most historians are not theoretical, but most comparative historians and, by extension, most comparative educational historians use theoretical insights, often derived from other disciplines. These could involve theories (such as functionalism, Marxism, modernization, or post-colonialism), or concepts of limited or more general applicability (e.g. class, capitalism, power, conflict, violence, reproduction, dependence, democratization, globalization, systematization, segmentation, habitus, etc.), which provide the lenses or the medium to select, organize and interpret the historical material.

In the past few decades, theoretical positions, more or less consistently adopted by individual historians of education and/or researchers in comparative education who make use of historical perspectives in their work, include the following (slightly modified from Kazamias' list):

- *Marxism/Critical Theory* (e.g. Simon 1970; Bowles & Gintis 1976; Silver 1977; Apple 2000). This approach emphasises economic factors and, especially, the influence of social class on both policy and practice. It is sometimes criticised for the air of inevitability that it introduces.
- *Dependency Theory/World Systems Analysis* (e.g. Wallerstein 1974; Meyer et al. 1992). These closely-related approaches are critical of the alleged hegemony over the 'developing world' exercised by the more developed nations, especially those of the 'West' and the 'North'. At times, however, work in this tradition appears itself to be

condescending and to assume wrongly that, simply because similar vocabulary is used (say, for the names of subjects in school curricula), outright copying of cargo-cult proportions has occurred.

- *Poststructuralism* (e.g. Ball 1994; Pennycook 1998). In academic circles, this approach has gained popularity over the past few decades. It has the advantage of permitting, even encouraging, subjective 'deconstructions' of policy and/or practice that are at odds with historical statements of intention. On occasions, its links with publicly verifiable evidence are, to say the least, tenuous.

- *Postmodernism* (e.g. Popkewitz 1994; Lowe 1996; Larsen 2009). Postmodernism, like its close relative Poststructuralism, provides its adherents with a flexibility of approach. It also provides a salutary corrective to rigidly linear and exclusively reason-based views of education (or anything else) that its adherents regard as typical of 'modernist' thinking first expressed in Europe during the Age of the Enlightenment. It offers opportunities for a multi-dimensional, impressionistic appreciation of realities, but tends to under-emphasise more conventional explanations of motivations, causes and effects. Some of its adherents fail to consider whether any approach could possibly be post-postmodernist and, at least in this sense, they are a-historical.

- *Postcolonialism* (e.g. Benton 1996; Tikly 1999; Sharma-Brymer 2009). This approach places colonialism and most especially its evils at the centre of attention. It has the value of challenging dated assumptions about alleged cultural and racial superiority, and it certainly recognises the possibility of incipient neocolonialism being practised in a range of mainly economy-related ways. As is the case with poststructuralism and postmodernism, the danger has occasionally existed that its adherents are more interested in political correctness than in actual evidence.

- *Feminism* (e.g. Stromquist 1990; Watts 1998b). This approach, too, has served the purpose of challenging and/or revealing unthinking prejudices, and therefore is to be welcomed as a healthy reminder about important aspects of education. At times, however, its advocates' understandable enthusiasms reach obsessive levels and some of the advocates may 'invent' or exaggerate past examples of male chauvinism or female exploitation for situations in which gender was not the main issue.

- *Neoliberalism/New Managerialism* (e.g. Townsend 1996; Reynolds 1998). These approaches seek historical evidence to illustrate the virtues of minimising government 'interference' in education and to recognise the positive values of the operation of market forces. Adherents tend to acknowledge rather limited concepts of 'effectiveness', whether applied to schools, teachers, students or policies, and to treat education itself essentially as a marketable commodity and not as an encounter or experience.

Some researchers, at least for substantial parts of their careers (e.g. Farrell 1986, p.8; but see also Farrell 2011, pp.65-69), have defiantly eschewed theory. They serve as counter-examples to the suggestions advanced by Kazamias (1961, pp.90-96; 2001, p.446) and Nóvoa and Yariv-Mashal (2003, p.430). Martin (2003) emphasised the similarity of the findings reached by such a theory-free approach (Farrell 1986) with those emerging from a theory-laden one (Jansen 1991). And few, if any, historians would deny making use of organising concepts such as class, capitalism, power, and conflict in the course of their work.

Characteristics of Modern Historical Analysis

Modern historiography has included much debate about the nature of historical explanation, especially in connection with the role, if any, played by 'Covering Laws' (Gardiner 1961; Roberts 1995; Haskell 1998; Fetzer 2000; Hamilton 2003). Although many historians resist the social science flavoured appeal of Covering Laws, most of them would accept that they have recourse to generalisations, especially in the form of organising concepts and especially as 'closed-class generalisations'. Thus, for historians, even such concepts as 'class', 'capitalism', 'power', etc. are to a significant extent historically contingent, with their precise meanings capable of change according to time, place, and context. Among historians of education and comparative education researchers with historical interests, Simon (e.g. 1970) has frequently focused on class, Bowles and Gintis (e.g. 1976) on capitalism, Silver (e.g. 1977) on opinion, Green (e.g. 1997) on state formation, Carnoy (e.g. 1974) on colonialism, Gray et al. (e.g. 1983) on reconstruction, and many others on education policy-making. The world of comparative education, generally, benefits from the light cast on these closed-class generalisations by historians. It also benefits from historians' use of 'colligation' (Walsh 1967). This is the process by which historians seek to establish, from several individual events, shared motives or purposes or significance, and thereby to link such events together as some movement or policy or trend. The comfortable affiliation (indeed, the compatibility) of comparative education research with the discipline of history is strengthened by the fact that the process of colligation essentially involves comparison (via interpolation into and extrapolation from a constructed series of events).

Other ways in which the usual practices of historians are capable of illuminating comparative studies of education derive from historians' concern for evidence, especially including primary sources, which, for many historians of modern periods/issues, include oral sources. For historians, primary sources are those that are contemporaneous with, and have become generated in the course of, the events under investigation. For this reason, what can be termed 'process sources' (e.g. eye-witness accounts, verbatim reports, agendas, correspondence, in-depth interviews) commonly receive greater attention than 'product sources' (e.g. actual legislative acts, finished reports). Even with process sources, however, most modern historians seek to cross-check (or 'triangulate') one set from a particular origin with one or more others from different origins. Moreover, primary sources of *information* become primary sources of *evidence* only once they are seen to help answer a specific, articulated question. More widespread adoption of such methodological rigour within the field of comparative education would at least reduce the number of descriptive, data-heavy, and ultimately pointless or misleading comparative education studies. Lack of clarity about purpose fuels comparisons dismissed by Cummings (1999, p.43) as 'senseless', including "those often used by international agencies, which report differences between aggregate statistical categories such as Asia, Africa, or Latin America … [because] there is too much variation within these categories". At the other extreme, comparisons bloated with extrinsic purpose (e.g. to confirm a particular paradigmatic stance or explanatory theory) may exhibit intellectual and methodological flabbiness untypical of historians. This becomes especially noticeable when such studies employ anachronistic or, in other ways, inappropriate definitions and/or make only selective use of evidence.

Historians' inclinations to view their sources from different viewpoints in order to accommodate different possible interpretations, together with their readiness to juxtapose different sources, characteristically encourages them not only to accept the likelihood of multiple causation, but also to feel comfortable with the prospect of multiple inter-pretations. As Farrell (1986, p.8) wrote about his own study:

> There is no claim here for a uniquely valid interpretation of what happened in Chile between 1970-1973, nor do I believe that there is, or can be, one. But the existence of a variety of interpretations is a benefit, except perhaps to those whose understanding of social real-ity is so rigidly narrow-minded that they regard any deviation from received truth, as they understand it, to be heresy which is only to be extirpated.

It is for these reasons (among others) that historical judgements tend to be tentative and historians argumentative. These are qualities that some workers in the field of comparative education would do well to adopt, and they seem especially suitable to deal with what King (2000, p.273) described as 'the globalization of many uncertainties'.

While revelling in tentativeness and argument, most historians are also interested in questions about the provenance, impact, longer-term seminality, and significance of events, movements or ideas. Many recog-nise that ostensibly clear statements about such matters which appear in official 'product-sources' may prove to be inaccurate, unfair, and/or in-complete, making, for example, erroneous attributions of agency. This lesson would be salutary for some comparative education researchers, encouraging greater scepticism with regard to public-relations-oriented pronouncements.

Similarly, in relation to causal analysis, historians are usually aware of the *post hoc ergo propter hoc* ("following x, therefore because of x") fal-lacy, though one cannot be quite so confident about the same awareness by some comparativists. Furthermore, many historians are suspicious of teleological explanations that depend on the assumption of some final end/grand intention. Again, comparative education researchers, seduced by conspiracy theories concerning, for example, colonial governments, would benefit from a healthy dose of historical scepticism, as sharpened by particular (rather than over-generalised) evidence.

A final characteristic of historical analysis to be discussed here is the predilection of many of the best modern historians to transcend pigeon-holes, to find connections between, say, accounts of developments in schooling with broader political, social, economic, religious and other cultural developments. In some cases, this recognition of connections is lacking in histories of education and comparative education studies. Thus, articles which include historical treatments of comparative education sometimes remain focused parochially on organisations, personalities and publications within the field of comparative education, omitting acknowledgement of the possibility that key developments in comparative education theory and methodology have been influenced by developments outside the field. These would include, for example, fashions in other academic fields, changes in the economy, life-style adaptations, technological innovations, political transformations, and even alterations in world-view and attitudes to the other gender or children. A more widespread acknowledgement of this possibility and plausible identification of specific connections would, of course, be in keeping with Sadler's (1900) dictum about the importance of "the things outside schools". As noted earlier, it also permits the comparison of education times/calendars with different, possibly cross-influencing times/calendars.

Strategies for Comparing Times

It may help to identify two main sub-divisions of such strategies: appropriate units of comparison, and possible structures for comparing times.

Units of Comparison

From the outset of published works in comparative education, the main unit of comparison has been the nation-state (Nakajima 1916; Kandel 1933) and, as several commentators (e.g. Cowen 2000, p.336; Nóvoa & Yariv-Mashal 2003, p.434) point out, it remains something like the default unit. On the other hand, in recent years, some researchers in comparative education (e.g. Bray & Thomas 1995; Sweeting 1999, p.270; Hawkins & Rust 2001, p.502) query the necessity and value of relying upon this default. The present book manifests the latter trend very clearly, showing as it does, that alternatives to the nation-state as the unit of comparison are not only locational (such as continents, regions, cities, and districts), but may properly include such education-related entities as cultures, values, curricula, policies, and ways of learning. Comparative studies may also focus on types of schools (e.g. grammar, vocational, international), individual schools, a whole range of communities (e.g. particular national minorities, Chinatowns), textbooks and/or other teaching/learning resources, and facilities for nonformal and informal education.

Structures for Comparing Times

Researchers utilise at least three different structural forms when seeking to compare times. These have been labelled *diachronic, synchronic,* and *quasi-synchronic* analyses (Sweeting 1993). The actual strategy adopted by a particular researcher depends, of course, at least partly on the nature of the subject. It also depends on the purpose(s) of the comparison, and on the researcher's personal preferences.

The first, diachronic analysis, is the most common – in histories of education, as well as in more general histories. Its main basis for organisation is chronological; thus, its main form is narrative. Typical examples include Aldrich (2002) and Farrell (1986). Metaphorically, such studies represent complete movies. The main advantage of this structure is its temporal clarity, which can emphasise both continuity and change, while offering a clear overview. Its main danger is that, if users seek to avoid the possible tedium of merely answering the typical story-listeners' questions ("and then?", "and then?") by inserting an element of 'plot' or design, they may actually distort realities by over-rationalising and exaggerating past-people's capacity to foresee the future (or even see clearly their present). Another danger is that the requirements of narrative flow may conflict with a comprehensive perception of the different levels and aspects of education and tempt the writer to resort exclusively to a macro-view of educational developments and to focus only on top-down initiatives.

Synchronic analyses, sometimes associated with structuralist thought, represent static snapshots. A classic study in English history is Namier's (1957) *The Structure of Politics at the Accession of George III.* In historical works focusing on education, scholars detailing particular legislation tend to adopt this sort of approach, as well as ones that juxtapose before/after situations (see e.g. Sweeting 1993, pp.14-40). Theoretically, at least, the approach would also appear to be encouraged by Cowen's (2002) focus on "moments of time". The advantage of this structure rests mainly in the room it offers for detailed analysis and exposition. Its main danger, even when two contrasting times are juxtaposed for the sake of impact, is that occurrences in the intervening period become unjustifiably undervalued.

The third form, quasi-synchronic or quasi-diachronic, encompasses a whole range of hybrids, especially those types of case studies that address policy episodes (e.g. Cheng 1987; Sze 1990). Metaphorically, they are closer to home-movies or brief television programmes. The advantage of these hybrid structures is that they are capable of combining the virtues of the two, more extreme, forms – offering some sense of continuity as well as the opportunity for case-study type detail. The main danger lies in the patchiness of coverage they provide and the likelihood that significant aspects of educational development will be omitted.

Problems when Comparing Times

It would be unrealistic and unhelpful to end this chapter without addressing the sorts of problems that arise in attempts to compare times. These form themselves into three clusters.

Problems of Sources

Access to sources (especially government archives) is, at times, problematic. Persistence often pays off, however, as do efforts to retrieve alternatives. Much the same may be said about the *incompleteness* of some sources. Again, alternatives and supplements (often from oral evidence) may serve the particular purpose. Relatively inexperienced researchers should also consider carefully the *nature* and, especially, the *variety* of the sources they use, ensuring that they are not too easily satisfied with the obvious (usually official and documentary) sources, but are also ready to incorporate oral, pictorial, statistical, and even personal sources. In this way, they are more likely to tackle effectively problems involving the *reliability* of evidence, especially via triangulation methods. They can also provide alternatives to seemingly endless pages of text, likely to be welcomed by readers.

Problems of Interpretation

These problems may be reduced through the triangulation of evidence, which is likely to provoke several different possible interpretations. Some, more specific interpretative problems involve the establishment of *provenance*. In these, as noted earlier, it is usually important to recognise that the official or conventional attribution of the origins of an idea or decision is not necessarily a full or even an accurate statement. Much the same is the case with judgements of *responsibility* or *agency*, as far as the formulation of, say, a policy is concerned, and with judgements of *potency*, as far as policy implementation is concerned. Frequently, for example, a commission, council or committee that has in actuality done nothing but 'rubber-stamp' a proposal receives credit for its creation. Similarly, official reports of widespread implementation of a particular, centre-endorsed policy need to be interpreted as self-serving until and unless compared with evidence about actual implementation practices at the periphery. Interpretation of the *significance* of formal declarations of *intentions* and *objectives* also benefits from caution and, especially, the recognition that the apparently 'logical' sequence of purpose-process-product is, in practice, often manifested chronologically in a different way, especially when the processes are piloted, the products evaluated, and the purposes retrospectively rationalised (Sweeting 2002). In other respects, interpretations of significance, like those of provenance, are aided by the use and triangulation of a range of sources. In all these cases, it is worth emphasising that history-focused commentators should use and not abuse their privilege of hindsight. Thus, researchers in comparative education need to be wary of the 'presentism' that seems to have regained acceptability in currently fashionable poststructuralist and post-modernist discourse (Lorringer 1996; Nóvoa & Yariv-Mashal 2003, p.430).

Problems of Periodisation

Periods, whether they are linked directly to time-words ('the 20th century', 'the 1960s'), indirectly ('The Victorian Age', 'Postwar Reconstruction', 'The Thatcher Years'), or only implicitly ('Retraction', 'The Rise of Neo-liberalism and New Managerialism') are artificial inventions (King 2000, p.267) and are used by historians and others as convenient forms of synthesis. When writers invent their own period-titles, they are seeking to encapsulate meaning, often via the process of colligation, and thus to transform a 'story' into the elements of a 'plot' (Forster 1953) or identifiable themes.

Problems associated with periodisation include the selection of *beginning-dates* and *end-dates*, decisions about *optimal duration*, and, for the historian of education, *links with other histories* – broader social, economic, political, regional, world histories, for example, data and insights that are *exogenous*, as well as *endogenous*, to education and/or the specific unit of comparison under investigation (Phillips 1994, 2002). The author's own work on education in Hong Kong included notions of periods borrowed from historians' terminology. In some cases (Sweeting 1998a, 1998b, 1999), for example, he felt it helpful to consider successive developments in university-level teacher education as:

- 'Pre-history' (pre-1917, when the first University department was established);

- 'Ancient History' (1917-1941, a time characterised by one full-time member of staff, assisted by a school-based "master of method");
- 'the Dark Ages' (late 1941-1951, from the Japanese invasion and closure of the University to the provisions to reopen the Department);
- 'the Renaissance' (1951-c.1976, from the rebirth of the Department up to the time it gained its independence from the Faculty of Arts);
- 'Modern Times' (c.1976-c.1998, with its higher technology and including Chaplinesque connotations).

A later publication (Sweeting 2004) used period-notions that were less open to criticism as being Eurocentric. After consideration of the advantages and disadvantages of long and short periods for a study of educational developments in Hong Kong 1941-2001, the following periodisation was used:

- Occupational Hazards (and 'therapy?') 1941-1945;
- Reconstruction, Expansion, and Transformation 1945-1964;
- Policy, Pressure Groups, and Papers – on the way to Mass Access 1965-1984;
- Planning for a More Certain Future 1985-1997; and,
- A More Certain Future – the Pleasures and Perils of Post-colonialism 1997 to the New Millennium.

Whatever the virtues and/or vices of the phrases used, all periods, apart from the first and last ones, do at least have the virtue of similar duration and of being marked at beginning and end by highly significant dates. In some (especially the second, third, and fourth), the basic grounds for periodisation were predominantly education-centred; in the first and last, the reasons were linked with broader matters, in which education was inevitably also involved. These examples apply to multiple aspects of education in a single society, studied over a relatively long period of time.

There are challenges and satisfactions involved, too, in the comparison of developmental periods in different places, as Phillips demonstrates in the cases of post-war Germany and England (Phillips 1994, p.270; 2002, pp.372-374). This may reinforce an understanding that comparison is involved in much of the historian's work. This is especially true with regard to colligation, the creation of coherent sequences, argument about alternative explanations and interpretations, and, as far as historians of education are concerned, the consideration of different levels or aspects of education (Westlund 2007).

Conclusions

With comparative education, as with almost all other activities, much depends upon purpose. If the purpose of the comparison is merely measurement, then comparing times may seem marginal – although, even in these cases, estimates of, say, rates of progress/decay over time could be rewardingly compared. When, however, the purposes of comparison include the identification of discrete phases of educational development, then comparing times is an integral part of the process.

Further explorations of comparing times could focus on the *comparing of important times* (emphasising especially, perhaps, Cowen's concept of transitologies) and the *timeliness of comparing importances* (possibly as an antidote to some poststructuralist, postmodernist, and often globalisation-heavy caricatures of educational systems). Both foci acquire a special pointedness in situations where reform initiatives are characteristically a-historical in approach. Thus, a deliberately historical comparative perspective provides a much-needed corrective. And more generally, in these and probably other ways, History's positive values of recognising the human and the humanistic (Kazamias 2001), reinforcing the crucial role of context (Crossley 2009), and offering alternatives to 'macro-mania' (Sweeting 1989) may fertilise the field of comparative education. Such an outcome is the ultimate justification of the *importance of comparing times*.

Editors' note: The basic text by the late Anthony Sweeting has been retained for this second edition of the book, but some updating of references has been undertaken by the editors.

References

Aldrich, Richard (1982): *An Introduction to the History of Education*. London: Hodder and Stoughton.

Aldrich, Richard (2002): *The Institute of Education 1902-2002: A Centenary History*. London: Institute of Education, University of London.

Altbach, Philip & Kelly, Gail (eds.) (1986): *New Approaches to Comparative Education*. Chicago: University of Chicago Press.

Apple, Michael W. (1999): *Power, Meaning, and Identity: Essays in Critical Educational Studies*. New York: Peter Lang.

Apple, Michael W. (2000): *Official Knowledge: Democratic Education in a Conservative Age*. New York: Routledge.

Archer, Margaret S. (1979): *Social Origins of Educational Systems*. London: Sage.

Ball, Stephen J. (1994): *Education Reform: A Critical and Post Structural Approach*. Buckingham: Open University Press.

Beech, Jason (2009): 'Who is Strolling through the Global Garden? International Agencies and Educational Transfer', in Cowen, Robert & Kazamias, Andreas M. (eds.), *International Handbook of Comparative Education*. Dordrecht: Springer, pp.341-357.

Benton, Lauren (1996): 'From the World-Systems Perspective to Institutional World History: Culture and Economy in Global Theory'. *Journal of World History*, Vol.7, No.2, pp.261-295.

Bereday, George Z.F. (1964): *Comparative Method in Education*. New York: Holt, Rinehart & Winston.

Bickley, Gillian (2002): *The Development of Education in Hong Kong 1841-1897: As Revealed by the Early Education Reports of the Hong Kong Government 1848-1896*. Hong Kong: Proverse Hong Kong.

Bolton, Kingsley (2002): *Chinese Englishes: A Sociolinguistic History*. Cambridge: Cambridge University Press.

Bowles, Samuel & Gintis, Herbert (1976): *Schooling in Capitalist America: Educational Reform and the Contradictions of Economic Life*. London: Routledge & Kegan Paul.

Bray, Mark (ed.) (2003): *Comparative Education: Continuing Traditions, New Challenges, and New Paradigms*. Dordrecht: Kluwer Academic Publishers.

Bray, Mark (2013): 'Control of Education: Issues and Tensions in Centralization and Decentralization', in Arnove, Robert F.; Torres, Carlos A. & Frantz, Stephen (eds.), *Comparative Education: The Dialectic of the Global and the Local*. Lanham: Rowman & Littlefield, pp.201-222.

Bray, Mark & Thomas, R. Murray (1995): 'Levels of Comparison in Educational Studies: Different Insights from Different Literatures and the Value of Multilevel Analyses'. *Harvard Educational Review*, Vol.65, No.3, pp.472-490.

Broadfoot, Patricia (2000): 'Comparative Education for the 21ˢᵗ Century: Retrospect and Prospect'. *Comparative Education*, Vol.36, No.3, pp. 357-372.

Broadfoot, Patricia (2003): 'Editorial: Post-Comparative Education?'. *Comparative Education*, Vol.39, No.3, pp.275-278.

Carnoy, Martin (1974): *Education as Cultural Imperialism*. New York: David McKay & Co..

Cheng, Kai Ming (1987): 'The Concept of Legitimacy in Education policy-making: Alternative Explanations of Two Policy Episodes in Hong Kong', PhD thesis, Institute of Education, University of London.

Cowen, Robert (2000): 'Comparing Futures or Comparing Pasts?'. *Comparative Education*, Vol.36, No.3, pp.333-342.

Cowen, Robert (2002): 'Moments of Time: A Comparative Note'. *History of Education*, Vol.31, No.5, pp.413-424.

Crossley, Michael (2009): 'Rethinking Context in Comparative Education', in Cowen, Robert & Kazamias, Andreas M. (eds.), *International Handbook of Comparative Education*. Dordrecht: Springer, pp.1173-1187.

Cummings, William K. (1999): 'The InstitutionS of Education: Compare, Compare, Compare!'. *Comparative Education Review*, Vol.29, No.3, pp.269-285.

Cunich, Peter (2012): *A History of the University of Hong Kong. Volume I. 1911-1945*. Hong Kong: Hong Kong University Press.

Curtis, S.J. (1967): *History of Education in Great Britain*. London: University Tutorial Press.

Dent, Harold Collect (1970): *1870-1970: Century of Growth in English Education*. London: Longman.

Epstein, Erwin (1987): Review of "The National Unified School in Allende's Chile". *Comparative Education Review*, Vol.31, No.3, pp.468-469.

Evans, Karen (2003): 'Uncertain Frontiers: Taking Forward Edmund King's World Perspectives on Post-compulsory Education'. *Comparative Education*, Vol.39, No.4, pp.415-422.

Farrell, Joseph P. (1986): *The National Unified School in Allende's Chile: The Role of Education in the Destruction of a Revolution*. Vancouver: University of British Columbia Press.

Farrell, Joseph P. (2011): 'Blind Alleys and Signposts of Hope', in Bray, Mark & Varghese, N.V. (eds.), *Directions in Educational Planning: International Experiences and Perspectives*. Paris: UNESCO International Institute for Educational Planning (IIEP), pp.63-87.

Fetzer, James H. (ed.) (2000): *The Philosophy of Carl G. Hempel: Studies in Science, Explanation, and Rationality*. Oxford: Oxford University Press.

Forster, E.M. (1953): *Abinger Harvest*. London: Edward Arnold.

Fraser, Stewart E. (1965): *Chinese Communist Education: Records of the First Decade*. Nashville: Vanderbilt University Press.

Fraser, Stewart E. (ed.) (1971): *Education and Communism in China: An Anthology of Commentary and Documents*. London: Pall Mall Press.

Gaither, Milton (2003): *American Educational History Revisited: A Critique of Progress*. New York: Teachers College Press.

Gardiner, Patrick (1961): *The Nature of Historical Explanation*. London: Oxford University Press.

Ginsburg, Mark B. (1995): *The Politics of Educators' Work and Lives*. New York: Garland.

Gordon, Peter & Szreter, Richard (eds.) (1989): *History of Education: The Making of a Discipline*. London: Woburn Press.

Gray, John; McPherson, Andrew F. & Raffe, David (1983): *Reconstructions of Secondary Education: Theory, Myth and Practice since the War*. London: Routledge & Kegan Paul.

Green, Andy (1997): *Education, Globalization, and the Nation State*. Basingstoke: Macmillan.

Green, Andy (2002): 'Education, Globalization, and the Role of Comparative Research'. Professorial Lecture. London: Institute of Education, University of London.

Grossman, David; Lee, Wing On & Kennedy, Kerry J. (eds.) (2008): *Citizenship Curriculum in Asia and the Pacific*. CERC Studies in Comparative Education 22, Hong Kong: Comparative Education Research Centre, The University of Hong Kong, and Dordrecht: Springer.

Hamilton, Paul D. (2003): *Historicism*. London: Routledge.

Haskell, Thomas L. (1998): *Objectivity is not Neutrality: Explanatory Schemes in History*. Baltimore: Johns Hopkins University Press.

Hawkins, John N. & Rust, Val D. (2001): 'Shifting Perspectives on Comparative Research: A View from the USA'. *Comparative Education*, Vol.37, No.4, pp.501-506.

Jansen, Jonathan D. (1991): 'The State and Curriculum in the Transition to Socialism: The Zimbabwean Experience'. *Comparative Education Review*, Vol.35, No.1, pp.76-91.

Jennings, Jack F. (ed.) (1995): *National Issues in Education: Elementary and Secondary Education Act*. Washington, DC: Phi Delta Kappa International.

Kallaway, Peter (ed.) (2002): *The History of Education under Apartheid 1948-1994: The Doors of Learning and Culture shall be Opened*. New York: Peter Lang.

Kandel, Isaac Leon (1933): *Studies in Comparative Education*. Boston: Houghton Mifflin.

Kazamias, Andreas M. (1961): 'Some Old and New Approaches to Comparative Education'. *Comparative Education Review*, Vol.5, No.1, pp. 90-96.

Kazamias, Andreas M. (1962): 'History, Science and Comparative Education: A Study in Methodology'. *International Review of Education*, Vol.8, Nos.3-4, pp.383-398.

Kazamias, Andreas M. (2001): 'Re-inventing the Historical in Comparative Education: Reflection on a *Protean Episteme* by a Contemporary Player'. *Comparative Education*, Vol.37, No.4, pp.439-450.

King, Edmund (2000): 'A Century of Evolution in Comparative Education'. *Comparative Education*, Vol.36, No.3, pp.267-278.

Kwo, Ora (ed.) (2010): *Teachers as Learners: Critical Discourse on Challenges and Opportunities*. CERC Studies in Comparative Education 26, Hong Kong: Comparative Education Research Centre, The University of Hong Kong, and Dordrecht: Springer.

Larsen, Marianne A. (2009): 'Comparative Education, Postmodernity and Historical Research: Honouring Ancestors', in Cowen, Robert & Kazamias, Andreas M. (eds.), *International Handbook of Comparative Education*. Dordrecht: Springer, pp.1045-1059.

Lau, Siu-kai (2002): *The First Tung Chee-hwa Administration: The First Five Years of the Hong Kong Special Administration Region*. Hong Kong: The Chinese University Press.

Lorringer, S. (ed.) (1996): *Foucault Live: Collected Interviews 1961-1984*. New York: Semiotexte.

Lowe, Roy (1988): *Education in the Post-War Years: A Social History*. London: Routledge.

Lowe, Roy (1996): 'Postmodernity and Historians of Education: A View from Britain'. *Paedagogica Historica*, Vol.32, No.2, pp.307-323.

Lowe, Roy (ed.) (2000): *History of Education: Major Themes*. London: RoutledgeFalmer.

Maclure, Stuart (1986): *Educational Documents: England and Wales, 1816 to the Present Day*. London: Methuen.

Maringe, F.; Foskett, N. & Woodfield, S. (2013): 'Emerging Internationalisation Models in an Uneven Global Terrain: Findings from a Global

Survey'. *Compare: A Journal of Comparative and International Education*, Vol.42, No.1, pp.9-36.

Martin, Timothy J. (2003): 'Divergent Ontologies with Converging Conclusions: A Case Study Comparison of Comparative Methodologies'. *Comparative Education*, Vol.39, No.1, pp.105-117.

McCulloch, Gary (1994): *Educational Reconstruction: The 1944 Act and the Twenty-first Century*. Ilford, Essex: Woburn Press.

Meyer, John; Kamens, David H. & Benavot, Aaron (1992): *School Knowledge for the Masses: World Models and National Primary Curricular Categories in the Twentieth Century*. London: Falmer Press.

Mok, Ka Ho (ed.) (2003): *Centralization and Decentralization: Educational Reforms and Changing Governance in Chinese Societies*. CERC Studies in Comparative Education 13, Hong Kong: Comparative Education Research Centre, The University of Hong Kong, and Dordrecht: Kluwer Academic Publishers.

Mok, Ka Ho & Welch, Anthony R. (2003): *Globalization and Educational Restructuring in the Asia Pacific Region*. Basingstoke: Palgrave Macmillan.

Morris, Paul; Kan, Flora & Morris, Esther (2001): 'Education, Civic Participation and Identity: Continuity and Change in Hong Kong', in Bray, Mark & Lee, W.O. (eds.), *Education and Political Transition: Themes and Experiences in East Asia*. CERC Studies in Comparative Education 1, 2nd edition, Hong Kong: Comparative Education Research Centre, The University of Hong Kong, pp.163-181.

Nakajima, Nanjiro (1916): *Comparative Study of National Education in Germany, France, Britain and the USA*. Tokyo: Kyouiku-shicho Kenkyukai. [in Japanese]

Namier, Lewis B. (1957): *The Structure of Politics at the Accession of George III*. London: Macmillan.

Ninnes, Peter & Burnett, Greg (2003): 'Comparative Education Research: Poststructuralist Possibilities'. *Comparative Education*, Vol.39, No.3, pp.279-297.

Noah, Harold J. & Eckstein, Max A. (1998): *Doing Comparative Education: Three Decades of Collaboration*. CERC Studies in Comparative Education 5, Hong Kong: Comparative Education Research Centre, The University of Hong Kong.

Nóvoa, Antonio & Yariv-Mashal, Tali (2003): 'Comparative Research in Education: A Mode of Governance or a Historical Journey?'. *Comparative Education*, Vol.39, No.4, pp.423-438.

Pennycook, Alastair (1998): *English and the Discourses of Colonialism*. London: Routledge.

Phillips, David (1994): 'Periodisation in Historical Approaches'. *British Journal of Educational Studies*, Vol.42, No.3, pp.261-272.

Phillips, David (2002): 'Comparative Historical Studies in Education: Problems of Periodisation Reconsidered'. *British Journal of Educational Studies*, Vol. 50, No.3, pp.363-377.

Popkewitz, Thomas S. (1994): 'Professionalization in Teaching and Teacher Education: Some Notes on its History, Ideology, and Potential'. *Teaching and Teacher Education*, Vol.10, No.1, pp.1-14.

Popkewitz, Thomas S.; Franklin, Barry M. & Pereyra, Miguel A. (eds.) (2001): *Cultural History and Education: Critical Essays on Knowledge and Schooling*. New York: RoutledgeFalmer.

Reynolds, David (1998): 'Schooling for Literacy: A Review of Research on Teacher Effectiveness and School Effectiveness and its Implications for Contemporary Educational Policies'. *Educational Review*, Vol.50, No.2, pp.147-162.

Roberts, Clayton (1995): *The Logic of Historical Explanation*. University Park: Pennsylvania State University Press.

Robertson, Susan (2012): 'Placing Teachers in Global Governance Agendas'. *Comparative Education Review*, Vol.56, No.4, pp.584-607.

Rusen, Jörn (1987): 'The Didactics of History in West Germany: Towards a New Self-consciousness in Historical Studies'. *History and Theory*, Vol.26, No.3, pp.275-286.

Rusk, Robert R. (1969): *The Doctrines of the Great Educators*. London, Macmillan.

Rust, Val D.; Soumaré, Aminata; Pescador, Octavio & Shibuya, Megumi (1999): 'Research Strategies in Comparative Education'. *Comparative Education Review*, Vol.43, No.1, pp.86-109.

Sadler, Sir Michael (1900): 'How Can we Learn Anything of Practical Value from the Study of Foreign Systems of Education?'. Reprinted 1964 in *Comparative Education Review*, Vol.7, No.3, pp.307-314.

Sharma-Brymer, Vinathe (2009): 'Reflecting on Postcolonialism and Education: Tensions and Dilemmas of an Insider', in Cowen, Robert & Kazamias, Andreas M. (eds.), *International Handbook of Comparative Education*. Dordrecht: Springer, pp.655-668.

Silver, Harold (1977): *The Concept of Popular Education: A Study of Ideas and Social Movements in the Early Nineteenth Century*. London: Methuen.

Simon, Brian (1970): *The Two Nations and the Educational Structure, 1780-1870*. London: Lawrence & Wishart.

Stromquist, Nelly P. (1990): 'Gender Inequality in Education: Accounting for Women's Insubordination'. *British Journal of Sociology of Education*, Vol.11, No.2, pp.137-153.

Sweeting, Anthony (1989): 'Snapshots from the Social History of Education in Hong Kong: An Alternative to Macro-mania'. *Education Research and Perspectives*, Vol.16, No.1, pp.3-12.

Sweeting, Anthony (1990): *Education in Hong Kong pre-1841 to 1941: Fact and Opinion – Materials for a History of Education in Hong Kong*. Hong Kong, Hong Kong University Press.

Sweeting, Anthony (1993): *A Phoenix Transformed: The Reconstruction of Education in Post-war Hong Kong*. Hong Kong: Oxford University Press.

Sweeting, Anthony (1998a): 'Teacher Education at Hongkong University: A Brief History (Part 1: 1917-1951)'. *Curriculum Forum*, Vol.7, No.2, pp.1-44.

Sweeting, Anthony (1998b): 'Teacher Education at the University of Hong Kong, A Brief History (Part 2: 1951 - circa 1976)'. *Curriculum Forum*, Vol.8, No.1, pp.1-32.

Sweeting, Anthony (1999): 'Teacher Education at the University of Hong Kong, a Brief History (Part 3: circa 1976 - circa 1998)'. *Curriculum Forum*, Vol.9, No.1, pp.1-44.

Sweeting, Anthony (2001): 'Doing Comparative Historical Education Research: Problems and Issues from and about Hong Kong', in Watson, Keith (ed.), *Doing Comparative Education Research: Issues and Problems*. Oxford: Symposium Books, pp.225-243.

Sweeting, Anthony (2002): 'Training Teachers: Processes, Products, and Purposes', in Chan Lau, Kit-ching & Cunich, Peter (eds.), *An Impossible Dream: Hong Kong University from Foundation to Re-establishment, 1910-1950*. Hong Kong: Oxford University Press, pp.65-97.

Sweeting, Anthony (2004): *Education in Hong Kong 1941-2001: Visions and Revisions*. Hong Kong: Hong Kong University Press.

Sze, Wai-ting (1990): 'The Cat and the Pigeons: relations between the Hong Kong Government and the Universities, in Anthony Sweeting (ed.), *Differences and Identities: educational argument in late twentieth century Hong Kong*. Hong Kong: Education Papers 9, Faculty of Education, the University of Hong Kong, pp.127-159.

Tikly, Leon (1999): 'Postcolonialism and Comparative Education'. *International Review of Education*, Vol.45, Nos.5-6, pp.603-621.

Townsend, Tony (1996): 'School Effectiveness and Improvement Initiatives and the Restructuring of Education in Australia'. *School Effectiveness and School Improvement*, Vol.7, No.2, pp.114-132.

Urban, Wayne J. (ed.) (1999): *Essays in Twentieth-Century Southern Education: Exceptionalism and its Limits*. New York: Garland.

von Borries, Bodo (1994): '(Re-)Constructing History and Moral Judgment: On Relationships between Interpretations of the Past and Perceptions of the Present', in Carretero, Mario & Voss, James F. (eds.), *Cognitive and Instructional Processes in History and the Social Sciences*. London: Lawrence Erlbaum, pp.339-355.

Wallerstein, Immanuel (1974): *The Modern World System: Capitalist Agriculture and the Origins of the European World Economy in the Sixteenth Century*. London: Academic Press.

Walsh, W.H. (1967): *An Introduction to Philosophy of History*. London: Hutchinson.

Watson, Keith (1998): 'Memories, Models and Mapping: The Impact of Geopolitical Changes on Comparative Studies of Education'. *Compare: A Journal of Comparative Education*, Vol.28, No.1, pp.5-31.

Watson, Keith (ed.) (2001): *Doing Comparative Education Research: Issues and Problems*. Oxford: Symposium Books.

Watts, Ruth (1998a): 'From Lady Teacher to Professional: A Case Study of Some of the First Headteachers of Girls' Schools in England'. *Educational Management and Administration*, Vol.26, No.4, pp.339-351.

Watts, Ruth (1998b): *Gender, Power and the Unitarians in England 1760-1860*. London: Longman.

Wegner, Gregory P. (2002): *Anti-Semitism and Schooling under the Third Reich*. New York: RoutledgeFalmer.

Westlund, Erik (2007): 'Time and Comparative and International Education'. *Research in Comparative and International Education*, Vol.2, No.2, pp.144-153.

Wilson, David M. (2003): 'The Future of Comparative and International Education in a Globalised World', in Bray, Mark (ed.), *Comparative Education: Continuing Traditions, New Challenges, and New Paradigms*. Dordrecht: Kluwer Academic Publishers, pp.15-33.

7

Comparing Race, Class and Gender

Liz JACKSON

As Mark Mason writes in this volume (p.253), "comparative educational research yields the most worthwhile results, from an ethical perspective at least, when researchers attempt, from the very conceptualisation of their projects, to identify the axes along which educational and other goods are differentially distributed, and to disaggregate their object of study along those axes".

Among the axes of educational inequality, race, class and gender are three of the most important, impacting on individual access and achievement across diverse societies. As such, these three factors arguably deserve more focus in comparative education research than they commonly receive. Definitions and significance of race, class and gender vary over time, however, and from one place to another. As subjective factors related to *identity* – another fluid concept – they can rarely be seen as functioning independently of one another, but are instead relational in their effects on educational access and equity. This chapter explores ways that race, class and gender can be investigated in comparative education research.

Race

When geographically separate groups encounter each other, their observations almost invariably focus on differences between themselves and the *others*. In such contexts, race and ethnicity are major categories for conceiving these differences (along with culture, discussed in this volume in Chapter 8). This section examines meanings of race and ethnicity, and the challenges that these concepts pose for comparative education research.

Race and Ethnicity: Fluid Conceptions
Racial classifications of humankind emerged in the 1600s (Keevak 2011). Attention focused on perceived physical and intellectual differences across groups, likening race to specie, under *essentialist racism*: "the belief that there are *essential* qualitative, biological differences between different races" (Kincheloe & Steinberg 1997, p.170). Western Europeans continually tested, defined and redefined these conceptions from the 17th to 20th centuries. Although they considered their research rigorous and objective, their studies enabled unequal treatment of individuals within and across societies, as most of their race categorisations were hierarchical (Keevak 2011). Social Darwinism in the late 19th and early 20th centuries depicted racial groups as evolving in parallel on one playing field, with 'whites' overtaking 'black', 'red', 'yellow' and 'brown' groups. Such racial lenses fuelled ghastly events across the world: Jim Crow Laws and eugenics in the United States, the Holocaust in Germany, and Apartheid in South Africa.

The question of the science of race re-emerges from time to time. As recently as 2006, the United States Food and Drug Administration approved a drug "designed for African Americans", supporting the idea of biological race (Takezawa 2011, p.13). However, since the mid-20th century, social scientists have increasingly portrayed race as a *social construction* rather than a biological trait. From a historical and cross-cultural viewpoint, it is hard to deny that race is socially constructed, given the myriad definitions of it across time and place. For instance, to be 'black' or 'coloured' in early United States history meant to have 'one drop' of 'black blood' – any semblance of African descent; while in Apartheid South Africa, blackness was defined *exclusively*, with 'one drop' of 'white blood' – any 'white' characteristics – marking a person as 'coloured', distinct therefore from 'black'. Early on, Europeans described Asians as "white, like ourselves", casting Asians as 'yellow' only after racial categorisations became popular in the late 1600s (Keevak 2011).

Against this backdrop, some people argue that race should no longer be treated as a serious category by researchers, particularly in the social sciences, or that researchers should strive to be 'colour blind'. Ravitch (1990, p.342), for example, has argued that:

No serious scholar would claim that all Europeans and white Americans are part of the same culture, or that all Asians are part of the same culture.... Any categorization this broad is essentially meaningless and useless.

Because individual identity is fluid, impacted by many factors beyond race (such as gender, religion, and even height and weight), some find race-related thought undesirable or even repulsive. In this context, Omi and Winant (1993) observed that it is "*conservatives* who argue that race is an illusion" (p.7), though some on the political left also challenge the use of racial thinking to defend or empower groups, such as in affirmative action programs for African Americans (Parekh 2000; McCarthy 2003).

Others argue that race continues to matter as a factor impacting on individual opportunity, despite awareness of its social construction. Critical race theorists elaborate *institutional racism* as a hurdle to equality and equity across societies even where *essential racism* among individuals appears rare, recognising the "continuing significance and changing meaning" of race in people's lives (Omi & Winant 1993, p.7). There is a kind of networking effect, as Kincheloe and Steinberg (1997, p.174) observed:

> Most institutions develop informal cultural practices that are internalized by their members. Such institutional cultures are diverse in their expression and specific to particular organizations; but they do tend to be white.... The organization "thinks" and carries on its business in a white manner. White people via their cultural experiences are perceived to be better suited for inclusion in these cultures, though class and gender issues obviously affect dimensions of "suitability" as well.

Others speak of an "invisible knapsack" of privileges that those cast as white in a society possess: benefits they receive from race, despite *de jure* racial equality. McIntosh (1990) listed numerous challenges of daily life rarely encountered by white people: from not being harassed while shopping for jewellery, to finding bandages that match skin colour. Personal experience (hooks 1994; Ladson-Billings 1998), representational analysis (McCarthy 2003; Takezawa 2011), and statistical data (Hacker 2003) suggest that race impacts life experiences and opportunities from birth. It can result in unequal treatment in various areas of social life, and therefore is an important factor in inequality, despite its socially constructed and fluid status.

In contexts where institutional racism seems to have replaced individual racism, Leonardo (2004, p.125) described *postmodern racism* as the sense of discomfort and inability of white people to engage with racial boundaries, given their "fragmented understanding of the world as it is racially structured" (see also Jackson 2009).

In a related way, Foster (1999) described *epistemological racism* in educational research, which stems from the fact that, "the social and behavioral science on which educational research has traditionally rested has been grounded in psychology, a field that has measured persons of color, women, and those from working class against a standard of White middle-class males" (pp.78-79). In her view, such epistemological racism plagues contemporary social science research, challenging scholars of colour constantly to defend their methods, while networking effects and related factors have kept their numbers low in academia in general.

Given this tense historical foundation and the controversial nature of identity politics, race discourse itself is taboo in some places. As Hollinger (2005, pp.225-226) observed:

> Almost everyone agrees that races do not exist in the sense so long assumed – biological entities carrying vastly different potentials for intelligence and social behavior, justifying the invidious treatment of inferior races – and almost everyone agrees, further, that the "racializing" of human beings, entailing their being treated differently on account of their perceived marks of descent, continues on a large scale. Yet some say that it is proper to denote as a "race" the people who have been racialized while others say not. To continue to speak of "races" ... perpetuates unintentionally too many of the old racist connotations. Better to speak of "racialized persons" or to diminish the invidiousness of *race* by speaking of *ethnoracial groups*.

Ethnicity approximates the concept of race, while acknowledging "the place of history, language and culture in the construction of subjectivity and identity, as well as the fact that all discourse is placed, positioned, situated, and all knowledge is contextual" (Hall 1995, p.226). Ethnicity has been used in countries such as the United States, where a racial binary of black/white failed to incorporate, include or effectively describe and classify growing populations such as Asians and Latinos.

Like race, ethnic categories change over time. For instance, 'Asian American' is increasingly broken down into categories such as 'East Asian', 'Indian' and 'Pacific Islander'. In the United States today, race, ethnicity and *descent* (as Latino or not Latino) are all currently considered in census data. 'Persons of colour' is also used to describe people not cast as *white* within or across societies, regardless of their racial or ethnic identity, though some feel that this obscures the greater challenges that black people have faced in some societies compared to ethnic minority groups (Hacker 2003). Hollinger favours *ethnoracial*, as it "denotes all descent-defined population groups, recognising that all have properties that sometimes have been called 'ethnic' and 'racial'" (2005, p.228). Leistyna favours "racenicity", to highlight the historical equation of "race and ethnicity within unsubstantiated claims that biological characteristics result in predisposed psychological, intellectual, and social behavior" (2001, p.425).

In other contexts, ethnicity is used similarly to race as the primary categorisation for internal social differences related to geographic, cultural or linguistic descent. As noted by Shih (2002, pp.13, 24), in China "ethnicity is defined in terms of blood, religion, language, and cultural proximity to the Han.... [It] is useful to those in the category to develop responses to their identity specification". Race and ethnicity are similarly conflated in Singapore (Bakar 2009) and Japan (Hirasawa 2009). 'Race' comes up more often in such settings when discussing groups regarded as outsiders to the national community; for instance 'White' and 'Chinese' may be considered as races in Hong Kong, with various ethnicities also held as important to identity among ethnic-Chinese people. In Indonesia, under Dutch colonialism races were given as European, Malay and Chinese; and within the Malay group, ethnicities were ascribed (Kuipers & Yulaelawati 2009, p.451). Today, Chinese Indonesians can also identify themselves as *ethnically* Chinese (Kuipers & Yulaelawati 2009, p.456).

Race, Ethnicity, and Comparative Education Research
In this context, comparative research on education focusing on race or ethnicity can be challenging. The following paragraphs begin with general points before turning to comparison of races across time and across place.

1. *Comparing 'Races'*: For centuries, different racial groups have been compared quantitatively in terms of achievement under 'racist epistemology' to legitimate essentialist racism and white supremacy. As critical race theorists point out, the Scholastic Aptitude Test (SAT), widely used in the United States to measure preparedness for higher education, was

originally modelled after intelligence tests designed "to perpetuate the notion that immigrants and Blacks were intellectually inferior for genetic reasons" (Roithmayr 1998, p.403). The creator of the SAT, Carl Brigham, believed that such tests should be used to justify restricting immigration and regulating reproduction by race in the United States.

In 1994, Herrnstein and Murray published *The Bell Curve*, which again suggested that intelligence was race-based. This book has been criticised (Kincheloe & Steinberg 1997, p.185) for discounting some factors related to race and uneven academic achievement, including family background and socioeconomic status, home environment and educational experience:

> One of the most important distortions of *The Bell Curve* involves the authors' analysis of the Minnesota Transracial Adoption Study, in which 100 children from varying ethnic backgrounds were adopted by white parents.... By the time the adoptees were sixteen, researchers Sandra Scarr and Richard Weinberg discovered that the non-white children's IQ scores had dropped an average of 17 points to 89. After analysing the situation, Scarr and Weinberg concluded that racial prejudice and discrimination at school had effected the 17-point decline.... [Yet] Herrnstein and Murray maintain that [the study] revealed little environmental impact on cognitive ability. Racial heredity, they maintain, determines a rank ordering of IQ that will become more pronounced as the adoptees grow older.

Though Herrnstein and Murray encountered much criticism for their interpretation of these results, the impact of genetic versus environmental factors on intelligence remains controversial and contested today.

Educational achievement is also compared by racial categories in quantitative research which aims to document institutional racism, tracking racialisation as a factor related to educational equity. The unequal distribution of educational resources across race lines is one point of comparison. Much research compares government and/or other spending on schools predominantly attended by different racialised groups within a society, considering educational finance important to achievement. Meek and Meek's (2008) study of South Africa compared per capita expenditure on education by race before and during Apartheid (pp.509, 519). They found that although public officials had claimed that education would increase equal opportunity in society, for most of the 20th century expenditure on schooling for Black South Africans was a small fraction of that provided for the minority Whites. Similarly, critical race theorists in the United States consider how "school funding is a function of institutional and structural racism," as schools are funded by property taxes in that country, within a historical context of racial oppression and race-based residential segregation (Ladson-Billings 1998, p.62).

UNESCO's World Inequality Database on Education (WIDE) offers data of educational achievement by ethnicity (among other indicators) in over 60 countries (UNESCO 2013). WIDE also makes it possible to understand how factors interrelate, permitting for instance examination of ethnicity alongside wealth, gender and region. Comparing such data can help researchers and policy makers to understand how ethnicity factors into educational opportunity and achievement.

Given the challenges to understanding the relationship between factors in this complex field, ethnographic approaches to comparing race focus on contextual issues impacting on educational equity. Heath's (1983) foundational study tracked children's school- and community-based language learning across two racially divided communities in the United States, showing how unequal access to resources such as books and different styles of communication at home influenced teacher effectiveness and the achievements of individual learners. Other ethnographic research in the United States has suggested that "current instructional strategies presume that African American students are deficient", often seen by white teachers as problems (Ladson-Billings 1998, p.61). However, the choice of focus can be contentious since the idea of the neutral, objective researcher may be challenged. For instance Villegas (1988, p.253) argued that focus on teachers' practices diverts attention from structural inequalities such as unequal distribution of educational resources across communities.

Additionally, the relationship of race and racism to educational achievement among other factors, such as gender and class, can be difficult to uncover. For example, Lamontagne's (1999) study of minority education in China found that gender disparities in China varied substantially by territory and ethnicity, such that race at the individual level often mattered less than gender. Thus, individuals' educational experiences are not necessarily similar within racial or ethnic groups.

2. *Comparing Race across Time*: Many studies compare educational achievements by race over time, particularly to measure outcomes of educational interventions for increasing equality. WIDE offers data on ethnicity over

three time periods (UNESCO 2013). However, caution is needed when conducting large-scale comparison over time, because racial and ethnic definitions can vary even at one site. Additionally, data are often scant. For example, many US states stopped tracking racial data in education after the 1954 *Brown versus Board of Education* lawsuit (Boozer et al. 1992). As observed in Sweeting's chapter on comparing times in this volume, synchronic analyses can capture before/after situations, but causal relationships – for instance, between educational interventions and outcomes – may be difficult to determine.

3. *Comparing Race across Place*: Though race and ethnicity undoubtedly impact on educational equality and equity around the world, comparing racial and ethnic-identity groups across countries is difficult. Contemporary definitions and categorisations of race and ethnicity vary in relation to societies' historical and demographic contexts. Though WIDE provides data on ethnicity and educational achievement by country for over 60 countries (UNESCO 2013), ethnic groups are given by country-level categorisations, precluding straightforward international comparisons of ethnic groups. Thus the data can be used to explore educational inequality and ethnicity across countries, but such comparisons should also attend to related factors, such as class and gender. In some countries official data on race or ethnicity and education are not available, such as France, where ethnicity is not recognised as "a valid way of categorizing a population" (Deer 2008, p.337). UNESCO's Education for All (EFA) Global Monitoring Reports (e.g. UNESCO 2012a) do not systematically compare ethnicity and educational equality across societies, though they identify numerous instances where ethnicity is significant in both rich and poor countries.

Comparisons of educational data by race and/or ethnicity across states, provinces, cities or school districts in one country are more common, and can clarify educational issues glossed over in country-level analyses. However, one should not presume that across a country racial or ethnic composition is uniform, or that local histories and political economies are equivalent. Rather, differences between locales should be examined while like groups are compared, to avoid oversimplification of findings. The United States National Opportunity to Learn Campaign (2013) compared how school closures in Chicago, New York City, and Philadelphia impacted on black, Latino and white students, also comparing the percentages of students in these groups with their representa-

tion in the cities overall. Such analyses can elucidate trends and disparities across locations.

Class

All societies have some conception of class or socioeconomic status (SES),
reflective of disparate relationships of individuals to income, wealth and
political-economic opportunity. Nonetheless, as with race, definitions of
class and SES vary by place and time, and in relation to societies'
make-up, economic dynamics and values. While research on the relationships between education and class is increasing in line with social
justice commitments to alleviating child poverty and improving equity,
the socially constructed aspects of class make it difficult to use coherently
across locations and time.

What is Class?

Many theoretical frameworks focus on the nature of class. In one group
are economic and sociological theorists who favour *functional* and *hierarchical* perspectives of class, defining it as natural, necessary financial and
occupational inequality resulting from progress and differentiation
within a capitalist society. Such analyses have traditionally regarded intelligence as naturally distributed unevenly within societies (Malott 2009,
p.285). Two of the best known historical proponents of this orientation,
Smith (1776) and Durkheim (1893), viewed early capitalism as excessive
or unbalanced in its differentiation of highly unequal social classes.
Nonetheless, they still viewed capitalism as the ultimate consequence of
the naturally diverse arrangement of human capital and material resources. Such views of inequality as natural or good are echoed by contemporary neoconservative ideologies which, for example, prioritise de-
creasing public expenditures on education and other social services over
heavily taxing wealthy individuals (Malott 2009, p.288).

Many disagree with this way of framing class, particularly because it
seems to condone the existence of grave inequalities. Marxist theorists
understand class as a "binary relation to the means of production" (Hill et
al. 2008, p.61), recognising two classes within capitalistic (private-
ownership) economic systems: those who own the means of production
(*bourgeoisie*) – factories, equipment, knowledge and so on – and those who
do not (*proletariat*). Within this framework, the need for skilled labour for
factories is highlighted as an original aim of universal education (com-

mon schools) in United States history. Althusser further argued (1971, p.132), that the education system reproduces class by teaching "submission to the ruling ideology for the workers, and ... the ability to manipulate the ruling ideology correctly for the ... ruling class". Within such views, ameliorating capitalism's impact on education is critical for equity.

Many contemporary sociologists of education concerned with the relationship between individuals and resources follow 'second-wave' Marxism, or 'neo-Marxism', broadening the view of class to be constituted by interrelated cultural and material aspects. Within such theories, the relationship between culture and material (economic) resources is complex and difficult to specify, as values assigned to many resources, including money, are socially constructed. Moreover, as Mason writes in this volume (p.227), culture is "not a fixed entity... [but] a dialectical process between people and their social environments", changing over time within communities. Different class-based communities can thus develop distinct orientations and values within a society. In this context, Bourdieu (1968, p.210) described cultural capital as "constellations" of interconnected aesthetic values linked to social status but not explicitly taught in schools or society. Thus, as Kincheloe and Steinberg (1997, p.106) wrote, "economic and occupational location in a social order is one of many factors that help to construct consciousness, perception of others, and relation to power". For example, in some societies teachers are viewed as more professional, and as part of a higher class, than in others. This status impacts on their identity and outlook on life. Given the relationship between identity and class, sociologists examining class often focus on the way that teachers treat students based on class indications, which can in turn help to shape students' behaviour, achievement and sense of self.

In an attempt to disaggregate cultural and ideological factors from economic ones, some favour using 'socioeconomic status' instead of class. Jacob and Holsinger (2008, p.14) distinguished class as an ascribed characteristic, in contrast to socioeconomic status which is fluid and can be changed through individual experiences. Still, socioeconomic status remains hard to define. Occupation, education, income and wealth are four common determinants, but also have complex relationships with each other and with other related factors. Additionally, such a conception of SES is quite dynamic, which can make it difficult to use. For instance, as noted by Grinberg et al. (2009, p.270), when students from middle class backgrounds work their way through college by taking jobs in the fast food industry, the jobs do not make the students working class. An individual's occupation, education, income and wealth may not all fit into a single classification.

Savage et al. (2013, p.28) reconceived class as three-pronged, consisting of:

- economic capital, i.e. income and wealth,
- cultural capital (echoing Bourdieu), i.e. interests and activities, and
- social capital, i.e. the make-up of one's social network.

Using this framing they identified seven social classes in the United Kingdom, including new social formations of the working class which had typically been seen as rather homogenous, stable and relatively immobile.

While useful for understanding how class operates in the United Kingdom, it would be difficult to export this model for international comparisons. As Ali and Dadush (2012) noted, for purposes of comparison most categorisations of class are unhelpful because of variations in socioeconomic and cultural contexts and methodological challenges in gaining accurate data. They proposed car ownership as a possible measure of membership in the middle-class or higher class levels, as "an unambiguous indication of the ability to purchase other luxury goods". However, even this may be an unreliable measure. In Hong Kong, for example, the availability of excellent public transport means that many high-income families choose not to own cars.

In educational research, class or socio-economic status is often conceived in terms of "family background", which focuses on the education, wealth, income, and occupation of parents, number of children, or other aspects related to family structure. Due to complications in labelling people according to these possibly divergent indicators, educational researchers may favour studying one or more of these variables independently – for instance, comparing educational achievement with family income, father's educational background and mother's educational background (see e.g. Hung & Cheng 2008). Alternatively class can be understood in terms of access to a computer at home, or eligibility for free school lunch or reduced tuition fees, though such factors are context-specific.

Two measures developed specifically for studying class in educational research include the index of economic, social and cultural status (ESCS), and the education Gini coefficient. The ESCS is a measure of individual status (OECD 2009, p.49) based upon the highest occupational status of parents from an international socioeconomic index, the highest educational level of parents, and the index of home possessions based on whether students had:

> a desk to study at, a room of their own, a quiet place to study, a computer they can use for school, any educational software, a link to the Internet, their own calculator, classic literature, books of poetry, works of art, books to help with their school work, a dictionary, a dishwasher, a DVD player or VCR, the number of cellular phones, televisions, computers, cars and books at home.

Such data can be difficult to gather, as they require interviews or surveys. A further challenge would lie in weighting items for international comparison.

The education Gini coefficient is based on the original Gini coefficient, which is a commonly-used measure of income distribution and inequality developed in the early 20th century by sociologist Corrado Gini (Burt & Park 2008). The education Gini coefficient is an equation based on distribution of educational attainment and average years of schooling for a population, the proportion of the population with given levels of schooling, and the number of years of schooling at each of the different educational levels. As with the original Gini coefficient, the index can be used to compare *populations* across places and times; but it does not specify the location of inequality within the distribution of the measured variable (Burt & Park 2008, p.264). While many Marxist sociologists of education argue that capitalism creates educational inequality (e.g. Hill et al. 2008; Malott 2009), the education Gini coefficient has been positively correlated with capital/income across countries (Jacob & Holsinger 2009, pp.10-12).

Class and Comparative Education Research
Multiple methods can be used to study class in comparative education, depending on context, units of comparison and research questions. As with the section on race, the following paragraphs begin with general points before turning to comparison of classes across time and across place.

1. *Comparing Classes*: Many studies compare educational equity by class or socioeconomic status within national, regional or local contexts. Depending on the focus for comparison, qualitative, quantitative or hybrid

methods may be preferred. Many qualitative researchers examine social reproduction of inequality through teacher-student interaction in schools. For instance, researchers might compare pedagogical strategies used in one school across classrooms with poor and middle-class students. Indeed, research along these lines has identified that teachers often regard economically disadvantaged students in "cold, impersonal ways" (Kincheloe & Steinberg 1997, p.128). Oakes' (1985) foundational work on tracking (streaming) in education found that often students are socialised differently through their educational experiences in ways echoing Marxist theorists' concerns about education as class reproduction. Curricula can also be examined for overt or subtle messages in textbooks or lessons which suggest particular orientations to social inequality.

Quantitative approaches can compare educational achievements (e.g. years of education or graduation rates) of students of different socio-economic groups. WIDE data enable comparison of educational achievements from the poorest 20% to the wealthiest 20% across different countries (UNESCO 2013), while the OECD (2007) has compared educational achievements with father's educational levels. Such approaches can yield relational data between class and educational equality. However, it can be difficult to decide which measures to use in such quantitative research, as common factors may be proxies for more particular, explanatory data. Thus multilevel or meta-analyses complementing quantitative data with qualitative findings can be included to help substantiate claims. In McInerney's (2010) study of Hong Kong, socioeconomic status, family background and family income were correlated with educational achievement. He used related research to illustrate (p.9) how these were causally related:

> Family income matters in terms of providing access to more expensive, higher-quality secondary schools and to extra tutorial support, enhancing the opportunity of students.... Among the potential liabilities of coming from low socio-economic backgrounds are more limited choice of schools, limited opportunity for private supplementary tutoring, less supervision of study time because parents work long hours, and financial stress that might provide a non-conducive learning environment at home.

2. *Comparing Class across Time*: WIDE and other data can also demonstrate how class factors relate to educational equity within communities or societies over time. However, it can be difficult to identify how changes in

the economy and/or the value of currency or other educational resources interact with class factors in time-based comparison. For instance, although the gap in educational achievements between the poorest and wealthiest 20% within a society may decrease, this would not necessarily indicate that educational achievements have increased. Research in Britain has shown that poorer students were more likely than previously to enter higher education, but that "the likelihood of them doing so relative to their richer peers is actually lower" (Hill et al. 2008, p.77). The policy implications of considering only one of these findings apart from the other could be quite different.

Additionally, definitions of terms such as 'poverty', and classifications of factors, may be fluid over time. Burt and Park's (2008) comparison of the education Gini coefficient over four decades in Korea used different categories for educational achievement based on the data available, which reflected different norms in achievement during the timeframe. For instance, in the 1970s and 1980s categories were "graduated," "not completed" and "never attended", whereas in the 1990s "general high school" and "vocational high school" were split. In 2000, "graduated" was split from "completed", while "graduated master's course", "graduated doctor's course", "dropped out of master's course", and "dropped out of doctor's course", were added (pp.264-265). Deciding how to deal with such shifts should be undertaken carefully with an eye to the research question.

3. *Comparing Class across Place*: Many studies compare education Gini coefficients, or the correlations between educational achievements and class indicators such as ESCS, family background, wealth, etc. in two or more places. The education Gini coefficient has been used to compare inequity across different regions within countries, such as Korea (Burt & Park 2008), and internationally (Jacob & Holsinger 2008; Thomas & Wang 2009). Additionally, it can be correlated to indicators of national wealth such as Gross Domestic Product (Jacob & Holsinger 2009). WIDE data enable comparison across percentiles of wealth across countries, though with such data sets it may be difficult to ensure that the information is accurate, or collected from the same time period. For instance, a 2010 UNESCO report compared educational achievement and wealth across several countries, using data from 2000 for Gabon and from 2007 for the Democratic Republic of Congo (p.140). Such representations better por-

tray broad themes across a wide variety of countries than they reveal the results of inputs or enable direct comparisons.

Gender

Often conflated with *sex*, which is determined by male or female physiological characteristics, *gender* can be defined as "an evolving relationship negotiated among your lived experiences, your context and your feelings about your body" (Airton 2009, p.224). Like race and class, gender is a dynamic social construct: what it means to be a man or women, or boy or girl, varies by context. Furthermore, alternative gender orientations can be found in traditional and modern contexts, which blur, dwell outside and conceptually challenge the traditional gender binary. Nonetheless, in comparison with race and class, gender is relatively easy to use for categorisation in research, as most people see themselves within the binary view of gender. As noted by Airton (2009, pp.223-224), because sex and gender "interact potently with each other as central components of our relationships with ourselves and the world", few educational studies "even define the terms sex, gender, boy, girl, male, female, etc., assuming that the meanings we attach to these words are universal and universally understood".

Historical research shows that gender equality in educational access and achievement improved dramatically in most countries during the 20th century, as the idea of females' general intellectual inferiority, commonplace in earlier time periods, was largely dismissed (Aiston 2010; Jones 2010). However, gender equality remains an official focus of many intergovernmental organisations, as girls' equal access and achievement in education remain far from universal, particularly in developing countries. Some researchers and policy makers approach these issues by focusing on parity in *access*. For example, the third of the United Nations' Millennium Development Goals (MDGs) established in 2000 was to eliminate gender disparity in primary and secondary education. Advocates also push for policies specifying educational rights of girls, because policies aimed at children in general can ignore or block gender equality (Hyer et al. 2008).

Comparative research on parity of educational access can analyse school enrolment or attendance of boys and girls, and societies' relevant rights provisions, policies and laws. For quantitative research, UNESCO's EFA Global Monitoring Reports use (among other measures) the Gender Parity Index (GPI), which indicates the proportions of boys and girls at different levels in education systems. The GPI is useful for comparing different countries, as well as for understanding how gender parity changes over time within a society. Policy analyses can also examine qualitatively how different countries give girls or all children equal rights to education.

However, when considering gender and educational inequality, researchers caution that parity in access does not necessarily lead to equality in terms of outcomes and achievement. As Hyer et al. (2008, p.133) observed:

> According to the MDG standards for gender parity in education, Morocco is doing fairly well with 83% of girls enrolled in primary school and a 0.79-to-1 ratio of men to women in literacy attainment for those between the ages of 15-24…. [Yet] although more and more girls are enrolling in school, few of them actually remain in school.

Likewise, provision of policies and legal rights for girls to access education hardly ensures that they will graduate, or even attend school.

Thus organisations and researchers increasingly focus on *achievement* of boys and girls, alongside parity of access, or in place of it in contexts where parity is stable. The Education for All (EFA) agenda, set in Jomtien, Thailand, in 1990 and renewed in 2000 in Dakar, Senegal (UNESCO 2012b), complemented the MDG by setting the target of "Eliminating gender disparities in primary and secondary education by 2005, and achieving gender equality in education by 2015, with a focus on ensuring girls' full and equal access to and achievement in basic education of good quality" (EFA Goal 5).

Quantitative research examining equality in achievement can compare boys' and girls' educational attainment or graduation rates across one or more schools, cities, regions or countries. Most countries collect data on educational attainment at various levels by gender, and studies sponsored by UNESCO (2010), the OECD (2007) and the Commonwealth (Menefee & Bray 2012) have compared male and female school graduation rates, often alongside attendance rates, by country and region. Studies can also compare achievement over time (e.g. Jones 2010).

Gender equality in achievement across countries or populations can also be compared with the Gender Equality Index (GEI) and Gender Equality in Education Index (GEEI). The GEI "is a composite index measuring gender parity in primary and secondary education and adult literacy" (Unterhalter & Oommen 2008, p.541), thus emphasising educational access as well as an outcome or capability which should result from access. The GEEI, developed in 2006, is more comprehensive, as it is based on girls' net attendance rate at primary school, survival rate over five years in primary schooling, net enrolment ratio in secondary school, and the gender development index (Unterhalter & Oommen 2008, p.543).

Though GEEI inputs can be weighted differently depending on the research context, the GEEI has been criticised for not capturing retention throughout primary school, which remains a significant problem in some African countries. Further, both the GEI and the GEEI are limited in their ability to depict the situation of girls and women in the most disadvantaged communities across societies, as girls' educational access and attainment can differ by socioeconomic status and across racial or ethnic lines. Indeed, gender can be seen as socially constructed differently across racial and class divides within a society in ways that make a difference for education (hooks 1994; Sewell 2004; Kincheloe & Steinberg 2009). Thus many see it as unhelpful to focus on girls and boys as simple groups, as these categories can mask a great deal of internal diversity in educational experiences. WIDE is useful here, as it includes primary school completion as an indicator, and compares outcomes by wealth, ethnicity and gender across countries. Concerning EFA Goal 5, for example, UNESCO (2013) has stated on the basis of WIDE data that in 10 countries 90% of the poorest young women have not completed primary school.

Qualitative research is also helpful for comparing experiences of different groups within a society – boys with girls, girls with girls, etc. – and for elaborating the extent to which girls in diverse societies equally receive 'good quality' education (as specified by the EFA agenda), in addition to their physical attendance in school. Ethnographic research comparing boys' and girls' experiences in education in a variety of contexts shows how schools socialise students to gender norms, just as they socialise them to participate in society generally, in ways that can impact on what girls (and boys) learn and the competencies they achieve. For instance, educators tolerating rowdiness among boys more than girls can stifle girls' development of assertive communication, while complimenting girls' writing more than their numeracy can discourage their engagement in mathematics, despite their possible interest or potential. Gordon et al. (2000) examined lessons and interviewed teachers and students about school practices regarding gender in London and Helsinki. They wrote (p.193) that:

> Gendered processes [in the research schools] largely followed the well known patterns that previous research has demonstrated: in general boys were at the centre of teachers' gaze and observation more often than girls, and teachers interacted more with boys than with girls [though] teachers made a conscious effort … to treat girls and boys in the same manner.

As with similar studies examining education and race or class, such ethnographic research can detail how individuals experience education differently due to gender, and can also focus more narrowly on experiences of students by gender, class and race/ethnicity. For instance Muravyeva (2010) compared the treatment of Russian women of different ethnicities and social origins in European universities in the late-19th century to highlight the diverse challenges faced by Russian women.

Other research examines the 'hidden curricula' of gender, such as observable background knowledge and attitudes that children and educators bring to school environments often unwittingly, which can impart unintentional lessons. For instance, in a study of children's independent play in United States schools, Thorne (1993) observed that boys and girls commonly taught each other gender norms without adult guidance and despite alternative messages from parents or teachers. Such research on children's background knowledge has led to questions on the role of popular and consumer culture in teaching about gender, as marketing to children is now commonplace in many societies (Stone 2000).

Qualitative research can also compare the nature and production of representations of gender (in images and text) in curriculum and school resources such as textbooks, which can be seen as a reflection of commonly accepted attitudes and educators' background knowledge. For example, textbook editors in Taiwan have expressed discomfort with the idea of including non-traditional gender roles in curricular materials (Peng & Huang 2012). Similarly, females have been much less visible than males in Iranian textbooks, and usually portrayed in subservient positions (Kheiltash & Rust 2008). While such findings may not reveal a causal relation between representation and educational inequality, they can illuminate informal lessons about gender that young people may experience through schooling.

Final Thoughts on Race, Class and Gender

As indicated, structural inequalities shape educational opportunities by race and ethnicity in relation to factors such as educator and societal prejudice, networking effects, the 'invisible knapsack' and so on. Class also impacts on educational equity, as youth have differential advantages and disadvantages related to family background and income, both of which have a clear facilitative role in enabling student educational achievement across societies. Finally, gender may structure educational expectations across diverse societies, barring girls' access to education, socialising boys and girls differently, and influencing trends in women's and men's educational attainment.

Race, class and gender have here mostly been discussed separately, to expose challenges for focus on any one of these categories. Yet, as noted by Kincheloe and Steinberg (2009, p.6), "educators should understand not only the dynamics of race, class, and gender but the ways their intersections in the lived world produce tensions, contradictions, and discontinuities in everyday lives". The significance of race, class and gender are highly dependent on social context, as are the ways that each impacts on the others.

Without considering the particular ways that race, class and gender interact in specific contexts, is it difficult to understand and ameliorate educational inequality. For example, 'affirmative action' enabling more equal higher education admission of prepared candidates by race as a means to reduce African American disadvantage in the United States has been described by many commentators as a failure, because most people who have gained from such programmes have been in the wealthiest groups (Jackson 2008). Although some socioeconomically disadvantaged African Americans have gained greater access to university entrance through such programmes, substantial numbers within this group have failed to attain their degrees due to disadvantages in preparedness and/or means to continued success, which come with class inequality rather than racial inequality. Without attention to the relationships between race and class, such policies and programmes are unlikely to succeed.

Likewise, research which focuses on gender can easily obscure important dynamics influencing girls' educational access due to race and class. In such complex territory, it is useful to ask how findings across gender reflect or obscure the importance of race and class – going beyond a simple understanding to yield effective educational findings and directions. Furthermore, as Fairbrother cautions in his chapter in this volume (p.77), "effort must be made to become conscious of … biases and to question one's own assumptions while trying to understand the assumptions underlying the societies and cultures which are the targets of research". Women of colour commonly observe that white women conceive of gender in ways which exclude the experiences of women of colour (hooks 1994). This observation again highlights the intertwining of variables.

In summary, although race, class and gender are three of the most significant social categories underpinning educational inequality and inequity across world regions, their complex interplay, dynamic meanings, and structural nature make them difficult to use in comparative education. Race and class are challenging to categorise and thus to analyse effectively across different social contexts; and while genders are easier to compare, they also are constructed differently within race, class and other categories of difference within societies. This feature means that 'women' cannot be viewed as a homogenous group even within one school or community. Furthermore, race, class and gender can impact on each other in ways that obstruct generalisability, creating new hurdles for researchers seeking answers to large-scale or global questions related to educational equality.

This chapter began with Mason's statement that "comparative educational research yields the most worthwhile results, from an ethical perspective at least, when researchers attempt, from the very conceptualisation of their projects, to identify the axes along which educational and other goods are differentially distributed, and to disaggregate their object of study along those axes". Comparative research on race, class and gender (and other personal identity characteristics, such as ability, religion and language) has a challenging task to compare categories within and across often-diverse schools and societies, without framing categories used as homogenous social groups (e.g. 'boys' and 'girls'). Conceiving comparative education, as Mason does (p.253), "as a critical social science, incorporating an emancipatory interest focused on the distribution of power and its associated attributes", comparative researchers should continually query the meanings and significance of race, class and gender as distinct but qualitatively compounding factors shaping individual access and achievement. They should compare contexts as well as social groups, to illustrate rather than obscure the difference that these factors can make in shaping people's lives.

References

Airton, Liz (2009): 'Untangling "Gender Diversity": Genderism and Its Discontents (i.e., Everyone)', in Steinberg, Shirley R. (ed.), *Diversity and Multiculturalism: A Reader*. New York: Peter Lang, pp.223-246.

Aiston, Sarah Jane (2010): 'Women, Education, and Agency, 1600-2000: An Historical Perspective', in Spence, Jean; Aiston, Sarah J. & Meikle, Maureen M. (eds.), *Women, Education, and Agency, 1600-2000*. London: Routledge, pp.1-8.

Ali, Shimel Se & Dadush, Uri (2012): 'The Global Middle Class is Bigger than we Thought: A New Way of Measuring Prosperity has Enormous Implications for Geopolitics and Economics'. *Foreign Policy*, 24 May.

Althusser, Louis (1971): *Lenin and Philosophy, and Other Essays*, trans. Ben Brewster. London: New Left Books.

Bakar, Mukhlis Abu (2009): 'Islamic Religious Education and Muslim Religiosity in Singapore', in Banks, James A. (ed.), *The Routledge International Companion to Multicultural Education*. New York: Routledge, pp.437-448.

Boozer, Michael A.; Krueger, Alan B. & Wolkon, Shari (1992): *Race and School Quality since Brown vs. Board of Education*. Princeton: Princeton University Press.

Bourdieu, Pierre (1968): 'Outline of a Theory of Art Perception'. *International Social Science Journal*, Vol.2, No.4, pp.589-612.

Burt, Matthew E. & Park, Namgi (2008): 'Education Inequality in the Republic of Korea: Measurement and Causes', in Holsinger, Donald B. & Jacob, W. James (eds.), *Inequality in Education: Comparative and International Perspectives*. CERC Studies in Comparative Education 24, Hong Kong: Comparative Education Research Centre, The University of Hong Kong, and Dordrecht: Springer, pp.261-289.

Deer, Cecile (2008): 'Different Paths, Similar Effects: Persistent Inequalities and Their Sources in European Higher Education', in Holsinger, Donald B. & Jacob, W. James (eds.), *Inequality in Education: Comparative and International Perspectives*. CERC Studies in Comparative Education 24, Hong Kong: Comparative Education Research Centre, The University of Hong Kong, and Dordrecht: Springer, pp.324-347.

Durkheim, Emile (1893/1984): *The Division of Labor in Society*, trans. Steven Lukes. New York: Free Press.

Foster, Michele (1999): 'Race, Class, and Gender in Education Research: Surveying the Political Terrain'. *Educational Policy*, Vol.13, No.1, pp. 77-85.

Gordon, Tuula; Holland, Janet & Lahelma, Elina (2000): 'From Pupil to Citizen: A Gendered Route', in Arnot, Madeleine, & Dillabough, Jo-Anne (eds.), *Challenging Democracy: International Perspectives on Gender, Education and Citizenship*. London: RoutledgeFalmer, pp. 187-202.

Grinberg, J.; Price, J. & Naiditch, F. (2009): 'Schooling and Social Class', in Steinberg, Shirley R. (ed.), *Diversity and Multiculturalism: A Reader*. New York: Peter Lang, pp.265-278.

Hacker, Andrew (2003): *Two Nations: Black and White, Separate, Hostile, Unequal*. New York: Scribner.

Hall, Stuart (1995): 'New Ethnicities', in Ashcroft, Bill; Griffiths, Gareth & Tiffin, Helen (eds.), *The Post-Colonial Studies Reader*. New York: Routledge, pp.223-227.

Heath, Shirley B. (1983): *Ways with Words: Language, Life, and Work in Communities and Classrooms*. Cambridge: Cambridge University Press.

Herrnstein, Richard J. & Murray, Charles (1994): *The Bell Curve: Intelligence and Class Structure in American Life*. New York: Free Press.

Hill, David; Greaves, Nigel M. & Maisuria, Alpesh (2008): 'Does Capitalism Inevitably Increase Inequality?', in Holsinger, Donald B. & Jacob, W. James (eds.), *Inequality in Education: Comparative and International Perspectives*. CERC Studies in Comparative Education 24, Hong Kong: Comparative Education Research Centre, The University of Hong Kong, and Dordrecht: Springer, pp.59-85.

Hirasawa, Yasumasa (2009): 'Multicultural Education in Japan', in Banks, James A. (ed.), *The Routledge International Companion to Multicultural Education*. New York: Routledge, pp.159-170.

Hollinger, David A. (2005): *Postethnic America: Beyond Multiculturalism*. New York: Perseus.

hooks, bell (1994): *Teaching to Transgress: Education as the Practice of Freedom*. New York: Routledge.

Hung, Chih-Cheng & Cheng, Sheng-Yao (2008): 'Access and Equity: Who Are the Students at Taiwan's Top Universities?', in Holsinger, Donald B. & Jacob, W. James (eds.), *Inequality in Education: Comparative and International Perspectives*. CERC Studies in Comparative Education 24, Hong Kong: Comparative Education Research Centre, The University of Hong Kong, and Dordrecht: Springer, pp.290-306.

Hyer, Karen E.; Ballif-Spanvill, Bonnie; Peters, Susan J.; Solomon, Yodit; Thomas, Heather & Ward, Carol (2008): 'Gender Inequalities in Educational Participation', in Holsinger, Donald B. & Jacob, W. James (eds.), *Inequality in Education: Comparative and International Perspectives*. CERC Studies in Comparative Education 24, Hong Kong: Comparative Education Research Centre, The University of Hong Kong, and Dordrecht: Springer, pp.128-148.

Jackson, Liz (2008): 'Reconsidering Affirmative Action in Education as a Good for the Disadvantaged'. *Journal of Critical Educational Policy Studies*, Vol.6, No.1, pp.379-397.

Jackson, Liz (2009): 'Reevaluating White Privileged Ignorance and Its Implications for Antiracist Education', in Glass, Ronald (ed.), *Philosophy of Education 2008*. Urbana, Illinois: Philosophy of Education Society, pp.301-304.

Jacob, W. James & Holsinger, Donald B. (2008): 'Inequality in Education: A Critical Analysis', in Holsinger, Donald B. & Jacob, W. James (eds.), *Inequality in Education: Comparative and International Perspectives*. CERC Studies in Comparative Education 24, Hong Kong: Comparative Education Research Centre, The University of Hong Kong, and Dordrecht: Springer, pp.1-33.

Jones, Claire (2010): 'Femininity and Mathematics at Cambridge Circa 1900', in Spence, Jean; Aiston, Sarah J. & Meikle, Maureen M. (eds.), *Women, Education, and Agency, 1600-2000*. London: Routledge.

Keevak, Michael (2011): *Becoming Yellow: A Short History of Racial Thinking*. Princeton: Princeton University Press.

Kincheloe, Joe L. & Steinberg, Shirley R. (1997): *Changing Multiculturalism*. Buckingham: Open University Press.

Kincheloe, Joe L. & Steinberg, Shirley R. (2009): 'Smoke and Mirrors: More than One Way to be Diverse and Multicultural', in Steinberg, Shirley R. (ed.), *Diversity and Multiculturalism: A Reader*. New York: Peter Lang, pp.3-22.

Kheiltash, Omid & Rust, Val D. (2008): 'Inequalities in Iranian Education: Representations of Gender, Socioeconomic Status, Ethnic Diversity, and Religious Diversity in School Textbooks and Curricula', in Holsinger, Donald B. & Jacob, W. James (eds.), *Inequality in Education: Comparative and International Perspectives*. CERC Studies in Comparative Education 24, Hong Kong: Comparative Education Research Centre, The University of Hong Kong, and Dordrecht: Springer, pp.392-416.

Kuipers, Joel C. & Yulaelawati, Ella (2009): 'Religion, Ethnicity, and Identity in Indonesian Education', in Banks, James A. (ed.), *The Routledge International Companion to Multicultural Education*. New York: Routledge, pp.449-460.

Ladson-Billings, Gloria (1998): 'Just What is Critical Race Theory and What's it Doing in a *Nice* Field Like Education?'. *International Journal of Qualitative Studies in Education*, Vol.11, No.1, pp.7-24.

Lamontagne, Jacques (1999): 'National Minority Education in China: A Nationwide Survey Across Counties', in Postiglione, Gerard A. (ed.), *China's National Minority Education: Culture, Schooling, and Development*. New York: Falmer.

Leonardo, Zeus (2004): 'The Souls of White Folk: Critical Pedagogy, Whiteness Studies, and Globalization Discourse', in Gillborn, David & Ladson-Billings, Gloria (eds.), *The RoutledgeFalmer Reader in Multicultural Education*. London: RoutledgeFalmer, pp.117-136.

Leistyna, Pepi (2001): 'Racenicity: Understanding Racialized Ethnic Identities', in Steinberg, Shirley R. (ed.), *Multi/Intercultural Conversations: A Reader*. New York : Peter Lang, pp.423-462.

Malott, Curry S. (2009): 'An Introduction to Social Class and the Division of Labor', in Steinberg, Shirley R. (ed.), *Diversity and Multiculturalism: A Reader*. New York: Peter Lang, pp.279-296.

McCarthy, Cameron (2003). 'After the Canon: Knowledge and Ideological Representation in the Multicultural Discourse on Curriculum Reform', in McCarthy, Cameron & Crichlow, Walter (eds.), *Race, Identity, and Representation in Education*. New York: Routledge.

McInerney, Dennis M. (2010): *The Role of Sociocultural Factors in Shaping Student Engagement in Hong Kong: An Ethnic Minority Perspective*. Hong Kong: Hong Kong Institute of Education.

McIntosh, Peggy (1990). 'White Privilege: Unpacking the Invisible Knapsack'. *Independent School*, Winter, pp.31-36.

Meek, Christopher B. & Meek, Joshua Y. (2008): 'The History and Devolution of Education in South Africa', in Holsinger, Donald B. & Jacob, W. James (eds.), *Inequality in Education: Comparative and International Perspectives*. CERC Studies in Comparative Education 24, Hong Kong: Comparative Education Research Centre, The University of Hong Kong, and Dordrecht: Springer, pp.506-537.

Menefee, Trey & Bray, Mark (2012): *Education in the Commonwealth: Towards and Beyond the Internationally Agreed Goals*. London: The Commonwealth Secretariat.

Muravyeva, Marianna (2010): 'Russian Women in European Universities, 1864-1900', in Spence, Jean; Aiston, Sarah J. & Meikle, Maureen M. (eds.), *Women, Education, and Agency, 1600-2000*. London: Routledge, pp.83-104.

Oakes, Jeannie (1985): *Keeping Track: How Schools Structure Inequality*. New Haven: Yale University Press.

OECD (2007): *Education at a Glance 2007*. Paris: Organisation for Economic Co-operation and Development (OECD).

OECD (2009): *Equally Prepared for Life? How 15-Year-Old Boys and Girls Perform in School*. Paris: Organisation for Economic Co-operation and Development (OECD).

Omi, Michael & Winant, Howard (1993): 'On the Theoretical Status of the Concept of Race', in McCarthy, Cameron & Crichlow, Walter (eds.), *Race, Identity, and Representation in Education*. New York: Routledge, pp.3-10.

Parekh, Bhikhu (2000): *Rethinking Multiculturalism: Cultural Diversity and Political Theory*. Cambridge: Harvard University Press.

Peng, Chih-ling & Huang, Shin-rou (2012): 'A Study of Gender Ideology in Taiwan Elementary School Textbooks: Perspectives from Textbook Editors and Reviewers'. *Philosophy of Education Society of Australasia*, Taiwan.

Ravitch, Diane (1990): 'Multiculturalism: E Pluribus Plures'. *The American Scholar*, Vol.59, No.3, pp.337-354.

Roithmayr, Daria (1998): 'Deconstructing the Distinction between Bias and Merit'. *La Raza Law Journal*, Vol.10, pp.363-421.

Savage, Mike; Devine, Fiona; Cunningham, Niall; Taylor, Mark; Li, Yaojun; Hjellbrekke, Johs; Le Roux, Brigitte; Friedman, Sam & Miles, Andrew (2013): 'A New Model of Social Class: Findings from the BBC's Great British Class Survey Experiment'. *Sociology*, Vol.47, No. 2, pp.219-250.

Shih, Chih-yu (2002): *Negotiating Ethnicity in China: Citizenship as a Response to the State*. New York: Routledge.

Sewell, Tony (2004): 'Loose Canons: Exploding the Myth of the "Black Macho" Lad', in Gillborn, David & Ladson-Billings, Gloria (eds.), *The RoutledgeFalmer Reader in Multicultural Education*. London: RoutledgeFalmer, pp.103-116.

Smith, Adam (1776/2009): *The Wealth of Nations*. Blacksburg, VA: Thrifty Books.

Stone, Lynda (2000): 'Embodied Identity: Citizenship Education American Girls', in Arnot, Madeleine & Dillabough, Jo-Anne (eds.), *Challenging Democracy: International Perspectives on Gender, Education and Citizenship*. London: RoutledgeFalmer, pp.73-86.

Takezawa, Yasuko (2011): 'Toward a New Approach to Race and Racial Representations: Perspectives from Asia', in Takezawa, Yasuko (ed.), *Racial Representations in Asia*. Kyoto: Kyoto University Press, pp.7-19.

Thomas, Vinod & Wang, Yan (2008): 'Distribution of Opportunities Key to Development', in Holsinger, Donald B. & Jacob, W. James (eds.), *Inequality in Education: Comparative and International Perspectives*. CERC Studies in Comparative Education 24, Hong Kong: Comparative Education Research Centre, The University of Hong Kong, and Dordrecht: Springer, pp.34-58.

Thorne, Barrie (1993): *Gender Play: Girls and Boys in School*. Rutgers University Press.

Unterhalter, Elaine & Oommen, Mora (2008): 'Measuring Education Inequalities in Commonwealth Countries in Africa', in Holsinger, Donald B. & Jacob, W. James (eds.), *Inequality in Education: Comparative and International Perspectives*. CERC Studies in Comparative Education 24, Hong Kong: Comparative Education Research Centre, The University of Hong Kong, and Dordrecht: Springer, pp.506-537.

UNESCO (2010): *Reaching the Marginalized: Education for All Global Monitoring Report 2010*. Paris: UNESCO.

UNESCO (2012a): *Youth and Skills – Putting Education to Work: Education for All Global Monitoring Report 2012*. Paris: UNESCO.

UNESCO (2012b): *World Atlas of Gender Equality in Education*. Paris: UNESCO.

UNESCO (2013): World Inequality Database on Education. Paris: UNESCO. http://www.education-inequalities.org

United States National Opportunity to Learn Campaign (2013). *The Color of School Closures*. www.otlcampaign.org/blog/2013/04/05/color-school-closures.

Villegas, Ana Maria (1988): 'School Failure and Cultural Mismatch: Another View'. *Urban Review*, Vol.20, No.4, pp.253-265.

8

Comparing Cultures

Mark MASON

"Were the British truly imperialist?" asked the respected travel writer, Jan Morris (2005, p.24). Does "The Chinese Learner" (Watkins & Biggs 1996) "invariably have a high regard for education"? Are "Asian students not only diligent, but also [possessed of] high achievement motivation" (Lee 1996, p.25)? Is there really "a distinct Chinese pedagogy", as Rao and Chan (2009, p.10) have intimated? Do Finnish students enjoy some cultural advantage that enables them to do well repeatedly – in 2000, 2003, 2006, 2009 and 2012 – in the league tables produced by the Programme for International Student Assessment (PISA) administered by the Organisation for Economic Co-operation and Development (OECD)? Was it appropriate for South Africa's 1951 Eiselen Commission to state that "education practice must recognise that it has to deal with a Bantu child, trained and conditioned in Bantu culture, endowed with a knowledge of a Bantu language and imbued with values, interests and behaviour patterns learned at the knee of a Bantu mother" (Kallaway 1984, p.175)? And was it valid then to declare, as did Hendrik Verwoerd, South African Minister of Native Affairs in 1954, that "there is no place for [the Bantu] in the European community above the level of certain forms of labour" (Kallaway 1984, p.173)?

Few would deny that cultural factors are associated with and influence many aspects of education. As Alexander (2000, pp.29-30) has observed:

> Life in schools and classrooms is an aspect of our wider society, not separate from it: a culture does not stop at the school gates. The

character and dynamics of school life are shaped by the values that shape other aspects of ... national life.

Alexander went further (p.30), writing that: "Culture, in comparative analysis and understanding, and certainly in national systems of education, is all."

When comparing one culture with another, however, researchers should tread with caution. They face possible accusations of stereotyping, of treating culture as monolithic, and of overstating its influence in a world of complex interactions and influences. Morris' (2005, p.24) response to her own question whether the British were truly imperialist was that:

some were, some weren't. It depended on class, age, temperament, religion, the state of the nation, the state of one's investments, the state of one's liver and all the myriad other factors that make national consensus about anything a nonsensical hypothesis.

In his chapter in the book, *The Chinese Learner*, Lee (1996) cited the claims of Ho (1986) and Yang (1986) about the diligence, motivation and high regard for education apparently typical of Chinese, and more generally, Asian students. Many who have taught in societies characterised by what are widely called "Confucian heritage cultures" have reported similar perceptions. How valid are these characterisations, and are the features unique to students in Confucian heritage cultures? Lee has cautioned readers about the risks of over-generalisation. He and Manzon remind readers in Chapter 9 of this volume that "[w]henever values are discussed collectively, they have to be examined in the context of individual choices of values". In *Revisiting the Chinese Learner*, Chan and Rao also warned readers of the risks in positing "a binary distinction between Chinese and Western students" and in "assum[ing] the homogeneity of the Chinese people" (2009a, p.318).

Concerning the performance of Finland's school children in the 2000 PISA study, Välijärvi (2002, p.45) has indicated that cultural influences were a significant element. One component, he has suggested, was cultural homogeneity: "it has been comparatively easy in Finland to reach mutual understanding on national education policy and the means for developing the education system". Välijärvi has also referred to students' engagement in reading, and cultural communication between parents and children; and he cited a great cultural emphasis in Finland on equal opportunity in education.

In related vein, Linnakylä's (2002) interpretation of the excellent performance of Finland's school children inferred that Finnish children in general have through centuries of cultural tradition long respected the ability to read. This is possibly because after the Protestant Reformation in northern Europe (1517-1648), in which the established practices of the European Catholic church were challenged by Martin Luther and others, it became increasingly acceptable and important for parents to read the Bible to their children (in contrast to the previously dominant Catholic practice that reserved the reading of the Bible for the priesthood). Since the 16ᵗʰ century in Finland, then part of Sweden, literacy had been a prerequisite for receiving the sacraments and contracting a Christian marriage. Children's reading skills were publicly assessed in the annual 'kinkerit', in which failure meant public disgrace and the denial of permission to marry (Linnakylä 2002, pp.83-85). This has meant that for several centuries almost all children in Finland have been raised in families where both parents are literate.

The last question raised at the beginning of this chapter – where cultural differences were used to justify apartheid education – contrasts sharply with the prior examples. However, apart from the transparently racist attitudes that served the economic and political interests of the elite in apartheid South Africa, many educational researchers would acknowledge substantial degrees of truth in the examples taken from Finnish and Confucian heritage cultures. As noted earlier, few would deny that cultural factors indeed influence many aspects of education; but most would flinch from asserting precisely what these factors are. Such factors are notoriously difficult to isolate, and assertions are often tenuous at best, given how easy it is not only to overstate the influence of a particular culture in a complex world, but also to get it wrong. Perhaps worse than this, researchers who attempt to describe the influence of cultural factors on education face accusations of stereotyping, even of racism. While *The Chinese Learner* (Watkins & Biggs 1996), *Teaching the Chinese Learner* (Watkins & Biggs 2001) and *Revisiting the Chinese Learner* (Chan & Rao 2009b) are respected volumes in the field of culture and pedagogy, publication of a volume entitled "The Black African Learner" would be scorned as racist. While the former three titles are not, in that they attempt to uncover the reasons behind the remarkable educational achievement of students in Confucian heritage cultures (which are also paradoxical, given educational policies, pedagogies and learning styles), the latter would be typical of the literature justifying colonial and apartheid education in South Africa: as if there were some phenomenon reducible to "*the* black African learner".

Bearing in mind such considerations, this chapter considers some philosophical and methodological challenges that face researchers who attempt to compare education across cultures. The two core sections respond to historical, philosophical, anthropological and sociological questions associated with the definition of culture, and to methodological questions associated with research across cultures. I attempt to sketch a more nuanced understanding of culture than is evident in much contemporary educational research by considering the work of writers such as Johann Herder, Raymond Williams, Robert Bocock, Stuart Hall, Geert Hofstede and Zygmunt Bauman. The methodological questions associated with cross-cultural educational research are addressed by reference in particular to the work of Robert LeVine, Joseph Tobin, Robin Alexander and Vandra Masemann.

Robust inferences from comparative studies would depend on comparison between entities that are both identifiable and discrete. If it is from comparison between two cultures that researchers wish to draw robust conclusions, they should be able at least to identify each culture, and to be sure about what marks each as distinct from the other. If they wish to claim, for example, that "Chinese learners invariably have a high regard for education", they should bear in mind that a claim as strongly put as this implies that *all* members of this group display this feature. The statement also implies that this feature is an *essential* attribute of the members of this group, and in turn that a high regard for education is a *necessary* condition for membership of the group described as Chinese.

Attention to this level of definitional constraint in comparative education research across cultures would increase rigour in the field. Comparisons of education across cultures are, after all, common. Two well-known examples are the cross-national studies of educational achievement conducted under the auspices of the IEA (International Association for the Evaluation of Educational Achievement) and PISA. Secondary analysis of these results frequently involves a challenging search for cultural factors associated with educational achievement – the immediately obvious first slippage being that from country to culture (and indeed, if the adjective "cross-national" is used, from nation to country). The assumption that nation, country and culture are synonymous is of course simply wrong. To assume that culture is a monolithic and discrete entity is equally wrong. The image of the pith-helmeted anthropologist cutting his way through jungles and traversing formidably mountainous terrain to 'discover' a remote tribe utterly isolated in its valleys in order to record its attributes and practices has possibly skewed contemporary views of cross-cultural comparison more than is normally realised. Questions about the validity and reliability of anthropological perspectives on educational comparison across cultures underlie much of the discussion in this chapter – that is, at least about the more outdated anthropological approaches that still seem to influence much comparative educational research across cultures. In a world where cultural isolation as per the mythic tribes of Borneo is increasingly impossible, some of these more outdated anthropological notions of culture might not serve as well in comparative research across cultures as other perspectives on culture might. I argue here that it is to sociological understandings of the concept of culture that researchers should turn for a more appropriate construction of culture in all its complexity in a world characterised by increasing degrees of plurality, multiculturalism, interdependence, hybridity and complexity.

Defining and Describing Cultures

The first major question, then, is about the very nature of culture. What is it, how can it be recognised, what are its consequences, and how is its influence expressed?

Raymond Williams, acknowledged as one of the greatest theorists of culture (see e.g. Williams 1981, 1982, 1985), has asserted (1985, p.87) that "culture is one of the two or three most complicated words in the English language". This is "partly because of its intricate historical development, in several European languages, but mainly because it has now come to be used for important concepts in several distinct intellectual disciplines and in several distinct and incompatible systems of thought".

A genealogy of culture

In its early uses, culture referred to "the tending of something, basically crops or animals" (Williams 1985, p.87). It was then extended by metaphor to the process of human development, as in Hobbes' "a culture of their minds" (1651), but it was not common in the English language until the mid-19th century. While the 'cultivation of the self' is familiar as a concept and value to scholars of Confucian heritage, Williams has pointed out that in 18th century England, 'cultivation' and 'cultivated' acquired class associations.

German borrowed the French *Culture*, spelling it *Kultur*, and implying a process of becoming civilized or cultivated. Bauman (2011, p.53), drawing on the work of Philippe Bénéton, has described how, at its inception, the idea of culture was characterised by:

> an assumption that the ideal of human nature … is the same for all nations, places and times; and eurocentrism, the conviction that that ideal was discovered in Europe and that it was there that it was defined by … the ways and models of individual and communal life.

Critically, however, both for the purposes of this chapter and as far as the historical development of the term is concerned, the late 18th century German philosopher Herder challenged this notion of a universal human development. He was scathing of "the very thought of a superior European culture" (cited by Williams 1985, p.89), choosing rather to draw distinctions between different cultures. This use of 'cultures' in the plural was, according to Williams (1985, p.89), Herder's "decisive innovation": not only "the specific and variable cultures of different nations and periods, but also the specific and variable cultures of social and economic groups within a nation". And at the same time, surely, questions would have been asked about comparison between and among them.

In addition to the use of culture to describe "a general process of intellectual, spiritual and aesthetic development" (Williams 1985, p.87), the modern social sciences employ the term in a line of reference that traces from Herder through Klemm's *General Cultural History of Mankind* (1843-52) and Tylor's *Primitive Culture* (1870). In these works, culture is commonly an independent noun, whether used generally or specifically, which indicates a particular way of life, of a people, a period, a group, or humanity in general. Of course culture frequently refers to "works and practices of intellectual and especially artistic activity: … culture is music, literature, painting and sculpture, theatre and film" (Williams 1985, p.90). This intellectual and aesthetic use of the term is, however, of less interest to us here. We need pause only to note that, if culture expresses so importantly in these ways the values of particular groups of people, Kluckhohn (1961) has suggested that it does this by responding to core human questions such as those about the character of human nature, the relationship of human beings to nature, the relationship of human beings to other human beings, and the relationship of human beings to work.

Most attempts to define a 'true', 'proper' or 'scientific' sense of the term have taken its use in North American anthropology as the norm. This is somewhat arbitrary, and this arbitrariness lies partly behind my defence of the use of contemporary sociological perspectives in comparing education across cultures, in preference to, for example, Masemann's (North American) anthropological perspective. Working towards an understanding of culture for comparative purposes, it is important to note Williams' (1985, p.91) remark that:

> in archaeology and in *cultural anthropology* the reference to culture or a culture is primarily to *material* production, while in history and *cultural studies* the reference is primarily to *signifying* or *symbolic* systems.

Comparison of education across cultures cannot avoid the study of both material production and symbolic systems. The curriculum is a good example of both material artefact and symbolic system, as are education policies, and pedagogical materials.

The field of symbolic (as opposed to cultural) anthropology has its primary focus signifying systems (as in cultural studies). A key text is Wagner's (1981) *The Invention of Culture*, which stresses that culture is not a fixed entity that shapes the lives of the individuals. It is more accurate to speak of a dialectical process between people and their social environments which involves also the shaping of the culture by those people as they manipulate its conventional symbols to create new meanings. Consider, for example, the different meanings associated with the terms denoting one who learns, each associated with a different set of values and each connoting a different role for the learner as cultural perceptions of learners change over time and across contexts: pupil, schoolboy, schoolgirl, trainee, apprentice, disciple, follower, scholar, critic, student, lifelong learner. People who share a particular culture construct these terms, or symbols, and each gives a different meaning to people who share that culture. Culture is, in other words, not a club, membership of which implied certain attributes. Culture functions more as a productive force constituted by a relatively amorphous aggregation of loosely bounded factors that both influence the lives of the individuals who share in it and are influenced by those individuals.

In summary, this discussion leads to two definitions of culture that are of most interest to social scientists. The first, commonly understood as the anthropological definition, indicates "a particular way of life, whether of a people, a period, a group, or humanity in general" (Williams 1985, p.90). This way of life would include the shared values and meanings common to members of the group. Drawing on Keesing's position that culture is "concerned with actions, ideas and artefacts which individuals in the tradition concerned learn, share and value" (1960, p.25), Masemann's anthropological approach to culture (2013, p.114) assumes that:

> Culture refers to all the aspects of life, including the mental, social, linguistic, and physical forms of culture. It refers to ideas people have, the relationships they have with others in their families and with larger social institutions, the languages they speak, and the symbolic forms they share, such as written language or art/music forms. It refers to their relationship with their physical surroundings as well as the technology that is used in any society.

The second definition of culture derives from its anthropological orientation, and also refers to shared meanings within groups, but differs in emphasis from the former by focusing more on "the symbolic dimension, and on what culture *does* rather than what culture *is*" (Bocock 1992, p.232). Here, in cultural studies (more than in cultural anthropology), culture is less importantly a distinctive way of life as understood, for example, by its material artefacts, and more importantly "the set of practices by which meanings are produced and exchanged within a group" (Bocock 1992, p.233). At the heart of these practices lies language, because the sharing of a common language system enables people to communicate meaningfully with one another. Language is here understood very broadly, to include all sign and symbol systems through which meaning is produced: "any system of communication which uses signs as a way of referencing objects in the real world; it is this process of *symbolisation* which enables us to communicate meaningfully about the world" (Bocock 1992, p.233).

These sign and symbol systems are most commonly understood as the words of a language, but they also include material objects. It is not least in the interpretation of the significance of the material object that this symbolic understanding of culture differs from, or at least extends, the anthropological understanding of culture. The uniforms that children wear to school, or, if uniforms are not required, the clothes that they choose to wear to school, with or without the logos of different fashion brands, function as 'signs' that express meaning.

In cultural anthropology, then, culture is understood as "shared meanings and ways of life"; in cultural studies and its associated fields, culture is understood as "the practices which produce meaning" (Bocock 1992, p.234). Again, the second draws on the first, and the first is interested also in the concerns of the second. It is more a matter of difference in emphasis: in the first, on the substantive contents of culture as a whole way of life; in the second, on the ways in which cultural practices produce meaning for those who share those practices. The approach to the analysis of culture typical of the second looks for the ways in which meaning is produced by "the arrangement, the pattern, the symbolic structure of an event" (Bocock 1992, p.235): hence the term 'structuralism'.

'National culture' in modern societies

Perhaps the most common expression of cultural identity in modernity is found in what is widely understood as 'national culture'. In pre-modern societies, cultural identity is typically constructed in terms of tribe, religion or region. With the nation-state the dominant political entity in modernity, these identities have in modern societies gradually given way to national cultural identity. 'Nation' (as in national, associated with a country) and 'culture' are, after all, often conflated in comparative education research that attempts to identify the cultural factors that might have contributed to, say, Finland's PISA success. The question then turns to the meaning of national culture.

Here I follow Hall (1994, p.292), for whom a national culture is a discourse – "a way of constructing meanings which influences and organizes both our actions and our conception of ourselves". National identity, Anderson (1983) has argued, is no more than an "imagined community". That does not mean that national identity and culture have no consequences in the real world; but before comparative education researchers undertake comparisons across cultures, they should consider not only the ways in which the discourse of national culture is represented, but also the power of those representations to win national allegiance and to define cultural identity.

This discussion focuses on national culture and identity because this concept has been of particular interest to comparative education researchers. There are, of course, many other cultural identities, and as a consequence of the processes associated with globalisation, national cultural identity has been reduced in significance to just one of many cultural discourses that constitute the individual in late modernity. National cultural identity has nevertheless been among the most powerful of these discourses in modern society.

What then is national cultural identity? Hall (1994, pp.292-293) has pointed out that:

> national identities are not things we are born with, but are formed and transformed within and in relation to *representation*. We only know what it is to be 'English' because of the way 'Englishness' has come to be represented, as a set of meanings, by English national culture. It follows that a nation is not only a political entity but something which produces meanings – *a system of cultural representation*. People are not only legal citizens of a nation; they participate in the *idea* of the nation as represented by its national culture.... National cultures construct identities by producing meanings about 'the nation' with which we can *identify*; these are contained in the stories which are told about it, memories which connect its present with its past, and images which are constructed of it. (emphases original)

National culture emerged with and helped to shape modernity by gradually displacing (but of course not entirely) the pre-modern discourses of identity mentioned earlier: tribal, ethnic, religious and regional. The ascendancy of national cultural discourses was heightened by the nation-state's establishment of a common language and a national education system that ensured, or at least aimed to ensure, universal literacy in that (now national) language. National culture was also promoted by museums, performing arts theatres, architectural icons such as palaces, castles and parliamentary buildings, and latterly, national sports teams and consumer brands marketed with national identities.

What are the origins of these representations that constitute and reflect the discourse of national culture? The narrative of national culture may be constructed through "an invocation of common roots and a common spirit" (Bauman 2011, p.73) that includes:

- "the narratives of the nation, as it is told and retold in national histories, literatures, the media and popular culture", which "provide a set of stories, images, landscapes, scenarios, historical events, national symbols and rituals which stand for, or represent, the shared experiences, sorrows, and triumphs and disasters which give meaning to the nation" (Hall 1994, p.293), and which "make up the threads which bind us invisibly to the past" (Schwarz 1986, p.155);

- an emphasis on "origins, continuity, tradition and timelessness" (Hall 1994, p.294), which represents national identity as primordial, "in the very nature of things" (Gellner 1983, p.48);
- the invention of 'tradition': as Hobsbawm and Ranger (1983, p.1) have pointed out, traditions which appear or claim to be old are often quite recent and sometimes invented;
- the creation of a "foundational myth", one which "locates the origin of the nation, the people and their national character so early that they are lost in the mists of, not 'real', but 'mythic' time" (Hall 1994, p.295; Hobsbawm & Ranger 1983, p.1); and
- the symbolic grounding of national identity on the idea of a "pure, original people" (Hall 1994, p.295; Gellner 1983, p.61).

My point in drawing on these authors to expose national cultural identity as more constructed than 'natural', more discursive than material, is to caution comparative education researchers about the shallowness and the arbitrariness of the 'foundations' of cultural identity. If a good first step in any comparative research is to isolate and define the entities being compared, it should be realised that the 'unit' of culture is one of the most difficult to identify and operationally describe. Certainly cultural identity is important and has real consequences; but inferentially locating the source of the significance of these consequences in culture is difficult indeed.

Beyond these questions about the rather arbitrarily constructed history of national cultural identity is a further problem: whether national identities really are as unified, coherent, consistent and homogeneous as appears in these representations of 'national culture'. The answer is that they are obviously not. As Hall (1994, p.297) has pointed out, "modern nations are all cultural hybrids". Most modern nations were, after all, born out of violent conquest of one or more groups by another. Gellner (1983) has reminded readers that, of the range of ethnic, religious and language groups that constituted early nineteenth century Europe, only some would become 'nations', in the process casting "other aspirants to nation status into ethnic minorities, other aspirants to the dignity of an official national language into dialects, and other candidates to the rank of national church into sects" (Bauman 2011, p.72).

National cultural identity is thus often constructed on a specious notion of race, marking as different those of different 'racial groups'. National identity is also often strongly gendered, excluding women from its patriarchal norms. Class is another powerful divider, and it is almost without exception the cultural capital of the elite groups in a society that represents the norm, that constitutes what is to be emulated and sought by all. The generalisation of the cultural norms of a society's elite groups to the level of 'national cultural identity' thus does what Bourdieu has called symbolic violence to the representations espoused in the cultural identity of other groups in society. These latter cultural representations become manifestations of mere "provincialism, parochialism or aberrant localism" (Bauman 2011, p.73). Differences in language, geographical region, tradition, religion, customs, and the like constitute further lines marking difference and exclusion. A key aim of the project of nation-building is, in Bauman's words, "to divest 'others' of their 'otherness'" (Bauman 2011, p.75). While it is thus the task of national cultural mythology to draw together the different identities and local communities of which a nation-state is constituted, "to make culture and polity congruent" under the same "political roof" (Gellner 1983, p.43), and to paper over the cracks that divide those who identify with Anderson's "imagined community" from those who are not subsumed under the state's hegemony, it is a brave researcher indeed who attempts to compare, say, South African cultural approaches to learning with Nigerian, Indonesian or Chinese ones.

'National culture' in an increasingly globalised world

I have argued that 'national culture' is somewhat arbitrary, probably best understood as myth, and not particularly successful at masking deep and cross-cutting social divisions. The process of globalisation has complicated matters even further. I turn now to the consequences of globalisation and its associated processes for national cultural identity. In a rather mixed geological metaphor, globalisation has marbled what has been sedimented and layered into the accepted truths of national cultural identity. The cultural hybridity of the modern nation-state, masked as a homogeneous unity by the myths of national culture, is exacerbated almost to the point of the displacement of the national culture by the processes of globalisation. One of these involves the mass 'unplanned' migration, driven by the increasing gap in wealth between rich and poor that is arguably the most stark of globalisation's consequences, of people from the previously colonised countries of the less developed world to the countries of the more developed world, frequently to the former colonial powers. If national cultural identity has been about attachment to an imagined community constituted and represented by a shared sense of place, historical narrative and discursively constructed events and symbols, globalisation is associated with, in part, a more universalist and deterritorialised form of identity.

For Waters (1995, p.3) globalisation is "a social process in which the constraints of geography on social and cultural arrangements recede and in which people become increasingly aware that they are receding". It is about, in Delanty's (2000, p.81) version, the diminishing importance of geographical constraints in defining the nature of economic, political, social and cultural interactions; in other words, about the transformation of space or, more specifically, the "deterritorialization of space". Cultures and civilisations are thus more exposed to each other, more likely to clash, or to merge, or to develop new hybrids or a universal culture, with as much impact on the local and specific as on the global and universal, as a consequence of the diminishing limits of geography. However, globalisation by no means leads necessarily to a global society, or even to a global culture, other than perhaps the rule of the market and its orientation towards global elites as a consequence of the transnationalisation of capitalism. Much of the literature points to increasing diversity and fragmentation as well as to increasing homogeneity.

Tendencies towards diversity and fragmentation are evident in, for example, Al Qaeda's rejection of Western consumer society and assertion of Islamic identity and culture. This fragmentation and emphasis on particular, local cultural identity is also evident in the resurgent expressions of nationalism that have been seen in central and eastern Europe since the late 1980s: typically, the Estonian, Latvian, Georgian, Kazakh, Uzbek and Tajik nationalisms (to name but a few) that contributed to the break-up of the Soviet Union; or, the expression of Slovenian, Croatian, Bosnian, and Serbian nationalism that contributed to the break-up of Yugoslavia. These struggles to assert a national cultural identity exemplified a search for an 'ethnically pure' heritage that had been 'lost', its most succinct and horrifying expression in the term synonymous with the recent Balkan wars, 'ethnic cleansing'. In Bauman's (1990, p.167) words:

> the 'resurgence of ethnicity' ... puts in the forefront the unanticipated flourishing of ethnic loyalties inside national minorities. ... Ethnicity has become one of the many categories or tokens, or 'tribal poles' around which ... communities are formed and in reference to which individual identities are constructed and asserted.

Examples of the homogenisation of culture are most evident in consumer culture, where (mostly) young people tend to define their identity – or at least a significant part of it – and 'lifestyle' in terms of shopping malls, Western-style jeans and T-shirts, Nike athletic shoes, Starbucks coffee shops, and so on. Ours is, after all, a consumers' society, in which culture, in Bauman's words, manifests itself as not too much more than "a repository of goods intended for consumption" (2011, p.14). The exploitation of just about everything that can be repackaged or pro-cessed and sold for a profit by means of 'adding value', in the process known as commodification, has contributed substantially to this ho-mogenisation of culture to an identity driven by consumerism and de-fined primarily in terms of choices made in the market place, or more specifically in the shopping mall. As Hall (1994, p.303) has put it:

> the more social life becomes mediated by the global marketing of styles, places and images, by international travel, and by globally networked media images and communications systems, the more identities become detached – disembedded – from specific times, places, histories, and traditions, and appear 'free-floating'. We are confronted by a range of different identities, each appealing to us, or rather to different parts of ourselves, from which it seems possible to choose. It is the spread of consumerism, whether as reality or dream, which has contributed to this 'cultural supermarket' effect.

Nevertheless, the consequences of globalisation are very unevenly dis-tributed. Defenders of the anthropological view of culture might point out that the consumer cultures of the USA and Japan are felt more strongly in Mexico and Hong Kong than they are in Bhutan or Myanmar. To use Wallerstein's (1974) terms, it is the cultural production of the 'Western' centre (including, of course, Japanese cultural capital) that dominates that of the periphery, and it is in the centre that the choice of identity with any number of 'cosmopolitan' or particular hybridities is indeed an option.

Of most interest for the purposes of this chapter are three processes associated with globalisation: first, national cultural identities are being rendered yet more tenuous than they already are; second, local and par-ticular identities are being strengthened as a consequence of resistance to the processes of globalisation; and third, these new hybrid identities are becoming, at the expense of national cultural identities, increasingly visi-ble. Ours is an "age of diasporas", Bauman has suggested: "an infinite archipelago of ethnic, religious and linguistic settlements.... Ways of life today drift in varied and not necessarily coordinated directions ... floating in a suspension of cultures" (2011, pp.35, 37). This is why Bauman has described what other authors refer to as 'postmodernity' or 'late modernity', as "liquid modernity" (2011, pp.11, 87): "like liquid, none of the [contemporary] forms of social life is able to maintain its shape for long" (2011, p.11). Perhaps the main point to be taken from all this is that the anthropological definition of culture starts to look methodologically suspect in all but the most homogeneous and isolated of cultures, if indeed any still exist. It is perhaps to cultural studies and to sociological more than anthropological understandings of culture in contemporary society that researchers need to turn for comparison of education across cultures.

At the same time, I add a word of caution: for all that I have said about the virtual impossibility of talking about a 'culture' any more, I have little choice but to use this term in what follows, for want of any other more appropriate and succinct terminology. Readers should perhaps, in every mention of culture that follows, imagine the word in scare quotes as 'culture'.

Comparing Education across Cultures

The second major question has to do with how researchers might set about comparing education across cultures. How, in short, can the particular influences of culture be isolated in attempts to explain institutions, arrangements and practices in education and to compare these with education in other societies?

Comparative research into the institutions and practices of education across cultures faces a problem commonly faced by ethnographic researchers: the problem of context. For comparative education researchers trying to identify the consequences of culture for education, the problem I have been indicating for much of this chapter thus far is, in many senses, one of context: what is the cultural context that produces the educational institutions and practices under study? Hammersley (2006, p.6) has asked two questions of central importance to ethnographers:

- How are we to determine the appropriate wider context in which to situate what we are studying?
- How are we to gain the knowledge we need about that context?

Can this wider context be limited to local cultural context? My arguments have indicated the limitations of this view of culture. Can the focus be isolated in terms of a national cultural context? I have suggested the virtual impossibility of this view of culture, given the influence of the processes associated with globalisation in rendering national cultural identities yet more tenuous than they already are, and in contributing to the increasing prevalence of culturally hybrid identities. And yet to give up and speak only of a 'globalised cultural context' is to ignore ways in which local and particular identities have been strengthened in resistance to the processes of globalisation. Perhaps more importantly, it is also to abandon the search for truths about the consequences of culture for education that are both evident to many people and productive of interesting insights.

With reference to his first question, Hammersley (2006, p.6) has asked a further question that reflects a central purpose of my analysis and deconstruction of culture thus far: "whether context is discovered or constructed; and, if it is constructed, whether it is constructed by the participants or by the analyst". I have argued that culture, or cultural context, is best understood in terms of what it *does*, rather than what it *is*; and that culture influences people as much as they shape culture. Hammersley (p.6) has pointed out one ethnographic approach to (cultural) context which argues that "it is generated by the people being studied, so that the analyst must discover and document context as this is constituted in and through particular processes of social interaction". Proponents of this approach would suggest that any attempt by researchers to impose their analytical frameworks onto the cultural meanings generated by the population under study would be an act of symbolic violence. Hammersley's response would be to ask (p.6) "whether it is the case that people always explicitly indicate the context in which they see themselves operating", and "whether it is right to assume that people know the context in which their activities can best be understood for the purposes of social science explanation".

With reference to the second question about how researchers can gain the knowledge they need about the wider context, Hammersley (2006, pp.6-7) has wondered whether ethnographic research might best rely on existing social theory, or be integrated with other kinds of social science research that are better suited to studying whole institutional domains, national societies, and global forces. He has at the same time cautioned that this could constrain the generation of grounded theory. The integration of research across cultures with contemporary social theory is certainly what I have been implying in this chapter. This of course raises questions about which social theoretical perspective might best inform comparative education research across cultures.

Ethnographic research has commonly been informed by several different approaches, including functionalist, structuralist, symbolic inter-actionist, and conflict or critical (whether Marxian, neo-Marxian, feminist, or other) perspectives. The choice between them is in my view best based less on evidence (on what evidential basis would researchers make sound choices?), and more on the researchers' value commitments in doing the research (see Sikes et al. 2003). Researchers might, for example, be com-mitted to educational equity, and would then seek to ascertain in their ethnographic research the axes along which educational goods are dif-ferentially distributed. Masemann's position on which theoretical per-spective most appropriately situates ethnographic research in its wider context is located in the paradigm of conflict theory. Calling for a "critical ethnography" (an anthropological methodology informed by critical theory) that avoids the assumptions of neutrality and objectivity of func-tionalist and positivist approaches, she has suggested (2013, p.113) that:

> although the ethnographic approach is necessary to explore the workings of culture in the classroom, school and administrative system, it should not constrain the researcher mainly to phenome-nological approaches or ones in which the focus is only the subjec-tive experience of the participants.... [A] critical or neo-Marxist ap-proach is necessary to delineate the connections between the mi-crolevel of the local school experience and the macrolevel of struc-tural forces at the global level that are shaping the delivery and the experience of education in every country, in even the most remote regions.

I am twice in agreement with Masemann: that comparative education research into culture not be restricted to phenomenology but be situated in a wider context of social theory; and that the most productive and morally justifiable theoretical perspectives are in the domain of conflict and critical theory. Masemann (2013, pp.117-118) has drawn on Durkheim and on Bernstein to defend this position, arguing that:

> it is the social class position of the students that ultimately deter-mines how they experience any form of pedagogy. The seeming variations in values are not merely cultural but are class-based. Thus the link is made between education, culture, and class in every so-ciety.... [Children's] experience of and reactions to their education

are not grounded only in culture and values that are perceived in the liberal tradition as unconnected to the material basis of their society (the world of work), but these experiences are also fundamentally shaped by the economic basis of their neighborhood, community, region, or country, and ultimately the global economy.

I add here that it would be a mistake for ethnographic researchers to assume that in their inductive generation of grounded theory from their empirical observations they were able to proceed a-theoretically in the first instance, as if they were able to enter their chosen site of study without any theoretical framework to 'bias' them. To put it more bluntly, we cannot see without theory.

But if researchers need a theoretical perspective in order to select and to interpret what they see, and if the choice of theoretical perspective is ultimately grounded in researchers' value commitments, researchers need also to be aware of the risk of systematic bias. Perhaps researchers cannot avoid what Hammersley (2006, p.11) sees as the inherent tensions in ethnographic research "between trying to understand people's perspectives from the inside while also viewing them and their behaviour more distantly, in ways that may be alien (and perhaps even objectionable) to them". Dealing with this tension methodologically is one of the challenges faced in this chapter, and one to which I shall shortly turn my attention.

An associated risk lies in the potential failure by researchers to recognise their own ethnocentric perspectives. It is not only that instruments need to be developed cross-culturally. Wagner (1981, pp.2-4) cautioned in his book *The Invention of Culture* that:

> since we speak of a person's total capability as 'culture', the anthropologist *uses his own culture to study others*, and to study culture in general (emphasis added). Thus the awareness of culture brings about an important qualification of the anthropologist's aims and viewpoint as a scientist: the classical rationalist's pretense of absolute objectivity must be given up in favour of a relative objectivity based on the characteristics of one's own culture. It is necessary, of course, for a research worker to be as unbiased as possible insofar as he is aware of his own assumptions, but we often take our own culture's more basic assumptions so much for granted that we are not even aware of them. Relative objectivity can be achieved through discovering what these tendencies are, the ways in which

one's culture allows one to comprehend another, and the limitations it places on this comprehension. (p.2) … The idea of 'relationship' is important here because it is more appropriate to the bringing together of two equivalent entities, or viewpoints, than notions like 'analysis' or 'examination', with their pretensions of absolute objectivity. (p.3) …

The only way in which a researcher could possibly go about the job of creating a relation between such entities would be to simultaneously *know* both of them, to realise the relative character of his own culture through the concrete formulation of another. … We might actually say that an anthropologist 'invents' the culture he believes himself to be studying…. It is only through 'invention' of this kind that the abstract significance of culture … can be grasped, and only through the experienced contrast that his own culture becomes 'visible'. In the act of inventing another culture, the anthropologist invents his own, and in fact he reinvents the notion of culture itself. (p.4)

Comparative research across cultures also involves phenomenology, the philosophical approach that aims to understand the world through the eyes of and as it is experienced by others. Phenomenological studies of values require researchers to bear in mind and to take methodological steps to counter as far as possible the fact that their values will to a significant extent shape their perceptions and observations, their descriptions and classifications, their conceptualisations, inferences, conclusions and predictions. Researchers need also to be aware of the ways in which their language shapes their view of reality. Translation of instruments and transcriptions adds another level of complexity to this question. Back-translation is of course one way to check the accuracy and equivalence of translations.

Hofstede's (2001) book, *Culture's Consequences*, is another landmark in the field of comparison across cultures, and few discussions of the field would be complete without reference to it. Hofstede examined differences in cultures among samples of employees of a large multinational corporation, IBM, in its offices in over 50 countries around the world. He considered cultural differences in terms of "five independent dimensions of national culture, each rooted in a basic problem with which all societies have to cope" (p.29):

- *power distance*, i.e. the extent to which the less powerful members of a culture accept and expect that power is distributed unequally, involving the degree of human inequality that underlies the functioning of each particular society;
- *uncertainty avoidance*, which has to do with levels of stress displayed by members of a society in the face of uncertainty;
- *individualism versus collectivism*, which describes the relationship between the individual and the collectivity that prevails in a given society;
- *masculinity versus femininity*, which has to do with the implications that biological differences between the sexes have for the emotional and social roles in a particular society; and
- *long-term versus short-term orientation*, which is related to the choice of focus for people's efforts: the future or the present.

Whether these five dimensions do indeed provide useful windows into culture's consequences, whether there are other dimensions conceptually and statistically independent from these five, and whether other and more finely-focused lenses might be of greater use to educational researchers are questions of less interest here than Hofstede's methodology. One criticism has been of the use of nations as a unit of analysis for studying cultures, and Hofstede himself admitted (2001, p.23) that "modern nations are too complex and subculturally heterogeneous for their cultures to be [described] … on the basis of [inductive inferences from] small samples studied in great depth", that being the methodological approach associated with much classical anthropological study. Jacob (2005, p.515) has agreed, pointing out that:

> cultural diversity can exist intranationally or within a single country, as well as across nations. Most significant studies have postulated typologies which treat countries as homogeneous cultural entities. … Since there is no such thing as cultural purity, what needs to be emphasized is that countries have different cultural mixes and people tend to be 'hybrids' who simultaneously hold membership in different cultural groups.

Not only is intra-cultural variation commonly greater than inter-cultural variation: there exist also trans-cultural universals, such as "that considerate leaders find greater acceptance than not-so-considerate leaders irrespective of culture" (Jacob 2005, p.516). If intra-cultural variation is so often greater than inter-cultural variation, and if trans-cultural universals threaten to make nonsense of cultural differences from the other direction, one has to wonder whether analysis at the level of culture is of any worth at all. My response, in defence of which I argue here, is that comparative analysis across cultures *can* reveal truths about cultural differences in education, if done sensitively and carefully.

What, then, are the possible methodological errors in attempting to replicate his study against which Hofstede himself has warned? "Confusing cultures with individuals", he has cautioned (2001, p.463), "is the first pitfall of cross-cultural research, especially tempting to psychologists from individualist countries". Cultures, Hofstede has further remarked (p.17) "are not king-size[d] individuals: they are wholes, and their internal logic cannot be understood in the terms used for the personality dynamics of individuals". Importantly, Hofstede (p.464) has warned against confusing national culture with other levels of culture, such as ethnic or regional cultures. It would be a naïve researcher indeed who tried to compare, say, cultural approaches to learning in the UK with those in south Asia. It makes more sense to compare, say, cultural approaches to learning in the Pakistani immigrant communities in the industrial cities of central England with those of traditional Pakistani communities in rural North Waziristan.

Hofstede (2001, p.20) has suggested that, methodologically, a multi-disciplinary approach is most appropriate for comparisons across cultures, because:

> at the level of (national) cultures, phenomena on all levels (individuals, groups, organizations, society as a whole) and phenomena related to different aspects (organization, polity, exchange) are potentially relevant. Crossing disciplines is essential.

At the risk of sounding trite, researchers in the field of comparative education are probably well suited for undertaking comparisons of education across cultures precisely because comparative education is more a field than a discipline: researchers in the field are often relatively comfortable with study that is informed by more than one disciplinary perspective. Perhaps comparative education research across cultures is best undertaken by teams of researchers who among them can draw on a range of disciplinary and field perspectives that include among others those from philosophy, history, geography, economics, political science, social theory, sociology, anthropology, cultural studies, psychology, theology, linguistics and educational studies.

Methodological approaches to comparing education across cultures

In his book, *Culture and Pedagogy*, Alexander (2000) presented a comparative analysis of primary education in five countries – England, France, India, Russia and the USA – which "exhibit marked contrasts in respect of their geographic, demographic, economic and cultural characteristics, while sharing a formal constitutional commitment to democratic values" (p.4). Focusing on educational policies and structures on the one hand, and school and classroom practices on the other, he aimed to "unravel further the complex interplay of policies, structures, culture, values and pedagogy" (p.4). In doing so, he realised that researchers on countries and cultures other than their own commonly become acutely aware of how little they know, and that "there is the constant spectre of seeming naïve, presumptuous or simply too tidy in the face of what even insiders find baffling or contrary". What is most elusive in this, he suggests, is how "the practice of teaching and learning ... relates to the context of culture, structure and policy in which it is embedded" (p.3).

Methodological thoroughness and the comprehensive gathering of data from as many sources as possible underlie Alexander's success in withstanding accusations of naivety, presumptuousness or tidiness to the point of simplicity. He collected data at three levels: the system, school and classroom. He used a mixture of interviews, semi-systematic observation and, for later transcription and analysis, videotape and audiotape. He supplemented these with school and country documentation, photographs and daily journal entries.

Alexander has made an interesting point about how the number of cultures, or countries, selected for study can influence the nature of the conclusions. Addressing the question why he chose five countries rather than just two or three, he responded (p.44) that:

> To compare two drops us into the polarizing mindset from which it is hard to escape. To compare three invites what Tobin (1999) calls 'the Goldilocks effect' (in respect of primary education this country is good, this one is bad but this one is just right). To compare five is more difficult but has the vital advantage of enabling one to present similarities and differences as continua rather than as poles. And if the five are sufficiently diverse it makes the uncovering of educational universals ... a realistic pursuit.

Also relevant to this discussion are LeVine's (1966) observations about outsiders' judgements in culture studies. LeVine highlighted the importance of the convergences that emerge from analysis of the views that members of different groups have about the particular culture under study. In the attempt to approximate truth in judgements across cultures, LeVine's concern was to enhance validity by this method of triangulation.

Tobin, Wu and Davidson (1989), and Tobin, Hsueh and Karasawa (2009) used LeVine's ideas in their studies of preschools in Japan, China and the USA. They set out to study preschools in the three cultures represented by the countries, but also the three cultures as seen through their preschools. Following LeVine, and also the Russian literary theorist, Mikhail Bakhtin (see Tobin et al. 2009, p.7), the researchers sought a "multivocal ethnography" (1989, p.4) in order to enhance by triangulation the validity of their conclusions about preschools in those three countries. This multivocal ethnography included (1989, pp.4-5):

> the voices of preschool teachers, parents, and administrators, who tell their own stories, creating their own texts (produced as descriptions of a videotape of the preschools under study in their and other societies) that discuss, deconstruct, and criticize [the researchers'] account of their schools. Each of these texts reacts to earlier texts while never entirely replacing, subsuming, or negating them.

Tobin et al. thus attempted to balance their judgements as anthropological researchers with those of 'cultural insiders' and other 'cultural outsiders'. They based their research on at least four narratives, shown diagrammatically in Figure 8.1.

Figure 8.1: Primary and Secondary Insiders and Outsiders in Ethnographic Research

	Outsiders	Insiders
Primary	Ethnographic researchers enter a cultural context, in this case a preschool classroom in another country, to film and study it from the outside. (First level narratives)	The teacher whose classroom is studied, and other early childhood educators from the same school, discussing the video made in a classroom in their school. (Second level narratives)
Secondary	Early childhood educators comment on videos made in preschools in other countries – in the process also providing insights for the researchers into their own cultural perspectives. (Fourth level narratives)	Early childhood educators from other cities in the same country discuss the video made in a school in their country, providing insights for the researchers into the question of typicality. (Third level narratives)

What the researchers chose to videotape in their visual ethnography of the preschools was the result of discussions between them and their hosts, "a compromise between what [the researchers] had come to the field hoping to film and what [their] hosts felt was important and appropriate for [them] to see". The researchers noted (1989, p.5) that:

> what preschool teachers, administrators, parents, and children feel free to say to visiting anthropologists is itself largely culturally determined. Notions of what it means to speak honestly, of what to show and say to a guest, of how frankly to criticize oneself and others vary widely from culture to culture and reflect changing political climates.

This multivocal ethnography was needed to provide different perspectives on the researchers' very ways of seeing, on their culturally biased selection and focus in the act itself of videotaping the three preschools. In their first (1989) study, they realised after their recording that when American team members were filming, they tended to focus more on individual students. By contrast, Chinese researchers tended in their filming to pan across large groups of students. The result, they acknowledged (1989, p.7), was "three videotapes that are very subjective, idiosyncratic, culture-bound".

Following their filming of three preschools in three cultures (which constituted the record of their primary outsiders' observations as ethnographic researchers), Tobin et al. (1989) sought a second narrative to lend perspective to their first, filmed, narrative. These were insiders' explanations: "Japanese, Chinese, and American preschool administrators', teachers', parents' [and children's] explanations of and reactions to the videotapes [that the researchers] shot in their schools" (1989, p.7). Audiences were asked to view the tapes of their preschools and to provide running commentaries – in the sense of both a narrative and an analysis – of the actions depicted in the tapes.

The researchers then sought a third narrative in their multivocal ethnography: (secondary) insiders' explanations that might address the problem of typicality. They asked other audiences associated with preschools in the same country how representative this preschool was of others in their society, and how atypical it was. Tobin et al. (1989) asked their third narrative participants, after they had viewed sections of the videotapes (made in the school in their own society) showing teachers dealing with issues involving discipline, questions such as: "Were the

teachers too strict, just right, or not strict enough?" (1989, p.9). The researchers presented the results of this third narrative both statistically
(using ratings sheets for responses to questions such as this one about
degree of strictness) and descriptively (using questionnaires that solicited
respondents' views about the purpose of preschools in a society, what
children should learn in preschool, the characteristics of a good preschool
teacher, and the like). These third narratives, of secondary insiders, contextualised and provided a further perspective on the first narratives of
the researchers, who could be described as the primary outsiders, and on
the second narratives, of the primary insiders. This strategy gave the researchers a better sense of the degree of homogeneity and of the range of
differences in practices and beliefs associated with institutions or social
arrangements in particular societies. It also enabled them to take into account questions about variation within each country's preschools (see
Tobin et al. 2009, p.10).

With respect to this problem of typicality, Alexander has located the
strength of Tobin et al.'s methods in their ability to render inferences
about what cultural values, ideas and experiences lie beneath observed
practices by accepting that culture is an integral part of, rather than an
extraneous factor contributing to, what goes on in schools and classrooms. Referring to their observations in a Japanese preschool, Alexander
stressed that their method enabled them to establish the *authenticity* of the
observed practices as *distinctive* (and indeed typical) of preschools in that
country. The problem of typicality was approached, in other words, by
assessing the extent to which observed practices were authentically distinctive through their seeking of first, second, third and fourth narrative
perspectives from primary and secondary insiders and outsiders. Alexander added (2000, p.267) that:

> The practices this particular research team witnessed and reported
> in Kyoto were certainly not identical to those in a nursery school
> down the road, let alone two hundred miles away, but their au-
> thenticity as distinctively and indeed typically Japanese pre-school
> practice stemmed from the extent to which any surface differences
> were outweighed by deeper and more abiding similarities which
> had their roots in the ideas, values and experiences which teachers,
> parents and children at the schools had *in common* – ideas, values,
> and experiences which the researchers' painstaking close-up meth-
> odology enabled them to explicate and examine in the round.

Approaching the problem of typicality by rendering a particular case *in-sightful* depends on two propositions, as Alexander has suggested (p.266), both of which are implicit in the previous paragraphs. First is that:

> the culture in which the schools in a country or state are located, and which its teachers and pupils share, is as powerful a determinant of the character of school and classroom life as are the unique institutional dynamics, local circumstances and interpersonal chemistries which make one school or classroom different from another. For culture is not extraneous to the school, nor is it merely one of a battery of variables that can be tidily stacked to await correlational analysis. Culture both drives and is everywhere manifested in what goes on in classrooms, from what you see on the walls to what you cannot see going on inside children's heads.

Alexander's second proposition (2000, p.266), so ably demonstrated both in his study and in that by Tobin et al., is that "the research methods used [should be] sufficiently searching to probe beyond the observable moves and counter-moves of pedagogy to the values and meanings which these embody". Key strengths of the conceptualisation of the studies by Tobin et al. and Alexander lie in the ability of their methodological approaches to render inferences about what cultural values, ideas and experiences lie beneath observed practices, because of their acceptance that culture is an integral part of, rather than an extraneous factor contributing to, what goes on in schools and classrooms.

Following LeVine's ideas on "outsiders' judgements" (1966), Tobin et al. (1989) sought a fourth narrative perspective by showing audiences in China, Japan and the USA videotaped footage of preschools in the two societies other than their own, and seeking their responses to these videotapes. These fourth narrative perspectives were gleaned from the same participants who provided the third narrative perspectives as secondary insiders on videotaped footage of the preschool in their own culture; but in this role as providers of a fourth narrative perspective, these participants might now be referred to as secondary outsiders. Their responses as secondary outsiders to the videotapes of preschools in the two other societies were stimulated and recorded in the same way as were their responses as secondary insiders.

This methodological focus on the different narratives of the observers should not lead researchers to overlook the importance of talking with and listening to the individuals under primary observation. Since language is an integral aspect of making meaning in any culture, researchers should look closely at the language used by teachers, pupils, administrators, parents, and so on. In his study, Alexander (2000, p.427) considered "the character of classroom language, the way that children are taught to use it, the kinds of learning it promotes, and how these three themes related to those wider, culturally embedded discourses about the nature and purposes of primary schooling".

The fourth narrative perspectives of the secondary outsider participants in the study by Tobin et al. (1989) provide insights into the beliefs and practices associated with the culture being described as well as insights into the cultural beliefs associated with those doing the describing. Both of these sets of insights permit the researchers to turn, full circle as it were, back to the perspectives of the primary outsiders themselves, to learn more about their own culturally biased perceptions: the problem of an ethnocentric perspective on the part of the researcher. As Tobin et al. (1989, p.9) put it:

> Ethnographic judgements, whether rendered by a layman or by an anthropologist, reflect an intermingling of the culture being described and the culture doing the describing. Thus statements by American preschool parents and staff about a Chinese preschool have something to teach us about both American and Chinese beliefs and values.

Comparative educational research across cultures will perhaps be stronger for its acknowledgement that it is not only research *about* two or more cultures, in the cross-cultural sense, but also, inevitably, research that is intercultural in nature, in that it is about perspectives *from* the cultures under study, and *from* the cultural perspectives of the researchers. The studies by Tobin et al. succeed in the best of both senses, and that was indeed their aim in undertaking them. In this regard they cite the point made by Marcus and Fischer (1986) that the study of other cultures functions also as "a form of cultural critique of ourselves".

In the design of their studies researchers should also bear in mind the objective of comparing across cultures only what is comparable. Thus it may not be meaningful, for example, to compare preschools in China with preschools in Gibraltar. In both their studies, Tobin et al. tried to record comparable situations, with children of comparable ages, in comparable institutions, in three different societies, but still acknowledged (1989, p.7) that "comparability across cultures can only be approximate at best". In their attempts to record at least one fight between children in each culture, and to record at least one instance of a child being disciplined by a teacher, they had to conclude that what constitutes fighting, or teacher discipline – in other words, the very definitions of the meanings of these actions – varied substantially across cultures.

Tobin et al. (1989) have reminded readers of the well-rehearsed critique of ethnographic research – that it offers a view of culture that is limited to a 'snapshot' of the cultural practices under study at only one particular point in time, thus leading too easily to descriptions of these cultural practices as ideal-typical, and of the culture itself as static. Tobin and his colleagues addressed these questions by undertaking a study of similar scale, again in preschools in China, Japan and the USA, some 20 years later, adding "a historical dimension that was not part of the first study" (Tobin et al. 2009, p.ix). Given, for example, the homogenising influences of globalisation, Tobin et al. were interested in ascertaining whether "Chinese, Japanese, and American early childhood education ideas and practices [had] grown more alike" (2009, p.4) than they were in their original study. The answers to their research questions are less important to this chapter than the methodological insights. The first caution that Tobin et al. offered with regard to diachronic ethnography (ethnographic research conducted at two points in time, or over a period – as opposed to synchronic ethnography, which is limited to one ahistorical 'snapshot') has to do with the challenge of adding a historical dimension "without placing the other cultures we study on *our* timeline" (2009, p.4). Readers would do well to note Sweeting's comments on this matter in his chapter in this volume. Researchers comparing across cultures and across time need to avoid assuming that all cultures are moving along the same trajectories of, say, "modernization, rationalization, or globalization" (Tobin et al. 2009, p.5). Theories about space, context and time need to hold all in relative balance simultaneously.

Researchers comparing education across cultures and across time should also be aware of the risks in evaluating change in any aspect of the system. Conclusions that things have got worse, or progressively better, over time, are difficult to sustain. It is probably more likely that any aspect of an education system simply reflects forces, processes and trends in the broader society and culture at that particular point in history. Tobin et al. have reminded readers (2009, p.247) that:

> Just as the cultural relativism that lies at the core of ethnography demands that we not view one culture as superior to another, so

should historical relativism warn us to steer clear of the dangers of narratives of both deterioration and linear progress. Just as cultural relativism is a corrective to ethnocentrism, historical relativism requires us to not judge – positively or negatively – one era from the perspective of another.

The most substantial methodological change made by Tobin et al. in their second study was to videotape in two preschools in each country, rather than in just one. This was of course not an attempt to generate a representative sample, but a way of considering space, context and time simultaneously. They did this by choosing a second preschool in each country that would give them insights into questions of continuity and change over time – to do with, for example, "the direction, pace, logic, regional specificity, and mechanisms of change" (Tobin et al. 2009, p.11) – and also into questions of typicality and variation.

Their criterion for selecting each of the three new preschools was "a program that thinks of itself and is thought of by others as representing a new direction in early childhood education" (Tobin et al. 2009, p.10). For example, to their original Chinese site, Daguan preschool in Kunming, the provincial capital of Yunnan in a fairly remote and rural part of Southwest China, they added Sinanlu preschool in Shanghai, "China's most economically developed and self-consciously and famously progressive and internationally minded city" (Tobin et al. 2009, p.11). The contrast between the two preschools, as well as between the videotapes from the 1989 and the 2009 studies (the original being shown to and considered by the same participants 20 years later) gave the researchers insights into degrees of continuity and change – not least in terms of the thesis about homogenising tendencies following sustained exposure to the processes of globalisation – and also into typicality and variation: 'typical' behaviours and practices would probably have endured more than 'atypical' ones.

In summary, Tobin et al. (2009) sought to understand processes of continuity and change in the three cultures under study in three ways: first, by replicating their 1989 study in the same three preschools; second, by showing the videotapes from their 1989 study to current and retired staff from each of the three original preschools, and asking them about what appeared to have changed, what appeared to have stayed the same, and why; and, third, by including in their 2009 study a second preschool in each of the three cultures, each representing new directions in early childhood education in each of the three countries. Tobin et al. described this method of simultaneously comparing across cultures and time as "video cued multivocal diachronic ethnography" (2009, p.21).

While the principal focus of this discussion has been on research methods rather than findings, it is worth noting their principal conclusion "that culture acts as a source of continuity and as a brake on the impacts of globalization, rationalization, and economic change, … that cultural practices are more resilient and resistant to change than is predicted by theories of economic determinism, modernization and globalization" (2009, pp.224, 225). And of course preschools are among the institutions that both "reflect and help to perpetuate the cultures and societies of which they are a part" (2009, p.225).

Conclusion: Values and Interests in Comparing Education across Cultures

The previous section on methodological issues in comparing education across cultures focused quite substantially on ethnographic issues and research methods. In this conclusion, it is appropriate to consider some serious concerns about ethnography as a method of research, at least one of which – its tendency to offer ahistorical perspectives – I alluded to earlier. Tobin et al. (1989, p.9) has summarised some of them as follows:

> Ethnography as a method of research and a mode of representation is vulnerable to the accusation of being static, ahistorical, ideal-typical, and conservative in its reification of the status quo. Ethnography tends to find order, function, and symmetry in institutions while missing conflict and dysfunction; ethnography highlights ritual, belief, and ethos while giving less attention to the issues of social class, politics, and power.

Hammersley (2006, p.5) has similarly pointed to ways in which "the shortness of much contemporary [ethnographic] fieldwork can encourage a rather ahistorical perspective, one which neglects the local and wider history of the institution being studied". This of course raises questions of sampling: how can researchers be sure that the temporal slice that they have selected indeed represents cultural patterns in the longer term? Following this are the obvious questions about the extent to which generalisation is possible.

In this regard, Tobin et al. admitted in 1989 that their videotapes, like other ethnographic narratives, "freeze people and institutions in time

and isolate them from their larger contexts", to the extent that their narratives, despite their being constituted by primary and secondary outsiders' and insiders' perspectives, "remain at risk of being essentially
timeless and contextless". Aware of these risks at the outset, they introduced into their earlier study what they called "a sense of time, place, and
social class" (1989, p.10). With respect to the historical context, Tobin et al.
situated their earlier study in China five years after that country's introduction of a one-child policy, when educators and parents would have
been considering how best to socialise the new generation of children
growing up without siblings. In similar vein they took account of the
spatial and geographic context of the schools that they studied, and also
of the class context. To a less apparent extent, Tobin et al. situated their
study with respect to gender issues (see, for example, the discussion of the
role of American mothers inside and outside the home [1989, pp.179-182]),
and far less so with respect to issues of race and ethnicity. And, as noted,
Tobin and his colleagues replicated and expanded their 1989 study in
2009 primarily to try to understand preschools in their historical as well as
their cultural contexts.

Tobin et al. acknowledged that they "tried to privilege those contexts that insiders in each culture see as being most important" (1989,
p.10). This is both a strength and a shortcoming of their approach. It is a
strength because it takes seriously the perspectives of cultural insiders.
But it is a shortcoming because insiders may prioritise and interpret aspects of their cultural context in a benignly functionalist manner – that is,
where they view the agents and institutions of their society as engaged in
essentially a cooperative endeavour to the good of all, and where the social arrangements of their society are ultimately oriented to this end. Researchers asking many white South Africans about the economic, political,
social and cultural arrangements of apartheid society could well have
received a conservative functionalist response to the effect that institutions of apartheid contributed most effectively to peaceful 'separate development' of the different racial groups, given the legacy inherited from
nearly three centuries of colonialism. Researchers may thus miss insiders
whose perspectives are grounded in critical theory, where the agents and
institutions of society are understood to be in conflict with each other over
limited resources, and the economic, political, social and cultural institutions are so arranged as to serve the interests of the privileged groups.

My own view here, as indicated earlier, is that researchers cannot
observe another society or culture a-theoretically, with the apparent aim,

as is espoused by much of the methodological literature in ethnography, of generating hypotheses inductively from 'a-theoretical' empirical observation. What we see, and what we do not see, is a consequence of our implicit theoretical perspectives and beliefs, whether or not we try to see without an explicit theoretical perspective. Without going into a long defence of this position, I simply cite the point made by Berger in his classic *Ways of Seeing* (1972, p.8), that "the way we see things is affected by what we know or what we believe".

Researchers need therefore to do more than "privilege those contexts that insiders in each culture see as being most important" (Tobin et al. 1989, p.10). They should acknowledge the implicit purposes, and particularly the moral and more broadly axiological purposes, that underlie their study. They need to ask why they are doing the study; what interests motivate them in carrying it out; and what values consequently inform the research. In this I follow Habermas' position elucidated most fully in his *Knowledge and Human Interests* (1971). For Habermas (p.197), "knowledge is neither a mere instrument of an organism's adaptation to a changing environment nor the act of a pure rational being removed from the context of life in contemplation". Habermas' concern, in other words, was not merely epistemological: it was with the cognitive interests, more broadly conceived than as in the interests of private individuals or those of politically motivated groups, that ultimately influence the constitution of knowledge. He identified (1971, p.308) three primary cognitive interests, the technical, practical, and the emancipatory, to which correspond three types of disciplinary field:

> The approach of the empirical-analytic sciences incorporates a *technical* cognitive interest; that of the historical-hermeneutic sciences incorporates a *practical* one; and the approach of the critically oriented sciences incorporates the *emancipatory* cognitive interest.

The empirical-analytic sciences, and the historical-hermeneutic sciences (which Habermas also described as the "systematic *sciences of social action*, that is economics, sociology and political science" [1971, p.310]) have, in Habermas' view, the goal of producing nomological knowledge, the laws of nature. But, he asserted (1971, p.310):

> a critical social science will not remain satisfied with this.... It is concerned with going beyond this goal to determine (not only) when theoretical statements grasp invariant regularities of social action, ... (but also, more importantly) when they express ideologically frozen

relations of dependence *that can in principle be transformed*. [emphasis added]

Much of what I have considered in this chapter has had implicitly to do with symbolic interactionism, which might lead readers to conclude that the field of comparative education might be best understood as a "historical-hermeneutic science" incorporating a "practical" interest corresponding to the field of human interaction. However, I wish to defend here the view that comparative education is best conceptualised as a critical social science, incorporating an emancipatory interest focused on the distribution of power and its associated attributes: economic wealth, political influence, cultural capital, social prestige and privilege, and the like. Comparative education research, and not only across cultures, has in my view its most worthwhile contribution to make in the domain of educational development. Indeed, it has been argued (e.g., Stromquist 2005) that this has been the area of greatest impact of research in the field.

From a 'raw' epistemological perspective, then, ethnographic researchers are at best naïve if they believe they can observe the practices and behaviours of another society or culture a-theoretically and make inductive inferences about the beliefs, about the patterns which supposedly underlie these practices, and about the ways in which these practices produce meaning, from an a-theoretical starting point. And if we follow Habermas and acknowledge that epistemology cannot be purely disinterested, then social science researchers are epistemologically and morally best informed and most responsible when they take care to identify what cognitive interests inform and motivate their research. My view in response to this question is that comparative education research yields the most worthwhile results, from an ethical perspective at least, when researchers attempt, from the very conceptualisation of their projects, to identify the axes along which educational and other goods are differentially distributed, and to disaggregate their object of study along those axes. As Bernstein has concluded (1976, pp.198-199), this emancipatory cognitive interest provides the epistemological basis for Habermas' understanding of critique. The emancipatory cognitive interest is the goal of critically oriented social science, of comparison across cultures to the end of educational equity.

References

Alexander, Robin (2000): *Culture and Pedagogy: International Comparisons in Primary Education*. Oxford: Blackwell.

Anderson, Benedict (1983): *Imagined Communities: Reflections on the Origins and Spread of Nationalism*. London: Verso.

Bauman, Zygmunt (1990): 'Modernity and Ambivalence', in Featherstone, Mike (ed.), *Global Culture: Nationalism, Globalization and Modernity*. London: SAGE, pp.143-169.

Bauman, Zygmunt (2011): *Culture in a Liquid Modern World*. Cambridge: Polity Press.

Berger, John (1972): *Ways of Seeing*. London and Harmondsworth: British Broadcasting Corporation and Penguin Books.

Bernstein, Richard J. (1976): *The Restructuring of Social and Political Theory*. Philadelphia: University of Pennsylvania Press.

Bocock, Robert (1992): 'The Cultural Formations of Modern Society', in Hall, Stuart & Gieben, Bram (eds.) *Formations of Modernity*. Cambridge: Polity Press, pp.229-274.

Chan, Carol K.K. & Rao, Nirmala (2009a): 'The Paradoxes Revisited: The Chinese Learner in Changing Educational Contexts', in Chan, Carol K.K. & Rao, Nirmala (eds.), *Revisiting the Chinese Learner: Changing Contexts, Changing Education*. CERC Studies in Comparative Education 25, Hong Kong: Comparative Education Research Centre, The University of Hong Kong, and Dordrecht: Springer, pp.315-349.

Chan, Carol K.K. & Rao, Nirmala (eds.) (2009b): *Revisiting the Chinese Learner: Changing Contexts, Changing Education*. CERC Studies in Comparative Education 25, Hong Kong: Comparative Education Research Centre, The University of Hong Kong, and Dordrecht: Springer.

Delanty, Gerard (2000): *Citizenship in a Global Age: Society, Culture, Politics*. Buckingham: Open University Press.

Gellner, Ernest (1983): *Nations and Nationalism*. Oxford: Blackwell.

Habermas, Jürgen (1971): *Knowledge and Human Interests*. Translated by Jeremy J. Shapiro. Boston: Beacon Press.

Hall, Stuart (1994): 'The Question of Cultural Identity', in Hall, Stuart; Held, David & McGrew, Tony (eds.) *Modernity and its Futures*. Cambridge: Polity Press, pp.273-325.

Hammersley, Martyn (2006): 'Ethnography: Problems and Prospects'. *Ethnography and Education*, Vol.1, No.1, pp.3-14.

Herder, Johann (1784-91): *Ideas on the Philosophy of the History of Mankind*. Translated by T. Churchill. London: Luke Hansard.

Ho, David Y.F. (1986): 'Chinese Patterns of Socialization: A Critical Review', in Bond, Michael Harris (ed.), *The Psychology of the Chinese People*. Hong Kong: Oxford University Press, pp.1-37.

Hobbes, Thomas (1651/1982) *Leviathan*. Harmondsworth: Penguin.

Hobsbawm, Eric & Ranger, Terence (eds.) (1983): *The Invention of Tradition*. Cambridge: Cambridge University Press.

Hofstede, Geert (2001): *Cultures Consequences: Comparing Values, Behaviours, Institutions, and Organizations across Nations*. 2nd edition. Thousand Oaks: SAGE.

Jacob, Nina (2005): 'Cross-cultural Investigations: Emerging Concepts'. *Journal of Organizational Change Management*, Vol.18, No.5, pp.514-528.

Kallaway, Peter (1984): *Apartheid and Education: The Education of Black South Africans*. Johannesburg: Ravan Press.

Keesing, Felix M. (1960): *Cultural Anthropology: The Science of Custom*. New York: Rinehart.

Klemm, Gustav F. (1843-52): *General Cultural History of Mankind*. Leipzig.

Kluckhohn, Florence (1961): 'Dominant and Variant Value Orientations', in Kluckhohn, Florence & Strodtbeck, Fred L. (eds.), *Variations in Value Orientations*. Westport: Greenwood.

Lee, Wing On (1996): 'The Cultural Context for Chinese Learners: Conceptions of Learning in the Confucian Tradition', in Watkins, David A. & Biggs, John B. (eds.), *The Chinese Learner: Cultural, Psychological and Contextual Influences*. Hong Kong: Comparative Education Research Centre, The University of Hong Kong, pp.25-41.

LeVine, Robert A. (1966): 'Outsiders' Judgments: An Ethnographic Approach to Group Differences in Personality'. *Southwestern Journal of Anthropology*, Vol.22, No.2, pp.101-116.

Linnakylä, Pirjo (2002): 'Reading in Finland', in Papanastasiou, Constantinos & Froese, Victor (eds.) *Reading Literacy in 14 Countries*. Lefkosia: University of Cyprus Press, pp.83-108.

Marcus, George E. & Fischer, Michael M.J. (1986): *Anthropology as Cultural Critique: An Experimental Moment in the Human Sciences*. Chicago: University of Chicago Press.

Masemann, Vandra Lea (2013): 'Culture and Education', in Arnove, Robert F.; Torres, Carlos Alberto & Franz, Stephen (eds.), *Comparative Education: The Dialectic of the Global and the Local*. 4th edition. Lanham: Rowman & Littlefield, pp.113-131.

Morris, Jan (2005): 'By Jingo, He's Got it: A Review of Porter, Bernard, *The Absent-Minded Imperialists: Empire, Society and Culture in Britain'. The Guardian Weekly*, January 14-20, p.24.

Rao, Nirmala & Chan, Carol K.K. (2009): 'Moving Beyond Paradoxes: Understanding Chinese Learners and their Teachers', in Chan, Carol K.K. & Rao, Nirmala (eds.) (2009): *Revisiting the Chinese Learner: Changing Contexts, Changing Education*. CERC Studies in Comparative Education 25, Hong Kong: Comparative Education Research Centre, The University of Hong Kong, and Dordrecht: Springer, pp.3-32.

Schwarz, Bill (1986): 'Conservatism, Nationalism and Imperialism', in Donald, James & Hall, Stuart (eds.), *Politics and Ideology: A Reader*. Milton Keynes: Open University Press, pp.154-186.

Sikes, Pat; Nixon, Jon & Carr, Wilfred (2003): *The Moral Foundations of Educational Research: Knowledge, Inquiry and Values*. Buckingham: Open University Press.

Stromquist, Nelly P. (2005): 'Comparative and International Education: A Journey toward Equality and Equity'. *Harvard Educational Review*, Vol.75, No.1, pp.89-111.

Tobin, Joseph; Wu, David Y.H. & Davidson, Dana H. (1989): *Preschool in Three Cultures: Japan, China, and the United States*. New Haven: Yale University Press.

Tobin, Joseph (1999): 'Method and Meaning in Comparative Classroom Ethnography', in Alexander, Robin; Broadfoot, Patricia & Phillips, David (eds.), *Learning from Comparing: New Directions in Comparative Education Research*. Vol. 1, Oxford: Symposium Books, pp.113-134.

Tobin, Joseph; Hsueh, Yeh & Karasawa, Mayumi (2009): *Preschool in Three Cultures Revisited: China, Japan, and the United States*. Chicago: The University of Chicago Press.

Tylor, Edward (1870): *Primitive Culture: Researches into the Development of Mythology, Philosophy, Religion, Language, Art and Custom*. London: J. Murray.

Välijärvi, Jouni (2002): *The Finnish Success in PISA – and Some Reasons behind it*. Jyväskylä: Institute for Educational Research.

Wagner, Roy (1981): *The Invention of Culture*. Chicago: The University of Chicago Press.

Wallerstein, Immanuel (1974): *The Modern World System: Capitalist Agriculture and the Origins of the European World Economy in the Sixteenth Century*. New York: Academic Press.

Waters, Malcolm (1995): *Globalization*. Cambridge: Polity Press.

Watkins, David A. & Biggs, John B. (eds.) (1996): *The Chinese Learner: Cultural, Psychological and Contextual Influences*. Hong Kong: Comparative Education Research Centre, The University of Hong Kong.

Watkins, David A. & Biggs, John B. (eds.) (2001): *Teaching the Chinese Learner: Psychological and Pedagogical Perspectives*. Hong Kong: Comparative Education Research Centre, The University of Hong Kong.

Williams, Raymond (1981): *Culture and Society, 1780-1950*. London: Fontana.

Williams, Raymond (1982): *The Sociology of Culture*. New York: Schocken.

Williams, Raymond (1985): *Keywords: A Vocabulary of Culture and Society*. New York: Oxford University Press.

Yang, Kuo-Shu (1986): 'Chinese Personality and its Change', in Bond, Michael Harris (ed.), *The Psychology of the Chinese People*. Hong Kong: Oxford University Press, pp.106-170.

9

Comparing Values

Wing On LEE & Maria MANZON

In the late 1980s, Cummings and associates highlighted a renaissance of interest in values education across the world. Their book, entitled *The Revival of Values Education in Asia and the West* (Cummings et al. 1988, p.3), contained rich information about how values education had penetrated the curriculum in 90 countries. Values education continued to 'revive', leading to another book entitled *Values Education for Dynamic Societies,* edited by Cummings and another group of associates (Cummings et al. 2001a). The book presented a study of values education in 20 settings in the Pacific Basin, showing in one way or another how values education remained a major concern to educational leaders. Asian scholarship has also contributed to the theme with a trilogy on citizenship education in Asia and Pacific (Lee et al. 2004; Grossman et al. 2008; Kennedy et al. 2010).

Although values are important to educators and researchers, the concept of values is both broad and elusive. Just as philosophy penetrates every area of studies, discussion of values can be found in nearly every discipline. It is almost impossible to pin down the scope of definitions of values, which extend from personal to collective levels and cover many forms of knowledge. For example, values can include self-actualisation, truth, goodness, individuality, justice, perfection, and meaningfulness (Heffron 1997, p.17).

People who see values from the personal perspective consider values education to be a form of moral and character development (Nucci 1989). By contrast, people who look at values from the collective perspective tend to focus on social values, cultural values, political values, citizenship, and belief systems such as religions and ideologies (Cheng 1997; Lee 1997; Beck 1998). Yet other scholars look at values from the perspective of forms of knowledge. In other words, they tend to look at the nature of the 'value realms', such as psychological, economic, ethical, aesthetic, poetic, literary, technological, and legal (Presno & Presno 1980). Nevertheless, since the concept of values is so broad, it is difficult for any author to confine discussion to a single framework. Whenever values are discussed collectively, they have to be examined in the context of individual choices. Likewise, whenever values are focused on individuals, they are never separable from the society at large. Even when values are discussed in the perspectives of value realms, they are in one way or another related to time differences and to individual and collective preferences. The interrelatedness of the personal, collective and value realms is highlighted in the work of Gardner et al. (2000) entitled *Education for Values: Morals, Ethics and Citizenship in Contemporary Teaching*.

This chapter focuses on studies of values that are comparative by design, analysing values in different social and political systems. These systems are variously called societies, nations or countries, depending on the foci of the researchers. The chapter reviews discussions of comparative methods and approaches in the study of values. The cases chosen mainly cover citizenship or civic-related matters, and illustrate typological variations. The 11 cases chosen can be grouped into four categories. Cases in Category A are related to size, scale and complexity of the research construct; cases in Category B are longitudinal analyses of textbooks; cases in Category C focus on convergent and divergent values; and cases in Category D are comparisons in qualitative studies.

Category A: Size, Scale and Complexity of the Research Construct

Case One: Large Scale, Multiple Researchers, and Multiple Dimensions and Instruments – The International Civic and Citizenship Education Study (ICCS)
The largest and most comprehensive international study of civic and citizenship education was conducted under the auspices of the International Association for the Evaluation of Educational Achievement (IEA) in 2009. The ICCS was the third IEA study on civics and citizenship education. The first was conducted in 1971 with nine countries participating, and the second in 1999 with 28 countries (Torney-Purta et al. 2001). The ICCS surveyed over 140,000 Grade 8 students and 62,000 teachers in 5,300

schools of 38 countries. Five countries were in Asia, 26 in Europe, six in Latin America, and one in Australasia. The data were augmented by contextual data collected from their respective school principals and national research centres.

The purposes of the ICCS (Ainley et al. 2013) were to examine:

- the ways in which countries prepare their young people to undertake their roles as citizens;
- student knowledge and understanding of civics and citizenship as well as student attitudes, perceptions, and activities related to civics and citizenship; and
- the differences among countries in relation to these outcomes of civic and citizenship education, and how differences across countries relate to student characteristics, school and community contexts, and national characteristics.

The study revolved around six research questions concerned with (1) variations in civic knowledge, (2) changes in content knowledge since 1999, (3) the interest and dispositions of students to engage in public and political life, (4) perceptions of threats to civil society, (5) features of education systems, schools, and classrooms that were related to civic and citizenship education, and (6) aspects of student background associated with the outcomes of civic and citizenship education (Schulz et al. 2011, p.15). In order to operationalize these questions, the ICCS team developed a civics and citizenship framework with three dimensions: content, affective-behavioural, and cognitive. In turn, each dimension was analysed by domains. 'Content' had four domains, namely civic society and systems, civic principles, civic participation, and civic identities. 'Affective-behavioural' domains comprised value beliefs, attitudes, behavioural intentions, and behaviours. The two cognitive domains were knowing and reasoning-and-analysing (Schulz et al. 2011).

Several instruments were administered. An international student cognitive test had 80 items measuring civic and citizenship knowledge, analysis and reasoning. A separate international student questionnaire collected data on perceptions about civics and citizenship and on students' backgrounds; and a set of regional instruments addressed particular issues related to civics and citizenship in Asia, Europe and Latin America. Teachers completed a questionnaire on perceptions of civic and citizenship education in their schools; and school principals completed a questionnaire on school characteristics and provision of civic and citizenship education. National research coordinators conducted an online survey among national experts, gathering information about the structure of the education system and the place of civic and citizenship education in the national curricula. This contextual information was published in the *ICCS 2009 Encyclopedia* (Ainley et al. 2013).

The study was organized by a consortium of three partner institutions: the Australian Council for Educational Research (ACER), the National Foundation for Educational Research (NFER) in the United Kingdom, and the Laboratorio di Pedagogia sperimentale (LPS) at the Roma Tre University in Italy. These institutions worked in close cooperation with the IEA Secretariat, the IEA Data Processing and Research Centre, and the study's national research coordinators from 38 countries.

Case Two: Small Scale, Multiple Researchers, and Simple Instruments – A Study of Teachers' Perceptions of Good Citizenship in Five Countries
Few comparative projects can achieve the scale of the IEA study; but not all scholars approve of the IEA approach. IEA studies have been challenged for their relatively simplistic interpretation of the complex data collected from a large number of countries with great variation in cultures, societies, economics and politics. They have also been questioned for the exclusivity of their choice of problems and countries for analysis. Buk-Berge (2006, p.543), commenting on IEA studies of civic education in post-communist countries, argued that they excluded countries that did "not exactly fit the template as created by the IEA", and that some country cases were "reflections of experts rather than representations of data".

An alternative extreme approach uses an instrument that is as simple as possible, to minimise variations in interpretation of the data from the participating countries. Lee and Fouts (2005) in their study of teachers' perceptions of good citizenship in the USA, England, Australia, Russia and China, conducted during 1995-1999, deliberately made this point (pp.11-12):

> Two specific and closely related challenges to this kind of study are, first, to do with the problem of conceptual constraints, and second, the problem of measurement. The problem with conceptual constraints is stated succinctly by Thomas (1990): "Many educational [and other] concepts do not have equivalent meanings across social or cultural groups or even across nations." Indeed, this fact is the basis for the project "Good citizenship" and it means different things to different people. But in a narrower sense, the problem is

one of ensuring that we are all talking about the same thing, not just about "good citizenship" but also about concepts used to define "good citizenship," such as moral education and patriotism....

In selecting the instrumentation and interview questions for this study, we did so with the recognition that the more complex the instruments and procedures, the greater the likelihood of translation difficulties and loss of comparability. For this reason, we have attempted to keep the survey and interview questions as basic and as straightforward as possible. While the instruments and interview questions may not be ideal or as elaborate as might be used in a single country study, we believe they will be adequate for our purposes, with some limitations, and allow for translations that will allow comparisons across countries.

In sharp contrast to the IEA study, this five-country study administered a simple two-page questionnaire to a convenient sample of about 500 teachers in each city of the participating countries, with follow-up interviews with some teachers. Rather than developing a complex schema that contained multiple dimensions of concepts, the study was confined to four questions about: (1) the qualities of a good citizen; (2) the influences on a person's citizenship; (3) threats to a child's citizenship; and (4) classroom activities that would help to develop a child's citizenship. The four questions were selected from a larger set of questions, many of which were discarded in the process of piloting and field test. The simple set of questions in the survey to enhance comparability was extended in the follow-up qualitative interviews. The US team started the trial, and their experience was consolidated and distributed to the other participating countries as a sample to be followed as closely as possible by the other participating countries for enhancing comparability.

Case Three: Large Scale, Single Researcher, Multiple Dimensions and Instruments – A Study of Political Socialisation in Five Countries
While many comparative studies of values have been undertaken by teams, Hahn (1998) conducted by herself a comparative study of political socialisation in England, Denmark, Germany, the Netherlands, and the USA. In her book *Becoming Political*, Hahn uses the first person singular – a refreshing departure from convention. For example, she explained (1998, pp.1-5) that:

I faced the difficult challenge of identifying a sample of adolescents in five countries. I began to contact people whom I met at various international conferences on social studies, citizenship, and global education.... I solicited and obtained classes of students, primarily ages fifteen through nineteen, in varied types of secondary schools in five countries.... I constructed a questionnaire with scales measuring political attitudes of interest, efficacy, trust, and confidence.... I conducted interviews with teachers and students to gain further insight into adolescent political attitudes and beliefs into the process of citizenship education in each country. I conducted interviews with small groups of from two to eight students and spoke with whole classes.... I analysed the quantitative data using factor analyses, item analyses, frequency distributions by item, means of items and scales, analyses of variance and effect sizes between means.... I analyzed each component of the qualitative data set (field notes, interviews, documents, and my field diary) using constant comparative analysis to generate themes from the raw data....

Since the study was ambitious, it is no wonder that it required 10 years to complete. Of course, Hahn did not work alone. She relied on many link persons in the respective countries, and she acknowledged many assistants in the process of data analysis. However, this represented individual effort in making decisions on when, where and how to work. Hahn's limitation was at the same time her strength. She did not have an international team to support her, and was therefore short of human resources and diversity in ideas for such a big study; but she did not need to cope with a cross-cultural team, worry about coordination, or ensure commonality across the country participants as in the two cases mentioned above. Hahn herself served as the overarching parameter, and performed the mediating role across the country cases.

Unlike Lee and Fouts, who minimised their scale and instrument in order to achieve the comparability that they perceived to be possible, Hahn adopted a comprehensive approach with complex methods. In respect to qualitative study, she analysed each component to generate themes from the raw data (including classroom observations, interviews of teachers and students, and documents, field notes and field diary). In respect to quantitative study, she adapted several scales and developed some of her own. The adapted scales included the Political Trust Scale, the Political Efficacy Scale, the Political Confidence Scale, and the Political Interest Scale. The items and scales developed by Hahn herself included the Future Political Activity Items, the Political Experience Item, the Freedom of Expression Scale, the Civic Tolerance Scale, and the Classroom Climate Scale. These scales were used to measure political attitudes of interest, efficacy, trust and confidence; political behaviours such as following news and discussing politics; attitudes towards free speech and press for diverse groups; beliefs in equal political rights for females as well as males; and perceptions of a classroom climate in which students were encouraged to express their beliefs about controversial issues (Hahn, 1998, pp.3-4). Hahn's major discovery from her 10-year multi-method study (pp.17-18) was of diversities within commonalities:

> Although we speak often of Western democracies, ... there is much variety among their political systems and cultures. At the same time that the forms of democratic structures and processes vary considerably, the citizens of these countries inherited enlightenment values of individual liberty.... [Nevertheless,] unique features of each national educational system evolved within shared ideas about the purposes and fundamental form of schooling.

Case Four: Small Scale, Multiple Researchers and Secondary Quantitative Analysis – A Study of Students' Views of Citizenship in Three Countries
Kennedy, Hahn and Lee (2008) conducted a secondary quantitative analysis of the 1999 IEA Civic Education data for Australia, Hong Kong and the United States, in order to compare students' values and attitudes both within and across the three societies. Each author had been a national research coordinator for the 1999 IEA study, so brought insiders' perspectives for their own societies as well as outsiders' perspectives towards the other two. Based on the nationally representative samples from the IEA international study, the authors used data from 1,000 randomly selected respondents in each weighted sample. They then employed the Statistical Package for the Social Sciences 12.0 to compute frequencies for each response category on every item of four scales chosen for each society. This was based on the assumption that the distribution of frequencies across response categories represented the emphases placed by students along the latent construct, and enabled cross-societal comparison of results. Finally, they related their findings to aspects of civic culture and values in the respective societies (pp.60-61).

This study drew a contextual 'map' of the three societies chosen for comparison, which justified the existence of sufficient commonalities to make their differences meaningful. The secondary analysis revealed some variations in student perceptions which would have been overshadowed in the original international large-scale analysis of the data by the IEA team. Moreover, the authors discovered some unexpected outcomes (p.88), noting that some similarities and differences among students could not easily be explained:

> The three societies are unique in historical, political, economic, and cultural terms. So why is it that in some cases Hong Kong students' attitudes are more like those of U.S. students while the attitudes of Australian students at times are completely different from those of their peers in the United States? At the present time we cannot explain such comparative results, but one important implication that flows from them is that political socialization appears to be a much more unpredictable process than traditional paradigms might suggest. Clearly, more work needs to be done in this area if we are to understand the subtle interplay of influences within local contexts that leads to unexpected and unplanned outcomes.

The above case illustrates a convergent outcome, in some instances, among rather divergent and distinctive societies.

Category B: Longitudinal Studies of Textbooks

Case Five: Multiple Countries, One Researcher, Quantitative – A Longitudinal Analysis of 465 Textbooks Worldwide

Bromley (2009) examined cross-national trends towards cosmopolitanism by employing a longitudinal content analysis of 465 high school textbooks of history, civics and social studies from 69 countries published between 1970 and 2008. The majority of the books were from Germany's Georg Eckert Institute for International Textbook Research. They were originally gathered for a research project on human rights education led by John Meyer and Francisco Ramirez (Meyer et al. 2010). Bromley coded each book on parameters designed to measure cosmopolitan emphases of universalism and diversity. Strategies to address challenges resulting from translation included the use of factual questions, employing fully-bilingual translators, and ensuring inter-rater reliability. The textbooks were divided into two main periods: 1970-1994 and 1995-2008, in order to capture the historical changes in Eastern Europe as well as to have an even divide of the sample data.

The study revealed a worldwide trend towards cosmopolitan emphases in civic education textbooks with the exception of Asia. The author recognised that this unexpected finding contradicted other in-depth studies of Asia. Bromley attributed this outlier outcome to the limitations of macro-level studies which failed to capture the nuances and meanings that individual and in-depth case studies bring to light (2009, p.39). The following case, similarly longitudinal in nature, demonstrates the benefits of a single case analysis seen in comparative perspective.

Case Six: One Country, Mixed Methods – A Longitudinal Analysis of Civic Education Textbooks
This study, while not explicitly comparative in the sense of cross-national comparison, deserves exploration here since it analyses a core theme of comparative education: the dialectic of the global and the local in the diffusion of educational ideas. Moon and Koo (2011) conducted a mixed-method study of citizenship education in South Korea, examining the way global trends on citizenship education interacted with local contextual factors. Using quantitative data from textbook content analysis, they described trends in 62 South Korean civic education textbooks from 1981 to 2004. They read each textbook, page by page, counting the number of keyword mentions (global vs. national) and obtaining an average number of keywords per page in order to identify trends over time. They complemented this analysis with qualitative data from 28 semi-structured interviews with local actors to elucidate how global citizenship emphases in the South Korean curriculum came about. Their study revealed interesting conclusions on the global-local dialectic in the diffusion and adoption of global citizenship concepts in South Korea. They claimed (p.595) that:

> global mechanisms were intimately tied to the chain of local developments that led to the successful incorporation of global citizenship themes in school textbooks. Local organizations, national political leaders, and government officials were closely linked to global models, and this linkage led to the diffusion and adoption of ideas of global citizenship within Korean society.

Category C: Studies of Convergent and Divergent Values

Case Seven: Studying Convergent Values – A Delphi Study on Policy Shapers in Nine Countries

Cogan (2000) and associates compared citizenship in England, Germany, Greece, Hungary, the Netherlands, Thailand, Japan, Canada and the USA from 1993 to 1997. Their method was a cross-cultural adaptation of an Ethnographic Delphi Futures Research model. The Delphi method is commonly used to tap long-term projections in order to develop appropriate policy directives. The method also helps to condense diverse data into consensus data, and to interpret those data by both the respondents and the researchers. The study obtained responses from 182 policy experts, and generated 900 draft Delphi statements, organised as trends, characteristics and educational strategies/approaches/innovations. The team developed a fine approach to determine significant weightings for grouping data (Kurth-Schai et al. 2000).

The process developed was in line with the purpose set for identifying convergence, particularly in setting specific criteria for selecting research partners and their respondents. Four criteria were developed to select research team leaders, namely demonstrated expertise in citizenship education and/or research methodology; a future-oriented vision; interest in the study; and a commitment to remain with the project. The four criteria for selecting expert panellists were future orientation; leadership in field of expertise; interest civic and public affairs; and knowledge of global trends and issues.

The criterion common to both groups led to a pattern in which future-oriented researchers studied future-oriented leaders. Using Berg-Schlosser's (2001) concept, this belonged to a 'similar systems, similar outcomes' approach. As a result, eight citizenship attributes were identified, and a schema of four dimensions was developed based on which a multidimensional citizenship model was constructed. However, the project team did not ignore non-consensus data. A specific chapter of the report examined non-consensual statements and the degree of disagreement. In general, the team identified many East-West differences, and noted that leaders in the East had a higher degree of agreement vis à vis their Western counterparts (Karsten et al. 2000).

Case Eight: Studying Divergent Values – A Sigma Study of Leaders in 11 Countries

In 1996, Cummings et al. initiated a project on the future focus of values education in the Pacific Rim. The study lasted for three years, and involved 11 countries. It started with a simple framework which focused on four core questions (Cummings 1998, p.1):

> **why** are values changing, **what** values should receive the greatest emphasis in values education, **who** should be the focus of values education, and **how** should these values be developed and transmitted?

At the outset, the team proposed a Delphi study, as it was an obvious approach for studying value orientations of leaders (Cummings et al. 1996). However, when the project started, and when country representatives met, the team members changed their minds. Cummings' working report noted (1998, p.1) that:

> This group [of country representatives] was appreciative of the recent trends and was especially conscious of the divergent positions in the region. At first the group considered ways to promote greater regional consensus. But then, in a surprising intellectual reversal, the group concluded that the diverging tendencies were a reflection of the emerging complexity of the contemporary life. Thus the group readjusted its focus, and agreed to join forces in developing a methodology for analysing the diverse patterns. The methodology involved a combination of national case and the international sigma survey.

Having acknowledged divergence as the defined nature for studying values across countries, the project dropped the idea of Delphi study and instead conducted a sigma study. The team argued that methodology for highlighting differences required a new survey approach, the Sigma International Elite Survey. In the final report, Cummings et al. (2001b, p.14) stressed that:

> The letter sigma is used by statisticians to symbolise variance. The sigma approach developed in this study seeks to highlight differences or variance. It should be contrasted with the Delphi approach, which seeks to develop consensus and thereby to reduce variance.

The special features of the Sigma Survey were said to be:

- the intentional selection of an elite sample from each setting that represents important points of variation in terms of political/ideological affiliation, social position, gender, and regional location;

- the development of questions that reflect the particular concerns of each setting;
- the use of a question format that requires respondents to clarify where they stand (e.g. rank-ordering from a list with many options); and
- follow-up questions to selected respondents who take exceptional positions on particular responses.

Having decided that the study was not to look for convergence, the project adopted a divergent approach to study divergent values (Cummings et al. 2001b, p.8):

> Recognising the impossibility of developing a meaningful definition of leaders that would fit the various countries and settings under consideration, no effort was made to choose a random sample. Rather each team was expected to choose those leaders that best reflected their setting, keeping in mind the common commitment to diversity. By social position, 6 percent of the sample are political leaders, 17 percent are central educational authorities, 5 percent are religious leaders, 11 percent are from related NGOs [Non-Governmental Organizations], 17 percent are intellectual leaders, 12 percent are academics, 18 percent are local school leaders, and 20 percent are curriculum designers or teachers of values education; 21 percent are women. This distribution was more or less similar for each setting, though the full details for the setting samples can be found in the respective chapters. In total, responses were obtained from 834 leaders.

According to Berg-Schlosser (2001), this arrangement adhered to the 'different systems, different outcomes' approach. The result of the analysis was the identification of patterns of variation in value orientation among the participating countries. The team conducted a multidimensional scaling of 15 rationales for values education, and located countries between two continua, namely individualism and collectivism, and diversity and nationalism. The team further identified four patterns that could locate the participating countries, namely Far West Liberals, Southeast Asian Moralists, Confucian Middle Way, and Former Socialist/ Centrists. Nevertheless, like Cogan and his associates, who could not ignore non-consensus data in the process of converging consensus data in the Delphi study, Cummings and his team could not ignore convergence in the process of studying divergence in values. The study concluded that the value areas receiving the most support were personal autonomy, moral values, civic values, and democracy. The value areas at the second level of support were work, ecology, family, peace, national identity, and diversity. The value areas receiving the lowest priority were gender equality, global awareness, and religion (Cummings 2001, pp.289-290).

Case Nine: Studying Divergence in Convergent Values – Asian Civic Values Study
Young and Tae (2013) undertook a cross-cultural comparison of lower-secondary school students' perceptions of Asian civic values in Taiwan and Hong Kong. They applied exploratory and confirmatory factor analyses to the ICCS 2009 Asian Regional Module data in order to explore the factor model that best fitted the three societies. Latent mean analysis was subsequently employed to compare between-society differences. The study revealed that, while there was an overall convergence among East Asian students' perceptions with respect to being averse to undemocratic and unfair practices as well as acceptance of Asian identity and democratic values, there were cross-national divergences in the degree of perception towards some civic values. This case illustrates Berg-Schlosser's (2001) typology of 'similar systems, different outcomes' in cross-case analyses.

Category D: Comparing Cases in Qualitative Studies
Case 10: A Study of School Cases in Six Societies
Cogan et al. (2002) compared civic education in six societies, namely New South Wales (Australia), Hong Kong, Japan, Taiwan, Thailand, and the American Midwest, in 1997-2000. Unlike the above-mentioned studies that employed a combination of quantitative and qualitative approaches, this study basically employed qualitative approaches, comprising historical overview, policy and documentary analysis, and case studies of schools in each participating society. The number of school cases selected ranged from two in Hong Kong to four in New South Wales. The resulting features of comparison also differed from the above-mentioned studies, as no quantitative data were compared. Instead, there was detailed description and analysis for each participating society, and the overall comparison took the form of statement juxtaposition. Three summary tables of comparison were provided in the final report, on (1) government policies, (2) knowledge/values promoted, and (3) civic values, highlighting major points judged to be important to the research team. The team

highlighted the term 'cross-case analysis' in their overview chapter, showing a distinctive kind of comparison. Moreover, the concept of case was multi-layered. The study was a comparison of comparative cases, or a study of case of cases. Each participating society identified school cases to be compared, and the team further compared the participating societies as individual case units. Moving even further, they developed them into cultural cases, such as 'the Asian societies' and 'the Western societies' (Morris et al. 2002).

This cross-case analysis identified both convergent and divergent values. On the side of convergence, the researchers identified eight clusters of values: self-cultivation, family values, democratic values, fair government, economic life, social cohesion/diversity, civil life and community, and national identity. However, the study identified much more divergence than convergence, and four sets of tensions across all the societies (Morris et al. 2002, p.174):

- the rights of the individual versus the interests of the community;
- maintaining social stability versus social change/reconstruction;
- social cohesion versus social diversity; and
- providing a body of received knowledge versus treating knowledge as provisional and constructed.

Another feature of the authors' comparative work was that, instead of presetting parameters for comparison, they chose the concept of minimal and maximal citizenship as a framework for locating their society cases.

Case 11: Secondary Qualitative Case Analyses
Another cross-case comparison is the IEA Civic Education Study. The study had two phases, with Phase 1 designed as a qualitative component that would help instrument construction for the quantitative survey in Phase 2. The research team formulated 18 framing questions to unify supply of background information, and the country representatives agreed to confine their analyses to the domains of democracy, national identity, and social cohesion and diversity. As a result, 24 qualitative case reports were produced. In order to make sense of these reports, and especially to inform Phase 2, the International Steering Committee invited a number of scholars to analyse the cases. The different methods and approaches of these scholars provided significant insight for qualitative comparisons.

These analyses were published in a book edited by Steiner-Khamsi et al. (2002a). The editors provided insightful discussion on the various comparative methods and approaches. One observation was related to the selection of cases. Most authors developed contextual sampling criteria that allowed them to concentrate on a few cases. The majority of authors reduced content by focusing either on specific core domains of civic education (democracy, national identity, or diversity/social cohesion) or levels of analysis (policy, practice, curriculum, etc.). Another method for narrowing the radius of the analysis was informed by controversies on theories of citizenship and civic education.

Two approaches were adopted in deriving the interpretation framework. One adopted a grounded-theory approach, by (1) identifying keywords from the case reports, (2) selecting a few themes for analysis, (3) choosing a focus developed from this process by ruling out themes that were non-comparable, and then choosing a theme that emerged in the process, and (4) reviewing the themes with relevant concepts in the literature. A few authors developed interpretive frameworks based on such literature reviews, trying to examine whether the cases matched the theoretical model. One author engaged in a meta-level analysis, reflecting on the process of how the qualitative data were collected and how that process differed from other studies in qualitative research or comparative education (Steiner-Khamsi et al. 2002b, pp.12-14).

When conducting the case comparison, these authors had varied views on what constituted a case. Some treated the country studies as units of analysis for cross-national comparison, whereas others regarded the country studies as bounded systems that represented different models of citizenship or civic education. Most authors used sampling criteria that clearly reflected the design of contrastive analysis. They selected cases that they perceived to be 'most different' from each other with regard to political system, educational system, or other criteria. The authors who reduced the sample of cases applied a contrastive method based on the 'most different systems and different outcomes' design. Steiner-Khamsi, for example, selected the reports on the United States, Romania, Germany and Hong Kong because she judged that these cases represented conceptions of citizenship, and she expected to find different outcomes with regard to civic education curricula (2002b, p.26).

The editors found that qualitative cross-national analysis provided room to address unexpected findings and that the case study material 'talked back'. While reviewing the qualitative data base, three authors found the original conceptual framework of the IEA Civic Education Study too narrow. Based on the case study analyses that they conducted independently, they suggested extension of the framework to cover economic and supranational aspects of citizenship.

Steiner-Khamsi et al. (2002b, p.34) commented that in many respects, qualitative researchers share the same methodological challenges of cross-national data analysis as quantitative researchers. For example, both need to deal with problems of sampling, reducing data, validity, and reliability. However, when qualitative comparativists analysed their case study material cross-nationally, they had to ensure that the 'texture' of the case study material was not harmed. The material needed a different treatment from open-ended questions in a survey. Steiner-Khamsi et al. (2002b, p.34) concluded that:

> Case studies are coherent stories, wrapped in theory. They tell us something about causal relations in a bounded system and are much more contextual than all open-ended questions in a survey combined. Not losing sight of contextuality appears to be a challenge that only qualitative comparative researchers are privileged to have.

Discussion and Conclusions

The above review shows that in comparative values, despite differences in the choice of methodology (such as quantitative and/or qualitative), the size of studies (such as the number of countries and cases), what values to look for (such as convergent and/or divergent values), and investigation approaches (such as inductive [observation derived from data] or deductive [verification of theories]), these studies invariably examined values by asking, even if not explicitly:

- What are the preferred values in society?
- What are the interactions between personal values and society values?
- Why are particular values emphasised (and very often understood in terms of cultural tradition and social change)?
- What explanatory tools can be adopted to understand these scenarios in terms of theorisation?
- How are these values disseminated in the education system?

- Is there a gap in policy (in terms of values espoused by policy makers) and implementation (in terms of values held by individuals, such as students and teachers, and the school)?

However, scholars approaching comparative study always face dilemmas in the choices of methods and approaches. Levi-Faur (2006) commented on some of these dilemmas, including the size of sample, the struggle between the quantitative-qualitative divide, and the choice of prioritising attention towards practicalities or ideologies. The 11 cases reviewed in this chapter show significant variations in approaches. In terms of size of sample, the number of countries ranged from one to 69. Most, with the exception of two huge cross-national analyses conducted by single individuals (Case 3, Hahn; Case 5, Bromley), adopted a team approach. Many favoured study of multiple dimensions, thus requiring complex instruments, though one reduced the instrument to its simplest form in order to promote ease of comparison.

Figure 9.1: Varied Methodological Emphases in Comparative Studies of Values

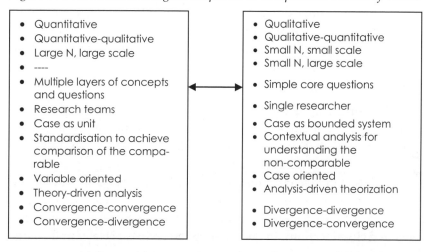

The cases also represented extremes in research paradigms. One extreme was entirely quantitative, which standardised variables using numerical methods; and the other extreme was entirely qualitative and sought to uncover the meanings of citizenship and values through case studies. In the quantitative studies, the topics were narrowed down by statistical methods such as factor analysis. In Case One, for example, final topics were knowledge of civic contents; interpretation of civic information; concepts of democracy, citizenship and government; and attitudes towards the nation, the government, immigrants, and women's political rights. These topics were derived from a broad initial focus, followed by detailed questionnaire survey. Cases Seven and Eight are similar. By contrast, the qualitative methods employed in Cases 10 and 11 included focus-group interviews and content analysis of textbooks and curricula.

Some of the studies (e.g. Case Six) used both approaches and lay between the two extremes. They reflected or represented efforts in comparative research in the field of social sciences to combine methods instead of dichotomising them. As noted by Coppedge (1997, p.1) large N and small N studies can be complementary:

> Small N Comparison tends to develop "thick" (complex, multidimensional, contextualised, or rich) concepts and theories that are well-suited for description and for making inferences about simple causation on a small scale or in a few cases; but thick concepts and theories are unwieldy when it comes to generalisation or rigorous testing of complex hypotheses. On the other hand, quantitative analysis is justifiably criticised for its "thin" (reductionist or simplistic) concepts and theories, but it is the best method available for testing generalisations, especially generalisations about complex causal relationships.

Coppedge further argued that thick concepts can be translated into the thin format of quantitative data, and that thin concepts can be thickened by employing qualitative methods to complement quantitative studies.

As illustrated by the cases reviewed in this chapter, comparative value studies tend to lean on the side of qualitative analysis, even though the quantitative component can also be emphasised (see e.g. Torney-Purta & Amadeo 2013, who stress the value of international large-scale assessments in civic education). In quantitative research, especially in the large IEA study, a country often constitutes one unit in the analytical framework, being grouped with the other countries with similar outcomes. However, this does not seem to be what most comparative value studies seek. Just knowing where one country is located alongside other countries does not seem to satisfy the researchers, who tend to ask what the values *mean* to the societies concerned. This question leads to a heavier emphasis on the qualitative approach, and contributes to emphasis on 'the ontology of kind' rather than 'methodology of size' (Levi-Faur 2006). Hahn (2010) likewise stressed the importance of intra- or sub-national comparisons by ethnic or other sub-groupings, since these may be more insightful than cross-national comparisons and also capture the voices of transnational youth communities. Hahn also called for more analysis of the interplay of global and local forces in shaping value orientations, an illustration of which is Case Six.

Some comparative studies look for convergence, but others seek divergence. It seems obvious that the starting points influence the choice of approaches, sampling of respondents, and the prediction of outcomes. However, two cases reviewed in this chapter show that convergent studies have to acknowledge divergence, and vice versa. Berg-Schlosser's analysis of comparative qualitative research designs (2001) identified a 2 x 2 matrix that distinguished between similarity of systems (cases) and predictions with regard to outcomes (variables), as shown in Figure 9.2.

Figure 9.2: Sampling Design in Case Study Format Research

Most similar systems + similar outcomes	Most different systems + similar outcomes
Most similar systems + different outcomes	Most different systems + different outcomes

Source: Berg-Schlosser (2001), p.2430.

In a different way, Levi-Faur (2006) observed that case-oriented comparative studies can be grouped into a difference-agreement matrix. This is shown in Figure 9.3.

Figure 9.3: Four Inferential Strategies in Case-oriented Comparative Research

	Difference	Agreement
Most similar system research design	Dealing with differences in similar cases: minimise variance of the control variables, maximise variance in the dependent variables	Dealing with similarities in similar cases: minimise variance of the control and dependent variables
Most different system research design	Dealing with differences in different cases: maximise variance of the control and dependent variables	Dealing with similarities in different cases: maximise variance of the control, and independent variables, minimise variance in the dependent variables

Source: Adapted from Levi-Faur (2006), p.59.

In the secondary qualitative analyses of the IEA Civic Education Study, most authors chose the 'most different systems, most different outcomes' approach. From the cases selected for discussion in this chapter, it seems that the more the study belonged to a qualitative case, the more divergence was identified. In the cross-case analysis conducted by Morris et al. (2002), the term 'variations' appears many times on a single page. This also shows that the more one looks into the context, the higher the tendency for the researchers to attend to 'thick descriptions' of the texture of the cases, and thus the higher degree of divergence. This phenomenon reflects findings about case-oriented approaches in social science research, which are characterised by 'small N, many variables' (Steiner-Khamsi et al. 2002a).

Approaches to analysing qualitative cases can also differ. The secondary qualitative analysis of the IEA cases included both grounded theory approaches and hypothesis-driven analyses. The former attempted a continued approach of narrowing down the scope of analysis until the researcher found a distinctive focus that was related to concepts of citizenship. The contextual analysis of concepts was further compared with existing theories for verification. The latter started with a certain theory or hypothesis whereby the choice of countries was made, and then tried to verify these cases with the theory (or vice versa). For example, Steiner-Khamsi (2002b, p.21) chose four societies for comparison, based upon her hypothetical model that distinguished four different spheres of citizenship – constitutional, economic, civic, and moral. She found that what she had anticipated did not in fact emerge from the data:

> Civic education curricula in Hong Kong are not particularly moralistic, German and Romanian curricula emphasize constitutional aspects no more than other countries, and civic education programmes in the United States do not place a particularly high priority on teaching about the economy nor do they engage students in civic actions. Moreover, in all four examined case studies, the political and economic spheres are inextricably linked.

Analysis of the studies identified in this chapter shows that comparative value studies have enriched the field of comparative education by showing complexities about values in context, how education interplays with these values, how values can be grouped by countries, and countries grouped by values, and how global values interact with local values. The attention to context is a natural orientation in value studies, and this has led to many surprises in the processes of comparison, including finding divergence in convergence and convergence in divergence. Moreover, the comparison is theory-rich, either from grounded approaches or theory-driven approaches, and theory advancement takes place in the process of theory verification. The comments of Levi-Faur (2006) best represent the features of the comparative studies reviewed in this chapter:

> To celebrate comparative research is to look for new languages, new terms, new procedures and new instruments of inference; it is, in short, to innovate and to move on with a critical view of the dominance of both case-studies and statistical approaches. It also implies an effort to bridge the divide between case- and variable-oriented research.

Indeed, all the comparative value studies reviewed in this chapter manifest attempts to find new languages, new terms, new procedures and new instruments of inference. They have enriched understanding in both contents and methods, and particularly in the varied ways to look at similar questions in relation to values.

References

Ainley, John; Schulz, William & Friedman, Tim (eds.) (2013): *ICCS 2009 Encyclopedia: Approaches to Civic and Citizenship Education around the World*. Amsterdam: International Association for the Evaluation of Educational Achievement (IEA).

Beck, John (1998): *Morality and Citizenship in Education*. London: Cassell.

Berg-Schlosser, Dirk (2001): 'Comparative Studies: Method and Design', in Smelser, Neil J. & Baltes, Paul B. (eds.), *International Encyclopedia of the Social and Behavioural Sciences*. Amsterdam: Elsevier, pp.2427-2433.

Bromley, Patricia (2009): 'Cosmopolitanism in Civic Education: Exploring Cross-National Trends, 1970-2008'. *Current Issues in Comparative Education*, Vol.12, No.1, pp.33-44.

Buk-Berge, Elisabeth (2006): 'Missed Opportunities: The IEA's Study of Civic Education and Civic Education in Post-Communist Countries'. *Comparative Education*, Vol.42, No.4, pp.533-548.

Cheng, Kai Ming (1997): 'Engineering Values: Education Policies and Values Transmission', in Montgomery, John D. (ed.), *Values in Education: Social Capital Formation in Asia and the Pacific*. Hollis, New Hampshire: Hollis Publishing Company, pp.173-184.

Cogan, John J. (2000): 'Citizenship Education for the 21st Century: Setting the Context', in Cogan, John J. & Derricott, Ray (eds.), *Citizenship for the 21st Century: An International Perspective on Education*. London: Kogan Page, pp.1-22.

Cogan, John J.; Morris, Paul & Print, Murray (2002): 'Civic Education in the Asia-Pacific Region: An Introduction', in Cogan, John J.; Morris, Paul & Print, Murray (eds.), *Civic Education in the Asia-Pacific Region: Case Studies across Six Societies*. New York: RoutledgeFalmer, pp.1-22.

Coppedge, Michael (1997): 'How the Large N Could Complement the Small N in Democratisation Research'. Paper presented at the annual meeting of the American Political Science Association, Washington, DC, August.

Cummings, William K. (1998): 'What should be the Future Focus of Values Education in the Pacific Rim: View of Educational Elites from Eleven Countries'. Unpublished working paper for the project "Building Bridges of Understanding and Belief in the Pacific Rim", funded by the Pacific Basin Research Centre, Soka University of America.

Cummings, William K. (2001): 'The Future of Values Education in the Pacific Basin', in Cummings, William K.; Hawkins, John & Tatto, Maria T. (eds.), *Values Education for Dynamic Societies: Individualism or Collectivism*. CERC Studies in Comparative Education 11, Hong Kong: Comparative Education Research Centre, The University of Hong Kong, pp.285-298.

Cummings, William K.; Gopinathan, Saravanan & Tomoda, Yasumasa (eds.) (1988): *The Revival of Values Education in Asia and the West*. Oxford: Pergamon Press.

Cummings, William K.; Hawkins, John & Steiner-Khamsi, Gita (1996): 'Building Bridges of Understanding and Belief in the Pacific Rim'. Proposal submitted to the Pacific Basin Research Centre, Soka University of America.

Cummings, William K.; Hawkins, John & Tatto, Maria T. (eds.) (2001a): *Values Education for Dynamic Societies: Individualism or Collectivism*. CERC Studies in Comparative Education 11, Hong Kong: Comparative Education Research Centre, The University of Hong Kong.

Cummings, William K.; Hawkins, John & Tatto, Maria T. (2001b): 'The Revival of Values Education in the Pacific Basin', in Cummings, William K.; Hawkins, John & Tatto, Maria T. (eds.), *Values Education for Dynamic Societies: Individualism or Collectivism*. CERC Studies in Comparative Education 11, Hong Kong: Comparative Education Research Centre, The University of Hong Kong, pp.1-17.

Gardner, Roy; Cairns, Jo & Lawton, Denis (eds.) (2000): *Education for Values: Morals, Ethics and Citizenship in Contemporary Teaching*. London: Kogan Page.

Grossman, David; Lee, Wing On & Kennedy, Kerry (eds.) (2008): *Citizenship Curriculum in Asia and Pacific*. CERC Studies in Comparative Education 22, Hong Kong: Comparative Education Research Centre, The University of Hong Kong & Dordrecht: Springer.

Hahn, Carole (1998): *Becoming Political: Comparative Perspectives on Citizenship Education*. New York: State University of New York Press.

Hahn, Carole (2010): 'Comparative Civic Education Research: What We Know and What We Need to Know'. *Citizenship Teaching and Learning*, Vol.6, No.1, pp.5-23.

Heffron, John M. (1997): 'Defining Values', in Montgomery, John D. (ed.), *Values in Education: Social Capital Formation in Asia and the Pacific*. Hollis, New Hampshire: Hollis Publishing Company, pp.3-27.

Karsten, Sjoerd; Kubow, Patricia; Matrai, Zsuzsa & Pitiyanuwat, Somwung (2000): 'Challenges Facing the 21st Century: Views of Policy Makers', in Cogan, John J. & Derricott, Ray (eds.), *Citizenship for the 21st Century: An International Perspective on Education*. London: Kogan Page, pp.109-130.

Kennedy, Kerry; Lee, Wing On & Grossman, David (eds.) (2010): *Citizenship Pedagogies in Asia and Pacific*. CERC Studies in Comparative Education 28, Hong Kong: Comparative Education Research Centre, The University of Hong Kong & Dordrecht: Springer.

Kennedy, Kerry; Hahn, Carole & Lee, Wing On (2008): 'Constructing Citizenship: Comparing the Views of Students in Australia, Hong Kong, and the United States'. *Comparative Education Review*, Vol.52, No.1, pp.53-91.

Kurth-Schai, Ruthanne; Poolpatarachewin, Chumpol & Pitiyanuwat, Somwung (2000): 'Using the Delphi Cross-culturally: Towards the Development of Policy', in Cogan, John J. & Derricott, Ray (eds.), *Citizenship for the 21st Century: An International Perspective on Education*. London: Kogan Page, pp.93-108.

Lee, Wing On (1997): 'Measuring Impact of Social Value and Change', in Montgomery, John D. (ed.), *Values in Education: Social Capital Formation in Asia and the Pacific*. Hollis, New Hampshire: Hollis Publishing Company, pp.113-134.

Lee, Wing On & Fouts, Jeffrey T. (eds.) (2005): *Education and Social Citizenship: Perceptions of Teachers in USA, Australia, England, Russia and China*. Hong Kong: Hong Kong University Press.

Lee, Wing On; Grossman, David; Kennedy, Kerry & Fairbrother, Gregory (eds.) (2004): *Citizenship Education in Asia and the Pacific: Concepts and Issues*. CERC Studies in Comparative Education 14, Hong Kong: Comparative Education Research Centre, The University of Hong Kong.

Levi-Faur, David (2006): 'A Question of Size? A Heuristics Stepwise Comparative Research Design', in Rihoux, Benoît & Grimm, Heike (eds.), *Innovative Comparative Methods for Policy Analysis: Beyond the Quantitative-Qualitative Divide*. Dordrecht: Springer, pp.43-66.

Meyer, John; Bromley, Patricia & Ramirez, Francisco (2010): 'Human Rights in Social Science Textbooks: Cross-National Analyses, 1970-2008'. *Sociology of Education*, Vol.83, No.2, pp.111-134.

Moon, Rennie J. & Koo, Jeong-Woo (2011): 'Global Citizenship and Human Rights: A Longitudinal Analysis of Social Studies and Ethics Textbooks in the Republic of Korea'. *Comparative Education Review*, Vol.55, No.4, pp.574-599.

Morris, Paul; Cogan, John & Liu, M.H. (2002): 'A Comparative Overview: Civic Education Across the Six Societies', in Cogan, John; Morris, Paul & Print, Murray (eds.), *Civic Education in the Asia-Pacific Region: Case Studies Across Six Societies*. New York: RoutledgeFalmer, pp. 167-189.

Nucci, Larry P. (ed.) (1989): *Moral Development and Character Education: A Dialogue*. Berkeley: McCutchan Publishing Corporation.

Presno, Vincent & Presno, Carol (1980): *The Value Realms: Activities for Helping Students Develop Values*. New York: Teachers College, Columbia University.

Schulz, Wolfram; Ainley, John & Fraillon, Julian (eds.) (2011): *ICCS 2009 Technical Report*. Amsterdam: International Association for the Evaluation of Educational Achievement (IEA).

Steiner-Khamsi, Gita; Torney-Purta, Judith & Schwille, John (eds.) (2002a): *New Paradigms and Recurring Paradoxes in Education for Citizenship: An International Comparison*. Oxford: JAI [Elsevier Science], pp.1-36.

Steiner-Khamsi, Gita; Torney-Purta, Judith & Schwille, John (2002b): 'Introduction: Issues and Insights in Cross-National Analysis of Qualitative Studies', in Steiner-Khamsi, Gita; Torney-Purta, Judith & Schwille, John (eds.), *New Paradigms and Recurring Paradoxes in Education for Citizenship: An International Comparison*. Oxford: JAI [Elsevier Science], pp.1-36.

Thomas, R. Murray (1990): 'The Nature of Comparative Education', in Thomas, R. Murray (ed.), *International Comparative Education: Practices, Issues and Prospects*. Oxford: Pergamon Press, pp.1-21.

Torney-Purta, Judith & Amadeo, Jo-Ann (2013): 'The Contributions of International Large-Scale Studies in Civic Education and Engagement', in von Davier, Matthias; Gonzalez, Eugenio; Kirsch, Irwin & Yamamoto, Kentaro (eds.), *The Role of International Large-Scale Assessments: Perspectives from Technology, Economy and Educational Research*. Dordrecht: Springer.

Torney-Purta, Judith; Lehmann, Rainer; Oswald, Hans & Schulz, Wolfram (eds.) (2001): *Citizenship and Education in Twenty-Eight Countries: Civic Knowledge and Engagement at Age Fourteen*. Amsterdam: International Association for the Evaluation of Educational Achievement.

Young, Cho & Tae, Kim (2013): 'Asian Civic Values: A Cross-Cultural Comparison of Three East Asian Societies'. *The Asia-Pacific Education Researcher*, Vol.22, No.1, pp.21-31.

10

Comparing Policies

Rui YANG

The word policy is commonly used in government documents, academic writings and daily conversations. The simplest definition of policy is "whatever governments choose to do or not to do" (Dye 1992, p.7), which indicates that policy is developed by government and involves both decision-making and non-decision-making. However, more detailed definitions of policy are highly contested. The nature of policy and the ways in which it can be researched, interpreted, and produced are open to debate. The literature that might assist in this matter is diverse, divided and to some extent inconclusive. In the words of Ball (1994, p.15), it contains "theoretical uncertainties".

Nevertheless, it is important to address these questions, in part because debates about educational policy around the world are becoming more intense. An increasing duality has become evident. On the one hand the way that policy is made is highly contextualised, and its implementation is even more context-dependent; and on the other hand policy travels globally and has profound impact in locations far removed from its origins. In such circumstances, much discussion surrounding educational policy is international in character, including comparative research on education policy, which is growing in relevance and interest.

This chapter discusses theoretical and methodological issues in comparative analysis of education policies. It begins with a description of the international policy environment, and then moves to debates about the definitions of policy. The chapter also illustrates ways in which education policies can be compared.

The Changing International Policy Environment

Policy does not exist in isolation. Since World War II, dramatic changes in the international policy environment have had a direct impact on how social policies are made, implemented and researched. The changes have of course been different in different parts of the world. The remarks that follow apply particularly to industrialised countries.

The first change has been economic. World War II was followed by an unprecedented boom during which many societies experienced strong economic growth. The period ended in the mid-1970s, and was followed by slow growth or stagnation. During times of slow growth, citizens become increasingly reluctant to pay taxes. Since the late 1970s, first the United States and then some other English-speaking countries have seen a series of low-tax movements and tax rebellions. Within such a climate, politicians have tried to reduce spending on public services.

The second change has been demographic, which significantly changed the composition of populations in the major wealthy societies. One phenomenon has been the baby-boom generation – people born between 1946 and 1964. As babies, as teens, and as young adults, this segment of the population had enormous impact on their nations. With the baby-boomers thinking about retirement, political leaders have needed to think about healthcare costs. Significant funds, both private and public, will have to be invested in the ageing populations over the coming decades, thereby reducing the money available for other public services.

The third change has been ideological. During the last quarter of the 20th century, a major shift in political ideas occurred first in the United States and the United Kingdom, then in other parts of the English-speaking world, and then in many other locations. In general, the focus of politics shifted from equality to excellence, accountability, and choice. Business leaders often advance these ideas in policy debates. They sometimes discern no difference between public and private institutions, and criticise public services for their alleged inefficiency and insensitivity to the market. The ideologies of both the business community and pressure groups such as the Religious Right in the USA lead them to be sceptical of government initiatives. Public services are a part of the government and are therefore automatically defined as part of the problem.

The fourth change has been the nation-state framework. Globalisation has challenged the assumed reality of sovereign policy formation as territorially bound within nation-states (Lingard & Rawolle 2011). Nation-states can no longer tightly control the global flow of people, information and capital. Some forms of traditional government politics can only operate well within the traditional international world system in which nation-states were the most important and powerful players. In the current global world system, national policies have demonstrated increasing limitations, while transnational forces and players have received increasing prominence.

The fifth change has been increased individualisation, which threatens public agencies and politics. The post-nation-state era is confronted with both a decline in the power of organised political bodies and the rise of individualisation. The former is caused by global capitalism and paves the way for further individualism, while the latter leads to further decline of political forces. Nowadays, there are neither clear identities of political parties and nation-states, nor universal social trust. Within this context, traditional government political structures are losing their capacity for integration.

The final change has been a sense of uncertainty and lack of trust in political decision-makers. Particularly in the West, people have gradually abandoned their strong belief in human rationality and the notion that knowledge is power or strength. Instead, people increasingly recognise uncertainties. Some even believe that human knowledge is a disastrous power. This sense of uncertainty leads to scepticism towards technocrats and political decision-makers.

Understanding Policy: Two Perspectives

The expansion of the policy field since the 1980s has brought debate about all aspects of analysis. The term policy derives from political science. It is a complex concept. Partly because of philosophical conflicts over the nature of individuals and society, people have different understandings of the meanings of power and the proper roles of government. Their perceptions of the meanings of policy, policy-making and implementation differ accordingly (Fowler 2013). Cunningham (1963) once suggested that policy was like an elephant – you recognise one when you see it, but it is somewhat difficult to define. Yet it may also resemble the elephant described by the blind men in the Indian fable, i.e. the one who felt the tail had a very different impression from the one who felt a leg, who in turn had a very different impression from one who felt the side, etc.. Similarly, the understanding of policies may mean very different things to different people.

Elaborating, policy can cover a very broad arena and can be understood and used in various ways, including plans, decisions, documents and proposals. In addition to written forms, policy can include actions, practices, and even the inactions of governments. The most popular of these definitions, amongst policy researchers and the public at large, defines policies as documents. Expanding the broad identification of policy documents, these representations can take various forms at different levels (Bowe et al. 1992): most obviously official legal texts and policy documents; formally and informally produced commentaries which offer to make sense of the official texts; the speeches and public performances of politicians and officials; and official videos.

Hogwood and Gunn (1984) identified nine possible contexts in which the word policy was used: a label for a field of activity, an expression of general purpose or desired a state of affairs, specific proposals, decisions of government, formal authorisation, theory or model, programme, output, and outcome. They proposed a tenth category of "policy as process" (p.19). Following on this, Taylor et al. (1997) classified policies into distributive or redistributive, symbolic or material, rational or incremental, substantial or procedural, regulatory or deregulatory, and top-down or bottom-up. Much depends on how allocation of resources or benefits is made, the extent of commitment to implementation, and the existence or otherwise of prescriptive stages for the development of policy. Such classification helps to define policy, although parts may be rather arbitrary.

Another classification, although increasingly blurred, is between public and private policy. The public sector represents a group of institutions which rely on, or justify their activities in terms of, the authority of the state. Based on the principle of equality of treatment of citizens, it is characterised by public accountability and more exposed to political direction and scrutiny than the private sector. The concepts of ownership of enterprise and profits have been traditionally missing from the public sector. The idea of a public sector embodies the principle that all public authority must only be used in the public interest. This contrasts with the scope for individuals and companies in the private sector to do anything that is not forbidden by the law to maximise their own advantage. Public policy is thus collective and cannot be easily separated as economic, environmental and educational. It is at the centre of major political struggles between those who see it only for its instrumental outcomes and those who see its potential for human emancipation.

As Dahrendorf (1959) explained, society has two faces: conflict, i.e. conflicts of interest; and consensus, i.e. value integration in society. Sociological theories can accordingly be classified into consensus and conflict perspectives (Jary & Jary 2000). Likewise, researchers have rational and conflict perspectives for viewing policy.

The Rational Perspective
The rational perspective, also called the traditional model of policy development and analysis, emphasises the technically best course of action to implement a decision or achieve a goal. This approach, it is suggested, enables governments to make the most cost-effective decisions. This positivist view believes in a value-neutral manner to avoid or simplify political complexities. It largely ignores issues of power and the way in which the state might exercise it. Its theoretical basis dates back to August Comte (1798-1857), who called sociology 'social physics' and insisted that the methods from natural sciences, including observation, experiment and comparison, should be used to study society.

Analysing decision-making processes, Simon (1960) proposed a rational policy production theory that was closely related to the stages of problem-solving first described by Dewey (1910, p.3): "What is the problem? What are the alternatives? Which alternative is the best?" This method of making decisions involves selecting from the alternatives that "will lead to the most complete achievement of your goals" (Simon 1945, p.240). It entails the choice of the 'best' course of action from all possible options, achieved through a systematic and sequential process.

The rational perspective sees the policy process as a sequence of events that occurs when a political system considers different approaches to public problems, adopts one of them, tries it out, and evaluates it. It suggests that the policy process is orderly and rational. It reflects functionalist assumptions about the way society works: underpinned by a value consensus in which the various institutions in society contribute to the ongoing stability of the whole.

A version of the rational model in the political science context was described by Anderson (1984) as having the following sequential steps of the policy process: (1) problem formulation including what policy problem is, what makes it a public problem, and how it gets on the government agenda; (2) formulation including how the alternatives for dealing with the problem are developed, and who participates in policy formulation; (3) adoption including how a policy alternative is adopted or enacted, what requirements must be met, and who adopts policy; (4) implementation including what is done, if anything, to carry a policy into effect, and what impact this has on policy content; (5) evaluation including how the effectiveness or impact of a policy is measured, who evaluates policy, what the consequences of policy evaluation are, and what demands are for change or repeal.

In a related vein, when singling out 'policy as process' as their preferred definition, Hogwood and Gunn (1984) compared the nine usages of policy they identified to still photographs – the statement of an objective, the moment of decision, a Bill becomes an Act, and so on. They suggested the desirability of the equivalent of a movie which permits study of the unfolding over time of the complexities of the policy-making. They went on to prescribe a policy-making framework and divided the process into nine stages: deciding to decide (issue search or agenda-setting); deciding how to decide (or issue filtration); issue definition; forecasting; setting objectives and priorities; options analysis; policy implementation, monitoring, and control; evaluation and review; and policy maintenance, succession, or termination.

Although this account seems to provide a clear framework to understand and investigate policy processes and how policy is made, the rational model has met much criticism because it suggests that the policy process is more orderly, has clearly defined stages, and is more rational than it really is (Rizvi & Lingard 2010). Indeed, each stage in policy-making involves complex processes. Even in the first stage – agenda setting – different people with different values and interests have different ideas about what should be on the policy agenda, what logic should inform the agenda, who decides priorities, and how the decision is made and why. Therefore, decision-makers are not faced with concrete, clearly defined problems because the rational model neglects the political nature of decision-making.

Moreover, the critics suggest, it is unrealistic to consider all possible alternatives and make a decision on which is the best option because there is always room for improvement. In any case, some decisions are made arbitrarily and illogically. These analyses of the first two stages show that they are closely related to each other and that agreement among different people cannot be reached easily. Their many uncertainties and complexities mean that they are almost impossible to separate from each other.

As for the last stage, while some policies may be purposely 'terminated' by other decisions or by new policies, the effects or the influences of terminated policies do not necessarily come to an abrupt end. Sometimes their influences can last a long time, and some effects, once realised, are hard to reverse. Even new policies can be greatly influenced by or derived from old ones. Furthermore, the effects of some policies fade away for various reasons, even if their makers are reluctant to admit this.

Intending to avoid the drawbacks of the rational model, Lindblom (1959) proposed an incremental approach to decision-making. The major difference between an incremental approach and a rational approach is that the decision-maker considers only some of the alternatives for dealing with a problem, and for each alternative only a limited number of important consequences are evaluated. Lindblom argued that incrementalism was a good description of how decisions and policies were actually made. He claimed that one advantage of 'muddling through' was that serious mistakes could be avoided if only incremental changes were made because it was easier to reach agreement among various disputing groups. Compared with a rational model, incrementalism is more realistic because it recognises the limitations of time, intelligence and other resources in policy-making processes.

Yet the incremental approach has also met criticism for being too conservative, helpless in dealing with crisis, and hence a barrier to innovation. Trying to avoid the weaknesses of rational and incremental models by combining the strongest features of the two, Etzioni (1967, p.389) put forward the approach of 'mixed-scanning'. His strategy was to include elements of both approaches by metaphorically employing two cameras: a broad-angle camera that would cover all parts of the sky but not in great detail and a second one which would zero in on areas revealed by the first camera as requiring closer examination. This was described by Smith and May (1980) as the 'third' approach, providing policy-makers with both rational and incremental approaches in different situations. It seems logical, because in practice it is not easy to decide which approach – rational or incremental – is most appropriate under specific situations.

Some scholars have argued that policy is both product and process, making it on-going and dynamic, and more complex, interactive and multi-layered than in rational models (Wildavsky 1979; Taylor et al. 1997). They suggest that policy processes accrue both prior to the production of policy texts and afterwards, through the stages of implementation and reinterpretation. This means that the text of policy, often in the form of written documents, is by no means the end of policy-making. The process of creating a final text is difficult enough. It is usually very hard to tell the specific reasons or intentions for initiating such a policy; and even if the reasons or intentions are clearly stated, they may not be the actual ones.

The research by Bowe et al. (1992) showed that policy is different in different contexts. In the context of influence, policy can be understood as intentions, ideas, aims, purposes, objectives or plans; in the context of policy-text production, policy can be written texts, products, documents and articles; and in the context of practice, policy can be actions, performances and activities. Indeed, policy can mean even more than these specific things, and involves various actions and processes. Recognising policy as a process places it in continuous, interrelated and reciprocally-influenced contexts, which should also be taken into consideration in policy-making and analysis. Policy is an outcome of the aggregate forces of all the three contexts. While each context is strongly related to process, the impact and effects of context are in practice different and unequal. Such differences and inequalities of weight in policy-making are derived from the nature of policy – an act of politics itself. This has been well explained in the 'conflict' perspective for viewing policy.

The Conflict Perspective

Critical theorists take a conflict approach. They see society as consisting of competing groups with different values and access to power. Policies do not emerge in a vacuum, but reflect compromises between the competing interests. Policy problems are thus too complex to be solved in simple technicist ways, and policy processes are interactive and multi-layered (Rizvi & Lingard 2010). Critical theorists note that the words policy and politics came from the same root, and that policy necessarily involves politics. Here, politics, with a small 'p', is about imposition of one interest over another, not necessarily about political parties.

A conflict perspective emphasises that authority "invariably becomes the determining factor of systematic social conflicts" (Dahrendorf 1959, p.165). Conflict theorists highlight the role of power in maintaining social order. Various positions that individuals inhabit within society have different amounts of authority, and some have more power and authority than others. However, a person of authority in one setting does not necessarily hold the same amount of authority in other settings. A conflict of interest is latent at all times, and "the legitimacy of authority is always precarious" (Dahrendorf 1959, p.268). Society experiences continuous social conflict because it is composed of individuals, groups and institutions with distinctive and conflicting interests. Authority shifts constantly among different settings. Policy is never static or permanent. It is valid only in certain contexts and within certain periods of time.

Fowler (2013) points out many similarities between policy processes and games: both have rules and players; both are complex and often disorderly; both are played in many arenas and involve the use of power; and both can have winners and losers. As in real games, in the game of policy "what is fair" is not always decided by all the players: fair for some players may be unfair to others. Policy is defined by the "rules of the game" (Offe 1985, p.106). But questions such as who makes the rules, how the rules are made, why the rules are made that way, and whether or not these rules are made fairly, raise further questions about individual values, interests and priorities.

At the institutional level, the power relations of policy settlements are "systematically asymmetrical", i.e. "different individuals or groups have a differential capacity to make a meaning stick" (Thompson 1984, p.132). Particular groups of people are institutionally endowed with power, while other groups are excluded or remain unable to access power. Due to the political nature of policy, "only certain influences and agendas are recognised as legitimate, only certain voices are heard" (Ball 1994, p.16). Policy is the outcome of conflict and struggle between interests in context.

Policy only represents the values of the interest group that possesses the authority in policy-making, although it often presents itself as universal, generalised and even commonsensical. Its interests and influence are invariably partial (Gale & Densmore 2003). It then makes sense to represent policy as the authoritative allocation of values. As Prunty (1985, p.136) argued, this view of policy "draws our attention to the centrality of power and control in the concept of policy; and requires us to consider not only whose values are represented in policy, but also how these values have become institutionalised".

Adopting a conflict view, Ball (1990) argued strongly that policy by no means stands for a consensus opinion of all social members. Policy-making, he asserted, never follows a rational or logical sequence. Rather, policy is derived as the consequence of endless struggles and compromises between various interest groups, and eventually makes a symbol of the dominant values of the group with authority. The values do not float free of their social context. It is therefore important to ask whose values are validated in policy, and whose are not. It would be both theoretically naïve and politically abhorrent to suggest that the policy process is democratic and that policy is produced through mutual agreement of elected representatives (Gale 2003). The conflict among different interest groups is the everlasting dynamic leading to change in society. The public decision-maker is usually confronted with a situation of value conflict rather than value agreement.

Interpretation of policy is a matter of struggle. Practitioners interpret policy with their own histories, experiences, values and purposes. Their responses to policy text are often constructed on the basis of "interpretations of interpretations" (Rizvi & Kemmis 1987, p.14). It is hard to control or predict the effect of a policy. Policy practitioners have unequal authority in different contexts. Legislators who have authority in the context of influence may lose (some of) their authority in the context of practice. The authority shifts from context to context. This is why policy effects are often quite unexpected and different from policy intentions. The authority of practitioners endows them with power to interpret policy according to their own understandings, which can be quite different and even opposite to those of the policy initiators.

In brief, the conflict perspective sees policy-making in complex societies as often unempirical and illogical, although policy-makers almost always claim otherwise. This conflict perspective is consistent with critical policy analysis which aims to identify who is advantaged, and who is not, by new arrangements. There is a fundamental need to explore the values and assumptions that underlie education policy by asking questions such as who are the winners and losers, and how their values are institutionalised (Taylor et al. 1997).

Making Sense of Comparing Education Policy: Uses and Abuses

Over two decades ago, Hallak (1991) pointed out that "comparative studies – carefully designed, conducted and used – are more than ever necessary for the improvement of educational policy and decision making" (p.1). Today, the concept of policy borrowing has become central to the work of comparative education researchers (Phillips & Ochs 2007; Steiner-Khamsi & Waldow 2012). Global policy agendas are steering education research as a means of shaping socioeconomic development within countries. A growing body of literature has discussed the increasingly intense cross-national travel of education policy. This literature is concerned with ways in which knowledge about policies, administrative arrangements, institutions and ideas in one political setting is used in the development of policies, administrative arrangements, institutions and ideas in other political settings.

Contemporary changes in geopolitical relations combined with the implications of the intensification of globalisation have heightened the significance of such relationships to the extent that the very conceptualisation of problems in comparative research needs fundamental change (Crossley & Watson 2003). Globalisation provides a new empirical challenge as much as a new theoretical frame for comparative education. Yet national contexts remain of great importance. It is highly risky to draw simplistic inferences from superficial inter-country comparisons of education policies.

Nevertheless, studies of education policy taken out of context remain common. A variety of uses and abuses of comparative education policy studies may be identified, despite the lack of a clear dividing line between them. Best uses and absolute abuses are extremes of the same continuum. Uses of comparing education policy studies have their prerequisites. Without meeting these prerequisites, uses commonly turn out to be abuses, which can easily be found in contemporary comparative studies of education policy.

The All-important Context

Many distinguished comparativists have long pointed out that major problems lie in any simplistic transfer of educational policy and practice from one socio-cultural context to another. To cite Sadler's (1900, p.310) seminal lecture:

> We cannot wander at pleasure among the educational systems of the world, like a child strolling through a garden, and pick off a flower from one bush and some leaves from another, and then expect that if we stick what we have gathered into the soil at home, we shall have a living plant.

This quotation is so well known in the field that the modern period of comparative education is widely considered to have started with Sadler. The field has always paid close attention to social, cultural, economic and political contexts. Looking into the future, the diverse and multidisciplinary traditions of comparative education make it especially well positioned to deal with the increasingly complex, global and cross-cultural issues that characterise the 21st century. The field has long recognised the significance of global forces in educational research and development, and has consistently examined the dilemmas associated with the transfer of educational policy and practice from one cultural context to another.

Globalisation has seriously challenged the way education policy is compared (Lingard & Rawolle 2011). This is because contemporary globalisation is reconstituting the power, functions and authority of national governments (Wiseman 2010). Given the changing global order, the forms and functions of the state have to adapt as governments seek coherent strategies to engage with a globalising world. Governments have become increasingly outward-looking as they seek to pursue cooperative strategies, but global agendas can only take effect when they are inserted into the policy and governance processes of established decision-making domains within nation states. As Arnove (2013) notes, there is a dialectic at work by which global forces interact with national and local actors and contexts to be modified and transformed. Through the processes of give-and-take and exchange, international trends are reshaped for local ends.

Such interplay between the global and the local, denominated as the "global-local nexus" (Robertson 1992, p.100), gives further measure to contexts, both local and global, in comparative education policy studies. Policy can only be understood, made and analysed in certain contexts. Hence, analysing policy is as much about understanding policy context as it is about understanding policy and policy processes.

With the increasing presence of policy networks and the geographic and conceptual border crossing of policy elites, efforts to globalise educational institutions have brought commonalities in the discourse on educational policy. However, this does not necessarily imply a transnational convergence of policy and practice in educational institutions. Rather, when global trends are encountered in the local context, some form of hybridisation results from a combination of elements to make up the final programme package for policy transfer (Well 2005). The convergence or divergence in education is the product of conscious adaptation, blind imitation, and pressure to conform (Stromquist 2002). Policies have undergone many transformations by the time they reach local educational institutions. The substantive elements of one programme, although successful in one location, may require fundamentally different delivery mechanisms to be effective in another. This 'missing piece' can be copied or emulated from a second location.

It is then erroneous to interpret the rise of international policy transfer as a global policy convergence in educational policy and practice. With increasing uncritical policy borrowing across national boundaries, the importance of not glossing over the complex and often contradictory national and local mediations of 'global' policy trends must be stressed. There is a constant need to navigate the local within the global as policies evolve. The processes of globalisation are complex, contested and often contradictory. The concept of globalisation, when it implies policy homogenisation, is arguably too blunt an instrument for critical analysis of education reforms. Too few studies on globalisation processes are grounded in detailed examinations of particular historical times and geographical spaces (Oke 2009).

The critical role of context undermines nation-states as the dominant unit of analysis in comparative studies in education policy. Global forces are dramatically changing the role of the state in education, and demanding increased attention to factors operating supra- and sub-national levels. National cultures can and do play a significant role in mediating global influences, but greater recognition is being given to other units of analysis (Bray & Thomas 1995; Bray 2003). Units of analysis that pay attention to the local effects of localisation should be prioritised.

For example, it can be very misleading to treat China as a single entity in comparative higher education studies. Disparities between urban and rural areas and between the rich and poor have historically been a longstanding issue in China. Disparities in receipt of education between China's different geographical areas and social classes are evident. The gap has widened since the late 1970s when China opened itself to the world and exploited the coastal east. The capacity of local governments in affluent areas to finance their higher education development is often many times more than that in the inland provinces. Higher education has developed far more vigorously in the thriving export-oriented coastal zones than that in the interior (Li & Yang 2013).

The continuing dominance of Anglo-American scholarship

The international knowledge system of people and institutions that create knowledge, and of structures that communicate knowledge, has divided nations into centre, semi-centre and periphery (Altbach 1998). Its function has been substantially strengthened by the exponential growth of the internet (DeNardis 2009), and by the fact that English has become a global language (Crystal 1997; Kayman 2004). In many ways, knowledge that is not part of Western networks in mainstream journals, books, and other indices of academic production is not considered to be real knowledge. The most recent innovations in scientific communications, databases and information networks are also located in the industrialised nations, especially the United States. The worldwide scientific communications system is centralised in and dominated by the research-producing nations. The unequal international knowledge network has also been manifested in comparative education policy studies. It is ironic that comparative education policy studies, as a field of research claiming to be defined by cross-cultural pursuits, is still impressively parochial (Welch 2003).

Since the effects of globalisation differ from place to place, attention needs to be drawn back to the nature and implications of the differential effects, even at the national level. Nevertheless, few empirical studies have compared these differences in any sustained way. Those that have been carried out have largely focused on Western industrialised societies. The impact of globalisation on the poorer, postcolonial societies of the 'South' has received much less attention, despite the dramatic implications for development processes in such contexts. For example, in today's interdependent wired world, the commitment by universities to advancing human knowledge means that they must engage in more extensive international cooperation. Scholarship and teaching require an international approach, to avoid parochialism and to stimulate critical thinking and enquiry into the complex issues and interests that bear on the relations among nations, regions and interest groups.

At the same time, against a backdrop of the aforementioned hegemony of Anglo-American knowledge and the English language, Asian countries including China are competing for leadership in the global, technologically oriented knowledge economy. A critical mass of non-Western scholarship is emerging in the field of comparative education, and beginning to force a reconsideration of traditional concepts and theories (Bray & Gui 2007; Manzon 2011). Important research is now done at more centres of scholarship than ever before, helping to offset the hegemony of European and North American scholarship (Arnove 2013).

It is thus useful to study higher education policy in different countries, especially in Asia, to facilitate understanding of changing higher education landscapes. The striking economic success of East Asian countries includes a key focus on education, especially plans to develop world-class universities (Liu et al. 2011). The rise of Asian universities has potential to alter the world higher education landscape. Yet, with the dominance of Anglo-American knowledge, East Asian researchers often look to their American and British counterparts for policy ideas. Analysis of the 114 education policy research articles carried during 2003-2004 by the *China Renda Social Science Information Centre-Education* showed that English dominance increased dramatically among their cited items in foreign languages (Yang 2006).

While the dominant Western (mainly American) policy research and theoretical constructions have propelled China's policy research forward, a shortage of comprehensive, systematic studies of the imported West-ernised theories and methods has led to superficial, fragmentary under-standings of them. In practice, the application of these seemingly 'ad-vanced' theories and methods often ends up with a blunder. Without deep knowledge of their localities, indiscriminate use of Western theories and methods has failed to help China define, recognise and formulate policy problems, let alone provide effective solutions. For instance, Chi-na's new millennium curriculum reform (Ministry of Education 2001) has been characterised by contradictions with little positive effect on practice (Ma & Cheng 2011). Blindly copying so-called advanced curriculum poli-cies in Western societies was a major reason for its lack of success.

Divides in the policy literature
As shown above, the scholarly world is highly divided in many ways. One of the ways is the deep yet often neglected divide within the indus-trialised, so-called Western world. Education policy studies are no excep-tion. One prominent example is those speaking various major world languages. For instance, Spanish-speaking people have their major aca-demic journals, cite overwhelmingly Spanish literature, and focus mainly on their own societies. Although various channels of communication between them and others remain, most social researchers who rely exclu-sively on the English literature have paid little attention to the vast Span-ish research circles and their products on education policy. Similar situa-tion exists in other linguistic regions such as Russian- and Chinese-speaking societies.

What is even more striking but little attended is the great divide within the English-speaking academic circles, especially between the United States-led North American circle and the United Kingdom-led camp consisting mainly of former British colonies including Australia, New Zealand and South Africa. Perhaps due to their self-centred mental-ities (at least partially), policy researchers in these countries tend to take sides: while US-based researchers do not seem to be aware of the vast policy literature produced elsewhere including other English-speaking countries, education policy researchers in Australia and New Zealand cite almost exclusively work from the United Kingdom, while many fewer publications produced by Australians and New Zealanders are cited by the British. This divide has far-reaching implications. International students trained within different camps usually establish their sense of belonging where they are based and then bring this sense back to their home societies. Academics visiting the camps from other (usually non-Western) societies, especially less academically sophisticated systems, are often similarly influenced. They bring back the partial they have seen and perceive it as the full of the contemporary world.

For instance, the edited volume *Shaping Education Policy: Power and Process* (Mitchell et al. 2011) has 13 chapters by 20 authors who are all based in the United States and have overwhelmingly cited literature produced by fellow US researchers. While a strong US focus may be quite legitimate, it is fair to question the range of its contributing authors' perspectives and frames of reference. A further example is *Policy Studies for Educational Leaders* by Fowler, which has been perceived well in North America. Its first three editions cited few studies by writers in countries other than the United States. The London-based, widely-cited education policy sociologist Stephen J. Ball only received passing reference in the fourth edition (2013), and was not mentioned in the list of major definitions of policy (Fowler 2013, pp.4-5).

Increasingly at odds with the spirit of the times, such divides could set unhealthy limits to research perspectives. In marked contrast to the aforementioned US-centred education policy literature, Ball has been very influential in the education policy literature produced by researchers in the United Kingdom, Australia and New Zealand – from prominent scholars to postgraduate research students. For example, in Gale's (2005) presidential address to the Australian Association for Research in Education, 24 out of the 37 cited items were directly on social and education policy. Among the 24, 15 references were authored by nine researchers in Australian institutions, and eight items were authored by researchers in British institutions. The only cited reference from an American scholar was a chapter by Schön (1979). In contrast, Gale cited four items by Ball, among which three were single-authored and one jointly.

A similar situation is common at the postgraduate research student level. For instance, Zhang's (2012) doctoral thesis on equity issues in

Chinese higher education policy through a case study of China's enrolment expansion starting from the late 1990s conducted at Monash University in Australia was entirely organised according to Ball's policy cycle framework: the 'context of influence', the 'context of policy text production', and the 'context of practice'. Zhang found Ball's work most generative because the rich conceptual framework helped him to interpret complexities in a comprehensive way. He emphasised (p.5) that "although Ball's theory was found in the context of the United Kingdom ... his notion of policy cycle worked as well for China as for other countries". Nevertheless, the thesis paid little attention to work by US authors, and also neglected the policy literature by Chinese researchers in its theoretical framework. It therefore had a rather limited base of policy literature.

Under-estimated Cultural Factors
Human behaviours are socio-cultural. As argued earlier, people are positioned differently in society with different interests. They view things differently based on where they are located socially and economically. This is especially true of policy, as policy has much to do with how a society is governed and what mode of governance is best perceived by its members. This becomes a particularly complex issue when policy travels across cultures. Due to different modes of cultural thinking, different nations appear to favour different ways of ruling and governance. What is widely accepted in one society is not necessarily received well in another. The impact of cultural influence on education policy permeates all aspects from agenda setting through decision-making to implementation. Considering the extent to which policy is culture-bound, it is surprising to see how cultural perspective has been neglected in the literature.

Comparative studies in education policy have, ironically, tended to fail to deal with real world cultural diversity. Without sufficient analysis of cultural factors, such studies are not only theoretically shallow, but also practically meaningless and even misleading. For instance, in comparison with their counterparts in many Western societies, Chinese people are much more accepting of government policies. Their definitions of policy are more in line with those of the governments at various levels (see e.g. Yuan 1998; Zhang 2002). However, the policy implementation gap between policy intention and effect is not necessarily narrower in China, as Chinese people also have their distinctive ways to distort policy implementation (Ding & Ding 2004; Ding 2011).

Another example is the Western concept of a university. Modern universities originated in Europe, and spread worldwide under the conditions of imperialism and colonialism. Even societies that escaped colonial domination adopted Western models (Altbach 2001). The idea of the university is arguably the most successful Western export to the rest of the world. Elements of the long traditions of universities directly affect global higher education and the international relations of academic institutions. Underpinned by its cultural values, the European model has never been tolerant of any alternative, allowing little room for other cultures to manoeuver. The export of the university, fuelled particularly by the rise of the English language, has helped the West to dominate world scholarship and cultural development, leading to the poor efficacy of universities in non-Western societies. Still, contemporary universities in non-Western societies often look to elite Western (usually American) counterparts for standards, policy innovations, and solutions to developmental problems (Teichler 2009; Yang 2013).

Conclusion

It is worth reiterating Ball's (1994) observation that the meaning given to policy affects the ways in which researchers undertake their work and interpret what they find. However, policy is so difficult to define that Kenway (1990, p.6) considered it more productive to think about 'the policy process', which involves a great deal of settlement, mostly political as well as economic and social, and is replete with differences in value orientation and unequal power relations. Policy is thus a process fraught with choices, and involves adopting certain courses of action while discarding others. It is the product of compromises between multiple agendas and influences, over struggles between interests in context. These struggles are generally conducted through discourses where conflicting points of view are heard or unheard by the policy-makers.

Through settlements and the other activities involved in policy development, the resulting policy text is commonly significantly modified from the original draft. As Rabb (1994, p.24) pointed out, "the pudding eaten is a far cry from the original recipe". With the increasing interdependence of countries, the emergence of transnational issues, and the growth of international organisations, comparing and sharing policy experience to resolve local problems becomes a necessary and an inevitable process. By the time policies reach local educational institutions they have been transformed many times.

The popular childhood game 'telephone' serves as a useful metaphor. In this game, one player whispers a message into a neighbour's ear. The action is repeated until each player has communicated the message, and the last one reveals it to the entire group. The message by the first person often undergoes a significant transformation by the time it reaches the last person, especially if the utterance is complex. A similar process occurs when educational policy constructed by global or transnational networks is transferred to regional, national and local levels (Well 2005).

Nevertheless, comparative and international education policy research is still littered with examples of the imposition of a 'one size fits all' development model and inappropriate application of 'world standards'. It remains difficult to convince some foreign consultants in development projects, especially ones funded by foreign donors that not all instruments that work in some parts of the world also work in the others.

Critical analysis of the global rhetoric is then needed at all levels of the policy-making process. The appropriate methods chosen to conduct such analysis vary, based on the different purposes of policy analysis, the policies themselves, the backgrounds of researchers, and the contexts in which the policies operate. The sorts of questions asked in policy analysis depend on its purpose, the position of the analyst, and the presence of constraints on the analyst (Taylor et al. 1997). Therefore, making judgements by applying one set of criteria to all policies is inappropriate and perhaps unattainable given the differing ideologies of differing analysts within the complex task of policy analysis. While meeting the above prerequisites does not necessarily guarantee best uses of comparative and international studies of education policies, failure to achieve even one of them certainly leads to abuses.

References

Altbach, Philip G. (1998): *Comparative Higher Education: Knowledge, the University, and Development*. CERC Studies in Comparative Education 3, Hong Kong: Comparative Education Research Centre, The University of Hong Kong.

Altbach, Philip G. (2001): 'The American Academic Model in Comparative Perspective', in Altbach, Philip G.; Gumport, Patricia J. & Johnstone, Bruce D. (eds.), *In Defence of American Higher Education*. Baltimore: Johns Hopkins University Press, pp.11-37.

Anderson, James E. (1984): *Public Policy-Making*. 3rd edition, New York: Holt, Rinehart & Winston.

Arnove, Robert F. (2013): 'Introduction: Reframing Comparative Education: The Dialectic of the Global and the Local', in Arnove, Robert F.; Torres, Carlos Alberto & Franz, Stephen (eds.), *Comparative Education: The Dialectic of the Global and the Local*. 4th edition, Lanham: Rowman & Littlefield, pp.1-25.

Ball, Stephen J. (1990): *Politics and Policy-making in Education: Explorations in Policy Sociology*. London: Routledge.

Ball, Stephen J. (1994): *Education Reform: A Critical and Post-Structural Approach*. Buckingham: Open University Press.

Bowe, Richard; Ball, Stephen J. & Gold, Anne (1992): *Reforming Education and Changing Schools: Case Studies in Policy Sociology*. London: Routledge.

Bray, Mark (ed.) (2003): *Comparative Education: Continuing Traditions, New Challenges, and New Paradigms*. Dordrecht: Kluwer Academic Publishers.

Bray, Mark & Gui, Qin (2007): 'Comparative Education in Greater China: Contexts, Characteristics, Contrasts, and Contributions', in Crossley, Michael; Broadfoot, Patricia & Schweisfurth, Michele (eds.), *Changing Educational Contexts, Issues and Identities: 40 Years of Comparative Education*. London: Routledge, pp.319-349.

Bray, Mark & Thomas, R. Murray (1995): 'Levels of Comparison in Educational Studies: Different Insights from Different Literatures and the Value of Multilevel Analyses'. *Harvard Education Review*, Vol.65, No.3, pp.472-490.

Crossley, Michael & Watson, Keith (2003): *Comparative and International Research in Education: Globalisation, Context and Difference*. London: RoutledgeFalmer.

Crystal, David (1997): *English as a Global Language*. Cambridge: Cambridge University Press.

Cunningham, Sir Charles (1963): 'Policy and Practice'. *Public Administration*, Vol.41, No.2, pp.229-237.

Dahrendorf, Ralf (1959): *Class and Class Conflict in Industrial Society*. Stanford: Stanford University Press.

DeNardis, Laura (2009): *Protocol Politics: The Globalization of Internet Governance*. Cambridge: The MIT Press.

Dewey, John (1910): *The Influence of Darwin on Philosophy and Other Essays.* New York: Henry Holt & Company.

Ding, Huang & Ding, Mingjie (2004): 'A Case Analysis of the Distorted Policy-Implementation Game and its Effects'. *Wuhan University Journal (Philosophy and Social Sciences)*, Vol.57, No.6, pp.804-809. [in Chinese]

Ding, Xiaojiong (2011): *Policy Metamorphosis in China: A Case Study of Minban Education in Shanghai.* Lanham: Lexington Books.

Dye, Thomas R. (1992): *Understanding Public Policy.* Englewood Cliffs: Prentice-Hall.

Etzioni, Amita (1967): 'Mixed-Scanning: A "Third" Approach to Decision-Making'. *Public Administration Review*, Vol.27, No.4, pp.385-392.

Fowler, Frances C. (2013): *Policy Studies for Educational Leaders: An Introduction.* 4th edition, Boston: Pearson.

Gale, Trevor (2003): 'Realising Policy: The *Who* and *How* of Policy Production'. *Discourse: Studies in the Cultural Politics of Education*, Vol.24, No.1, pp.51-66.

Gale, Trevor (2005): 'Towards a Theory and Practice of Policy Engagement: Higher Education Research Policy in the Making'. President's Address, Australian Association for Research in Education Conference, University of Western Sydney, 27 November-1 December.

Gale, Trevor & Densmore, Kathleen. (2003): *Engaging Teachers: Towards a Radical Democratic Agenda for Schooling.* Buckingham: Open University Press.

Hallak, Jacques (1991): *Educational Policies in a Comparative Perspective: Suggestions for a Research Agenda.* Paris: UNESCO International Institute for Educational Planning (IIEP).

Hogwood, Brian & Gunn, Lewis (1984): *Policy Analysis for the Real World.* Oxford: Oxford University Press.

Jary, David & Jary, Julia (2000): *Collins Dictionary of Sociology*, 3rd edition, Glasgow: Harper Collins.

Kayman, Martin A. (2004): 'The State of English as a Global Language: Communicating Culture'. *Textual Practice*, Vol.18, No.1, 1-22.

Kenway, Jane (1990): *Gender and Education Policy: A Call for New Directions.* Geelong: Deakin University Press.

Li, Mei & Yang, Rui (2013): 'Interrogating Institutionalised Establishments: Urban-Rural Inequalities in China's Higher Education'. *Asia Pacific Education Review*, Vol.14, No.1, pp.315-323.

Lindblom, Charles (1959): 'The Science of Mudding Through'. *Public Administration Review*, Vol.19, No.1, pp.79-85.

Lingard, Bob & Rawolle, Shaun (2011): 'New Scalar Politics: Implications for Education Policy'. *Comparative Education*, Vol.47, No.4, pp.489-502.

Liu, Niancai; Wang, Qi & Cheng, Ying (eds.) (2011): *Paths to a World-Class University*. Rotterdam: Sense.

Ma, Huifang & Cheng, Dongya (2011): 'Curriculum Reforms in Basic Education: Evaluations and Reflections', *Education and Training Research*, Vol.25, No.11, pp.12-15, 30. [in Chinese]

Manzon, Maria (2011): *Comparative Education: The Construction of a Field*. CERC Studies in Comparative Education 29, Hong Kong: Comparative Education Research Centre, The University of Hong Kong, and Dordrecht: Springer.

Ministry of Education (2001): *The Curriculum Reform Guidelines for the Nine-Year Compulsory Education (Trial Version)*. Beijing: Beijing Normal University Press. [in Chinese]

Mitchell, Douglas E., Crowson, Robert L. & Shipps, Dorothy (eds.), (2011): *Sharping Education Policy: Power and Process*. New York: Routledge.

Offe, Claus (1985): *Disorganised Capitalism: Contemporary Transformations of Work and Politics*. Cambridge: Polity Press.

Oke, Nicole (2009): 'Globalizing Time and Space: Temporal and Spatial Considerations in Discourses of Globalization'. *International Political Sociology*, Vol.3, No.3, pp.310-326.

Phillips, David & Ochs, Kimberly (2007): 'Processes of Policy Borrowing in Education: Some Explanatory and Analytical Devices', in Crossley, Michael; Broadfoot, Patricia & Schweisfurth, Michele (eds.), *Changing Educational Contexts, Issues and Identities: 40 Years of Comparative Education*. London: Routledge, pp.370-382.

Prunty, John J. (1985): 'Signposts for a Critical Educational Policy Analysis'. *Australian Journal of Education*, Vol.29, No.2, pp.133-140.

Raab, Charles D. (1994): 'Where we are Now: Reflections on the Sociology of Education Policy', in Halpin, David & Troyna, Barry (eds.), *Researching Education Policy: Ethical and Methodological Issues*. London: Falmer Press, pp.17-30.

Rizvi, Fazal & Kemmis, Stephen (1987): *Dilemmas of Reform: The Participation and Equity Program in Victorian Schools*, Geelong: Deakin Institute for Studies in Education.

Rizvi, Fazal & Lingard, Bob (2010): *Globalising Education Policy*. London: Routledge.

Robertson, Roland (1992): *Globalisation: Social Theory and Global Culture*. London: Sage.

Sadler, Sir Michael (1900): 'How Far can we Learn Anything of Practical Value from the Study of Foreign Systems of Education?'. Reprinted 1964 in *Comparative Education Review*, Vol.7, No.3, pp.307-314.

Schön, Donald (1979): 'Generative Metaphor: A Perspective on Problem-Setting in Social Policy', in Ortony, Andrew (ed.), *Metaphor and Thought*. Cambridge: Cambridge University Press, pp.254-283.

Simon, Herbert (1945): *Administrative Behaviour: A Study of Decision-making Processes in Administrative Organisation*. 3rd edition, New York: The Free Press.

Simon, Herbert (1960): *The New Science of Management Decision*. Englewood Cliffs: Prentice Hall.

Smith, Gilbert & May, David (1980): 'The Artificial Debate between Rationalist and Incremental Models of Decision-Making'. *Policy and Politics*, Vol.8, No.2, pp.147-161.

Steiner-Khamsi, Gita & Waldow, Florian (eds.) (2012): *World Yearbook of Education 2012: Policy Borrowing and Lending in Education*. London: Routledge.

Stromquist, Nelly P. (2002): *Education in a Globalised World: The Connectivity of Economic Power, Technology, and Knowledge*. Lanham: Rowman & Littlefield.

Taylor, Sandra; Rizvi, Fazal; Lingard, Bob & Henry, Miriam (1997): *Educational Policy and the Politics of Change*. London: Routledge.

Teichler, Ulrich E. (2009): 'Internationalisation of Higher Education: European Experiences'. *Asia Pacific Education Review*, Vol.10, No.1, 93-106.

Thompson, John B. (1984): *Studies in the Theory of Ideology*. Cambridge: Polity Press.

Welch, Anthony R. (2003): 'The Discourse of Discourse Analysis: A Response to Ninnes and Burnett'. *Comparative Education*, Vol.39, No.3, pp.303-306.

Well, Traci (2005): 'Educational Policy Networks and their Role in Policy Discourse, Action, and Implementation'. *Comparative Education Review*, Vol.49, No.1, pp.109-117.

Wildavsky, Aaron (1979): *Speaking Truth to Power: The Art and Craft of Policy Analysis*. Boston: Little Brown.

Wiseman, Alexander W. (2010): 'The Uses of Evidence for Educational Policymaking: Global Contexts and International Trends'. *Review of Research in Education*, Vol.34, No.1, pp.1-24.

Yang, Rui (2006): 'Education Policy Research in the People's Republic of China', in Ozga, Jenny; Popkewitz, Thomas & Seddon, Terri (eds.) *The*

World Yearbook of Education 2006: Education Research and Policy. London: Routledge, pp.270-284.

Yang, Rui (2013): 'Indigenising the Western Concept of University: The Chinese Experience'. *Asia Pacific Education Review*, Vol.14, No.1, pp.85-92.

Yuan, Zhenguo (1998): *Educational Policy*. Nanjing: Jiangsu Education Publishing House. [in Chinese]

Zhang, Hongzhi (2012): *Equity Issues in Chinese Higher Education Policy: A Case Study of the Enrolment Expansion Policy*. PhD Thesis, Faculty of Education, Monash University.

Zhang, Letian (2002): *Educational Policy and Regulations: Theories and Practices*. Shanghai: East China Normal University. [in Chinese]

11

Comparing Curricula

Bob ADAMSON & Paul MORRIS

Many stakeholders in education undertake comparisons of curricula. Governments compare their states' curricula with overseas models when searching for new initiatives and when attempting to enhance international competitiveness; parents compare the offerings of schools in order to choose suitable institutions for their children; students look at the range of courses available when they select electives; academics seek to understand the dynamics of curriculum construction and implementation to increase knowledge and assist policy makers; and all parties except possibly the students make comparisons between current curricula and those which operated in earlier historical periods.

The field of curriculum studies provides many of the theoretical and methodological tools for comparing curricula. Indeed, it could be argued that all curriculum research involves some degree of comparison – one is always (at least implicitly) referring to some 'Other' when analysing a phenomenon. For every 'What is?', there exists implicitly the Other 'What isn't?'. Thus, for example, research on how content is assessed in one context might be seen as implicitly comparing the assessment approach with a range of alternative approaches. Another form of implicit comparison is between 'What is the reality?' and 'What is intended?'. A study of teachers' enactment of a particular syllabus might incorporate an implicit comparison with a desired outcome. However, explicit comparison heightens the contrasts and reveals similarities by "making the strange familiar, and the familiar strange" (see Spindler & Spindler 1982, p.43; Bray 2004, p.250). The focus of this chapter, therefore, is on research that is based on explicit comparisons of curricula, such as those across cultures and subjects.

These comparisons take diverse forms, partly because the purposes of the stakeholders are different, and partly because the underlying conceptions of what actually constitutes a curriculum vary greatly. While this chapter does not adopt the broadest of these conceptions, it does accept that curriculum is complex and multifaceted, operating at a variety of focal points and in diverse manifestations. This creates a critical problem of scope for comprehensive analysis and comparison, although it is less of a concern to stakeholders seeking answers to specific, narrowly focused questions (such as students comparing elective courses). The complexity and diversity constrains the capacity of researchers to capture the whole picture, and one usually has to be satisfied with a partial snapshot, even with multilevel analyses. However, the constraints add to the interest and value of the insights that they permit. Comparing curricula is an on-going investigation of a complex, dynamic entity, and these insights continue to challenge beliefs and understandings that shape and are shaped by curricula.

This chapter begins by examining the conceptions of curriculum in the literature. It then offers a tripartite framework for approaching comparisons of curricula. The framework is applicable for research that involves multilevel or more narrowly focused analyses. The chapter also presents examples of research that have compared curricula, to bring out the complexity of the undertaking and to demonstrate some ways of tackling it.

The Nature of Curriculum

The word *curriculum* originates from the Latin for a short running track, but this metaphor is tantalisingly imprecise. Applying the metaphor by equating curriculum with a 'course' of study does not really help to understand the meaning of the word. The term has been applied to the academic disciplines, school and syllabus subjects, teaching, and formal and informal learning experiences and assessments. Seven broad conceptions of curricula have been identified by Marsh and Willis (1995), each of which is a potential focus for comparative study:

- *Classical heritage.* This view of curriculum refers to time-honoured subjects or content – such as grammar, reading, logic, rhetoric, mathematics, and the greatest books of the Western world – that are deemed to embody essential knowledge. In this sense, the notion of curriculum is very narrow, culture-bound, conservative and inflexible. It can only be transferred in a limited sense to other cultural traditions. For instance, the content of learning in schools in imperial China was limited to a few canonical works of classical literature; and the question arises as to who determines what should be considered as essential knowledge or skills, and how they might be accessed and mastered.

- *Established knowledge*. In this conception, the curriculum is again viewed in terms of subjects and content. The choice of subjects on offer is based around the established academic disciplines which have emerged as the components around which educational institutions are organised. Examples are arts, sciences, humanities and languages, each of which defines what constitutes the key knowledge and skills that pupils should learn.

- *Social utility*. This view of curriculum is also subject-based, but is oriented towards the subjects that are considered most useful for life in contemporary society. Such a view suggests that modernity has a higher value than tradition, and that a curriculum should pass on skills and knowledge which are chosen because they will be useful when the pupils leave school.

- *Planned learning*. A slightly broader view of curriculum embraces the planned learning outcomes, such as critical thinking and tolerance, for which a school is seen to be responsible. These would include aspects such as the subjects on offer, as well as the extra-curricular activities and other types of learning organised by the school. One limitation of this definition (which is equally applicable to the previous three) is the assumption that planned learning equates to actual learning. It omits unplanned learning experiences, and focuses on outcomes rather than processes of learning.

- *Experienced learning*. This conception encompasses all the experiences – both planned and unplanned, and desirable and undesirable – that a learner has within the context of an educational institution. In addition to the planned learning experiences, this conception includes the learner's experiences of the hidden curriculum, which refers to those social values (both negative and positive) that are wittingly or unwittingly reinforced through the construction of planned learning and other institutional modes of communication.

- *Personal transformation*. This view resembles the previous one, but includes the transformation that the teacher undergoes through participating in the learning and teaching processes, as well as the learner's experience.
- *Life experiences*. An even broader conception views all life experiences as constituting the curriculum. This would not distinguish between planned or experienced learning in educational institutions and other real life contexts.

These views of what constitutes a curriculum reflect different emphases. The first two focus on the content of what is taught, and the third and fourth on the goals of education. The last three are concerned with the processes of change experienced by those involved in educational undertakings. One viewpoint, linked to the experiential notion, sees curriculum as text. Pinar and Reynolds (1992, p.7) emphasised the value of conceiving curricula as phenomenological and deconstructed texts as a means to "present the multivocality, multiperspectivity, and 'lived' aspects of textbooks and classrooms". For the purposes of this chapter, the last two conceptions (personal transformation and life experiences) are too unwieldy and all-embracing. Instead, the chapter considers curriculum as operating in educational settings, encompassing planned and experienced learning for pupils. This view excludes studies which focus on measuring pupil learning outcomes, for instance, and this area is discussed elsewhere in this book, particularly Chapter 14.

The various conceptions of the curriculum are shaped by, or derived from social ideologies that are underpinned by normative views and beliefs about the desired role of schooling in society, the nature of knowledge and learning, and the roles of teachers and learners. At least six different ideologies can be identified (Table 11.1), some of which may compete with each other:

- *Academic rationalism*. This ideology stresses the importance of inducting learners into the established academic disciplines (such as physics or mathematics), and equipping them with the concepts and intellectual rigour associated with these disciplines. Academic rationalism is essentially conservative, being concerned with the preservation and transmission of established knowledge through

Table 11.1: Curriculum Ideologies and Components

component ideology	Intentions	Content	Teaching/ learning methods	Assessment
Academic rationalism	To enhance learners' intellectual capabilities and cognitive skills, and to teach them how to learn	Focus on the knowledge, skills and values derived from the academic disciplines	Focus on exposition and didactic teaching, and on promoting inquiry skills	Emphasises testing of learners' knowledge and skills, and on academic rigour
Social and economic efficiency	To provide for the current and future human capital needs of a society	Focus on knowledge and skills which are relevant to future employment	Emphasises application and skill mastery	Emphasises assessing learners' ability to apply knowledge and skills
Social reconstruc-tionism	The curriculum serves as an agent for social reform, changes and criticism	Focus on social needs, issues and ideals	Focus on interaction, group work and learners' involvement in community activities	Focus on the need to involve learners in their own assessment
Orthodoxy	To induct learners into a particular religious or political orthodoxy	Focus on the beliefs and practices of those holding the particular orthodoxy	Focus on didactic teaching, and on promoting requisite beliefs and practices	Focus on learners' adherence to belief system and related practices
Progressivism	To provide learners with opportunities for enhancing their personal and intellectual development	Focus on knowledge as integrated holistic entity and on the process of learning	Emphasises learners' activity and self-learning, and the teacher as facilitator	Focus on the qualitative measures that attempt to analyse the process of learning
Cognitive pluralism	To provide a wide range of competencies and attitudes	Negotiated content and diversity of input and outcomes	Emphasises learners' activity and self-learning, and the teacher as facilitator	Focus on the qualitative measures that attempt to capture the diversity of learning

didactic teaching. It tends to emphasise the differences among elements of the curriculum, rather than making cross-curricular connections. Learners are often ascribed a passive role in the teaching-learning process.

- *Social and economic efficiency*. This perspective views the development of human capital as the main role of education. Taking society's needs as the starting point, the curriculum is designed to prepare responsible citizens who have the necessary attributes to contribute to the well-being and growth of the economy. Social and economic efficiency seeks to develop learners' mastery of knowledge and skills that are deemed relevant for future employment, and desirable civic attitudes and values. Teaching and learning is seen as a moulding exercise that allows little scope for learner autonomy.

- *Social reconstructionism*. This ideology envisages education as the means for bringing about social change and improvement. It assumes that society is essentially problematic, and addresses issues such as social injustice, problems and inequities. It seeks to improve society by making learners aware of such issues, and by empowering them to take action to create a better society. The issues provide the focal point of the curriculum, and the learners are actively involved in investigating and finding solutions to the problems.

- *Orthodoxy*. This perspective sees the primary function of schooling as the propagation of a particular orthodoxy. Through the curriculum, the learners are initiated into a fundamental belief system, either religious (such as Christianity or Islam) or political (such as communism, fascism or nationalism). Learners are expected to be relatively passive and uncritical, and successful learning is considered to have taken place when the learners display adherence to the beliefs and practices advocated. By definition, orthodoxy does not recognise the need for change or tolerate diversity.

- *Progressivism*. This ideology is learner-centred, with the curriculum focused on the needs, interests and abilities of the individual. Often associated with constructivist models of learning, progressivism encourages learners to explore and develop autonomously, and to be active constructors of their own learning.

- *Cognitive pluralism.* The curriculum is seen as catering to multiple forms of intelligence, such as those identified by Gardner (1985), and a diversity of competencies and attitudes. Cognitive pluralism can be associated with a reaction against specific vocational training as a society's human capital needs become less predictable in times of rapid social change and technical innovation. Learners are viewed as learning in many different ways and becoming skilled to cope with the demands of ever-changing environments.

Clearly, these ideologies can be exclusive in principle and practice. A curriculum could be constructed that is driven by a single ideology, such as fascism. However, in pluralistic societies and institutions, the curriculum is influenced by a combination of ideologies – and these may be contradictory rather than consistent. There is also a tendency for curricula to maintain links to traditions, even though radical changes may be incorporated in curricular reform. As a result, a curriculum is often a complex set of tensions and contradictions that is shaped by ideological, historical and educational forces (Luke 2008). The Australian Curriculum Studies Association (ACSA), for example, recognises the complexity of the curriculum and places it within its socio-political contexts. The Association portrays the curriculum as an interactive structuring phenomenon, both explicit and implicit, experienced by all individuals and groups (ACSA 2005). The Association also describes curriculum as a social and historical construction, and observes that it involves notions of social change and the role of education in the reproduction and transformation of society.

The lack of conciseness and the variety of definitions surrounding the curriculum are best interpreted as a manifestation of the perennial dilemmas of schooling and the increasingly complex roles which educational institutions and their curricula are expected to undertake in post-industrial and increasingly pluralistic societies. The main implication is that a comprehensive comparison of curricula would be a major undertaking which would range from analysing what is planned, what is learned that is planned, and what is learned that is not planned. Few studies — even those involving multilevel analyses — have attempted such an undertaking.

Cross-national comparative studies such as the collection by Benavot and Braslavsky (2006), which focused on school subjects, and the study by Woolman (2001) on systems of curriculum development, commonly investigate the first two levels. The study by Alexander (2000) also involved cross-national comparisons, but the focus was on the pedagogy implemented in schools and its connections to national cultures. The cross-national studies of civic education by Cogan et al. (2002) involved the analysis and comparison of each of these levels, while the national studies presented in Moyles and Hargreaves (1998) compared broader childhood experiences as well as the planned curriculum and implemented pedagogy.

Approaching Comparisons of Curricula

Figure 11.1 presents a framework for shaping comparative curricular inquiry. The three dimensions – purpose and perspective, curriculum focus, and manifestations – are interlinked. The framework is based on the premise that the inquirer has a purpose, be it utilitarian (e.g. policy-making) or the generation of new understandings. Having a purpose implies the adoption of a perspective. The purpose also informs the question(s) that the inquirer wishes to answer, which in turn would suggest a focal point – an aspect or component of the curriculum – for the inquiry. Data would then be collected from relevant curricular manifestations, which could include documents or behaviours. Each of the three dimensions is discussed in the following sections.

Figure 11.1: A Framework for Comparing Curricula

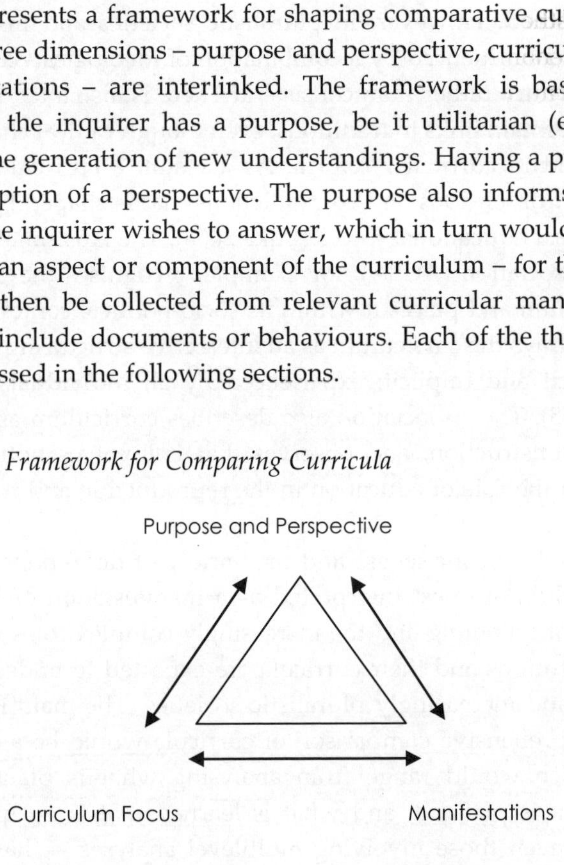

Purpose and Perspective

Curriculum Focus   Manifestations

Purpose and perspective
As noted earlier, stakeholders carry out a comparison of curricula for a variety of reasons. Short (1991), for example, identified 17 forms of cur-

riculum inquiry, all of which have (and would benefit from) comparative applications:

- analytical,
- ampliative (i.e. challenging implicit assumptions and seeking valid alternatives),
- speculative (i.e. collecting evidence in order to provide warnings or guidance),
- historical,
- scientific (i.e. quantitative-oriented),
- ethnographic,
- narrative (i.e. biographical),
- aesthetic (i.e. qualitative-oriented),
- phenomenological (i.e. studying stakeholders' perceptions),
- hermeneutic (i.e. looking at deeper meanings),
- theoretical (i.e. seeking valid concepts),
- normative (i.e. establishing justifications),
- critical,
- evaluative,
- integrative (i.e. seeking emergent themes, understandings or hypotheses),
- deliberative (i.e. focusing on resolving a specific issue), and
- action (i.e. seeking to align actions with goals).

These forms of inquiry may be loosely categorised in three perspectives that commonly underpin comparisons of curricula in the literature: evaluative, interpretive and critical. These are discussed below with examples.

Evaluative perspective
An evaluative perspective would be adopted when seeking evidence in order to make informed decisions about the curriculum (in whatever manifestation). Governments creating league tables of schools based on their performance in order to allocate resources, parents choosing suitable schools for their children, teachers selecting the set book from an array of textbooks, and students voting for a Teacher of the Year award, are all undertaking evaluative comparisons of aspects of the curriculum.

The studies of pupil performance conducted in the Programme for International Student Assessment (PISA) are evaluative in that the data are used to influence policy decisions about aspects of the curriculum (see e.g. Andere 2008). Thus the overall poor performance in PISA studies by pupils in Western societies compared to Asian societies resulted in a range of curriculum reforms in the former 'borrowed' from the latter with the intention of rectifying the situation (Morris 2012).

The increasing tendency to borrow, learn, reference or appropriate curricular practices from elsewhere since the advent of international tests of pupil achievement has created a standardized global reform agenda that has replaced appeals to ideology and history as the public rationale for identifying, initiating, or legitimating curriculum reform. The source of 'borrowed' policies is not limited to other education systems—a network of intermediate agencies who interpret educational policies and practices, and promote reform agendas to policy makers, has emerged. It includes international agencies (e.g. World Bank, UNESCO), multi- or trans-national companies (e.g. Pearson), consultants (e.g. advisory groups comprising academics and stakeholders), and policy think tanks (e.g. McKinsey, PricewaterhouseCoopers).

When policies are 'borrowed', they are often adapted or not implemented, or they simply serve primarily as symbolic references in the process of policy making. A number of scenarios might occur. First, System A may be attracted by the good test outcomes in System B. Taking the rhetoric of policy documents from System B, System A borrows the ideas for its own rhetoric. In this case, the implemented reality in both System A and System B are not considered, and the policy borrowing occurs primarily at the policy rhetoric level. An alternative scenario is that System A gets a detailed understanding of the contextual factors that contribute to System B's results and extracts elements that are compatible with its own context, thereby ensuring that the appropriation occurs at the policy implementation level. Between these two scenarios are a range of forms of cross-system policy engagements. In any curriculum reform, there is often slippage between the rhetoric of policy planning and the realities of implementation. This slippage might be exacerbated if the policy is transplanted from another system without consideration of its appropriateness for the recipient cultural context (Hantrais 2008).

Phillips and Ochs (2007) constructed a four-stage model for understanding policy borrowing. In the first stage, policy makers in a system are attracted to cross-national borrowing. They then make a decision to borrow. The borrowed policy is implemented in the third stage, and finally it undergoes a process of synthesis or indigenisation as it interacts with existing contextual features. An alternative approach would allow greater prominence for the local context. First the policy makers would assess features of the policy that attracts them. Then the policy makers would align compatible features of this policy with the salient features of the context in which the borrowed policy is to be implemented before making systemic adjustments, allocating resources, and setting out the policy detail (Adamson 2011).

Interpretive perspective

The interpretive perspective, which is also known as the hermeneutic perspective, endeavours to analyse and explain phenomena. Examples of comparisons of aspects of the curriculum would include research into the history of a curriculum at different points in time, or into curricular phenomena as socio-cultural artefacts. A classic example is Alexander's (2000) study of pedagogy in different cultures, which is discussed in greater detail in Chapter 12. Alexander compared primary education in France, Russia, India, the United States of America and England. The key data were semi-systematic classroom observations captured on videotape and audiotape, complemented by interviews, policy documentation, photographs and journal entries. The study compared state provision of education, the physical and logistical organisation of schools, school-community relations, and pedagogy (in terms of lesson structure, organisation and nature of learning activities, routines, interaction and learning discourse). The study had implications for policy makers, and Alexander specifically identified issues relating to his own country, England. However, its primary purpose was to provide a better understanding of pedagogic approaches and how they reflect those societies' cultures.

A challenge facing researchers who adopt an interpretive approach is the subjective nature of interpretation (Andrade 2009). Studies that compare curricula as lived experiences have to rely on building a case in which the evidence is persuasive rather than proof (Guba & Lincoln 1994) because the underlying assumption is that reality tends to be complex, multifaceted and ambiguous. The researcher should seek to make a case 'beyond reasonable doubt', to use an English legal phrase. To achieve credibility, as well as transferability, dependability and confirmability, the researcher should strive to incorporate strategies such as triangulation, thick description, prolonged engagement with the case, and an audit trail in the research design (Krathwohl 2009).

Louv
orr
Bowes etc.

Critical perspective

A critical approach involves interrogating curricula from a previously determined framework, such as postcolonial, feminist or social equity perspectives. This approach might be appropriate to researchers interested in issues of equity, justice or social reconstruction, for instance. The purpose of such research is to bring out features of curricula that are present either by design or by accident and that may be perceived as desirable or undesirable. The benefit of adopting a comparative study of curricula when using a critical perspective is the potential to bring out such features in sharp relief.

Within the curriculum, textbooks are one area of particular focus. As Apple and Christian-Smith (1991, pp.1-2) argued, textbooks reveal:

> the results of political, economic, and cultural activities, battles, and compromises. [These texts] are conceived, designed, and authored by real people with real interests. They are published within the political and economic constraints of markets, resources and power. And what texts mean and how they are used are fought over by communities with distinctly different commitments and by teachers and students as well.

Sleeter and Grant (1991) analysed the portrayals of race, class, gender and disability in 47 textbooks for social studies, reading and language arts, science, and mathematics in the USA. They devised six categories of analysis – picture analysis, anthology analysis, 'people to study' analysis, language analysis, story-line analysis, and miscellaneous – and used either tallying or discourse analysis to describe how the textbooks treated different racial groups, different genders, different social classes, and the disabled. The researchers discerned little diversity in the textbooks. Instead, they found a common bias towards Whites and males, and against Americans who were people of colour, female, poor and/or disabled. They argued that since textbooks are instruments of social control, they should reflect diversity and give attention to the accomplishments and concerns of all groups.

The critical perspective involves risk-taking. It does not claim to be objective: the researcher openly embraces an ideological standpoint that represents particular interests (Foley & Valenzuela 2005). This can bring about a tension between the researcher's desire to change society—which often involves adopting a controversial and political stance—and the desire for academic security (Bailey 2010). Weak evidence and theorising might undermine any research approach, but this is particularly evident in critical research.

Table11.2: Curriculum Manifestations and Typical Research Methods

Aspect of curriculum	Typical manifestations	Typical research methods	Examples
Ideology	books; academic papers; policy and curriculum documents	discourse analysis	Millei (2011)
Planned/ intended	policy and curriculum documents; prospectuses; teaching materials; lesson plans; assessment materials; minutes of meetings; notices	discourse analysis; interviews	Grossman, Lee & Kennedy (2008)
Enacted	teacher and student action (e.g. use of time and resources); roles of teachers and students; student interest and involvement; classroom interaction (e.g. questioning patterns; use of group work); school interaction; student output	Lesson observations; teacher's log; interviews; ethnography; activity records	Alexander (2000)
Experienced	change in student attitude and/or behaviour; change in teacher attitude and/or behaviour; student's cognitive processes	questionnaires; interviews; autobiographical narratives; reflections; psychometric tests	Included in Cogan et al. (2002) and Moyles & Hargreaves (1998)

Curriculum focus and manifestations

Since curricula may be amorphous and spread over various aspects of planned and unplanned experiences, for the purposes of obtaining a research focus it is necessary to identify distinct elements or aspects for comparison. These could include:

a) the ideologies and societal cultures that influence the curriculum;
b) curriculum development and planning systems – the processes and products of curriculum development;
c) curriculum implementation – the modes of delivery of teaching and learning experiences; and

d) experience – planned and unplanned events, values, and messages that are experienced by the learner.

Each of these elements of curriculum has tangible and intangible manifestations, some of which are identified in Table 11.2.

An extra dimension to these four aspects is the 'null' curriculum
(Posner 2004), which refers to what is wittingly or unwittingly omitted
from a particular curriculum. Obviously, tangible manifestations are easier for researchers to access. For instance, policy documents can be obtained from various sources, such as government offices, educational institutions, the authors, and the internet. Likewise, it is usually reasonably
straightforward to obtain the teaching materials that are used in particular contexts. Teaching and learning experiences are less readily obtainable
for analysis – not just logistically, in the sense of gaining access to classrooms or other education sites, but also analytically. This is because such
experiences are less tangible than printed materials, and are available to
the researcher in highly subjective and indirect manifestations such as
behavioural responses or post-lesson reflections on the experiences.

Research Methods in Comparing Curricula

As in most fields of research, a range of qualitative and quantitative
methods can be used in comparisons of curricula. The research methods
to be adopted in any study obviously depend on the research perspective
(evaluative, interpretive or critical); the curriculum focus; and the curricular manifestations that are available. Many studies use mixed methods
to capture the richness of curricula-in-context. For example, Alexander's
(2000) study described above blended a more holistic, ethnographic approach with an atomistic focus on discrete aspects of pedagogy in order to
establish a multi-dimensional portrayal of classroom events. Other studies may be mainly concerned with specific details, such as a critical inquiry comparing the number of teacher questions directed to boys with
those directed to girls. In this case, a quantitative observation instrument
might be the main data collection instrument, although some ethnographic or phenomenological data might be collected if, for example, an
interpretive perspective is also being adopted.

Based on the three general perspectives (evaluative, interpretive and
critical) identified above, the following examples of comparative curriculum research used a variety of methods. They have been included in this

chapter to illustrate processes in action and to highlight some of the issues that the researchers need to address.

Evaluative study

An example of this kind of study is an evaluation of models of trilingual education in primary schools in ethnic minority regions of China (Adamson, Feng & Yi 2013). The purpose of the evaluation is to identify the factors shaping and sustaining different models of trilingual education and also to evaluate their comparative strengths and weaknesses in fostering trilingualism (in the minority language, Chinese and English) in pupils. The evaluation covers the planning, enactment and experience of these models, with a major focus on the curriculum design.

A representative sample of nine schools in each of the ethnic minority regions involved in the project was selected. A typical study of each single school would include:

- focus group interviews with community leaders, education officials
- school leaders, teachers, students, former students and parents
- documentary analysis of policy papers, syllabuses, timetables, learning resources and curriculum materials
- lesson observations
- questionnaire surveys focusing on language attitudes and views of trilingual education among students, teachers and school leaders
- field notes (e.g. observations of the school buildings and wall decorations, of languages used in the school outside of the classroom and of language use in the community.

To guide the study, coherence in the research questions was devised by adapting the four critical dimensions of policy making identified by Elmore and Sykes (1992), namely the nature of policy, the sources or origins of the policy, the forms of action and the impact (Figure 11.2).

Figure 11.2: Evaluation of Models of Trilingual Education in China

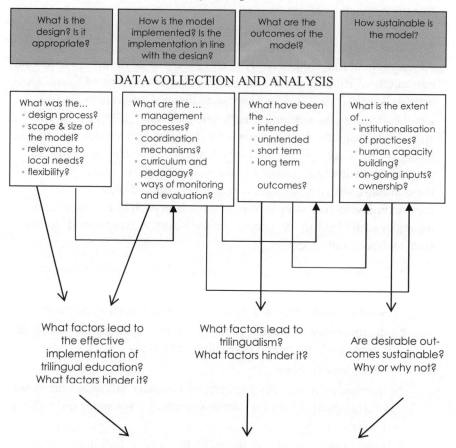

| What is the design? Is it appropriate? | How is the model implemented? Is the implementation in line with the design? | What are the outcomes of the model? | How sustainable is the model? |

DATA COLLECTION AND ANALYSIS

What was the...
◦ design process?
◦ scope & size of the model?
◦ relevance to local needs?
◦ flexibility?

What are the ...
◦ management processes?
◦ coordination mechanisms?
◦ curriculum and pedagogy?
◦ ways of monitoring and evaluation?

What have been the ...
◦ intended
◦ unintended
◦ short term
◦ long term

outcomes?

What is the extent of ...
◦ institutionalisation of practices?
◦ human capacity building?
◦ on-going inputs?
◦ ownership?

What factors lead to the effective implementation of trilingual education? What factors hinder it?

What factors lead to trilingualism? What factors hinder it?

Are desirable outcomes sustainable? Why or why not?

Lessons learned: What factors are the facilitators of and barriers to the planning and implementation of an effective trilingual education model?

Source: Adapted from Adamson, Feng & Yi (2013, p.6)

The first two dimensions were merged: the study was trying to find out whether the implemented models matched the overall objectives of the trilingual education policy, and if so, whether they were designed in a feasible manner given the constraints of time and resources. The *forms of action* dimension was interpreted as incorporating both the curriculum delivery and the management of the curriculum. The impact dimension was also divided into two: the outcomes of the trilingual model, and the likely prospects for sustainability. The overarching comparative perspective makes clear which practices were effective and which problems were evident in more than one context.

The evaluative framework, on the surface, seems to suggest a rational, linear approach to curriculum policy-making and implementation. The reality is that most policy processes are complex, reiterative and messy. The framework is concerned with evaluating the coherence of the settlements or compromises that have been made in the design, implementation and sustaining of positive outcomes, rather than imposing a rigid linearity on the process.

Interpretive study

An example of an interpretive study is a research project (Tong et al. 2000) that examined how task-based learning was planned, implemented and experienced in two different subjects in the Hong Kong school curriculum – Chinese Language and English Language – and sought reasons for these realisations. The study compared task-based learning in the two subjects in three different manifestations, thus setting up a horizontal comparison across the subjects and a vertical comparison within each subject. The three manifestations were the policy documents, commercially published textbook resources, and lessons in classrooms.

The description of tasks in the policy documents was analysed using a conceptual framework that was based on a continuum (focus on individual grammar at one end, and focus on realistic language in use at the other end) derived from a study of definitions in the literature on task-based learning in language teaching. The same framework was used for the analysis of the tasks published in various sets of textbooks and other resources in the two subjects. The manifestations of task-based learning in the classroom were studied by classroom observations that provided notes taken regularly during the lessons on the nature and purpose of each learning activity, the roles of the learners and the teachers, and the kinds of interaction that took place among them. This data collection was supplemented by semi-structured interviews with publishers, textbook writers and teachers that included questions on the nature of task-based learning as conceived by the informants, on how they went about producing the textbook resources or lessons, on the principles that they used to guide the process, and on the experiences gained by the informants in the process.

Figure 11.3: Interpretations of Task-Based Learning from Policy Intention to Implementation

Source: Tong et al. (2000, p.167).

The study found that tasks were interpreted differently both across the two subjects and also in the different manifestations within the subjects (Figure 11.3). The two subjects, Chinese Language and English Language, had emerged from very disparate pedagogical traditions in Hong Kong. This partly reflected the natures of the languages (for instance, Chinese using characters and English using phonological script) and partly reflected the functions of the two languages in Hong Kong society (Chinese as mother tongue for the vast majority of the population, and English as a language of officialdom and international trade). The two traditions led to differing interpretations of task-based learning in the policy documents and at the chalkface. Meanwhile, textbook writers and publishers were faced with commercial realities, which constrained the extent to which they complied with policy documents. They preferred to address the needs and requests of teachers, who were the main stake-holders in each school's choice of textbook resources. These historical, socio-cultural, economic and pedagogical forces brought about a variety of interpretations of the 'official' definitions of task-based learning.

The interpretive outcomes of the study also had an evaluative edge. They demonstrated the problems facing curriculum planners of achieving coherence as a reform progresses from intention to implementation, and highlighted the need to take into account the historical, socio-cultural, economic and pedagogical contexts in which curricula operate. Designing an 'ideal' curriculum on the basis of uncontextualised theory only creates a 'fantasy' curriculum that results in disappointment when the antici-pated outcomes are not realised.

Critical study

An example of a critical study is Hickling-Hudson and Ahlquist's (2003) analysis of the discourses of ethnicity in school curricula provided to in-digenous children in four primary schools, two in Australia and two in the USA. The critical dimension of the research drew attention to the questions of who defines the curriculum and whose interest is served (Hickling-Hudson & Ahlquist 2003, p.65), with a view to remedying the situation:

> The overarching concerns [of the researchers] are with how school-ing may help children of color to develop identities that are not distorted by the colonizing identity of Eurocentrism, and how teachers can learn to challenge assimilationist curricula and teach instead about the diverse histories, sciences, and arts of people of color in the world.

The researchers identified a school in each country in which the curricu-lum exhibited what they felt were poor practices, and a school in each country that displayed good practices. This arrangement therefore set up international and intranational comparisons. On field visits to the schools, classes were observed, staff and students were interviewed, and notes were made concerning the library facilities, wall displays and other curricular artefacts. In the schools identified as exhibiting poor practice, the researchers found that the curriculum was grounded in White culture: Aboriginal children in the Australian school were observed decorating Christmas trees, or being encouraged to read European fairy tales, while the walls were decorated with Disney characters; in the US school, the corridors were lined with pictures depicting White histories, and literacy lessons were focused on the demands of state tests. The researchers felt that such schools were "perpetuating a European industrial factory model of schooling that regiments learners and disregards their interests and backgrounds" (Hickling-Hudson & Ahlquist 2003, p.80). In contrast, the researchers visited a school in each country that challenged the Euro-centric view, with posters and library resources that celebrated indige-nous culture, and lessons that were grounded in the students' life expe-riences. Unlike the other two, these schools enjoyed strong community support and involvement.

Conclusions

To guide the researcher embarking upon comparative curricular inquiry, this chapter has identified some of the pitfalls and possible directions. It has proposed three interlinked considerations for approaching the task: determining the purpose and perspective of the study, selecting apposite points of curricular focus, and identifying the relevant curricular mani-festations.

Curriculum is a complex, multifaceted and dynamic concept, and covers such a broad range of stakeholders, perspectives, processes and manifestations that it is barely feasible to encompass all aspects compre-hensively in a single project. Some comparisons, often carried out for utilitarian purposes, do not aspire to be comprehensive, being only con-cerned with answering narrowly focused questions. However, when broader questions are investigated, it is important that the limitations of scope are acknowledged and that appropriate caveats are issued to guard against over-generalisation of the findings. For instance, the results of an interpretive comparative study of curriculum planning processes are not necessarily applicable to the implementation of those curricula in class-rooms. Different influences and tensions come into play, as demonstrated by the example concerning task-based learning in Chinese Language and English Language in Hong Kong. Another major problem arises from the variety of contexts of time and place. It is very difficult to make generalisations about the curriculum without taking full account of those contexts. Broad international comparisons of trends in school curricula, for instance, are only truly meaningful if the interpretation of subjects is similar in each context. A subject might be labelled 'History' in two different countries, but the nature and content of the subject might vary so much as to render comparison futile.

The dynamic nature of curriculum arising from the human interactions that occur at its many focal points of planning, implementation and experience, together with the regularity with which curriculum reform is undertaken, means that comparisons of the curriculum will always be a work-in-progress. This does not mean that comparisons of curricula are without value. When used with circumspection they permit useful transfers of good practice, allow informed decision-making, and deepen understandings of the interactions between education and its social, economic and political contexts.

References

Adamson, Bob (2011): 'Embedding Assessment for Learning', in Berry, Rita & Adamson, Bob (eds.), *Assessment Reform in Education: Policy and Practice.* Dordrecht: Springer, pp.197-203.

Adamson, Bob; Feng, Anwei & Yi, Yayuan (2013): *A Framework for the Study of Policy Design and Implementation of Models of Trilingual Education.* Technical Paper, Models of Trilingual Education in Ethnic Minority Regions of China Project. Hong Kong: Hong Kong Institute of Education.

Alexander, Robin (2000): *Culture and Pedagogy: International Comparisons in Primary Education.* Oxford: Blackwell.

Andere, Eduardo (2008): *The Lending Power of PISA: League Tables and Best Practice in International Education.* CERC Monograph Series in Comparative and International Education and Development 6, Hong Kong: Comparative Education Research Centre, The University of Hong Kong.

Andrade, Antonio Diaz (2009): 'Interpretive Research Aiming at Theory Building: Adopting and Adapting the Case Study Design'. *The Qualitative Report*, Vol.14, No.1, pp.42-60.

Apple, Michael & Christian-Smith, Linda K. (1991): 'The Politics of the Textbook', in Apple, Michael & Christian-Smith, Linda K. (eds.), *The Politics of the Textbook*. London: Routledge, pp.1-21.

Australian Curriculum Studies Association (ACSA) (2005): *ACSA Policy Statement*. http://www.acsa.edu.au/.

Bailey, Carol, A. (2010): 'Public Ethnography', in Hesse-Biber, Sharlene N. and Leavy, Patricia (eds.), *Handbook of Emergent Methods*. New York: The Guildford Press, pp.265-281.

Benavot, Aaron & Braslavsky, Cecilia (eds.) (2006): *School Knowledge in Comparative and Historical Perspective: Changing Curricula in Primary and Secondary Education*. CERC Studies in Comparative Education 18, Hong Kong and Dordrecht: Comparative Education Research Centre, The University of Hong Kong and Springer.

Bray, Mark (2004): 'Methodology and Focus in Comparative Education', in Bray, Mark & Koo, Ramsey (eds.), *Education and Society in Hong Kong and Macao: Comparative Perspectives on Continuity and Change*. 2nd edition. CERC Studies in Comparative Education 7, Hong Kong: Comparative Education Research Centre, The University of Hong Kong, pp.237-250.

Cogan, John J.; Morris, Paul & Print, Murray (2002): *Civic Education in the Asia-Pacific Region*. New York: RoutledgeFalmer.

Elmore, Richard & Sykes, Gary (1992): 'Curriculum Policy', in Jackson, Philip W. (ed.), *Handbook of Research on Curriculum*. New York: Macmillan, pp.185-215.

Foley, Douglas & Valenzuela, Angela (2005): 'Critical Ethnography: The Politics of Collaboration', in Denzin, Norman K. & Lincoln, Yvonna S. (eds.), *The Sage Handbook of Qualitative Research*. 3rd edition, Thousand Oaks, CA: Sage, pp.217-234.

Gardner, Howard (1985): *Frames of Mind: The Theory of Multiple Intelligences*. London: Paladin.

Grossman, David; Lee, Wing On & Kennedy, Kerry J. (2008): *Citizenship Curriculum in Asia and the Pacific*. CERC Studies in Comparative Education 22, Hong Kong and Dordrecht: Comparative Education Research Centre, The University of Hong Kong and Springer.

Guba, Egon G. & Lincoln, Yvonna, S. (1994): 'Competing Paradigms in Qualitative Research', in Denzin, Norman K. & Lincoln, Yvonna S. (eds.), *Handbook of Qualitative Research*. Thousand Oaks, CA: Sage, pp.105-117.

Hantrais, Linda (2008): *International Comparative Research: Theory, Methods and Practice*. New York: Palgrave Macmillan.

Hickling-Hudson, Anne & Ahlquist, Roberta (2003): 'Contesting the Curriculum in the Schooling of Indigenous Children in Australia and the United States: From Eurocentrism to Culturally Powerful Pedagogies'. *Comparative Education Review*, Vol.47, No.1, pp.64-89.

Krathwohl, David R. (2009): *Methods of Educational and Social Science Research: The Logic of Methods*. Long Grove Illinois: Waveland Press.

Luke, A. (2008): 'Curriculum in Context', in Connelly, F. Michael; He, Ming Fang & Phillion, JoAnn (eds.), *The Sage Handbook of Curriculum and Instruction*. Thousand Oaks, CA: Sage, pp.145-150.

Marsh, Colin & Willis, George (eds.) (1995): *Curriculum: Alternative Approaches, Ongoing Issues*. Englewood Cliffs: Prentice Hall.

Millei, Zsuzsa (2011): Governing Through the Early Childhood Curriculum, 'The Child', and 'Community': Ideologies of Socialist Hungary and Neoliberal Australia. *European Education*, Vol.43, No.1, pp. 33-55.

Morris, Paul (2012): 'Pick n' mix, Select and Project; Policy Borrowing and the Quest for 'World Class' Schooling: An Analysis of the 2010 Schools White Paper'. *Journal of Education Policy*, Vol. 27, No.1, pp. 89-107.

Moyles, Janet & Hargreaves, Linda (eds.) (1998): *The Primary Curriculum: Learning from International Perspectives*. London: Routledge.

Phillips, David & Ochs, Kimberley (2007): 'Processes of Policy Borrowing in Education: Some Explanatory and Analytical Devices', in Crossley, Michael; Broadfoot, Patricia & Schweisfurth, Michele (eds.), *Changing Educational Contexts, Issues and Identities: 40 Years of Comparative Education*. London: Routledge, pp.370-382.

Pinar, William F. & Reynolds, William M. (1992): 'Introduction: Curriculum as Text', in Pinar, William F. & Reynolds, William M. (eds.), *Understanding Curriculum as Phenomenological and Deconstructed Text*. New York: Teachers College Press, pp.1-14.

Posner, George J. (2004): *Analyzing the Curriculum*. 3rd edition. New York: McGraw-Hill.

Short, Edmund C. (1991): 'Introduction: Understanding Curriculum Inquiry', in Short, Edmund C. (ed.) *Forms of Curriculum Inquiry*. Albany: State University of New York Press, pp.1-25.

Sleeter, Christine E. & Grant, Carl A. (1991): 'Race, Class, Gender and Disability in Current Textbooks', in Apple, Michael & Christian-

Smith, Linda K. (eds.), *The Politics of the Textbook*. London: Routledge, pp.78-110.

Spindler, George & Spindler, Louise (1982): 'Roger Harker and Schönhausen: From Familiar to Strange and Back Again', in Spindler, George (ed.), *Doing the Ethnography of Schooling: Educational Anthropology in Action*. New York: Holt, Rinehart & Winston, pp.20-46.

Tong, Siu Yin Annie; Adamson, Bob & Che, Mary Man Wai (2000): 'Tasks in English and Chinese Language', in Adamson, Bob; Kwan, Tammy & Chan Ka Ki (eds.), *Changing the Curriculum: The Impact of Reform on Primary Schooling in Hong Kong*. Hong Kong: Hong Kong University Press, pp.145-173.

Woolman, David C. (2001): 'Educational reconstruction and post-colonial curriculum development: A comparative study of four African countries'. *International Education Journal*, Vol.2, No.5, pp.27-46.

12

Comparing Pedagogical Innovations

Nancy LAW

Innovation seems to be a constant – and necessary – theme in education. A common underlying rationale is that changes in education of all levels and types prepare citizens for life in the knowledge society. The contexts include intensifying globalisation, progressively shorter half-lives of knowledge, and economic competitiveness which requires increased collaboration and different ways of working (Hershock et al. 2007; Scardamalia & Bereiter 2010). As the creation and dissemination of knowledge are perceived to be of paramount importance, education requires new goals and processes. This view is applicable both in economically advanced countries (e.g. European Round Table of Industrialists 1997; OECD 2004) and in less developed countries (e.g. UNESCO 2003; Kozma 2008).

Changes in education policy around the world are coupled inextricably with the increasing importance of, and changing perspectives on, Information and Communication Technology (ICT). Computers were first introduced in classrooms around the early 1980s to give students opportunities for *learning about ICT* as a subject in the school curriculum. Later came the additional goal of bringing about more effective *learning with ICT*, including multimedia, the internet and the web. During the 1990s, policy priority for ICT use in schools began to shift towards *learning through ICT*. This demanded the integration of ICT as an essential tool into curricula to introduce teaching and learning activities that would be impossible without it. Towards the end of the decade, the educational role of ICT began to be perceived as indispensable for nurturing new competencies for the 21ˢᵗ century, and is evident in many of the ICT masterplans (e.g. Denmark 1997; Singapore 1997; Hong Kong 1998; Finland 2000; Korea 2000; Singapore 2008; US Department of Education 2010).

Against this background, comparative research on pedagogical innovations has developed with corresponding speed. This chapter begins by reviewing research on educational change, reform and innovation. It then turns to research that has compared pedagogical practices, and presents three studies with different approaches. One used video recordings of lessons to compare pedagogical practices in three countries, another used multiple approaches to compare pedagogical practices in five countries, and the third used video recordings in one education system.

Turning from studies of pedagogical practices to work that has been specifically concerned with pedagogical innovations, the next section presents another three studies. These were selected because they represent different methodological approaches, address different research questions, and serve different goals. They are the:

- Second Information Technology in Education Study (SITES) conducted by the International Association for the Evaluation of Educational Achievement (IEA) in 28 countries;
- Scalability of Creative Classrooms Study (SCALE CCR) conducted by the Institute for Prospective Technological Studies of the European Commission's Joint Research Centre (JRC-IPTS) comparing seven studies of innovations in Europe and Asia; and
- Innovative Teaching and Learning Research (ITL) sponsored by the Microsoft Partnership in Learning Program in collaboration with educators in seven countries.

All of the studies reviewed in the chapter use multilevel analyses that may be related to the cube developed by Bray and Thomas (1995) and highlighted in the Introduction of this book. They show the value of multilevel approaches, and also show how concepts maybe operationalised. The chapter closes with a discussion of the methodological contributions of the two sets of studies not only to research on comparative pedagogical innovations but also to wider policy and practice.

Research on Educational Change, Reform and Innovation

Changes take place in organisations for many reasons, and may be reactive rather than purposive (Dill & Friedman 1979). Innovation is a specific subset of change. It may be defined as a tangible product or procedure that is new and intentional, and that aims to be beneficial (Barnett 1953; King & Anderson 1995). Reforms typically refer to innovations that are initiated from the top of organisations or from the outside (Kezar 2001).

Within this broad framework of seeing innovation as deliberate change with specific goals, different operational definitions have been adopted. Research on the degree of change has distinguished between first-order changes involving minor adjustments in one or a few dimensions of the organisation, and second-order transformational changes involving the underlying mission, culture, functioning processes and structure of the organisation (Goodman 1982; Levy & Merry 1986). Another major research orientation focuses on innovation as a process, examining behaviours and incidents that occur over time. Some researchers have focused on stages of innovation adoption at an individual level (e.g. Hall & Loucks 1978; Hall et al. 1979). Others have presented models of innovation diffusion through organisations (e.g. Rogers 1995) and at system level (e.g. Reigeluth & Garfinkle 1994).

Until the 1990s, research on educational change focused more strongly on reform than innovation. A significant shift in both educational policy and research was evident in the CERI/OECD (1999) report arising from a workshop on "Schooling for Tomorrow". Many of the system-level reforms in the 20th century changed procedures, regulations and formal curriculum specifications, but changing teachers' practices was much more difficult (Cros 1999). Reforms need ownership and creative engagement from the grassroots to realise changes in learning and teaching practices. There is a tension between system-level reform efforts through policy stipulations and bottom-up innovations from teachers and/or schools, though these need not be in opposition to each other (Hargreaves 1999).

Methods for Comparing Pedagogical Practices

Many educational innovations reported in the literature involve pedagogical changes. Some of these studies focus on innovations that share similar pedagogical philosophies, methods and/or contexts, and are reported in literature on learning theories and pedagogy. Comparative studies that focus on pedagogical characteristics of innovations and encompass diverse approaches and philosophies were rare until the 2000s.

Alexander (2000, p.510) suggested two reasons for the lack of comparative research on pedagogy: such comparison "demands kinds and levels of expertise over and above knowledge of the countries compared, their cultures, systems and policies", and pedagogy is a large and complex field of study in its own right. In this section, three comparative studies of pedagogy differing greatly in scale, purpose, research paradigm and method are featured to highlight the diversity in the literature.

Video-Studies of Teaching as Surveys of Instructional Practice
The video studies of the Third International Mathematics and Science Study (TIMSS) are among the best-known examples of comparative pedagogical studies at the level of classroom interactions (Stigler et al. 1999; Stigler & Hiebert 1999; Hiebert et al. 2003). These studies can be described as 'video surveys' in that they employed random samples of Grade 8 mathematics lessons to secure descriptions of how mathematics was taught. They included indicators of statistical errors of the descriptive parameters and confidence levels of hypotheses about cross-national comparisons.

The TIMSS 1995 video study presented data from 231 Grade 8 mathematics lessons in Germany, Japan and the United States. First, nationally representative samples of teachers were randomly selected. One lesson was then randomly selected per sampled teacher to yield national-level descriptions and comparisons of individual lessons. All lessons were transcribed and then analysed on a number of dimensions by teams of coders who were native speakers of the relevant languages. Analyses were based on weighted data. They focused on the content and organisation of the lessons, and on the instructional practices used by teachers during the lessons. Stigler et al. (1999) and Hiebert et al. (2003) discussed the issues of standardisation in the collection, storage, processing and analysis of qualitative data to yield statistical results similar to those commonly found in surveys. Their goal was to reach normative descriptions of pedagogical practice at a national level.

Linking Pedagogy with School- and System-Level Characterisations
Alexander's (2000) "Five Cultures" study took an entirely different approach. Alexander challenged the idea that characterisations of pedagogical practices derived from a small sample of classroom observations

across different subjects could be taken as typical of a culture. His study was conducted between 1994 and 1998 in England, France, India, Russia and the United States. It described, analysed and explained the similarities and differences within and between the approaches to primary education through the examination and cross-referencing of data at the levels of system, school and classroom.

The work was underpinned by a strong belief that what teachers and students do in classrooms both reflects and shapes the values of the wider society. From this followed the view that comparative studies of pedagogy should not be confined to what happens within classrooms, but should be comprehended as practices within the school, local and national contexts. Comparison at the system level examined the history, policy, legislation, governance, control, curriculum, assessment and inspection in each country, since these were expected to exert powerful pressures towards similarity in pedagogy within each country. At the school level, Alexander identified characterisations along four organisational dimensions: space, school time, people and external relationships, and a conceptual dimension on values and functions of schools as perceived by the teachers. At the classroom level, the pedagogical features included lesson structure and form; classroom organisation, tasks and activities; differentiation and assessment of pupils; routines, rules and rituals; the organisation of interactions; timing and pacing; and how learning is scaffolded through the learning discourse. Alexander's work illustrates how studies of pedagogy can move between the different levels of interacting contexts from the classroom to the system level.

Revealing Diversity in Pedagogy and its Relationship with School Factors
Detailed study of educational phenomena within a particular national or cultural setting is an important category of research in the comparative education literature. The research by Law et al. (2000) on good practices in using ICT in Hong Kong is an example of a study that encompassed a comparison of pedagogical practices at the levels of classroom and school. Like Alexander's work (2000), this study was underpinned by a belief that pedagogical practices are strongly influenced by and can only be appropriately interpreted within the context of school- and system- level factors and characteristics. However, unlike the Five Cultures and TIMSS video studies which aimed to identify characterisations of pedagogical practice at a general cultural level, this study sought to understand the diversities in pedagogy that emerge during a period of flux – when the emphasis in

the goals of education shifts towards the development of lifelong learning capability, and the availability of ICT in classrooms to support teaching and learning is increasing.

The study recorded wide diversity in pedagogies, and explored possible links between pedagogical differences and school-level contextual factors such as leadership and school culture. Since the use of ICT was a focal feature of the practices studied, random selection of lessons for classroom observation was not appropriate. Instead, the study used purposive sampling based on the preliminary characteristics of cases collected from a network of informants knowledgeable about the status of ICT adoption in Hong Kong schools.

For the classroom-level analysis, Law et al. (2000) identified typologies of pedagogy based on coding of videotaped lessons along six key aspects: roles of the teachers; roles of the students; roles of technology; the interactions between teachers, students and technology; interactions between students; and the exhibited competences of students. Based on the grounded theory approach (Strauss & Corbin 1990), the team further identified five typologies, or *pedagogical approaches*, from analysis of the 46 lessons. At the school level, the study analysed the key distinguishing features characterising different models of school change, and found that in addition to the perceived role of ICT and its impact on the school, the vision and values of the school and its established culture and reform history played important roles in the way that ICT was integrated into the pedagogical practices.

The three studies presented above demonstrate that the method considered appropriate for comparing pedagogical practices depends on the research questions, the unit of analysis, and the purpose and scale of the study. While most data collected in these studies were qualitative, the analysis could take a quantitative, positivistic orientation or an interpretive one. Further, analyses may aim at characterisations of what is typical or representative, assuming that the system studied is relatively stable; or, conversely, analyses may reveal diversity and seek characterisations that illuminate the models of change and associated outcomes.

International Comparisons of Pedagogical Innovations

From the previous section about research on pedagogical practices, this section turns to research that has specifically focused on pedagogical innovations. Again it highlights three studies, doing so in more depth than the previous section because pedagogical innovations are the principal concern of the chapter. The increasing interest in pedagogical innovations is motivated by a desire to understand the characteristics of innovations that emerge as a complex interplay between local and broader contextual factors rather than as a phenomenon to be understood at the individual teacher level. In line with this, all three selected studies placed strong emphasis on data beyond the classroom level to shed light on the con-textual factors as well as the policies and strategies in place at various levels (school, regional, national and/or cross-national) that influence the emergence, sustainability and scalability of the innovations. In two of the studies, data about each case were collected over extended periods of time.

For each study, the following features of the methodological ap-proach and design are described:

- Research context and questions,
- Definition and selection of innovation cases,
- Methodological approach, research design and instrumentation,
- Analytical methods and key outcomes, and
- Contributions and limitations of the study.

SITES M2—Characterizing Classroom and School Level Typologies of ICT-enabled Pedagogical Innovations

The Second Information Technology in Education Study was designed as a three-module study, the second of which, Module 2 or SITES M2, com-pared cases of Innovative Pedagogical Practices Using Technology (Kozma 2003a). The study was preceded by SITES Module 1, which was a 1998 survey of principals and technology coordinators in schools in 26 countries. It documented the extent to which schools had adopted ICT in teaching and learning (Pelgrum & Anderson 2001). The findings revealed cross-national differences in the levels of ICT infrastructure, the kinds of ICT-using learning and teaching activities observed, and the obstacles experienced. Responses to an open-ended question in the principals' questionnaire indicated that the use of ICT had contributed to the emer-gence of new curriculum approaches, different roles of teachers, and productive learning activities for students.

Research context and questions

The positive impact of ICT does not arise as an automatic consequence of IT adoption in the classroom. Rather, it requires significant changes in pedagogical practice, including the roles of teachers and students (Bransford et al. 2000). SITES introduced the concept of *"emerging pedagogical paradigm"* (Pelgrum & Anderson 2001) to highlight the expectation that new pedagogical practices must accompany the implementation of ICT in teaching and learning if new goals of education are to be achieved. SITES M2 was designed to study the transformative changes that ICT brought to classrooms to prepare students for the future, and the school conditions that nurture them. In particular, the study explored the conditions for sustainability and scalability of ICT-supported pedagogical innovation through case studies in countries around the globe.

Definition and selection of innovation cases

The selection of innovation cases from each country was based on two stipulations. First, the selection was made by a national team comprising education professionals such as government officers, school principals, information technology coordinators, experienced teachers, and university researchers. Second, the selected cases satisfied four agreed international criteria: (1) evidence of significant change in the roles of teachers and students, curriculum goals, assessment practices, and/or educational materials and infrastructure, (2) technology played a substantial role in the practice, (3) evidence of measurable positive student outcomes, and (4) likelihood of being sustainable and transferable. In addition, the cases had to be considered innovative based on a set of *nationally* established criteria, as relevant to the cultural, historical and developmental contexts.

The International Study Consortium offered some criteria for innovation: providing students with information and media skills; promoting active, independent and self-directed learning; engaging students in collaborative, complex, real-world problems; 'breaking down the classroom walls' in the learning processes; promoting cross-curricular learning; addressing individual learner differences; providing students with individualised self-accessed learning opportunities; addressing equity issues; and improving social cohesiveness and understanding.

The criteria for case selection did not specify the origins of the innovations. Thus the selected cases might have resulted from top-down initiatives at the national or regional level, or bottom-up innovations initiated by classroom teachers. Both types of innovation were present among the 174 case studies reported by the 28 country teams.

Methodological approach, research design and instrumentation
SITES M2 was based on in-depth case studies, i.e. intensive descriptions and analyses of bounded systems or units to gain deep understanding of the situations and meanings for those involved. Case studies are particularly suited when the research interest is in studying process, in describing and analysing the context rather than specific variables, and in discovery rather than confirmation (Merriam 1998). The approach is especially useful for uncovering the interaction of significant factors characteristic of situations or phenomena where the variables involved cannot be delineated from their contexts (Yin 2009). The case studies in SITES M2 were designed and analysed using an *instrumental* approach, so as to generalise beyond specific cases to shed light on underlying issues, relationships and causes to address the research questions (Kozma 2003b).

In case study research, much of the analysis is usually done in the course of writing the case report (Miles & Huberman 1994). For reasons of language and resources, the case reports formed the sole basis for international cross-case analyses in SITES M2. Each case report was submitted in two formats: narrative and data matrix. The narrative format is the most common in case study research, and usually comprises a combination of description and analyses. In the SITES M2 design, the main emphasis of the narrative report was on description. The data matrix component of the report was designed as a 'slot-filling' approach, i.e. the report comprised short answers to a series of structured questions organised around the conceptual framework and presenting evidence on classroom practice. The 174 case reports can be found at the SITES M2 Study website, http://sitesm2.org/sitesm2_search.

Analytical methods and key outcomes
In addition to analyses in the international research report for SITES M2 (Kozma 2003a), in-depth national and international cross-case analyses published by the national teams in Israel and Hong Kong are briefly described in this section.

Clustering of all case features. As an instrumental case study, the SITES M2 International Study Centre focused on deriving typologies of innovation across the entire set of 174 case studies using statistical cluster analysis. Cluster analysis is an exploratory statistical method to identify relatively homogeneous groups of cases (or variables) based on selected characteristics (Aldenderfer & Blashfield 1984; SPSS Inc. 1999). Kozma and McGhee (2003) looked for the prominent pedagogical typologies in these case studies through K-means cluster analysis on 38 features categorised along four dimensions: *teacher practices* (nine features including methods, roles and collaborations), *student practices* (10 features including activities and roles), *ICT practices* (eight features including the roles and functions played by ICT in the case studies) and the *kinds of ICT* used in schools (11 features encompassing both hardware and software tools). K-means clustering is an interpretive quantitative procedure that computes iteratively, after being given the assumed number of clusters (N), to provide at the end N cluster means each with their respective cluster membership such that the sum of squared distances of the cluster members from the cluster means of the respective clusters was minimised.

Kozma and McGhee (2003) decided on an eight-cluster solution and used the most prominent features for each cluster as its label, such as tool use, student collaborative research, information management, and teacher collaboration. Thirty-one cases (18% of the total) could not be meaningfully characterised. Furthermore, this analysis was not particularly helpful in providing a characterisation beyond surface level descriptions of the innovative pedagogical practices collected.

Clustering of features related to teachers' roles and students' roles separately. Law et al. (2003) took a more judicious approach to cluster analysis of the SITES M2 case study data. Instead of clustering on all the coded pedagogical features, they conducted cluster analysis separately on each of two sets of features – teachers' roles (13 features) and students' roles (17 features) – on the basis that the changes in pedagogical roles lie at the core of pedagogical innovations, and changes in one may not necessarily link with changes in another (Law 2004).

This analysis led to five clusters of teacher roles: present, instruct and assess; provide learning resources; administer learning tasks; guide collaborative inquiry; and facilitate exploratory learning. It also led to five clusters of student roles: listening and following instructions; engaging in low level project work involving the completion of well-defined instructional tasks, and searching and presenting information; engaging in productive learning involving the design and creation of various types of media products or reports; engaging in online enquiry with remote peers; and engaging in general enquiry.

These two sets of clusters revealed that some role clusters such as the teacher presenting/instructing and the students following instructions were rather traditional. Nevertheless, there was clear evidence of some emerging roles such as the teacher facilitating exploratory learning and the students engaging in online inquiry with remote peers. It also revealed that in some cases, even though the teachers were primarily playing traditional roles such as providing learning resources, they had given students opportunities to venture into more innovative roles such as the creation of media products and artefacts (Law et al. 2011).

Comparing the extent of pedagogical transformation brought by the use of ICT. Mioduser et al. (2003) devised an analysis scheme to compare the extent of pedagogical transformation in the 10 cases of innovation collected in Israel. Their analysis was underpinned by the assumption that changes resulting from technology adoption would develop from a preliminary level of alterations to the school's routine to achieve an initial *assimilation* of ICT, through a *transitional* level, to achieving far-reaching *transformations* in pedagogical practices and learning processes. They developed a rubric comprising nine aspects grouped under four different *domains of innovation* within a school's milieu (time/space configuration, students' roles, teachers' roles, and the impact of ICT on aspects of the curriculum) and three levels of innovation (assimilation, transition, transformation) to reflect the extent to which the use of ICT triggered a gradual departure from previous patterns of work.

Using this framework, Tubin et al. (2003) analysed the 10 Israel cases collected in SITES M2. A mean overall 'level of innovation' was computed for each school across all nine aspects. The analysis found large variations in scores, and in most schools the extent of change was not the same for the nine aspects of change analysed. This means that the overall 'level of innovation' may not be easily interpretable since it is an aggregate score derived from rather different domains. Another noteworthy finding was that the levels of innovation in the various domains were highly correlated, except that the extent of ICT use in teachers' communication and work patterns had little correlation with changes brought about by ICT in the other aspects.

Comparing pedagogical innovativeness with ICT as one comparative dimension. Being wary of the assumption that the extent of pedagogical innovation is necessarily correlated with ICT adoption, Law, Chow and Yuen (2005) designed a comparison of pedagogical innovativeness across the international case studies that considered ICT use as only one of six dimensions of innovation. The other five dimensions were *student practices, teacher practices, curriculum goals, multidimensionality of the observable learning outcomes* and the *connectedness* of the classrooms. They constructed a rubric for assessing the level of innovativeness for each dimension independently, specifying the respective pedagogical features along a continuum of innovativeness on a seven-point Likert scale from the most traditional to the most innovative.

Using this method, Law et al. (2003) reported large diversities along each of these six dimensions across 130 of the SITES M2 international case studies. Some cases had features that resembled traditional practices, while others had innovative features rarely found in everyday classroom practices. The research team did not consider it appropriate to compute an aggregate innovation score for each case out of the six innovation scores, but developed a graphical representation to provide a bird's eye view of the team's rating for the extent of innovativeness of each case along the six dimensions. The study found that cases rated as highly innovative in all six dimensions were rare, and that many were highly innovative in only one or a few dimensions. This probably indicates that in experimenting with novel ways of organising teaching and learning, the change agents in the different practices did not give the same priority to the six dimensions.

Among the six dimensions of innovation, ICT sophistication had the highest mean innovation score as well as the smallest standard deviation. This indicates that while the overall ICT availability differs greatly around the world (Pelgrum & Anderson 2001), the cases selected as innovative by the different countries were much more similar in terms of the technology used than in any of the other dimensions. On the other hand, the connectedness of the classrooms had the largest standard deviation, indicating that connectedness was possibly more dependent on other factors, such as the prevalent classroom culture, than hardware/software availability and connectivity (Law 2008).

Using the innovation scores developed as a measure of the extent of innovativeness, Law, Chow and Yuen (2005) revealed similarities and differences across geographical regions. The multidimensionality of learning outcome score had the lowest mean score for nearly all regions and was below the mid-point score of 4 for all regions except Western Europe. This indicates that assessment practices had undergone the least change among the six pedagogical dimensions. Furthermore, the study found that Western Europe had the highest mean innovation scores for all dimensions, except for the dimension ICT sophistication. On the other hand, with the exception of the ICT sophistication dimension, the mean innovation scores for Asia were below 4 for all the other five dimensions.

Such findings can be followed up by in-depth explorations of the regional/cross-national differences. For example, starting from the observation that the Asian case studies were lowest in connectedness while the Western European ones were most connected, Law, Kankaanranta and Chow (2005) conducted further qualitative analysis to reveal significant differences in the roles played by ICT in the innovation cases collected from Hong Kong and Finland. In the Hong Kong innovations, ICT was used mainly as a learning and productivity tool for information search through the internet. Even though internet access was available in all of the Hong Kong innovation schools, the only communication tools used were emails and a discussion forum. By contrast, all the Finnish innovations adopted online learning environments that formed an important information and communication infrastructure to scaffold *both* the learning activities *and* the collaborative interactions (i.e. connectedness) between the various parties involved in the innovations.

Contributions and limitations of the study
SITES M2 was the first large international comparative study of pedagogical innovations. It pioneered a number of methodological innovations in case study research, and provided rich datasets. The findings reported to date based on the SITES M2 study have been largely descriptive, but some explanatory studies have also been conducted. They include explorations into possible factors contributing to the regional differences in innovation characteristics between European and Asian cases (Law, Kankaanranta & Chow 2005), and the sustainability and scalability of ICT-supported pedagogical innovations (Law 2008).

Obviously, as a pioneering study, there was much room for methodological improvement. In particular, the study did not really take account of the multilevel nature of the education system even though the conceptual framework stated that "innovative pedagogical practices are embedded in a concentric set of contextual levels that affect and mediate change" (Kozma 2003a, p.10) and data were collected at the classroom (micro), school (meso) and national (macro) levels. Inadequacies in the SITES M2 design prevented the analyses from truly revealing the multi-level interactions and relationships. First, while the data collection for each case included school-level information, only one innovative practice was selected within each school. This effectively reduced schools to the same level as the classroom in terms of data collection, as it did not permit analysis at multiple nested levels. Second, data collection in SITES M2 was confined to in-depth qualitative interviews and class observations involving a few individuals within each school, and only a few schools within each country. The fact that each level of context had only one or a few data points effectively collapsed the data from the various levels into one. In the ITL study described below, these design limitations were overcome, resulting in more powerful findings.

Another feature, which may or may not be seen as a limitation, is that all cases were defined around a single classroom practice, even though some of them may have been part of local, national or international initiatives. While the data collection did include such contextual links and some mentioned the contribution of such contextual backgrounds, the lack of information about other classrooms and schools within the same initiative meant that the researchers did not have access to an understanding of the specific case within the full richness of the broader innovation context. The possibility and advantages of studying pedagogical innovations with cases defined at vastly different grain sizes is discussed at greater detail through the SCALE CCR below.

SCALE CCR—Comparing Vastly Different Grain Sizes of Innovation "Cases" from Asia and Europe to Explore Conditions for Sustainability, Scalability and Impact from an Ecological perspective

As SITES M2 demonstrates, it is not the extent of innovativeness per se which is the most important for long term impact on the education system, but the sustainability and scalability of the innovations (Kozma 2003a). Decades of study of educational change have led many to adopt an ecological perspective to understanding and promoting change as a complex, evolving process (Hargreaves 2003; Coburn 2003; CERI/OECD 2010; Law et al. 2011). Change is not one-off but ongoing, and for change to be sustainined the entire education ecology, including infrastructure, culture, curriculum and other school and system level factors, needs to evolve.

Since the turn of the century, many large-scale pilots have been conducted on the use of ICT to support learning in various contexts, with differing levels of policy involvement and support. The Information Society Unit at JRC-IPTS launched in 2011 the project "Up-scaling Creative Classrooms in Europe" (SCALE CCR) on behalf of the European Commission. The work culminated in a report on the conditions for sustainability, scalability and impact at system level of ICT-enabled innovations for learning, based on in-depth comparisons of case studies selected from Europe and Asia (Kampylis et al. 2013). The methods used are described in this section.

Research context and questions
The core part of the SCALE CCR study sought better understanding of the innovation aims, outcomes, impacts, and pedagogical, technological and organisational nature of ICT-enabled learning innovations. The researchers examined the implementation and dissemination strategies of ongoing innovations that had already achieved significant scale and/or impact. The study investigated the conditions for ICT-enabled learning innovations to achieve sustainability, scalability and significant impact at the system level, and effective policies and strategies for mainstreaming ICT-enabled learning innovations. The focus was on supporting policy reform through building an evidence base and theory construction.

Definition and selection of innovation cases
Unlike the usual practice in conducting comparative case studies where the cases are defined to be of similar grain sizes, the seven cases selected in the SCALE CCR study – three from Europe and four from Asia – represent enormous diversity. The range in scale was from a single school to a multinational project involving more than 200,000 registered teachers in 33 countries. Such diversity was intentional, to provide authentic "life histories" of the ongoing ICT-enabled learning innovations to facilitate an ecological exploration that confronts and learns from real innovations in different countries with its usual messiness and complexities.

In SITES M2, the focus was a curriculum unit selected as a pedagogical innovation. The case boundaries were clearly defined at two levels, the classroom and the school to which it belonged, even though the innovation may have been part of a bigger national or international network. In contrast, the focus in SCALE CCR was on theory building around the problem of scalability and systemic impact of ICT-using learning innovations. The scale or nature of the innovation served as a "variable", indentifying whether and how the different histories, contexts and scales of the innovation interacted and impacted on the issue of scalability. A case in this study was taken as a "project" in its broadest possible definition around a common theme and structure, and included all levels of stakeholders and interactions that impinged on the nature as well as the changes and development of the innovation. For the purpose of theory building, purposive sampling was adopted, i.e. cases were selected for their potential to illuminate and extend the relationships among the identified constructs for the study (Eisenhardt & Graebner 2007).

The three European cases selected were:

- *eTwinning*. This was a network of teachers who used the European Schoolnet portal as a safe online environment for cross-border classroom projects and teacher professional development. Started in 2005, by 2013 this initiative had over 200,000 registered teachers in 33 European countries. It was supported by a Central Support Service at the European level and by National Support Services at the country level. eTwinning was selected on the basis of its scale and the recognition achieved in enhancing intercultural awareness among European school communities and teachers.
- *1:1 learning in Europe*. This collection of 31 projects was launched in 19 European countries to equip all students of specific classes, schools, or age groups with a portable computing device, in order to bring about pedagogical change and innovation. The diversity of approaches to implementation, financing models and mainstreaming strategies in these 31 initiatives shed valuable light on how these factors influenced the projects and their scalability.
- *Hellerup School in Denmark*. This innovative public school built in 2000-2002 had successfully adapted its pedagogy and reinvented its physical spaces to promote diversity, flexibility, and creativity in student learning, fully embracing ICT-possibilities. It also catered for diverse learning strategies and styles. The school adapted its entire ecosystem to achieve sustainability, and had significant influence on other school ecologies.

The following four Asian cases were selected for inclusion:

- *Renovating Education of the Future Project (CoREF).* This project, launched in 2010, aimed to change Japanese teacher-centred education into more student-centred, socio-constructivist learning. It adopted a specific pedagogical method, the knowledge construction jigsaw, led by a university-based consortium and supported by District Education Boards. CoREF reached about 770 schools in 2013, and was expected to provide evidence-based recommendations on educational policies, including the national standards, school grading systems and curriculum development.
- *Digital Textbook Project in South Korea.* This was a pilot project of the South Korean Ministry of Education to develop digital textbook contents that were accessible and easy to use. It leveraged mobile devices and social network service tools to provide students with interactive, authentic, and rich learning experiences. The project was part of the South Korean ICT masterplan.
- *e-Learning Pilot Scheme in Hong Kong.* This three-year scheme was launched by the Hong Kong government as part of its Third IT in Education Strategy to explore suitable modes and necessary support measures for the development of effective e-Learning solutions that are sustainable, transferable and scalable. It consisted of 21 projects selected by the government's Education Bureau, involving a variety of subject domains and 61 schools.
- *Third Masterplan for ICT in education (mp3), Singapore.* This initiative of the Singapore government targeted the entire school population and sought to "enrich and transform the learning environments of students and equip them with the critical competencies and dispositions to succeed in a knowledge economy". The project had already reached the mainstreaming stage, building on the vision and outcomes of the first and second masterplans.

The above list shows that "polar" cases were selected in terms of scale (a single school vs 200,000 teachers in 33 countries), focal source of agency (school-based vs European level initiative) and maturity (an initial pilot vs mainstreaming a national initiative with 15 years of history). The list matched the design of case studies for theory building, where "each case serves as a distinct experiment that stands on its own as an analytic unit" and the emphasis is "on developing constructs, measures, and testable theoretical propositions" (Eisenhardt & Graebner 2007, p.25).

Methodological approach, research design and instrumentation
In most case study research, data collection begins after the research design has been finalized. In this particular study, no primary data collection was involved. Instead, individual researchers or a team of researchers who were knowledgeable about and had access to research reports and key people related to the selected case were identified to author the 'case report' for each of the seven selected cases. Each case author was provided with a template for reporting so that each case could be mapped onto a conceptual framework. The framework has five dimensions, each defined with a label for the two extremes and the midpoint of a continuous scale for mapping of any innovation involving changes in pedagogy:

1. Nature of innovation (from incremental to radical to disruptive),
2. Implementation phase (from pilot to scale to mainstream),
3. Access level (from local to regional/national to cross-border),
4. Impact area (from processes to services to organization), and
5. Target (from single actor to multiple actors to a wide range of actors).

These five dimensions were designed to capture not only the differences across different innovations but also the dynamic aspects of change during the life histories of the innovations. Figure 12.1 shows the resulting mapping of the seven cases on this framework.

Figure 12.1: The Seven Cases of Innovation Mapped onto the Framework Developed by Kampylis et al.

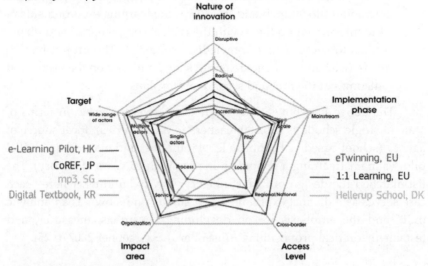

Source: Kampylis et al. (2013), p.6.

Analytical methods and key outcomes

SCALE CCR identified conditions for innovations to have significant impact on learning outcomes based on replicated observations across the seven cases, which were consistent with findings from the literature. This section describes how two trend observations were derived from examining the relationships between constructs varying across a wide scale.

<u>Does the choice of technology affect pedagogical innovativeness?</u> One of the observations concerns the relationship between the sophistication of the technology used and the role played by technology in the context of the innovation. The study found that single or multiple pieces of technology tend to serve as either add-ons or a focal reason for an innovation project. However, for technology to have the possibility of serving as a lever for deep pedagogical change, it needs to be a digital infrastructure that *integrates* the hardware, networks and devices with the online learning environment and resources.

<u>An innovation's participation threshold for strategic alignment and its scalability.</u> Underpinning the creation of this construct is the assumption that innovation can be initiated bottom-up or top-down, and that often both kinds of strategies are in operation in any specific innovation. For any innovation, irrespective of the nature, scale or primary source of agency, there must be a common basis accepted by everyone participating in that innovation. For some, this *participation threshold for strategic alignment* can be very low, such as using the eTwinning portal to communicate with classrooms in other European countries, or making use of 1:1 learning devices. Alternatively, it can be much higher such as the adoption of a common pedagogical model as in CoREF or in pursuing a disruptive school vision involving physical spaces, curriculum, timetabling, etc. that are totally different from the mainstream, as in the Hellerup School. Using this framework, the study mapped the *participation threshold for strategic alignment* of each case to its *scale* (i.e. its access level according to the innovation mapping framework described above). Figure 12.2 shows that overall, innovations with a larger scale tend to have a lower participation threshold for strategic alignment.

Contributions and limitations of the study

This kind of work demonstrates the methodological potential for using cases at different levels of scale for the purpose of achieving multilevel understanding when the phenomenon under investigation involves complex, hierarchical interactions, and interdependent feedback. Here, the boundaries of the cases are fluid and organic – they change with time. The study leverages the case authors' deep knowledge and connections with the selected cases to craft the case reports on the basis of a secondary analysis of a rich collection of in-depth reports according to the defined template. This design made it possible for the study to have larger geographic and participant coverage, and cover longer durations than are normally feasible.

Figure 12.2: Plot of the Participation Threshold for Strategic Alignment vs its Access Level in the SCALE CCR Study

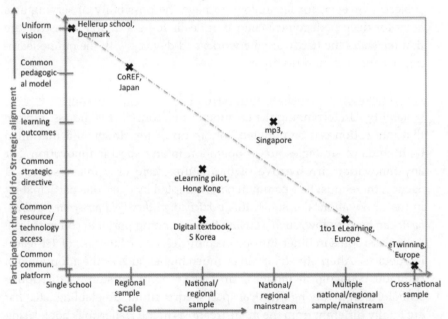

Source: Kampylis et al. (2013), p.128.

   In addition, the evidence gathered through the cases has been used to develop policy recommendations for the further mainstreaming and up-scaling of ICT-enabled systemic innovations (Brečko et al 2013). The final analyses are potentially ecologically valid as they take account of the dynamic and evolving nature of ongoing innovations, but at the same time raise methodological challenges as to what counts as criteria for ecological validity.

While a negative relationship is clearly discernible from Figure 12.2, there are important deviations. For example, both the eLearning Pilot in Hong Kong and the Third Masterplan for IT in Education in Singapore built on initiatives that started around the same time, but the latter has achieved much greater scale and a higher participation threshold for strategic alignment. Due to the absence of information on the organic evolution of these different innovations to illuminate the static snapshots represented in Figures 12.1 and 12.2, the core reasons for such deviations cannot be clearly identified. Understanding of the contextual and/or strategic differences that have contributed to different pathways of change and their evolution may require further methodological advances in the comparative study of pedagogical innovations.

ITL—Investigating Conditions for ICT Use to Foster Students' 21st Century Skills from an Ecosystem Perspective

The Innovative Teaching and Learning Research (ITL), conducted in 2010-2011, was led by SRI International and sponsored by Microsoft® (Shear et al. 2011). This study, underpinned by an ecosystem conceptual framework, investigated supports for innovative pedagogies enabled by ICT use and how these led to students' learning outcomes. ITL was conducted in seven countries with wide geographic, cultural and socio-economic diversity: Australia, England, Finland, Indonesia, Mexico, Russia, and Senegal. The focus was not on comparison as ranking, but comparison for identifying similarities in the relationships among the interacting conditions within each education system that impacted on innovative teaching practices and students' outcomes.

Research context and questions

The ITL study addressed three research questions (Shear et al. 2010):

- To what extent are innovative teaching practices associated with 21st century learning outcomes?
- What school-level conditions are associated with innovative teaching practices?
- What national or regional programme supports are associated with innovative teaching practices?

The findings were used to inform a later phase of the research, which focused on support for teaching practices. Like SITES M2, the ITL research was coordinated by a global research team responsible for global design, analysis and reporting. In each country a local research partner took responsibility for local adaptations and data collection.

Definition and selection of innovation cases

For an ecologically grounded study, case study is the most appropriate method to provide holistic understanding. As the focus was on innovative teaching practices, cases were purposively sampled. Again like SITES M2, case selection in each country was carried out by a nominating committee of three or four members able to identify 12 innovative schools and 12 comparison schools. Innovative schools were defined as those judged to have high levels of innovative teaching practices. Innovative teaching practices were characterised by three key constructs: student-centered pedagogies, learning outside the classroom, and integration of ICT into teaching and learning (Gallagher et al. 2011).

Methodological approach, research design and instrumentation

The ITL research employed an instrumental comparative case study method with two levels of comparison. First, comparisons across the schools within each country were made to explore the three descriptive research questions. The findings from each of the seven countries were then compared to identify relationships that were significant in the over-all dataset and also significant in at least three countries.

Four kinds of data were collected in this study – survey of teachers and school leaders; classroom observations; interviews of school leaders, teachers and student focus groups; and analysis of Learning Activities and Student Work (LASW) – to yield multiple sets of indicators related to innovative teaching. Among these, LASW was the primary objective measure for both teacher practices and student outcomes (Gallagher et al. 2011). The use of LASW for large-scale international comparison of pedagogical innovation was relatively new and is described in some detail here.

A learning activity is a piece of work that the teacher assigns to students within or outside the classroom as part of the learning process. Student work samples are artifacts produced by students such as essays, presentations, worksheets or multimedia products such as podcasts and videos during the process of completing a learning activity. In LASW, samples of learning activities and student work were collected as evidence of teaching practice and learning outcomes that reflected what was happening in authentic classroom settings. This method was developed on the basis of prior work on authenticity and intellectual complexity of assigned work (Bryk et al. 2000), rigor and relevance (Mitchell et al. 2005), and 21st century learning opportunities (Shear et al. 2009).

In the ITL year 1 study, samples of learning activities and student work were collected from eight humanities or science teachers of students aged 11 to 14 in each of six schools from the 12 sampled innovative schools in each country. Each selected teacher provided four to six samples of learning activities (LAs), which the teacher considered to have provided the best learning opportunities for students over different periods of the school year. The criterion for best was left to the teachers, and thus reflected their beliefs about quality teaching.

In addition to submitting samples of learning activities, each selected teacher was asked to submit, for four of the learning activities they provided, six randomly-selected samples of student work (SW). The random sampling was usually done by the local research partner based on the list of student names for the class associated with the learning task. The LA samples were first coded for the extent to which they provided opportunities for students to build the skills. The associated SW samples were then coded to reflect the extent to which the students were actually able to demonstrate the skills targeted.

Analytical methods and key outcomes
Here, only analysis involving the LASW data is presented, since the analyses of the survey and interview data were similar to used in SITES M1 and M2. The LASW samples were coded by teachers recruited and trained separately by the local research teams (Gallagher et al. 2011). LA samples were coded on five dimensions (collaboration, knowledge building, use of ICT for learning, real-world problem-solving and innovation, and self-regulation) to provide measures of the extent to which teachers provided their students with opportunities to develop 21st century skills. SW samples were coded on a parallel series of four dimensions (coding was on skilled communication rather than self-regulation, no coding for the collaboration dimension), to reveal the extent to which the students' work exhibited the respective skills. Coding was done on a four-point scale, and inter-rater reliability was computed for 20% of the samples.

Four types of analysis were conducted on the coded LASW data: descriptive statistics of the weighted scores, intraclass correlation coefficient of the SW scores, ordinal regression analysis of the LA and SW scores (weighted and adjusted for standard errors), and a linear regression analysis of the mean weighted scores collapsed across LA dimensions and the mean weighted scores collapsed across SW dimensions. The LASW data for the teachers were also used in ordinal regression models to examine the relationship between LASW scores and the teachers' scale scores on the survey data.

Shear et al. (2011) reported several important findings:

a) Innovative teaching practices were positively associated with 21st century learning outcomes, the development of which is most influenced by the design of learning activities;

b) Innovative teaching practices were more likely to be found when there are opportunities for teachers to collaborate; when teachers experience sustained and hands-on methods of professional development; and within school-wide cultures that support innovation;

c) Teacher use of ICT in their teaching was more common than student use of it in their learning;

d) Innovative teaching practices were found in all countries. These tended to be isolated occurrences resulting from individual motivated teachers' efforts and disconnected from other parts of the education ecosystem such as student assessment and teacher appraisal. There were wide intra-school variations in teaching, and consistent school-wide innovative practices were rare.

Contributions and limitations of the study
ITL provided clear evidence on the links between innovative teaching practices and students' development of the skills that would be useful to them in their future lives and work. Through the nested structure of sampling teachers in a selection of schools in each participating country, the study revealed strong similarities in the ecological status in relation to ICT use and pedagogical innovation. The finding d) above, as well as the observation of all of the four key findings across the seven countries with diverse backgrounds, would not have been possible without the nested case study design.

Nevertheless, ITL also had weaknesses. In particular, the limited scale of data collection and the lack of a strict adherence to the sampling design constrained the generalisability of the findings within each country and the ability to make cross-country comparisons (Gallagher et al. 2011).

Methodological Advances and Challenges to Comparing Pedagogy and Pedagogical Innovations

The key difference between comparisons of pedagogical innovations and comparisons of pedagogy is that the former focuses on understanding the tip of the pedagogical "iceberg" – the fluid pedagogical changes taking place in classrooms as part of the broader contextual background and forces – while the latter focuses on the more stable, representative picture of pedagogical practices within specific contexts. Comparative studies of pedagogy aim to identify and understand pedagogical differences and relate these to socio-cultural, historical and economic contexts. Here comparison is the focal interest. In contrast, comparative studies of pedagogical innovations primarily aim to develop better theories and models for sustaining and up-scaling pedagogical innovation. Comparison is used instrumentally as a method to answer questions related to change and innovation at different levels of education systems.

The shift from comparing pedagogy to comparing pedagogical innovations raises methodological issues that are also relevant to other domains of comparative education research. They include the purpose of comparison, how to handle context, and how to conduct comparative studies of dynamic educational phenomena that are rooted in hierarchically nested systems.

Limited Utility of Static, Decontextualised Comparisons of Pedagogy
The TIMSS video study was designed to understand the differences in mathematics performance between the USA, Germany and Japan, i.e. three economically developed countries that occupied different positions on the TIMSS mathematics league table. The key finding was that the inter-country differences were much greater than the intra-country differences – to the extent that Stigler et al. (1999) claimed that each country's mathematics teaching could be represented in the form of a script, much like the mathematics achievements of the students could be represented by the means and standard deviations of the test scores. This was an interesting and perhaps surprising finding, the validity and utility of which could be challenged. The finding stands in sharp contrast to the ITL study, which found wide diversities in teaching practices even within

schools. It also found relationships between teaching practices and contextual factors that were similar across countries that differed widely in curriculum and socio-economic and cultural backgrounds.

During periods of flux, before the tipping point is reached, instruments that aim to measure the central tendency are blunt in detecting change. For example, SITES 2006 reported that teachers' pedagogical practices were still very traditional, and the pedagogical innovations identified in the SITES M2 cases collected in 2000 were still rare (Law et al. 2008). Study designs that are essentially snapshots such as the TIMSS video study would not be able to capture changes unless repeated.

From Contextual Mapping to Ecosystem Modelling
Unlike the TIMSS video study, the other five studies reviewed in this chapter paid much attention to contextual data. However, conceptualisations and approaches to study of context differed. In the work of both Alexander (2000) and Law et al. (2000), context was taken to include the multi-faceted school and system level factors, such as school vision and leadership, and the cultural and economic background. In both studies, typologies of pedagogical practices and contextual conditions were developed on the basis of in-depth, iterative analysis of the qualitative data. These studies constructed 'contextual maps' to complement the qualitative descriptions of pedagogical practice.

SITES M2 went further with an explicit conceptual model of the hierarchical, nested structure of the contextual factors at macro and meso levels that influence the characteristics of pedagogical innovations at the micro level. However, the research design did not permit a true ecosystem model of pedagogical innovations to be derived as there was only one or a few data points at each level.

ITL had the most sophisticated design to capture the hierarchical complexity of data at different levels. It was hence able to provide interesting observations about the relationships between the innovation characteristics and the contextual factors at different levels in each country.

The SCALE CCR study also had an innovative design in its definition of a case. Wide diversities in grain sizes were included, and the comparisons were made on analytical rather than descriptive dimensions. This offered an alternative design to explore pedagogical innovations as multilevel phenomena.

Building dynamic ecosystem models of pedagogical innovation

Rudimentary attempts have been made to capture the dynamic aspects of pedagogical innovation in both the SCALE CCR and ITL studies, though in very different ways. By analysing a cross section of 'projects' at different granularities and developmental histories, statistical models could be designed on how different kinds of projects developed over time in terms of the extent of innovativeness (represented by the participation threshold for strategic alignment) and the scale of influence of the innovation. However, the models are still relatively static and do not shed light on the mechanisms and conditions for projects and their subunits to change along these two dimensions.

The ITL project spanned three years. The review reported in this chapter was on the findings from the second year (the first year having been a pilot to refine the research design and instrumentation). The third year was not designed as a 'normal' longitudinal evaluation, but as a study to develop and implement interventions and to investigate the resulting changes. This arrangement allows for more dynamic explorations of the complex interactions and interdependencies at various levels of the education ecosystem within which pedagogical innovations take place.

Looking ahead

Much advance has been made in this sub-field in research design and instrumentation. In particular, clear advances have been achieved in case study methods for building multilevel ecological models of change. Given the strong interests in comparative studies of pedagogical innovations worldwide to inform policy at different levels, further methodological advances in this area may be expected, particularly in developing dynamic models of change that take account of context as nested within complex interacting and interdependent hierarchical structures.

References

Aldenderfer, Mark S. & Blashfield, Roger K. (1984): *Cluster Analysis*. Beverly Hills: SAGE.

Alexander, Robin J. (2000): *Culture and Pedagogy: International Comparisons in Primary Education*. Oxford: Blackwell.

Barnett, Homer (1953): *Innovation*. New York: McGraw-Hill.

Bransford, John D.; Brown, Ann L. & Cocking, Rodney R. (eds.) (2000):

How People Learn: Brain, Mind, Experience, and School. Washington DC: National Academy Press.

Bray, Mark & Thomas, R. Murray (1995): 'Levels of Comparison in Educational Studies: Different Insights from Different Literatures and the Value of Multilevel Analyses'. *Harvard Educational Review*, Vol.65, No.3, pp.472-490.

Brečko, Barbara N.; Kampylis, Pan & Punie, Yves (2013): *Mainstreaming ICT enabled Innovation in Education and Training in Europe: Policy Actions for Sustainability, Scalability and Impact at System Level*. Luxembourg: Publications Office of the European Union.

Bryk, Anthony S.; Nagaoka, Jenny K. & Newmann, Fred M. (2000): *Chicago Classroom Demands for Authentic Intellectual Work: Trends from 1997-1999*. Chicago: Consortium on Chicago School Research.

CERI/OECD (1999): *Innovating Schools*. Paris: Centre for Educational Research and Innovation (CERI), Organisation for Economic Co-operation and Development (OECD).

CERI/OECD (2010): *Inspired by Technology, Driven by Pedagogy: A Systemic Approach to Technology-Based School Innovations, Educational Research and Innovation*. Paris: Centre for Educational Research and Innovation (CERI), Organisation for Economic Co-operation and Development (OECD).

Coburn, Cynthia E. (2003): 'Rethinking Scale: Moving Beyond Numbers to Deep and Lasting Change'. *Educational Researcher*, Vol.32, No.6, pp.3-12.

Cros, Françoise (1999): 'Innovation in Education: Managing the Future?', in CERI/OECD (ed.), *Innovating Schools*. Paris: Centre for Educational Research and Innovation (CERI), Organisation for Economic Co-operation and Development (OECD), pp.59-78.

Denmark, Ministry of Education (1997): *Information Technology and Education*. www.uvm.dk/eng/publications/9Informationtec/eng_it.htm, accessed 4 October 2005.

Dill, David D. & Friedman, Charles P. (1979): 'An Analysis of Frameworks for Innovation and Change in Higher Education'. *Review of Educational Research*, Vol.49, No.3, pp.411-435.

Eisenhardt, Kathleen M. & Graebner, Melissa E. (2007): 'Theory Building from Cases : Opportunities and Challenges'. *Academy of Management Journal*, Vol.50, No.1, pp.25-32.

European Round Table of Industrialists (1997): *Investing in Knowledge: The Integration of Technology in European Education*. Brussels: European

Round Table of Industrialists.

Finland, Ministry of Education. (2000): *Information Strategy for Education and Research 2000-2004 Implementation Plan*. Helsinki: Ministry of Education.

Gallagher, Larry; Shear, Linda; Patel, Deepa & Miller, Gloria (2011): *ITL Research Phase I Technical Supplement*. Menlo Park: SRI International.

Goodman, Paul S. (1982): *Change in Organizations: New Perspectives on Theory, Research, and Practice*. San Francisco: Jossey-Bass.

Hall, Gene E.; George, Archie A. & Rutherford, William L. (1979): *Measuring Stages of Concern about the Innovation: A Manual for the Use of the SoC Questionnaire*. Austin: The University of Texas, Research and Development Center for Teacher Education.

Hall, Gene E. & Loucks, Susan (1978): 'Teacher Concerns as a Basis for Facilitating and Personalizing Staff Development'. *Teachers College Record*, Vol.80, No.1, pp.36-53.

Hargreaves, David H. (1999): 'Schools and the Future: The Key Role of Innovation', in CERI/OECD (ed.), *Innovating Schools*. Paris: Centre for Educational Research and Innovation (CERI), Organisation for Economic Co-operation and Development (OECD), pp.45-58.

Hargreaves, David H. (2003): *Education Epidemic: Transforming Secondary Schools through Innovation Networks*. London: Demos.

Hershock, Peter D.; Mason, Mark & Hawkins, John N. (eds.) (2007): *Changing Education: Leadership, Innovation and Development in a Globalizing Asia Pacific*. CERC Studies in Comparative Education 20, Hong Kong: Comparative Education Research Centre, The University of Hong Kong, and Dordrecht: Springer.

Hiebert, James; Gallimore, Ronald; Garnier, Helen; Givvin, Karen Bogard; Hollingsworth, Hilary & Jacobs, Jennifer E. (2003): *Teaching Mathematics in Seven Countries: Results from the TIMSS 1999 Video Study*. Washington DC: National Center for Education Statistics.

Hong Kong, Education & Manpower Bureau (1998): *Information Technology for Learning in a New Era*. Hong Kong: Education & Manpower Bureau.

Kampylis, Panagiotis; Law, Nancy & Punie, Yves (eds.) (2013): *ICT-enabled Innovation for Learning in Europe and Asia: Exploring Conditions for Sustainability, Scalability and Impact at System Level*. Luxembourg: Publications Office of the European Union.

Kezar, Adrianna J. (2001): *Understanding and Facilitating Organizational Change in the 21st Century: Recent Research and Conceptualizations*. San

Francisco: Jossey-Bass.

King, Nigel & Anderson, Neil (1995): *Innovation and Change in Organizations*. New York: Routledge.

Korea, Republic of; Ministry of Education (2000): *Adapting Education to the Information Age: A White Paper*. Seoul: Korea Education and Research Information Service.

Kozma, Robert B. (ed.) (2003a): *Technology, Innovation, and Educational Change: A Global Perspective*. Eugene: International Society for Technology in Education.

Kozma, Robert B. (2003b): 'Study Procedures and First Look at the Data', in Kozma, Robert B. (ed.), *Technology, Innovation, and Educational Change: A Global Perspective*. Eugene: International Society for Technology in Education, pp.19-41.

Kozma, Robert B. (2008): *ICT, Education Reform, and Economic Growth: A Conceptual Framework*. San Francisco: Intel Corporation.

Kozma, Robert B. & McGhee, Raymond (2003): 'ICT and Innovative Classroom Practices' in Kozma, Robert B. (ed.), *Technology, Innovation, and Educational Change: A Global Perspective*. Eugene: International Society for Technology in Education.

Law, Nancy (2004): 'Teachers and Teaching Innovations in a Connected World', in Brown, Andrew & Davis, Niki (eds.), *Digital Technology, Communities and Education*. London: RoutledgeFalmer, pp.145-163.

Law, Nancy (2008): 'Technology-Supported Pedagogical Innovations: The Challenge of Sustainability and Transferability in the Information Age', in Ng, Chi-hung Clarence & Renshaw, Peter D. (eds.) *Reforming Learning: Issues, Concepts and Practices in the Asian-Pacific Region*. Dordrecht: Springer, pp.319-344.

Law, Nancy; Chow, Angela & Yuen, Allan H.K. (2005): 'Methodological Approaches to Comparing Pedagogical Innovations using Technology'. *Education and Information Technologies*, Vol.10, Nos.1-2, pp.7-20.

Law, Nancy; Kankaanranta, Marja & Chow, Angela (2005): 'Technology-supported Educational Innovations in Finland and Hong Kong: A Tale of Two Systems'. *Human Technology*, Vol.1, No.2, pp.176-201.

Law, Nancy; Pelgrum, Willem J. & Plomp, Tjeerd (eds.) (2008): *Pedagogy and ICT Use in Schools around the World: Findings from the IEA SITES 2006 Study*. CERC Studies in Comparative Education 23, Hong Kong: Comparative Education Research Centre, The University of Hong Kong, and Dordrecht: Springer.

Law, Nancy; Yuen, Allan; Chow, Angela & Lee, Yeung (2003): *SITES*

Module 2 Hong Kong Study Centre Secondary Analysis. Hong Kong: Centre for Information Technology in Education, The University of Hong Kong.

Law, Nancy; Yuen, Hoi Kau; Ki, Wing Wah; Li, Siu Cheung; Lee, Yeung & Chow, Yin (eds.) (2000): *Changing Classrooms and Changing Schools: A Study of Good Practices in Using ICT in Hong Kong Schools.* Hong Kong: Centre for Information Technology in Education, The University of Hong Kong.

Law, Nancy; Yuen, Allan & Fox, Bob (2011): *Educational Innovations Beyond Technology: Nurturing Leadership and Establishing Learning Organizations* New York: Springer.

Levy, Amir & Merry, Uri (1986): *Organizational Transformation: Approaches, Strategies, Theories.* New York: Praeger.

Merriam, Sharan B. (1998): *Qualitative Research and Case Study Applications in Education.* San Francisco: Jossey-Bass Publishers.

Miles, Matthew B. & Huberman, A. Michael (1994): *Qualitative Data Analysis: An Expanded Sourcebook.* 2nd edition, Thousand Oaks: SAGE.

Mioduser, David; Nachimias, Rafi; Tubin, Dorit & Forkosh-Baruch, Alona (2003): 'Analysis Schema for the Study of Domains and Levels of Pedagogical Innovation in Schools using ICT'. *Education and Information Technologies*, Vol.8, No.1, pp.23-36.

Mitchell, Karen; Shkolnik, Jamie; Song, Mengli; Uekawa, Kazuaki; Murphy, Robert; Garet, Mike & Means, Barbara (2005): *Rigor, Relevance, and Results: The Quality of Teacher Assignments and Student Work in New and Conventional High Schools.* Washington, DC: American Institutes for Research and SRI International.

OECD (2004): *Innovation in the Knowledge Economy: Implications for Education and Learning.* Paris: Organisation for Economic Co-operation and Development (OECD).

Pelgrum, Willem J. & Anderson, Ronald E. (eds.) (2001): *ICT and the Emerging Paradigm for Life-long Learning: An IEA Assessment of Infrastructure, Goals and Practices in Twenty-six Countries.* 2nd edition, Amsterdam: International Association for the Evaluation of Educational Achievement (IEA).

Reigeluth, Charles M. & Garfinkle, Robert J. (eds.) (1994): *Systemic Change in Education.* Englewood Cliffs: Educational Technology Publications.

Rogers, Everett M. (1995): *Diffusion of Innovations.* New York: Free Press.

Scardamalia, Marlene & Bereiter, Carl (2010): 'A Brief History of Knowledge Building. *Canadian Journal of Learning and Technology*, Vol.36,

No.1, pp.1-16.

Shear, Linda; Means, Barbara; Gorges, Torie; Toyama, Yukie; Gallagher, Larry; Estrella, Gucci & Lundh, Patrik (2009): *The Microsoft Innovative Schools Program Year 1 Evaluation Report*. Seattle: Microsoft.

Shear, Linda; Novais, Gabriel & Moorthy, Savitha (2010): *ITL Research: Pilot Year Findings and Lessons Learned*. Menlo Park: SRI International.

Shear, Linda; Gallagher, Larry & Patel, Deepa (2011): *Innovative Teaching and Learning Research 2011 Findings and Implications*. Menlo Park: SRI International.

Singapore, Ministry of Education (1997): *Masterplan for IT in Education*. Accessed 10 May 2002, http://www1.moe.edu.sg/iteducation/masterplan/summary.htm.

Singapore, Ministry of Education (2008): *Press Release: MOE Launches Third Masterplan for ICT in Education*, http://www.moe.gov.sg/media/press/2008/08/moe-launches-third-masterplan.php

SPSS Inc. (1999): *SPSS Base 10.0 Applications Guide*. Chicago: Statistical Package for the Social Sciences.

Stigler, James W.; Gonzales, Patrick; Kawanaka, Takako; Knoll, Steffen & Serrano, Ana (1999): *The TIMSS Videotape Classroom Study: Methods and Findings from an Exploratory Research Project on Eighth-grade Mathematics Instruction in Germany, Japan, and the United States*. Washington DC: National Center for Education Statistics.

Stigler, James W. & Hiebert, James (1999): *The Teaching Gap: Best Ideas from the World's Teachers for Improving Education in the Classroom*. New York: Free Press.

Strauss, Anselm L. & Corbin, Juliet (1990): *Basics of Qualitative Research: Grounded Theory Procedures and Techniques*. Newbury Park: SAGE.

Tubin, Dorit; Mioduser, David; Nachimias, Rafi & Forkosh-Baruch, Alona (2003): 'Domains and Levels of Pedagogical Innovation in Schools Using ICT: Ten Innovative Schools in Israel'. *Education and Information Technologies*, Vol.8, No.2, pp.127-145.

US Department of Education, Office of Educational Technology (2010): *Transforming American Education: Powered by Technology*. Washington, DC: US Department of Education, Office of Educational Technology.

UNESCO (2003): *Building the Capacities of Curriculum Specialists for Educational Reform: Final Report of the Regional Seminar Vientiane, Lao PDR, 9-13 September 2002*. Bangkok: UNESCO.

Yin, Robert K. (2009): *Case Study Research: Design and Methods*. Beverly Hills: SAGE.

13

Comparing Ways of Learning

David A. WATKINS & Jan VAN AALST

The authors have investigated ways of learning in different cultures for several decades. This chapter describes some of the methodological problems we have faced, and some of our findings. In particular, the chapter notes what types of comparisons of learning can be justified, and the analytic methods appropriate for conducting such comparisons.

Our early work was informed by our backgrounds in scientific disciplines, particularly cognitive psychology. In psychology, cross-cultural research has always raised a fundamental problem. Psychology is basically the study of individual differences in behaviour, so the natural unit of analysis is the individual. Aggregating the responses of individuals from one culture to represent that culture's score on a variable of interest can lead to what has become known as the ecological fallacy (van de Vijver & Leung 1997).

To illustrate the problem, consider the correlation between death rates resulting from heart attacks and strokes. Both involve blood vessels and may have similar causes, but a stroke is an attack on the brain rather than the heart. At the individual level the correlation between death rates from heart attacks and strokes is zero since people do not die from both events. However, at a country level a considerable correlation is found between the pair of problems: in most affluent countries, both causes of death are typically higher than in less developed ones.

Similarly, it became apparent in the 1990s that the laboratory studies of human verbal learning and animal maze learning that had dominated psychology had little to say about learning in classrooms (Brown 1992).

Experimental studies of learning typically tried to copy the laboratory conditions of the physical sciences by attempting to control all variables except for a few independent ones, which were manipulated to observe their effect on a dependent variable. For example, patterns of reinforcement could be varied to observe their effect on the number of nonsense syllables a research subject could learn in a fixed period. Too often, such research seemed to focus on testing complex theories of unimportant types of learning in artificial conditions, and typically with samples of only Caucasian white American college students.

From this background developed the research agenda that is described in this chapter. Reflecting our own interests and expertise, the chapter especially focuses on comparison of ways of learning by students in Chinese and Western societies. It begins with the foundational literature on learning approaches, and then turns to comparisons of correlates of learning strategies noting matters of conceptual equivalence, reliability, and within-construct validity. The chapter then focuses on the so-called paradox of the Asian learner, indicating what the paradox is and how it could be explained. A further section addresses conceptions of teaching from a Chinese perspective, before the chapter rounds up in conclusion.

Learning Approaches

The first author was first drawn into research on the learning ecology by two seminal papers (Biggs 1979; Marton & Säljö 1976), which are among the most widely cited items in the literature on educational psychology. Biggs, Marton and Säljö wanted to find out about learning *from the learner's perspective* rather than from that of the researcher. This has become known as the *second order perspective* (Marton & Booth 1997).

These researchers, though all from a psychological background, approached their task in very different ways. Marton and Säljö asked Swedish university students to read an academic article and then answer questions about what they had learned and how they had learned it. During in-depth interviews, students reported two main ways of tackling the task. Some tried to memorise details or key terms in order to be able to answer subsequent questions. These students tended to focus on the reading at word or sentence level. Most of the other students tried to understand the message that the passage was trying to impart. They tended to focus on the themes and main ideas, and generally tried to process the reading for meaning.

These intentions and their associated reading strategies were called 'surface' and 'deep' approaches to learning. Significantly, the researchers also found qualitative differences in learning outcomes, depending on the approach to reading that had been utilised. Students who had adopted a surface approach typically could not explain the authors' message and could only recall isolated factual fragments of the passage. Those adopting a deep approach were able to provide a more sophisticated overview of the authors' intentions, and frequently used extracts from the article to support their reasoning.

The Swedish researchers went on to develop a qualitative research approach that they called 'phenomenography' (Marton 1981). This approach aims to understand how students perceive the content and process (the 'what' and 'how') of learning. The underlying rationale is the phenomenological notion that people act according to their interpretations of a situation rather than to 'objective reality'.

Biggs in Australia and Entwistle in the United Kingdom independently developed learning process inventories which owed a debt both to the paper by Marton and Säljö (1976) and to later phenomenographic writing, and adopted the 'surface/deep' and 'approaches to learning' terminology. Biggs (1987), in his Learning Process Questionnaire (LPQ) and its tertiary counterpart, the Study Process Questionnaire (SPQ), and Entwistle and Ramsden (1983) in their Approaches to Studying Inventory (ASI) added a third approach, 'achieving'. Students adopting this approach tried to achieve the highest possible grades by such strategies as working hard and efficiently, and by being cue conscious. They would use any strategy, including rote memorising many facts and understanding basic principles, that they perceived would maximise their chances of academic success.

Watkins followed the approach of Biggs and Entwistle, and provided some of the early supporting reliability and validity evidence for their questionnaires. While much of his early work had investigated factors influencing the learning of Australian university students, he undertook parallel studies at a university in the Philippines. He was able to confirm the psychometric properties of the questionnaire for Filipino students (factor validity and reliability), but this still left open the question of comparing the raw scores of Australian and Filipino students. In the cross-cultural psychology literature this is known as the problem of measurement equivalence. As argued by Hui and Triandis (1985), when psychological measuring instruments are used in different cultures, range of types of equivalence need to be demonstrated, each of which could justify corresponding types of interpretations. At the most basic level, the concepts involved must be equivalent in both cultures so that researchers can use such questionnaires to compare the cultures.

The highest level of equivalence is known as *metric equivalence*. This means that the raw score of a respondent from one culture is equivalent mathematically to that from another culture. For example, a score of 19 by a Nepalese student on the Surface Strategy scale of the SPQ means that that student's use of surface strategies is the same as an Australian student who also scores 19 on that scale. Unfortunately such metric equivalence is almost impossible to demonstrate, and there is one major reason why it should not be assumed: the existence of response sets that operate differently across cultures. Thus whatever questions are asked, respondents from different cultures are likely to differ in the extent that they will agree with the question statement, provide socially desirable responses, or use extreme rating points. While such response sets tend to cancel out within a culture, they tend to confound cross-cultural comparisons of raw scores (see van de Vijver & Leung 1997). In addition, the statistical tests typically used to compare means assume that random sampling has been used, which is seldom possible in real-life classrooms. Moreover, when comparisons are made across cultures, the samples need to be representative of students and teachers in these cultures. This is seldom achieved, and so such comparisons must therefore be treated with caution.

At an intermediate level of equivalence, if responses to the instrument can be shown to be reliable and valid for each culture, then correlations can be compared between the constructs measured and other variables within each culture. For example, a comparison can be made of the correlations between scores on the LPQ Deep Strategy scale and academic achievement of like students in the Philippines and Australia. Such correlations allow comparison of the relationships between approaches to learning and other important psychological and educational variables across different cultures. The technique further allows testing of the validity of a number of Western theoretical propositions in non-Western cultures. Work in this arena by the first author led to a series of papers and to a long-term research programme labelled 'cross-cultural meta-analyses' (e.g. Watkins 1998; 2001).

Comparing Correlates of Learning Strategies

The first stage in this research programme established that the concepts involved were relevant for different cultures, and that the instruments used were reliable and valid for use with respondents from these cultures. This required attention to conceptual equivalence, reliability, within-construct validity, and a number of other matters.

Conceptual equivalence

The notions of conceptual equivalence are closely related to 'etic' and 'emic' approaches to research (Berry 1989). The etic approach seeks to compare cultures on what are thought to be universal categories. In contrast, the emic approach uses only concepts that emerge from within a particular culture. It is associated with the traditions of anthropology, but also more recently those of indigenous psychology (Kim & Berry 1993). Triandis (1972) pointed to the dangers of 'pseudo-etic' research, which involves the imposition of the concepts of one culture upon another as if they were universal without any prior research into the veracity of this assumption.

Psychologists claim that they can identify problems with conceptual equivalence by comparing the distribution of responses to a questionnaire by respondents from different cultures (van de Vijver & Leung 1997). The methods of item-bias analysis that they advocate can indeed highlight problems with the wording of different items. However, this approach missed the central question: *Are the concepts equivalent?*

It seems clear that assessment of the conceptual equivalence of the constructs underlying learning instruments such as the SPQ require qualitative analysis, such as phenomenography. Studies in non-Western cultures have been conducted with non-Western students in Mainland China, Hong Kong, Japan, Malaysia, Nepal and Nigeria, and at the University of the South Pacific.

To illustrate, several studies support the proposition that the concepts underlying the theorising of Biggs and Entwistle are relevant to Nigerian students. An ethnographic study based on 120 hours of observations in primary schools in Lagos found that Nigerian pupils were trained to believe that getting the right answer by any means, even cheating, was the essence of learning (Omokhodion 1989). Neither the teachers nor the pupils considered that the processes of understanding the problem and of obtaining the solution were important. Omokhodion concluded that a superficial, surface approach to learning was encouraged. Further evidence came from a study in which 250 Nigerian university students responded to the question "What strategies do you use to study?" (Ehindero 1990). Content analysis revealed three main themes: diligence, building up understanding, and memorising content material without understanding. These themes appeared to correspond to the notions of achieving, deep, and surface approaches to learning.

Qualitative investigations of the learning approaches and conceptions of Chinese learners in Hong Kong and China (e.g. Kember & Gow 1991; Marton et al. 1996; Dahlin & Watkins 2000) have partially supported the conceptual validity of the constructs of deep and surface approaches for Chinese students. However, all of these studies have concluded that Chinese students tend to view memorisation as relevant to both approaches, whereas Western students are more likely to view memorisation as characteristic of a surface approach. Research in Nepal (Watkins & Regmi 1992, 1995) found that while deep and surface approaches were relevant for the sampled Nepalese students, the concept of learning as character development emerged at a lower cognitive level than in Western studies. Thus while the constructs of deep and surface approaches to learning are relevant to non-Western cultures, culturally specific aspects must also be considered.

Reliability
The responses to any measuring instrument must be assessed for reliability in the culture in which it is to be used. There is fairly strong support for the reliability of responses of the SPQ, LPQ, and ASI in a range of cultures. Watkins (2001) obtained coefficient alphas for responses to the SPQ scales by 14 independent samples of 6,500 university students from 10 countries generally exceeding .50. This magnitude is widely considered acceptable for a research instrument used for group comparisons, but well below the level required for important academic decisions about an individual student (Nunnally 1978). Not surprisingly, the reliability estimates were slightly higher for Australian students for whom these instruments were originally developed. They were particularly low for the Nepalese for whom the concepts may not have been as relevant and whose level of English competence was relatively low.

Within-construct validity
The within-construct validity of the LPQ and SPQ has been demonstrated by comparing the results of internal factor analysis of responses to the

LPQ and SPQ scales for different cultures both with each other and with the theoretical model expected. Thus, confirmatory factor analysis of responses to the LPQ, which shares the same underlying motive/strategy model as the SPQ, by 10 samples of school students from six different countries confirmed the two basic factors of deep and surface approach (Wong et al. 1996). A review of the factor analytic studies by Richardson (1994) also supported the cross-cultural validity of the ASI as a measure of deep and surface approaches.

The cross-cultural meta-analysis
Cross-cultural meta-analysis employs quantitative synthesis methods in the meta-analytic tradition (Glass et al. 1981; Rosenthal & DiMatteo 2001) to test the cross-cultural relevance of variables proposed in learning theory to be significantly correlated with surface, deep, and achieving approaches to learning. According to Biggs (1987), how a student learns depends on presage factors related to both the person and the learning environment. In particular, the following relationships have been examined from a cross-cultural perspective:

- *Correlates with academic grades.* Students' approaches to learning are expected to influence their academic performance. In particular, it is predicted that in any culture use of a surface approach is negatively correlated with academic achievement, and use of deep and achieving approaches is positively correlated with grades (Biggs 1987; Schmeck 1988). However, an assumption underlying these predictions is that higher quality learning outcomes are rewarded by the assessment system, which often is not the case.

- *Correlates with self-concept and locus of control.* Students who are more self-confident, particularly about their academic abilities, and who accept greater responsibility for their own learning outcomes, are more likely to adopt deeper, more achieving approaches to learning. These approaches require them to rely more on their own understanding of the course materials, rather than to rely greatly on the teacher and textbook (Biggs 1987; Schmeck 1988).

The first stage of any meta-analysis is to select the studies to be quantitatively synthesised. A decision to be made at this stage is whether only studies satisfying some predetermined quality criteria should be included. A further decision, of course, is what the criteria should be.

Watkins conducted a cross-cultural meta-analysis using formal searches of established CD-ROM databases and informal searches of the extensive journal collection in the library of the University of Hong Kong. He also sought relevant published and unpublished material at international conferences, and sent letter and e-mail appeals to established researchers in the area. All studies which reported correlates of at least one approach to learning and measures of self-esteem, locus of control, and/or academic achievement (or where it was possible statistically to estimate such correlations from the data provided) were included in the meta-analysis, provided responses to the scales showed a reasonable level of internal consistency (alphas of at least .50) for the culture being studied. These criteria led to four studies being discarded.

An issue in this type of meta-analysis is whether scales from different instruments are really measuring the same variables and thus can be combined. In this meta-analysis a number of different learning process instruments were assumed to be assessing a student's approach to learning as their test constructors claimed. In addition, different measures of self-esteem, locus of control, and academic achievement (measured by school tests, grade point average, standardised achievement tests, etc.) were assumed to be measuring the same variable.

Once all the studies to be included had been identified and the relevant correlations obtained, average correlations were calculated. A major aim of meta-analysis is not just to obtain an overall estimate of the strength of a relationship, but, more importantly, to find out if the relationship varies according to the characteristics of the sample. Thus, it was hoped that the analysis would provide insight into the nature of the relationship. The study sought to find out whether the relationships between approaches to learning and the other variables of interest varied between Western and non-Western samples and at school and university levels.

The average Pearson correlation coefficients between approaches to learning and academic achievement, self-esteem, and internal locus of control, respectively, are shown in Table 13.1. Separate analyses were carried out for school and university students and different measures of the variables concerned.

- *Approaches to learning and academic achievement.* The average correlations based on data from 28,053 respondents (55 independent samples from 15 countries) were -.11, .16, and .18 with surface,

deep and achieving approaches respectively. The average correlation coefficients appeared to be somewhat higher (particularly
at school level) for Western samples. While the relatively low
correlations between approaches to learning and academic
achievement were disappointing, this was not unexpected because school and university grades often reward superficial
learning outcomes. The relationship between deeper approaches
to learning and higher quality learning outcomes has been shown
to be much stronger (Watkins & Biggs 1996).

*Table 13.1: Average Correlations between Learning Approach Scales and Aca-
demic Achievement, Self-Esteem and Locus of Control*

Groups	Sample Size	Surface Approach	Deep Approach	Achieving Approach
Academic Achievement				
Western	11,023	-.13	.18	.21
Non-Western	17,030	-.10	.14	.16
Total	28,053	-.11	.16	.18
Self-Esteem				
Western	5,478	-.03	.33	.30
Non-Western	3,232	-.08	.27	.25
Total	8,710	-.05	.30	.28
Locus of Control				
Western	4,339	-.15	.10	.15
Non-Western	8,673	-.22	.09	.11
Total	13,012	-.20	.09	.12

Source: Adapted from Watkins (2001).

- *Approaches to learning and self-esteem.* The average correlations
  based on data from 8,710 respondents (involving 28 independent
  samples in 15 countries) were -.05, .30, and .28 with surface, deep,
  and achieving approaches respectively. The average correlations
  with deep and achieving approaches exceeded .25 for all sub-
  samples, but were particularly strong (.33) for Western university
  students with deep approaches.
- *Approaches to learning and internal locus of control.* The average correlations based on data from 13,012 respondents (involving 27 independent samples in 11 countries) were -.20, .09, and .12 with
  surface, deep and achieving approaches respectively. Further analysis showed that the negative correlations with surface approaches
  were larger than those with the other approaches for non-Western

and Western school samples. However, at the university level correlations with both deep and achieving approaches were much higher for Western samples.

In summary, this cross-cultural meta-analysis showed that the correlates of approaches to learning and academic achievement, self-esteem, and locus of control were similar across a range of Western and non-Western schools and universities, and also across a range of measuring instruments. The findings support the cross-cultural validity of Western theorising in this area, and suggest that Western interventions designed to improve the quality of learning strategies based on such theorising may also be appropriate for non-Western students.

The Paradox of the Asian Learner

The value of qualitative methods for interpreting comparisons of student learning across cultures may be illustrated by research into the so-called 'paradox of the Asian learner'. This paradox starts with a seemingly simple syllogism:

1. Asian students use rote learning more than Western students.
2. Rote learning leads to poor learning outcomes.
3. Therefore, Asian students have poorer learning outcomes than Western students.

The problem is that international comparisons of educational performance show that the reverse is true: e.g. students from Singapore, Japan, Taiwan and Hong Kong consistently outperform students from almost all other countries participating in the Trends in Mathematics and Science Study (TIMSS) and Programme for International Student Assessment (PISA) (Mullis et al. 2008; OECD 2010; Martin et al. 2012). Such results have been remarkably stable despite curriculum reforms that have attempted to 'Westernise' education. Results for these education systems in the Progress in International Reading Literacy Study (PIRLS) also are above the international average (Mullis et al. 2012). It seems that the conclusion of the above syllogism is incorrect, and so must be at least one of the premises.

The evidence for the claim about rote learning comes from reports of examiners and teachers of such students in Asian as well as Western countries. For example, examiners in various subjects at the main public examinations in Hong Kong often complain about the model answers given by candidates – in some cases hundreds of students from the same school giving the same long answer. Western university lecturers have also commented that students prefer rote learning and are disinclined to question readings or the lecturer.

As Biggs (1996) argued, such observations often reveal what he called 'Western misperceptions of Confucian learning culture' (p.45), and are not consistent with findings from qualitative studies. For example, the TIMSS Video Study, which analyzed Grade 8 mathematics lessons in the United States, Germany and Japan (Stigler & Hiebert 1999), showed that teaching in Japanese schools is not generally oriented toward rote learning. Japanese mathematics lessons tended to begin with a brief review of the previous lesson, and then had students solve challenging problems – first individually and then in small groups – and present their solutions to the class; at the end of lessons teachers summarised the main points. Japanese lessons were more likely to contain high-level mathematical content, and had more seatwork that involved thinking and invention. However, there also were deviations from these patterns, and Japanese lessons dealt with some content via lectures and asking students to commit content to memory. Stigler and Hiebert noted that these different approaches often co-existed in the same lesson (p.49). A study of the teaching of Pythagoras' theorem involving Grade 8 students in Shanghai, Hong Kong and the Czech Republic (Huang & Leung 2002) found that the Shanghai teacher provided the most challenging problems: students not only made conjectures based on drawings and calculating, but also explored multiple mathematical proofs of the theorem. The students were "quite involved in the process of learning such as putting up and presenting diagrams and explaining their understanding" (p.276). We have observed similar lessons in Hong Kong (van Aalst 2010).

Further, as Wong (2004) has observed, Chinese learners tend first to commit new information to memory, then to understand and apply it, and only then question and modify it. And Li's (2009) studies of the beliefs about learning of American and Chinese university students identified the following positive affects in Chinese learners: commitment to learning, thirst for learning, respect for teachers and knowledge, and humility. Learning "aims at breadth and depth of knowledge, its application to real-life situations, and the unity of one's knowledge and moral character" (Li 2009, p.61). 'Respect' does not mean that students uncritically accept what the teacher says but that they are receptive and sincere toward the teacher, and students remain 'humble' after learning to stay alert to complacency and then continue their journey of self-perfection. In a study that compared peer interaction in Australian and Taiwanese middle-school science classrooms, Wallace and Chou (2001) found that Taiwanese students talked, during interviews, about their peers as sources of help for learning, while Australian students "seemed more interested in the importance of relationships for their own sake" (p.704). These authors further observed that when students in Taiwanese classes worked in groups, they remained focused on the learning task and leaned their bodies toward each other to maximise eye contact – a state of cognitive engagement. Finally, in comparison studies involving the LPQ and SPQ questionnaires, Australian students self-reported the use of surface learning strategies more often than Asian students from Hong Kong, Malaysia, and Nepal (Kember & Gow 1991; Watkins et al. 1991).

The aforementioned findings do, in our opinion, debunk the Western misperceptions of the learning behaviours of Asian students that led to the first premise. However, it is unclear whether Confucian-heritage beliefs about learning will endure in the face of continuing exposure to Western values. Chan and Rao (2009), re-examining the notion of a distinctly Asian learner, argued that it is more accurate to refer to *contexts* in which Confucian values are important, and that these contexts are changing in response to global developments.

The affects identified by Li (2009), such as the extent of commitment to learning and desire to learn, are likely to be important factors in explaining the positive results of East Asian learners on international comparisons of achievement. However, Asian learners do memorise, and a culturally sensitive understanding of the relationship between memorisation and understanding also seems necessary for resolving the paradox.

While Western education has in the past depended on rote learning, Western educators today reject such learning. In doing so, many have failed to draw a distinction between *rote* learning, i.e. memorising "without thought or understanding" (*Oxford English Dictionary*), and *repetitive* learning, i.e. learning in order to enhance future recall alongside understanding. Memorising without understanding undoubtedly leads to very limited learning outcomes, but many Western teachers mistakenly assume that when Chinese students memorise, they are rote learning at the expense of understanding. In fact, Chinese students frequently learn repetitively, both to ensure retention *and* to enhance understanding. On the basis of in-depth interviews with teachers and students in Hong Kong and China, it has become clear first that many teachers and better students do not see memorising and understanding as separate but rather as *interlocking* processes, and second that high quality learning outcomes usually *require* both processes as complements to each other (Marton et al. 1996; Marton et al. 1997). This is purportedly the solution to the paradox. Students in Confucian-heritage cultures are correctly observed as making great use of memorisation, but they are not necessarily rote learning, as their Western teachers have supposed. Many such students actually develop understanding through the process of memorisation, and so can perform well academically.

Dahlin and Watkins (2000) investigated this possibility empirically. Through in-depth interviews with students attending international schools and public secondary schools, they showed that students in China, unlike their Western counterparts, used repetition for two different purposes. On the one hand it was associated with creating a 'deep impression', and thence with memorisation; but on the other hand it was used to deepen or develop understanding by discovering new meaning. The Western students on the other hand tended to use repetition only to check that they had really remembered something. This finding was consistent with another cross-cultural difference identified by Dahlin and Watkins (2000). Whereas Western students see understanding as usually a process of sudden insight, Chinese students typically think of understanding as a long process that requires sustained mental effort.

Conceptions of Teaching: A Chinese Perspective

In their earlier research, Watkins and Biggs (1996) focused on Chinese students, but also recognised that Chinese teachers must be doing something right to help bring about learning outcomes that are frequently superior to those in Western schools. It did not take long to realise that the relationship between teacher and student is fundamental to understanding the role of the teacher in Chinese classrooms. According to Chinese tradition, the relationship between teachers and students is akin to that of parents and their children. This is an area where Western observers often see only part of the picture. Thus, the comment by Ginsberg (1992, p.6) that a lecturer in China is an authority figure, 'a respected elder transmitting to a subordinate junior', certainly has a ring of truth. However, the typical method of teaching is often not simple transmission of superior knowledge but utilises considerable interaction in a mutually accepting social context.

Ho (2001) presented an important cross-cultural difference in perceptions of what is involved in good teaching. She used a survey to compare Australian and Hong Kong secondary school teachers, and found that while the former saw their role as restricted primarily to instruction within the classroom, the latter saw their role as extending to the students' domestic problems and behaviour outside the school.

Further research confirmed the widespread conception that Chinese teachers should be of good character as well as concerned with the moral development of their students (Gao & Watkins 2001). A major aim of that study was to develop a model of conceptions of teaching appropriate for secondary school physics teachers in China's Guangdong Province. After numerous in-depth interviews, classroom observations and a pilot quantitative survey, Gao and Watkins developed a model with five basic conceptions (knowledge delivery, examination preparation, ability development, attitude promotion, and conduct guidance). The first two of these were grouped into a higher order 'moulding' orientation which corresponded fairly well with the 'transmission' dimension identified in Western research (e.g. Kember & Gow 1994). Gao and Watkins grouped the remaining three lower-level conceptions into a higher-order 'cultivating' orientation. This not only involved a concern with developing student understanding and higher quality learning outcomes, as in the 'facilitating' dimension of Kember and Gow, but broadened it to focus on affective outcomes such as developing the student's love of science and moral (not ideological) aspects such as their responsibilities to their families and society as a whole.

Cultural differences were further exposed by a study of British and Chinese secondary school students by Jin and Cortazzi (1998). In this study, which employed both survey and observational methods, British students characterised a good teacher as one who is able to arouse the students' interest, explain clearly, use effective instructional methods, and organise a range of activities. These are very much the skills taught in typical Western teacher-education method courses. The Chinese students, by contrast, preferred the teacher to have deep knowledge, be able to answer questions, and be a good moral model. In terms of teacher-student relationships, the British students liked their teachers to be patient and sympathetic with students who had difficulty following the lesson, whereas the Chinese students considered that their relationship with a good teacher should be friendly and warm well beyond the classroom.

This perception of Chinese teachers as friendly and warm has been noted by a number of researchers and linked to the Confucian concept of *ren* (仁) (Jin & Cortazzi 1998; Gao & Watkins 2001), which translates as something like human-heartedness or love. Indeed, according to Jin and Cortazzi (1998), all education in Mainland China is based on Confucian principles even though the teachers and students are often unaware of it. These principles include that education is highly valued by society; learning involves reflection and application; hard work can compensate for lack of ability; the teacher is a model both of knowledge and morality; and learning is a moral duty and a responsibility to the family (see also Lee 1996; Li 2001).

Another study in this area showed how quantitative and qualitative methods can be combined to provide a better understanding of how the good teacher is viewed in different cultural contexts (Watkins & Zhang 2006). The great majority of their 128 respondents were Chinese students but studying either in regular Hong Kong Chinese secondary schools or American international secondary schools in Hong Kong. In the latter case most of the teachers were American, and the pupils studied in English using an American syllabus. Following the approach to research utilised by Beishuizen et al. (2001), the students were first each asked to write a short essay about 'The Good Teacher'. These essays were then content analysed, and the constructs utilised were identified. Each essay was then re-scored '0' or '1', depending on whether that essay used each of these constructs in turn. Thence dual scaling was used to identify dimensions of the good teacher used by these respondents. Two dimensions were easily identifiable. The first referred to characteristics such as keeping promises, being responsible, and being honest, while the second referred to having deep knowledge, organising a variety of learning situations, and giving students freedom. Consistent with previous findings, the international school students scored much higher on the second dimension but lower on the first. Thus it seems that just contact with a Western educational context was sufficient for these Chinese students to view teaching from a more 'Western' perspective.

Conclusions

This chapter has illustrated some methodological issues involved in comparing learning across cultures by describing some of our own and colleagues' work. Much of the literature in this area uses the methods and theories of psychology. We have shown how, once educational psychologists emerged from the laboratory and started using second-order research methods based on the perspective of actual students and teachers, researchers were able to make real progress in understanding the processes of learning in Western classrooms. However, most of this work has used the individual students or teachers as the unit of analysis. Thus, like psychology in general, these methods are not so suitable for comparisons across cultures.

In our opinion, comparisons of means from instruments designed to measure most, if not all, psychological constructs related to learning must be questioned due to problems of metric equivalence and sampling. Fortunately, testing whether most theories and training programmes are appropriate in different cultures requires only comparisons of correlations across cultures (see Table 13.1) or of means within cultures. Such analyses require less stringent tests of conceptual equivalence and the reliability and validity of the instrument(s) for respondents of each culture being studied.

We have also shown how a qualitative approach (or a combination of quantitative and qualitative) can be adopted to explore the meaning of concepts such as learning across and within cultures (and thus of testing conceptual equivalence). Such in-depth research, in our view, is required if we are validly to compare the processes of learning across cultures. It may also be the best hope to provide the basis for developing training programmes suitable for improving the quality of learning outcomes in different cultures.

References

Beishuizen, J.J.; Hof, E.; van Putten, C.M.; Bouwmeeter, S. & Asscher, J.J. (2001): 'Students' and Teachers' Cognitions about Good Teachers'. *British Journal of Educational Psychology*, Vol.71, No.2, pp.185-202.

Berry, John W. (1989): 'Imposed Emics – Derived Etics: The Operationalisation of a Compelling Idea'. *International Journal of Psychology*, Vol.24, No.6, pp.721-735.

Biggs, John B. (1979): 'Individual Differences in Study Processes and the Quality of Learning Outcomes'. *Higher Education*, Vol.8, No.4, pp. 381-394.

Biggs, John B. (1987): *Student Approaches to Learning and Studying*. Melbourne: Australian Council for Educational Research.

Biggs, John B. (1996): 'Western Misperceptions of Confucian-heritage Learning Culture', in Watkins, David A. &. Biggs, John B. (eds.), *The Chinese Learner: Cultural, Psychological and Contextual Influences*. Hong Kong: Comparative Education Research Centre, The University of Hong Kong, pp.45-67.

Brown, Ann L. (1992): 'Design Experiments: Theoretical and Methodological Challenges for Creating Complex Interventions in Classroom Settings'. *The Journal of the Learning Sciences*, Vol.2, No.2, pp.141-178.

Chan, Carol K.K. & Rao, Nirmala (eds.) (2009): *Revisiting the Chinese Learner: Changing Contexts, Changing Education*. CERC Studies in Comparative Education 25, Hong Kong: Comparative Education Research Centre, The University of Hong Kong, and Dordrecht: Springer.

Dahlin, Bo & Watkins, David (2000): 'The Role of Repetition in the Processes of Memorising and Understanding: A Comparison of the Views of German and Chinese Secondary School Students in Hong Kong'. *British Journal of Educational Psychology*, Vol.70, No.1, pp. 65-84.

Ehindero, O.J. (1990): 'A Discriminant Function Analysis of Study Strategies, Logical Reasoning Ability and Achievement across Major Teaching Undergraduate Curricula'. *Research in Education*, Vol.44, No.1, pp.1-11.

Entwistle, Noel J. & Ramsden, Paul (1983): *Understanding Student Learning*. London: Croom Helm.

Gao, Lingbiao & Watkins, David A. (2001): 'Identifying and Assessing the Conceptions of Teaching of Secondary School Physics Teachers in China'. *British Journal of Educational Psychology*, Vol.71, No.3, pp. 443-469.

Ginsberg, E. (1992): 'Not just a Matter of English', *HERDSA News*, Vol.14, No.1, pp.6-8.

Glass, Gene V.; McGaw, Barry & Smith, Mary Lee (1981): *Meta-Analysis in Social Research*. Beverly Hills: SAGE.

Ho, Irene T. (2001): 'Are Chinese Teachers Authoritarian?', in Watkins, David A. & Biggs, John B. (eds.), *Teaching the Chinese Learner: Psychological and Pedagogical Perspectives*. Hong Kong: Comparative Education Research Centre, The University of Hong Kong, pp.99-114.

Huang, Rongjin & Leung, Frederick K.S. (2002): 'How Pythagoras' Theorem is Taught in Czech Republic, Hong Kong and Shanghai: A Case Study'. *Zentralblatt für Didaktik der Mathematik*, Vol.34, No.6, pp. 268-277.

Hui, C. Harry & Triandis, Harry C. (1985): 'Measurement in Cross-Cultural Psychology: A Review and Comparison of Strategies'. *Journal of Cross-Cultural Psychology*, Vol.16, No.2, pp.131-152.

Jin, Lixian & Cortazzi, Martin (1998): 'Expectations and Questions in Intercultural Classrooms'. *Intercultural Communication Studies*, Vol.7, No.2, pp.37-62.

Kember, David & Gow, Lyn (1991): 'A Challenge to the Anecdotal Stereotype of the Asian Student'. *Studies in Higher Education*, Vol.16, No.2, pp.117-128.

Kember, David & Gow, Lyn (1994): 'Orientations to Teaching and their Effect on the Quality of Student Learning'. *Journal of Higher Education*, Vol.65, No.1, pp.58-74.

Kim, Uichol & Berry, John W. (eds.) (1993): *Indigenous Psychologies: Research and Experience in Cultural Context*. London: Sage.

Lee, Wing On (1996): 'The Cultural Context for Chinese Learners', in Watkins, David A. & Biggs, John B. (eds.), *The Chinese Learner: Cultural, Psychological and Contextual Influences*. Hong Kong: Comparative Education Research Centre, The University of Hong Kong, pp. 25-41.

Li, Jin (2001): 'Chinese Conceptualization of Learning'. *Ethos*, Vol.29, No.2, pp.111-137.

Li, Jin (2009): 'Learning to Self-Perfect: Chinese Beliefs about Learning', in Chan, Carol K.K. & Rao, Nirmala (eds.), *Revisiting the Chinese Learner: Changing Contexts, Changing Education*. CERC Studies in Comparative Education 25, Hong Kong: Comparative Education Research Centre, The University of Hong Kong, and Dordrecht: Springer, pp.35-69.

Martin, M.O.; Mullis, I.V.S.; Foy, P. & Stanco, G.M. (2012): *TIMSS 2011 International Results in Science*. Chesnut Hill: TIMSS & PIRLS International Study Center, Boston College.

Marton, Ference (1981): 'Phenomenography: Describing Conceptions of the World around Us'. *Instructional Science*, Vol.10, No.2, pp.177-200.

Marton, Ference & Booth, Shirley (1997): *Learning and Awareness*. Mahwah: Lawrence Erlbaum.

Marton, Ference & Säljö, Roger (1976): 'On Qualitative Differences in Learning – I: Outcome and Process'. *British Journal of Educational Psychology*, Vol.46, No.1, pp.4-11.

Marton, Ference; Dall'Alba, Gloria & Tse, Lai Kun (1996): 'Memorizing and Understanding: The Keys to the Paradox?', in Watkins, David A. & Biggs, John B. (eds.), *The Chinese Learner: Cultural, Psychological and Contextual Influences*. Hong Kong: Comparative Education Research Centre, The University of Hong Kong, pp.69-83.

Marton, Ference; Watkins, David A. & Tang, Catherine (1997): 'Discontinuities and Continuities in the Experience of Learning: An Interview Study of High-School Students in Hong Kong'. *Learning and Instruction*, Vol.7, No.1, pp.21-48.

Mullis, I.V.S.; Martin, M.O. & Foy, P. (2008): *TIMSS 2007 International Mathematics Report: Findings from IEA's Trends in International Mathematics and Science Study at the Fourth and Eighth Grades*. Chestnut Hill: TIMSS & PIRLS International Study Center, Boston College.

Mullis, I.V.S.; Martin, M.O.; Foy, P. & Drucker, K.T. (2012): *PIRLS 2011 International Results in Reading*. Chestnut Hill: TIMSS & PIRLS International Study Center, Boston College.

Nunnally, Jum C. (1978): *Psychometric Theory*. 2nd edition, New York: McGraw Hill.

OECD (2010): *PISA 2009 Results: What Students Know and can Do – Student Performance in Reading, Mathematics and Science (Volume I)*. Paris: Organisation for Economic Co-operation and Development (OECD).

Omokhodion, J. Otibhor (1989): 'Classroom Observed: The Hidden Curriculum in Lagos, Nigeria'. *International Journal of Educational Development*, Vol.9, No.2, pp.99-110.

Richardson, John T.E. (1994): 'Cultural Specify of Approaches to Studying in Higher Education: A Literature Survey'. *Higher Education*, Vol.27, No.4, pp.449-468.

Rosenthal, R. & DiMatteo, M.R. (2001): 'Meta-Analysis: Recent Developments in Quantitative Methods for Literature Reviews'. *Annual Review of Psychology*, Vol.52, No.1, pp.59-82.

Schmeck, Ronald R. (ed.) (1988): *Learning Strategies and Learning Styles*. New York: Plenum.

Stigler, James W. & Hiebert, James (1999): *The Teaching Gap: Best Ideas from the World's Teachers for Improving Education in the Classroom*. New York: Free Press.

Triandis, Harry C. (1972): *The Analysis of Subjective Culture*. New York:

John Wiley.

van Aalst, Jan (2010): 'Gaining an Insider Perspective on Learning Physics in Hong Kong', in Gomez, K.; Lyons, L. & Radinky, J. (eds.), *Proceedings of the 9th International Conference of the Learning Sciences* Chicago: International Society of the Learning Sciences, pp. 881-888.

van de Vijver, Fons & Leung, Kwok (1997): *Methods and Data Analysis for Cross-Cultural Research*. London: SAGE.

Wallace, John & Chou, Ching-Yang (2001). 'Similarity and Difference: Student Cooperation in Taiwanese and Australian Science Classrooms.' *Science Education*, Vol.85, No.6, pp.694-711.

Watkins, David A. (1998): 'Assessing Approaches to Learning: A Cross-Cultural Perspective on the Study Process Questionnaire', in Dart, Barry & Boulton-Lewis, Gillian (eds.), *Teaching and Learning in Higher Education*. Melbourne: Australian Council for Educational Research, pp.124-144.

Watkins, David A. (2001): 'Correlates of Approaches to Learning: A Cross-Cultural Meta-Analysis', in Sternberg, Robert & Zhang, Li-fang (eds.), *Perspectives on Thinking, Learning, and Cognitive Styles*. Mahwah: Lawrence Erlbaum, pp.165-196.

Watkins, David A. & Biggs, John B. (eds.) (1996): *The Chinese Learner: Cultural, Psychological and Contextual Influences*. Hong Kong: Comparative Education Research Centre, The University of Hong Kong.

Watkins, David A. & Regmi, Murari (1992): 'How Universal are Student Conceptions of Learning? A Nepalese Investigation'. *Psychologia*, Vol.35, No.2, pp.101-110.

Watkins, David A. & Regmi, Murari (1995): 'Assessing Approaches to Learning in Non-Western Cultures: A Nepalese Conceptual Validity Study'. *Assessment and Evaluation in Higher Education*, Vol.20, No.2, pp.203-212.

Watkins, David A.; Regmi, Murari & Astilla, Estela (1991): 'The Asian-Learner-as-a-Rote-Learner Stereotype: Myth or Reality?'. *Educational Psychology*, Vol.11, No.1, pp.21-34.

Watkins, David A. & Zhang, Q. (2006). 'The good teacher: a cross-cultural perspective,' in Inerney, D.M., Dowson, M. & van Etten, S. (eds.), *Effective Schools*. Charlotte: Information Age Publishing, pp.185-204.

Wong, Ngai-Ying (2004): 'The CHC Learner's Phenomenon: Its Implications on Mathematics Education', in Fan, L.H., Wong, N.Y., Cai, J.F. & Li, S.Q. (eds.), *How Chinese Learn Mathematics: Perspectives from Insiders*. Singapore: World Scientific, pp.503-534.

Wong, Ngai-Ying; Lin, Wai-Ying & Watkins, David A. (1996): 'Cross-Cultural Validation of Models of Approaches to Learning: An Application of Confirmatory Factor Analysis'. *Educational Psychology*, Vol.16, No.2, pp.317- 327.

14

Comparing Educational Achievements

Frederick K.S. LEUNG & Kyungmee PARK

When George Bereday, the famous comparative educator from Columbia University in New York (see e.g. Bereday 1964), first heard of the work of the International Association for the Evaluation of Educational Achievement (IEA) in the early 1960s, he said that the IEA researchers were comparing the incomparable. Perhaps he meant that it was impossible to compare pupils and schools from different cultures. Perhaps he meant that there were so many differences between systems of education that it was impossible to compare them. After all, the pupils begin school at different ages, the curricula are different, the ways in which teachers are trained are different, and, and, and, ...!

Bereday might have asked whether, for example, it was 'fair' to compare the achievement of a Japanese 10 year old with the achievement of a Netherlands pupil of the same age. On the one hand they have different numbers of years of schooling, different curricula, and they are spread across a different number of grades because of grade repeating, and therefore it is not 'fair'. On the other hand they can be regarded as being the same age, and what is really being judged is what a system of education does with the children in an age cohort under its authority. These are some of the issues that will be addressed in this chapter.

Why Compare Achievements?
Before beginning to examine some of the techniques associated with comparing, it would be wise to ask why researchers and policy makers

wish to compare achievements among countries. The major reasons for comparison can be phrased as a Minister of Education might ask:

- Is our achievement higher, the same as, or lower than that in comparable points in other systems?
- How do the inputs and processes in other systems, especially those achieving better than ours, compare with our inputs and processes, and what are the costs?
- How different or similar are schools in other systems compared with ours? Is there much variation among schools?
- How large are the differences between sub-groups of students (gender, socio-economic groups, urban/rural, and so on) in other systems, and how do these differences compare with those in our system?

There are other questions, but these are the main ones. They can all be summed up as: 'What can we learn from other systems?'.

While international studies always compare between countries, some also make comparisons within countries. The questions posed within countries typically focus on the magnitude of differences in achievement within and among classes, within and among schools, and between gender or other groups. Comparing achievement implies that there is a common understanding on the nature the subject(s) being compared. It also assumes that comparable groups of students or schools are being compared.

What are the Procedures for Measuring Achievements?

Comparing educational achievements may seem at first sight to be simple. If the aim of the study is to compare the mathematics achievements of Grade 8 students in, say, Germany and Chile, isn't it simply a matter of administering a mathematics test to some Grade 8 students in the two countries and then comparing the test results? In practice, it is not as simple as that. Several pages below are devoted to this topic because it is so often underestimated by comparative educators.

In any study of achievement, whether national or international, the first step is to create a framework that describes and defines the subject area and produces a test blueprint. The second step is to produce a test; and the third is to produce a score for each student. This section deals with each of these aspects, beginning with the following set of questions:

- How is the subject matter defined?
- What kinds of summary scores are needed?
- What is the blueprint like?
- What kinds of items are used?
- Who writes and checks the items?
- How are the items translated?
- How are the items trialled?
- How do the final tests look?

How is the subject matter defined?

If mathematics achievement is taken as an example, the first step is to 'define' mathematics. Does mathematics mean the same thing in Germany and in Chile? There is a need for a common understanding of what actually is being measured.

In some of the older IEA studies (see e.g. Husén 1967; Comber & Keeves 1973), the work began with a content analysis of the curriculum in each of the relevant grades in each country. After much debate, an agreed framework describing the subject area was produced. An example of the kind of debate that ensued came from the mathematics framework for the Third International Mathematics and Science Study (TIMSS). For the content area of geometry, some countries included Euclidean geometry, others transformational geometry, and yet other countries what became known as the intuitive approach. Which were to be included?

On the basis of the framework, a test blueprint must be produced. In the early IEA mathematics and science studies, the blueprint consisted of different content areas on the vertical axis and a set of taxonomic behaviours on the horizontal axis. In some later studies such as TIMSS 1995, the dimension of 'perspectives' was added (Robitaille et al. 1993, p.44). These perspectives were attitudes, careers, participation, increasing interest, and habits of mind.

Another example is the Programme for International Student Assessment (PISA) study conducted under the auspices of the Organisation for Economic Co-operation and Development (OECD), in which an exhaustive exercise was undertaken in order to reach consensus on what knowledge and skills would be required by 15 year olds in the areas of reading literacy, mathematical literacy and scientific literacy (OECD 1999). For example, according to one specification (OECD 2009, p.14), mathematical literacy was defined as "an individual's capacity to identify and understand the role that mathematics plays in the world, to make well-founded judgements and to use and engage with mathematics in ways that meet the needs of that individual's life as a constructive, concerned and reflective citizen". This was different from the approach taken by the IEA studies.

In addition, TIMSS and PISA differ in content areas. In the mathematics assessment framework at Grade 8 for TIMSS 2011[1], the content dimension was organized around four strands: number, algebra, geometry, and data & chance. PISA, on the other hand, set up four overarching ideas: space and shape, change and relationships, quantity, and uncertainty. These four overarching ideas constitute a good coverage of the school curriculum, and correspond roughly to the strands geometry, algebra, number, and data & chance respectively. The correspondence is not sharp because PISA intentionally set up somewhat blurred outskirts that allow for intersection with other contents. One of the salient features of PISA is an encompassing set of phenomena and concepts that make sense and can be encountered in real world situations. Thus PISA addresses overarching ideas in place of the traditional content areas (see Figure 14.1).

Figure 14.1: Components of the Mathematics Domain in PISA

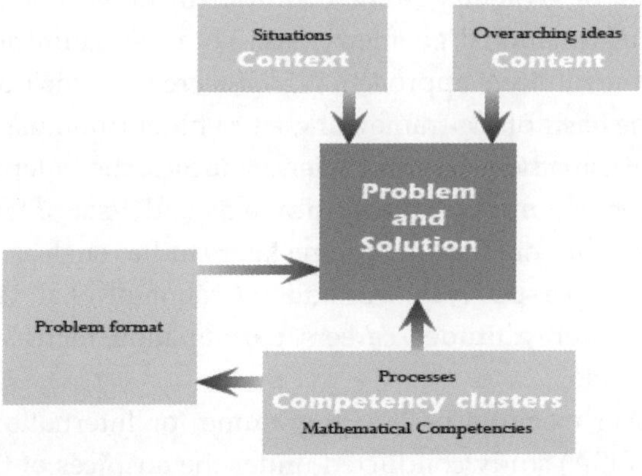

Source: OECD (2010a), p.90.

In the projects of the Southern and Eastern Africa Consortium for Monitoring Educational Quality (SACMEQ), attention has focussed on

---

[1] TIMSS was the Third International Science and Mathematics Study in 1995 and 1999, but in 2003 was renamed the Trends in International Science and Mathematics Study.

the hierarchical categories of competency skills in reading and mathematics. This is because the users of the research report can easily see which percentage of students have achieved which levels of skills. This is more meaningful than, say, a score of 487 (Postlethwaite 2004).

There is no right or wrong in this definition of subject matter. The definition is decided by the curriculum specialists participating in the study. Obviously, when interpreting results it is important to refer back to the definition of the subject matter. Since it is impossible to construct a blueprint which is fair to all countries, it is often said that the final blueprint is "equally unfair to all countries".

What kinds of summary scores are needed?

If the reporting of the test results will have not only a total score but also domain scores, then it is important to ensure that there are enough items in the relevant domains to be able to generate the domain sub-scores. If items are to be written for different levels of skills in the subject matter, then these levels must also be determined in advance. Thus, it is important to identify the kinds of scores that will be needed because this will determine the kinds of items to be written and at what levels of difficulty.

If, say, reading and mathematics have to be measured, then it is usual to have a total score for reading and a total score for mathematics. It is also usual to have domain scores such as narrative prose, expository prose, and document reading in reading literacy; and number, measurement, and space in primary school mathematics. The notion of skill levels is less well known. Skill levels are hierarchical in difficulty/complexity. For example, the science literacy skills in PISA 2009 for 15 year olds are shown in Table 14.1. In this type of assessment, the percentages of pupils achieving each level are reported. This form of reporting is felt to be more important than total scores or even domain scores, because it informs the policy makers and curriculum developers of the kinds of science literacy that have or have not been achieved.

What is the blueprint like?

While a framework provides the scope of the test, a blueprint encapsulates the emphasis in the various parts of the framework. A blueprint consists of the areas to be tested (based on the framework), the item type(s) to be used, and the relative emphasis on different parts of the framework (number of items and the total score in each area). An example of a test blueprint from TIMSS 2011 is given in Table 14.2.

Table 14.1: A Hierarchy of Science Literacy Skills

Science Skill Levels	
Level 1	Students have such a limited scientific knowledge that it can only be applied to a few, familiar situations. They can present scientific explanations that are obvious and follow explicitly from given evidence.
Level 2	Students have adequate scientific knowledge to provide possible explanations in familiar contexts or draw conclusions based on simple investigations. They are capable of direct reasoning and making literal interpretations of the results of scientific inquiry or technological problem solving.
Level 3	Students can identify clearly described scientific issues in a range of contexts. They can select facts and knowledge to explain phenomena and apply simple models or inquiry strategies. Students at this level can interpret and use scientific concepts from different disciplines and can apply them directly. They can develop short statements using facts and make decisions based on scientific knowledge.
Level 4	Students can work effectively with situations and issues that may involve explicit phenomena requiring them to make inferences about the role of science or technology. They can select and integrate explanations from different disciplines of science or technology and link those explanations directly to aspects of life situations. Students at this level can reflect on their actions and they can communicate decisions using scientific knowledge and evidence.
Level 5	Students can identify the scientific components of many complex life situations, apply both scientific concepts and knowledge about science to these situations, and can compare, select and evaluate appropriate scientific evidence for responding to life situations. Students at this level can use well-developed inquiry abilities, link knowledge appropriately and bring critical insights to situations. They can construct explanations based on evidence and arguments based on their critical analysis.
Level 6	Students can consistently identify, explain and apply scientific knowledge and knowledge about science in a variety of complex life situations. They can link different information sources and explanations and use evidence from those sources to justify decisions. They clearly and consistently demonstrate advanced scientific thinking and reasoning, and they use their scientific understanding in support of solutions to unfamiliar scientific and technological situations. Students at this level can use scientific knowledge and develop arguments in support of recommendations and decisions that centre on personal, social or global situations.

Source: OECD (2010a), p.144

Table 14.2: Number of Mathematics Items of Each Type and Score Points, by Reporting Category, Grade 8

Reporting Category		Multiple-Choice	Constructed-Response	Total Items
Content domain	Number	31 (31)	30 (36)	61 (67)
	Algebra	37 (37)	33 (39)	70 (76)
	Geometry	25 (25)	18 (19)	43 (44)
	Data and chance	25 (25)	18 (20)	43 (45)
	Total	118 (118)	99 (114)	217 (232)
Cognitive domain	Knowing	53 (53)	27 (30)	80 (83)
	Applying	47 (47)	38 (44)	85 (91)
	Reasoning	18 (18)	34 (40)	52 (58)
	Total	118 (118)	99 (114)	217 (232)

Score points are shown in parentheses.

Source: Mullis et al. (2012), p.427.

What kinds of items are used?

Several kinds of items can be used, ranging from fully open-ended to multiple-choice. The test designers must decide on the kinds of items they will use. Many international studies use multiple-choice items. They are not easy to write, especially if they are also to be diagnostic items where the kind of wrong thinking can be inferred from the wrong answers chosen.

In the mid-1990s there was a movement in favour of so-called performance items. Multiple-choice items, it was said, only required pupils to recognise right answers, and guessing could be involved; what was important was to have pupils develop the right answers. However, multiple-choice items have the advantage that they are cheap to score. Short-answer items have become more common, and good optical scanning devices allow scoring by computer. True/false items are rarely used because of the problem of guessing.

The problem with many performance items is that they have to be scored by teams of markers, often with complicated scoring systems. This is costly and requires extensive training of scorers. An example of the scoring criteria for a performance item on "Pulse" in the TIMSS 1995 Performance Assessment is shown in Figure 14.2.

Figure 14.2: An Example of Scoring Criteria for a Performance Item

---

Criteria for Fully-Correct Response

Item 1 – Measure pulse rates and record in table.
Response is scored for both the quality of the presentation and the quality of data collection.

Quality of presentation. i) Presents at least two sets of measurements in table. ii) Measurements are paired: time and number of pulse beats. iii) Labels table appropriately: data entries in columns identified by headings and/or units; units incorporated into headings or placed beside each measurement; headings or units for the number of pulse beats include the time interval.
Total Possible Points: 2

Quality of data. i) Makes at least five measurements (at rest, and four or more during exercise). ii) Pulse rates are plausible: 7 to 25 counts per 10 seconds (40-150 pulse beats per minute). iii) Pulse rate increases with exercise (may level off or slow near the end).
Total Possible points: 3

Source: Harmon et al. (1997), p.15.

Who writes and checks the items?

In an international study, it is normal to have item writing groups within each national centre. Once the blueprint is known, then the national teams are asked to contribute items either from existing tests or by writing new ones. The items are sent to an international test committee which decides which ones to select, perhaps with modification. The proposed items are checked by the national committees again, and finally, after negotiation, agreed upon.

How are the items translated?

Translation of instruments (test items and questionnaire questions) is more than simply a technical issue, for the accuracy of the translation affects both the substance of what is being tested and the comparability of the results. For an international study, one language must be chosen as the working language, and the tests (and other instruments such as questionnaires) are usually constructed in that language. When translating the test items into other languages, it is important to ensure that the sense is the same, the difficulty-level in the language is about the same, and the cognitive processes required from the students to answer the questions as similar as possible.

This work is not easy, especially if many countries are involved. In TIMSS 1995 for example, 31 different languages were involved, and the international study centre had teams of professional translators checking the accuracy, sensitivity and equivalence of the translations. In the PISA project, a number of quality assurance procedures were implemented in order to ensure equivalence between all national versions of the test and questionnaire materials used by participating countries (Adams & Wu 2002; Grisay 2003; OECD 2010c). These included:

- providing two parallel source versions of the material (in English and French), and recommending that each country develop two independent versions in their instruction language (one from each of the source languages), and then reconcile them into one national version;
- adding systematic information on the Question Intent to the test and questionnaire materials to be translated, in order to clarify the scope and the characteristics of each item, and extensive Translation Notes to draw attention to possible translation or adaptation problems;
- developing detailed guidelines for the translation/adaptation of the test material, and then for revising it after the Field Trial, as an important part of the PISA National Project Manager Manuals;
- training key staff from each national team on the recommended translation procedures; and
- appointing and training a group of international verifiers (professional translators proficient in English and French, and with native command of each target language), in order to verify the equivalence of all national versions against the source versions.

It can be seen that translation is neither easy nor inexpensive; but it is something that international test constructors cannot ignore.

How are the items trialled?
Normally, three to five times more items are required for any one cell in the blueprint than will be actually needed for the final test. These items are split into a number of trial forms, and each trial form is then administered to a judgement sample of about 200 pupils from the defined target population.

The test data are then entered into a database, and item analyses conducted. The analyses are usually those of classical and item response theory. Checks are made that the items measure one underlying trait for the measure in question, and that the items do not favour one group versus another (e.g. boys versus girls, or rural versus urban children). Scores derived from the tests must be deemed to be reliable and valid. In some cases, further item writing and trialling are required. A final set of items is then agreed upon.

How do the final tests look?

Items are assembled into a test more or less in ascending order of difficulty. Depending on the subject area, the number of items required to cover the content of the blueprint may be too many for a test of, say, 60 to 90 minutes. In this case rotated tests can be used. Several tests are created, but with items that are common to each test which allow for calibration later on. These tests are then rotated over pupils within schools. Through this method it is possible to create school scores, but often it is not possible to create individual pupil scores on the same items.

Whom to Compare?

After deciding what is to be compared, the next major question is whom to compare. This requires consideration of age versus grade groups, and raises questions of the defined population.

Age versus grade groups

Comparative studies usually specify an age level or a grade level, or sometimes a combination of both. The PISA study, for example, tested 15 year olds. Measuring an age group gives information on what the system has done to an age cohort under its care. However, in some countries the official age of entry to school is relatively young (e.g. four years old in the Netherlands), and in other countries students enter school much later (e.g. six, or seven, or even eight years old in some South American and African countries). So is it fair to compare the nine year olds in the Netherlands who have had five years of schooling with the nine year olds in South American countries who have just started school?

   Age-based definitions also face practical complications. For the PISA study, 15 year olds may have been in two grades at the time of testing for some countries, but in countries with frequent grade repetition the 15 year old pupils may have been in several grades. This makes the sampling and testing very complicated and hence expensive.

Whereas the concept of age is not ambiguous, the concept of grade is. Does Grade 4 mean the same thing in different countries? Some education systems have a number of years of preschool before students start Grade 1, and it is simply a matter of tradition that the first year of primary or elementary school is called Grade 1. At the other end of the scale, if researchers decide to test students in their final year of schooling (as was the case in the IEA's Second International Mathematics Study), some systems of secondary schooling end at Grade 10 and others at Grade 13. Three years difference in the number of years of schooling is likely to make a lot of difference to achievement, and therefore, it is argued, they should not be compared.

Further, the dropout rate is very different between systems. Even if all systems have the same number of years of schooling, the percentages of an age group remaining in school may be very different. In the United States, about 90 per cent of age groups remain in school until Grade 12, but in some other countries it is as low as 20 per cent. However, if a subject such as Physics is taken, even in the United States only 5 per cent specialise in Physics. In other countries the percentage of an age group specialising in Physics may be between 7 and 35 per cent. Are these parts of an age or grade group therefore comparable?

For TIMSS 1995, to overcome this difficulty a grade-age definition was used in the first two of the three populations tested. The first population, for example, was defined as those students in the two adjacent grades with the most nine year olds. Even this definition was not totally satisfactory, because the nine year olds in some countries had substantially fewer years of education than the nine year olds in other countries. In choosing between a grade definition and an age definition, the essential question to ask is whether the researchers are more interested in the effect of schooling (in which case they should use a grade definition) or of maturity (in which case they should choose an age definition).

Defined population
Even when a fairly good description of the desired target population for comparison has been achieved, such as 'All pupils in Grade 5 in full time schooling on 25 April in government and non-government schools', there is still the problem of what constitutes 'all pupils'. For example, should the following Grade 5 pupils be included:

- pupils who live in very remote areas, to whom access is difficult and the costs of testing may be very high;

- minority groups who speak different languages from the majority in the population;
- pupils who follow curricula that are different from the majority of the population (e.g. because they are in international schools); and
- children with severe disabilities such as mental handicap?

Normally exclusions are allowed, usually on the grounds of cost. However, the excluded population should never exceed 5 per cent of pupils in the desired population. Arriving at the defined population (i.e. the desired population minus the excluded population) requires a very good comparative educator who knows the systems to be compared.

Once the defined population has been identified, the populations may or may not need to be sampled. In an international study conducted under the auspices of SACMEQ, the Seychelles did not need to be sampled because it is a small country in which the researchers could relatively easily access all the children. Thus, in this case the researchers tested the whole population of Grade 6, which contained about 1,500 students (Leste et al. 2005). However, in most cases the population is large, and it is too costly to test all. In this situation, sampling is used.

The number of pupils to be sampled depends on the standard error of sampling required. In most international studies it is common to aim for a standard error of sampling to be 0.05 of the standard deviation of the measure. In this case, a sample equivalent to at least 400 randomly-selected pupils is needed. Since it is virtually impossible to draw a simple random sample of all pupils in a particular grade in a country, often two-stage sampling is used: the primary sampling unit is the school, and the second stage of sampling is the pupil. Schools are typically sampled with a probability proportional to the enrolment of the grade that is the focus of the study.

In some studies, intact classes of pupils within schools are drawn; and in other studies a random sample of pupils across classes within the focal grade is drawn. In the former case more meaningful multivariate analyses can be undertaken, but the variance within school is inevitably underestimated. There is also the problem of defining a class. Where teaching for all subjects is done in intact classes, the answer is easy; but in some countries students are grouped in different ways for instruction in different subjects. These problems need to be addressed, and a common procedure agreed.

After the data have been collected, recorded and cleaned, the next problem concerns the shortfall of pupils (or schools) in one or more of the strata used in the sampling frame. If there has been shortfall, then corrections need to be made by using sampling weights for correcting for disproportionality between strata. The weights are calculated and then added to the data file.

Comparing Levels and Equity of Performance

Pupils within schools
Most teachers (and many parents) are eager to know the strengths and weaknesses of pupils in different subject areas. This is true whether the study is national or international. It is very important for researchers to give feedback to the teachers and schools. Among other benefits, it increases the willingness of schools to cooperate in future studies. The teachers may well ask:

- What are my pupils' achievements on specific sub-dimensions of mathematics and science?

Where whole classes have been tested, it is possible to give feedback to schools about sub-scores and skill scores for pupils in a class; but this is not the case if the tests have been rotated.

An example of feedback to a class for the first four pupils is presented in Table 14.3. From such a table it can be seen that Pupil 1 was the best in both subjects, and that Pupil 3 had a higher score in mathematics than in reading. It would also be possible to compare the class with similar classes in the country and with the average score of classes in the international study.

Table 14.3: Sub-scores for First Four Pupils in a Class

Pupil	Reading Sub-scores			Mathematics Sub-scores		
	sub-score A (Max = 20)	sub-score B (Max = 20)	sub-score C (Max = 20)	sub-score A (Max = 15)	sub-score B (Max = 15)	sub-score C (Max = 15)
1	17	15	10	12	13	12
2	10	9	9	7	8	9
3	6	5	7	12	14	13
4	7	8	9	10	12	11

Levels of school performance

The school principal's question may be something like:

- On which sub-domains of which subject areas and at which grade levels is my school doing well or poorly in comparison with similar schools in my country and with all schools in my country?

To address this kind of question, the principal needs one or more points of comparison. One would be a 'relative' level of performance which focuses on the performance of the school with respect to similar schools or even all schools in the target population in the country.

Table 14.4 illustrates this point with data from Hong Kong, and shows the mean and standard deviation of the TIMSS 1999 Rasch scores (with mean 150 and standard deviation 10) for a Grade 8 class in a certain school for mathematics and science. These results enable the principal to compare the school's performance with that of similar schools and all other schools in the target population.

Table 14.4: Results for a Relative Comparison of a School with Similar Schools and all Schools in Hong Kong

Schools	Mathematics		Science	
	Mean	SD	Mean	SD
This school				
Boys	160.3	8.1	158.6	7.2
Girls	162.5	8.3	154.6	8.3
Total	161.4	8.2	156.7	7.9
Similar schools				
Boys	159.1	7.9	159.0	8.6
Girls	157.4	8.5	154.8	7.8
Total	158.4	8.2	157.4	8.5
All schools				
Boys	150.5	10.4	151.4	10.7
Girls	150.4	9.5	149.3	9.0
Total	150.5	9.9	150.4	10.0

In this case, the mathematics and science scores of the school are better than the average scores of all schools in Hong Kong, so the principal should be heartened to find that pupils in this school are performing well in these two subjects. When compared with similar schools, pupils in this school still did better in mathematics, but they did less well in science.

An unambitious principal would be contented that the pupils in the school are doing well, especially in mathematics. But a more ambitious principal who wanted the school to be a leader would attempt to find out the cause of relatively poor science performance and how it could be improved. Is it that the science teachers in the schools are too conservative in their teaching methods, or is it that this school lacks good science laboratories? The principal would have to carry out separate investigations. This would require the principal to review the school's science education programme and facilities, and could require the principal to visit similar schools to see what they were doing that would be worth copying.

When the gender differences are examined, it can be seen that in this school the differences for both mathematics and science are comparable to those in similar schools. However, when compared to all schools in Hong Kong, the gender difference is larger in this school. Whether this difference is tolerable may depend on the philosophy of the school and the principal.

It should also be noted that compared to other schools, this school is distinctive in that girls do better than boys in mathematics. The fact that the pupils in this school do so well in mathematics implies that there are some very good mathematics programmes in the school, but that somehow the boys are not benefiting as much as the girls.

Since TIMSS is an international study, the authorities are often very interested in how their schools compare with all other schools in the study, or at least with the schools in nearby countries. Since the international scores were calculated using plausible values (with a mean of 500 and standard deviation of 100) while Rasch scores were used in the between school comparison in Hong Kong, we cannot simply add rows of results to the table. However, the principal can still gain a sense of the 'international standing' of a particular school by combining the information in Table 14.4 with the information in Table 14.5 (extracted from Martin et al. 2000; Mullis et al. 2000).

Table 14.5: Achievement of Hong Kong Students in TIMSS 1999 Compared with International Averages

	Mathematics		Science	
Hong Kong Averages	mean	standard error	mean	standard error
Boys	581	5.9	537	5.1
Girls	583	4.7	522	4.4
Total	582	4.3	530	3.7
International Averages				
Boys	489	0.9	495	0.9
Girls	485	0.8	480	0.9
Total	487	0.7	488	0.7

Levels of regional performance

It is likely that the authorities will wish to know if there are any differences between regions with different characteristics. A typical question is:

- Do regions with different characteristics differ in achievement?

Table 14.6 is an example of differences in PISA 2006 scores in Korea at the regional level. In Korea, most ordinary high schools (except several special high schools for Science, English, etc.) are located in either "standard" regions or "non-standard" regions. In standard regions, the majority of the students are assigned to one of the nearby high schools, while schools in non-standard regions may select students for admission. Student achievements are more even among schools in standard regions. Most large cities including Seoul and Busan are standard regions, while many small cities and rural areas are non-standard regions. There used to be a huge gap between students' overall achievements in these two kinds of regions, but Korea has been in transition from the non-standard region system to the standard region system since the late 1970s, and the achievement gap has reduced.

Table 14.6 shows the PISA 2006 results in reading, mathematics and science by these two kinds of regions in small and mid-sized cities. The number of ordinary high schools (special high schools were excluded in this analysis) in standard regions is 25 (845 students), and that in non-standard regions is 20 (652 students). There was not much difference

Table 14.6: Pupil Reading, Mathematics, Science Scores in PISA 2006 by the Characteristics of Region (Korea)

	Standard/ Non-standard Regions	Reading		Mathematics		Science	
		Standard	Non-standard	Standard	Non-standard	Standard	Non-standard
10th	Mean	476.2	485.0	470.5	468.6	441.9	445.9
	SE	8.2	13.3	8.8	13.3	9.0	12.2
25th	Mean	527.1	531.7	521.4	515.4	492.2	497.0
	SE	6.8	11.0	6.6	12.2	5.9	11.5
50th	Mean	579.7	581.4	576.8	575.8	546.4	552.0
	SE	7.0	9.8	5.7	14.1	5.3	12.5
75th	Mean	627.4	627.6	628.3	633.2	597.8	609.6
	SE	8.4	7.9	4.1	10.9	4.4	9.3
90th	Mean	667.6	666.8	668.6	679.0	637.1	663.0
	SE	8.1	7.4	5.9	10.5	6.2	11.3

Source: Kim et al. (2010), p.85.

between students' reading scores in standard regions and those in non-standard regions across all the percentiles. In mathematics, at the 75th and 90th percentiles students in non-standard regions scored higher than their counterparts in standard regions, but the scores were reversed in the lower percentiles. In science, students in non-standard regions outperformed those in standard regions in all the percentiles.

In Table 14.6, the standard errors of sampling have been reported together with the estimates of means. These standard errors are important when generalising from the sample to the target population. For example, if researchers wish to assess the accuracy of the 90th percentile science mean of 663.0 for non-standard regions, and if they wish to be sure 19 times out of 20 or at the 95 % level of confidence, then they multiply one standard error by 1.96. The standard error is 11.3, so 1.96 times the standard errors is 22.1. Thus the researchers can be sure 19 times out of 20 that the real mean value lies between 663.0 ± 1.96*(11.3) or 663.0 ± 22.1 or between 640.9 and 685.1. This in turn allows the researchers to compare scores to see if they differ by more than sampling error.

One could ask whether the 90th percentile students in non-standard regions scored higher in science than those in standard regions. The population mean for the standard region lies between 637.1 ± 1.96*(6.2) or between 624.9 and 659.3. As noted, the 90th percentile science mean for the non-standard region was between 640.9 and 685.1. The lower limit of the real value of the 90th percentile science mean for the non-standard regions was within the bounds for the standard regions, and hence the researchers cannot say that the difference is greater than sampling error. So, there was no significant difference in the 90th percentile science scores between the two kinds of regions.

Important information at the national level
Typical questions posed at the national level include:

- What percentages of pupils in our school system reach different skill levels?
- What percentages of pupils reach specified benchmark levels such as 'being able to cope in society' or 'being able to study at the next level of education without difficulty'?
- How does our country's achievement compare with that of similar pupils in other countries?

For skill levels, an example from Vietnam has been presented in Table 14.7. The levels range from very simple tasks to quite complex tasks for Grade 5 pupils. In reading it can be seen that 19 per cent of pupils did not get further than Level 2, and it is often said that reading to function well in the society begins at Level 3. The levels were identified by the primary school reading and mathematics experts at the Ministry of Education. They examined the Rasch difficulty levels for items in the test, and were then able to examine clusters of items at a particular difficulty level and state what it was that the items were measuring. The advantage of these kinds of analyses is that the curriculum development specialists can easily see the kinds of skills that have been mastered and not mastered by pupils in the country as a whole. The calculations could also be made for the regions and provinces.

The second kind of information referred to in the national questions is the so-called benchmark information. Again an example from Vietnam illustrates the point. In the Grade 5 survey, two benchmarks were established. The first benchmark was based on a pupil's ability to use a set of reading and mathematics skills needed to function in Vietnamese society. Those below this benchmark were described as 'pre-functional'. A second benchmark was based on an estimation of a pupil's ability to cope with the reading and mathematics tasks in the next grade of education, Grade 6, which is the first year of secondary education. The two benchmarks helped to identify three groups of pupils. Those below the first benchmark would need considerable help to enable them to function and participate fully in Vietnamese society. Those above this benchmark but below the second needed assistance to help them cope with the reading and mathematics involved in secondary education. Pupils above the second benchmark were expected to be able to cope with the reading and mathematics involved in secondary education.

Each item was rated twice. The first was the probability that a person who could adequately function in Vietnamese society could obtain the correct answer to each item. The second was the probability that a pupil who had adequate skills to cope with Grade 6 learning could obtain the correct answer to each item. In each case, the probabilities were summed using an Angoff approach to establish the cut-off points. A detailed description of how the benchmarks were conceptualised and calculated has been given in the Grade 5 Vietnam study (World Bank 2004). The benchmarks were:

Table 14.7: Percentages of Grade 5 Vietnamese Pupils Reaching Different Skill Levels in Reading and Mathematics

Reading Skill Levels	%	SE
Level 1 Matches text at word or sentence level aided by pictures. Restricted to a limited range of vocabulary linked to pictures.	4.6	0.17
Level 2 Locates text expressed in short repetitive sentences and can deal with text unaided by pictures. Type of text is limited to short sentences and phrases with repetitive patterns.	14.4	0.28
Level 3 Reads and understands longer passages. Can search backwards or forwards through text to for information. Understands paraphrasing. Expanding vocabulary enables understanding of sentences with some complex structure.	23.1	0.34
Level 4 Links information from different parts of the text. Selects and connects text to derive and infer different possible meanings.	20.2	0.27
Level 5 Links inferences and identifies an author's intention from information stated in different ways, in different text types and in documents where the message is not explicit.	24.5	0.39
Level 6 Combines text with outside knowledge to infer various meanings, including hidden meanings. Identifies an author's purposes, attitudes, values, beliefs, motives, unstated assumptions and arguments.	13.1	0.41
Mathematics Skill Levels	%	SE
Level 1 Reads, writes and compares natural; numbers, fractions and decimals. Uses single operations of +, -, x and : on simple whole numbers; works with simple measures such as time; recognises simple 3D shapes.	0.2	0.02
Level 2 Converts fractions with denominator of 10 to decimals. Calculates with whole numbers using one operation (x, -, + or :) in a one-step word problem; recognises 2D and 3D shapes.	3.5	0.13
Level 3 Identifies place value; determines the value of a simple number sentence; understands equivalent fractions; adds and subtracts simple fractions; carries out multiple operations in correct order; converts and estimates common and familiar measurement units in solving problems.	11.5	0.27
Level 4 Reads, writes and compares larger numbers; solves problems involving calendars and currency, area and volume; uses charts and tables for estimation; solves inequalities; transformations with 3D figures; knowledge of angles in regular figures; understands simple transformations with 2D and 3D shapes.	28.2	0.37
Level 5 Calculates with multiple and varied operations; recognises rules and patterns in number sequences; calculates the perimeter and area of irregular shapes; measurement of irregular objects; recognised transformed figures after reflection; solves problems with multiple operations involving measurement units, percentage and averages.	29.7	0.41
Level 6 Problem solving with periods of time, length, area and volume; embedded and dependent number patterns; develops formulae; recognises 3D figures after rotation and reflection and embedded figures and right angles in irregular shapes, data from graphs and tables.	27.0	0.6

1. *Benchmark 1*: A group of pupils was described as pre-functional because they had not yet reached a benchmark demonstrating reading or mathematics required for everyday activities in Vietnamese society. The label pre-functional does not mean that a pupil is illiterate or non-numerate. There are basic skills that these pupils can demonstrate, but the skill level is not yet deemed by experts to be at a sufficient level to enable the person to be an effective member of Vietnamese society. A second group of pupils was identified as those who could demonstrate the kinds of skills needed to cope with life in Vietnam. They were found to be above this lower benchmark but had not yet reached the second benchmark. These pupils were designated as functional in terms of their capacity to participate in Vietnamese society. However it was deemed that this group would need some remedial assistance to be able to cope with the reading and mathematics required at Grade 6.

2. *Benchmark 2*: Pupils who performed above the second benchmark were described as demonstrating the kinds of skills that were desirable in order to learn independently at the next level of schooling without needing remedial assistance. The label used in the tables was 'independent'.

Table 14.8 presents the results for Vietnam Grade 5 as a whole. The expectations for reading, as measured by the reading test, were higher than for mathematics, as measured by the mathematics test. Only 51 per cent of pupils in Grade 5 were deemed to be able to study independently in Grade 6 given their reading ability in Grade 5. This was important feed-

Table 14.8: Percentages and Sampling Errors of Pupils Reaching Functionality Levels in Reading and Mathematics, Vietnam

Functionality		Reading		Mathematics	
		%	SE	%	SE
Independent	Reached the level of reading and mathematics to enable independent learning in Grade 6	51.3	0.58	79.9	0.41
Functional	Reached the level for functional participation in Vietnamese society	38.0	0.45	17.3	0.36
Pre-functional	Not reached the level considered to be a minimum for functional purposes in Vietnamese society	10.7	0.3	2.8	0.13

back to the Ministry of Education about how the system was preparing its pupils for society and for the next grade level. It was not a surprise to the authorities in Vietnam, who had been revising the curriculum for some time in order to improve the reading levels in Grade 5.

How these benchmarks were met in the different regions can be seen in Table 14.9, to which an extra column has been added. For the Red River Delta it can be seen that 95.0 per cent of pupils were at the functional level – the addition of the per cent functional (31.6) and the per cent independent (63.4) together make 95.0 per cent. It can be seen that the problem areas for reading were the Northwest and Mekong Delta regions.

Although this kind for information is important, it must be recognised that only brave Ministries undertake such calculations. They are very instructive data for a Ministry to know, but could easily stimulate a member of parliament of the opposition party to ask why, after five years of schooling, 10 per cent of pupils are still at the pre-functional level of reading.

The third kind of question that Ministries often ask is:

• How well is our country doing compared with similar countries?

Table 14.9: Percentages and Sampling Errors of Pupils at Each Benchmark by Region, Vietnam

	Pre functional		Functional				Independent
			--------- Reading ---------				
	%	SE	%	SE	%	SE	%
Red River Delta	5.0	0.37	31.6	1.10	63.4	1.35	95.0
Northeast	12.0	0.63	34.8	0.95	53.2	1.13	88.0
Northwest	16.6	1.92	38.6	2.26	44.9	2.79	83.5
North Central	8.8	0.95	35.7	1.52	55.5	2.09	91.2
Central Coast	10.9	0.91	41.2	1.23	48.0	1.65	89.1
Central Highlands	12.2	1.78	33.9	2.16	53.9	2.95	87.8
Southeast	7.0	0.56	39.9	1.34	53.1	1.51	93.0
Mekong Delta	17.6	0.66	46.3	0.81	36.1	1.06	82.4
Vietnam	10.7	0.30	38.0	0.45	51.3	0.58	89.4
			--------- Mathematics ---------				
Red River Delta	1.7	0.24	11.2	0.67	87.1	0.83	98.3
Northeast	3.6	0.32	18.0	0.72	78.4	0.88	96.5
Northwest	7.8	1.42	19.3	1.82	72.9	2.72	92.2
North Central	1.8	0.40	12.0	1.00	86.3	1.22	98.2
Central Coast	1.6	0.24	15.5	0.85	82.9	0.96	98.4
Central Highlands	2.9	0.60	13.7	1.59	83.5	2.05	97.1
Southeast	1.9	0.21	15.9	0.78	82.2	0.85	98.1
Mekong Delta	4.6	0.30	28.6	0.86	66.8	0.93	95.4
Vietnam	2.8	0.13	17.3	0.36	79.9	0.41	97.2

This is where involvement in international studies is important. The PISA study was concerned with 15 year olds wherever they might be in the system of education. In Table 14.10, some results from the 2009 PISA study have been presented. These are of interest because countries want to know what the general level of education is likely to be for the future work force. It is quite clear that the Asian countries far out-distanced their European and American counterparts. One notable exception was Finland, which performed well in all the three subjects and in all the PISA cycles, and its education system has drawn huge attention from the international community. Germany on the other hand, which is traditionally known for its good technical work, had much lower scores. This score provoked a big debate on education in that country when the first PISA results were released.

These kinds of results only inform a country how it compares with other countries. They do not tell a country how to improve itself or even which malleable factors are most associated with variation in pupil achievement. But if this information is coupled with the skills levels approach, benchmark approach and multivariate analyses approach, then the studies can yield information of great benefit to those responsible for the system of education.

Returning to an earlier point, great care must be taken when there are very different proportions of a cohort still in school. This is the case with Population 3 in the IEA studies. This is usually the last grade in secondary schools; but the grade itself differs. In TIMSS Advanced 2008 (Table 14.11), the last grade for some countries (e.g. Armenia) is Grade 10,

Table 14.10: Selected Results from PISA 2009

	Mathematics literacy		Reading literacy		Scientific literacy	
	Mean	SE	Mean	SE	Mean	SE
Shanghai	600	2.8	556	2.4	575	2.3
Japan	529	3.3	520	3.5	539	3.4
Korea	546	4.0	539	3.5	538	3.4
Finland	541	2.2	536	2.3	554	2.3
Germany	513	1.9	497	2.7	520	2.8
United Kingdom	492	2.4	494	2.3	514	2.5
United States	487	3.6	500	3.7	502	3.6
OECD average	496	0.5	493	0.5	501	0.5

Source: OECD (2010b), pp.56, 135, 152.

and in others it is Grade 13 (e.g., Italy). Also, the average ages of the students at the time of taking the test ranged from 16.4 (Philippines) to 19.0 (Italy). Some countries have nearly 100 per cent of the final cohort still in school, but others have less than 20 per cent. The percentages can also differ where subject specialisation occurs. For example, the percentages of those studying mathematics in the last grade in school in TIMSS Advanced 2008 are given in Table 14.11. They ranged from 1.4% in the Russian Federation to 40.5% in Slovenia. This is a considerable range, and the scores should be interpreted in that light.

Table 14.11: TIMSS Advanced 2008 Distribution of Achievement in Advanced Mathematics

Country	Advanced Mathematics Achievement	Country Context for Achievement		
	Average Scale Score	Advanced Mathematics Coverage Index	Years of formal Schooling**	Average Age at Time of Testing
Russian Federation	561 (7.2)	1.4%	10/11	17.0
Netherlands*	552 (2.6)	3.5%	12	18.0
Lebanon	545 (2.3)	5.9%	12	17.9
TIMSS Advanced Scale Average	500			
Iran, Islamic Rep.of	497 (6.4)	6.5%	12	18.1
Slovenia	457 (4.2)	40.5%	12	18.8
Italy	449 (7.2)	19.7%	13	19.0
Norway	439 (4.9)	10.9%	12	18.8
Armenia	433 (3.6)	4.3%	10	17.7
Sweden	412 (5.5)	12.8%	12	18.8
Philippines	355 (5.5)	0.7%	10	16.4

*   Met guidelines for sample participation rates only after replacement schools were included.

** Represents years of schooling counting from the first year of primary or basic education (first year of ISCED Level 1).

Source: Extracted from Mullis et al. (2009), Exhibit 2.1, p.65.

How equitable is achievement among schools?

The above results have been concerned with the *levels* of achievement in this school, in similar schools, in this region, and in the nation. The Ministry of Education planners are also interested in the extent to which schools differ in the country as a whole. To what extent are differences in pupil scores a function of differences among schools and among pupils within schools? Where intact classes have been tested, then the focus of interest becomes the extent to which the differences in scores among pupils are a function of between schools, between classes within schools, and between pupils.

In the first case, an easy summary statistic is the intra-class correlation. In the Vietnam Grade 5 survey, this statistic was 0.58 – indicating that 58 per cent of the variance was between schools, and therefore only 42 per cent was within schools. But, if the interest was in, say, differences among provinces, among schools, among classes within schools, and among pupils within classes, then using a multi-level analysis it was possible to show that for reading achievement in Grade 5 in Vietnam it is as shown in Figure 14.3.

Figure 14.3: Pupil Reading Achievement Variance Partitioned by Province, School, Class within School, and Pupils within Classes, Vietnam

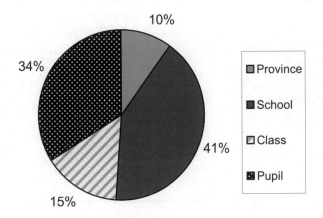

In this case it can be seen that 10 per cent of the variance was due to differences between provinces, 41 per cent between schools, 15 per cent to classes within schools, and 34 per cent to pupils within classes. This is a more differentiated picture. Strikingly, the large difference in Vietnam is between schools. Within each of these levels within a school system it is possible to determine which province, school, class or pupil variables play a role in explaining the variance within each level.

The intra-class correlation is a good statistic to use for comparing within-country school variations among countries. The intra-class correlations for Grade 8 mathematics in the TIMSS 2007 survey for a number of countries are shown in Table 14.12. For Korea, for example, this statistic was 0.083 – indicating that only 8.3% of the variance was between schools, and therefore 91.7% was within schools.

The above finding shows that the variation between schools is very small in Korea, only 8.3% of the variance is due to differences between schools, in contrast to 46% in the US. When equity is considered to be politically important, countries often want to know the variation between schools.

Table 14.12: TIMSS 2007 Intra-class Correlations for Grade 8 Mathematics for a Number of Countries

	Korea		Taiwan		United States		Israel		Singapore	
	Variance	%	Variance	%	Variance	%	Variance	%	Variance	%
Within school	7204.2	91.7	8483.3	73.4	3630.7	71.0	5484.2	64.2	4381.4	54.0
Between school	649.4	8.3	3075.0	26.6	1480.6	29.0	3059.6	35.8	3737.7	46.0
Total	7853.6	100.0	11558.3	100.0	5111.3	100.0	8543.8	100.0	8119.1	100.0
Intra-Class Correlation	0.083	8.3	0.266	26.6	0.290	29.0	0.358	35.8	0.460	46.0

Source: Kim et al. (2012), p.193.

Conclusions

This chapter has provided information about the problem of measuring achievement when comparing pupils, schools, provinces or regions within a country, and countries. At the country level it dealt with information concerning skill levels, benchmarks, and overall scores.

The construction of achievement measures is very difficult. If this hurdle is overcome and the sampling and data collection are well conducted, then the information can be of great use to the educational planners. However, care must be exercised when comparing countries, especially at the end of secondary school where many features of the target populations are different.

Whereas comparing achievement is an important first step in these kinds of studies, it is only a first step. No country is good at everything: they all have their strong and weak points in achievement. But they also want to know what they might do to improve education in one or more aspects. For this they need to know which variables are associated with variation in achievement so that they can think of what action to take to ameliorate the situation. This means that the studies have to be designed in such a way to measure likely factors in the system that might be associated with achievement variance among pupils, among schools, among region and among countries. But, how to do that is another story!

Editors' note: This chapter for the second edition of the book was written by Frederick Leung and Kyungmee Park based on the chapter written by the late T. Neville Postlethwaite and Frederick Leung for the first edition.

References

Adams, Ray & Wu, Margaret (2002): *PISA 2000 Technical Report*. Paris: Organisation for Economic Co-operation and Development (OECD).

Bereday, George Z.F. (1964): *Comparative Method in Education*. New York: Holt, Rinehart & Winston.

Comber, L.C. & Keeves, John (1973): *Science Education in Nineteen Countries: An Empirical Study*. New York: Wiley.

Grisay, Aletta (2003): 'Translation Procedures in OECD/PISA 2000 International Assessment'. *Language Testing*, Vol.20, No.2, pp.225-240.

Harmon, M.; Smith, Teresa A.; Martin, Michael O.; Kelly, D.L.; Beaton, Albert E.; Mullis, Ina V.S.; Gonzalez, Eugenio J. & Orpwood, G. (1997): *Performance Assessment in IEA's Third International Mathematics and Science Study*. Chestnut Hill, MA: International Study Center, Boston College.

Husén, Torsten (1967): *International Study of Achievement in Mathematics: A Comparison of Twelve Countries*. Stockholm: Almqvist and Wiksell.

Kim, S., Kim, H., Park, J., Jin, E., Lee, M., Kim S., & Ahn, Y. (2012): *Trends and International Comparative Analysis of Educational Environment in TIMSS*. Seoul: Korea Institute of Curriculum and Evaluation. RRE 2012-4-1.

Kim, K., Si, K., Kim, M., Kim, B., Ok, H., Yim, H., Yun, M., & Park, S. (2010). *An Analysis of Higher Achievement of Korean Students in OECD PISA*. Seoul: Korea Institute of Curriculum and Evaluation. RRE 2010-14.

Leste, A.; Valentin, J. & Hoareau, F. (2005): *The SACMEQ II Project in Seychelles: A Study of the Conditions of Schooling and the Quality of Education*. Harare: Southern and Eastern Africa Consortium for Monitoring Educational Quality.

Martin, Michael O.; Mullis, Ina V.S.; Gonzales, Eugenio J.; Gregory, Kelvin D.; Smith, Teresa A.; Chrostowski, Steven J.; Garden, Robert A. & O'Connor, Kathleen M. (2000): *TIMSS 1999 International Science Report: Findings from IEA's Repeat of the Third International Mathematics and Science Study at the Eighth Grade*. Chestnut Hill, MA: International Study Center, Boston College.

Mullis, Ina V.S.; Martin, Michael O.; Gonzales, Eugenio J.; Gregory, Kelvin D.; Garden, Robert A.; O'Connor, Kathleen M.; Chrostowski, Steven J. & Smith, Teresa A. (2000): *TIMSS 1999 International Mathematics Report: Findings from IEA's Repeat of the Third International Mathematics and Science Study at the Eighth Grade*. Chestnut Hill, MA: International Study Center, Boston College.

Mullis, Ina V.S.; Martin, Michael O.; Robitaille, David F. & Foy, Pierre (2009): *TIMSS Advanced 2008 International Report: Findings from IEA's Study of Achievement in Advanced Mathematics and Physics in the Final Year of Secondary School*. Chestnut Hill, MA: TIMSS & PIRLS International Study Center, Boston College.

Mullis, Ina V.S.; Martin, Michael O.; Ruddock, Graham J.; O'Sullivan, Christine Y.; Preuschoff, Corinna (2009): *TIMSS 2011 Assessment Frameworks*. Chestnut Hill, MA: TIMSS & PIRLS International Study Center, Boston College.

Mullis, Ina V.S.; Martin, Michael O.; Foy, Pierre, Arora, Alka (2012): *TIMSS 2011 International Results in Mathematics*. Chestnut Hill, MA: TIMSS & PIRLS International Study Center, Boston College.

OECD (1999): *Measuring Student Knowledge and Skills: A New Framework for Assessment*. Paris: Organisation for Economic Co-operation and Development (OECD).

OECD (2010a): *PISA 2009 Assessment Framework: Key Competencies in Reading, Mathematics and Science*. Paris: Organisation for Economic Co-operation and Development (OECD).

OECD (2010b): *PISA 2009 Results – What Students Know and Can Do: Student Performance in Reading, Mathematics and Science*. Paris: Organisation for Economic Co-operation and Development (OECD).

OECD (2010c): *Translation and Adaptation Guidelines for PISA 2012*. Paris: Organisation for Economic Co-operation and Development (OECD).

Postlethwaite, T. Neville (2004): *Monitoring Educational Achievement.* Fundamentals of Educational Planning 81, Paris: UNESCO International Institute for Educational Planning (IIEP).

Robitaille, David F.; Schmidt, S.R.; McKnight, C.; Britton, E. & Nicol, C. (1993): *Curriculum Frameworks for Mathematics and Science.* Vancouver: Pacific Educational Press.

World Bank, The (2004): *Vietnam Reading and Mathematics Assessment Study.* Vols. 1-3. Report No.29787-VN, Hanoi: Vietnam Culture and Information Publishing House.

III: Conclusions

15

Different Models, Different Emphases, Different Insights

Mark BRAY, Bob ADAMSON & Mark MASON

This final chapter pulls together some themes from earlier chapters, and in a sense makes a comparison of comparisons. The earlier chapters have addressed a range of foci within a variety of paradigms. Using insights from the book, this final chapter begins with a discussion of models for comparative education research. It then makes some remarks about emphases, before concluding with comments about the insights than can be gained from comparative approaches and methods in educational research.

Models for Comparative Education Research

This book has shown that many models exist for comparative study of education. They cannot all be listed here, but some examples from the previous chapters deserve highlighting and elaboration. This section begins by remarking on the number of parallel units for comparison. It then looks again at the cube designed by Bray and Thomas noted in the Introduction, before turning to relationships with epistemological issues.

The number of units for comparison
Manzon's chapter on comparing places commenced with the classic model presented by Bereday (1964) for comparison of education in two countries. The model has been widely cited and appreciated. Because it

focuses on only two countries, the model permits considerable depth of analysis.

Taking an example from East Asia, within the present volume several chapters have referred to a book which in many respects echoes the Bereday model. The book focused on a pair of Special Administrative Regions (SARs) within a single country rather than on a pair of countries; but the SARs operated with strong autonomy in many domains including education, and in this respect were arguably similar to countries. The book, edited by Bray and Koo (2004), focused on Hong Kong and Macao. It contained 15 chapters focusing on sub-sectors of education (including preschool education; primary and secondary schooling; and teacher education), political, economic and social issues (including church, state and education; higher education and the labour force; and language and education); curriculum policies and processes (including curriculum reform; and civic and political education); and a concluding section (with chapters on methodology, and on continuity and change in education). A book with 323 pages focusing on two small places is able to cover its subject in considerable depth. Figure 15.1 is a representation of such a 'thick' two-location study.

Figure 15.1: Diagrammatic Representation of a Two-Location Comparative Study

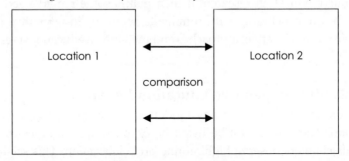

An alternative model puts education in one location at the centre of analysis and then makes comparisons as appropriate with other locations. Taking another example which concerns Hong Kong, a special issue of the journal *Comparative Education* illustrates this model. Entitled *Education and Political Transition: Implications of Hong Kong's Change of Sovereignty* (Bray & Lee 1997), the work focused on Hong Kong's 1997 transition at the close of the colonial era, and contained comparisons with transitions of other colonies including Fiji, Nigeria, Rhodesia and Singapore. Data on the territory at the focus of discussion were detailed, while the data on other places were thin. Figure 15.2 is a representation of a comparative study of this type.

Figure 15.2: Diagrammatic Representation of a Comparative Study with a Single Location in the Centre

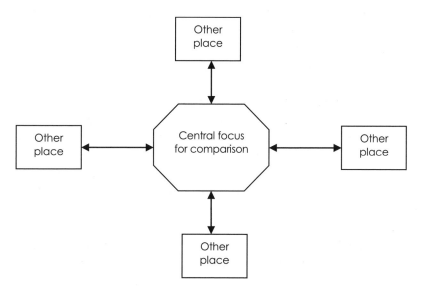

A third variation resembles the Hong Kong and Macao comparison but has more locations. An example is a book entitled *Education and Development in East Asia* (Morris & Sweeting 1995), which has separate chapters on China, Hong Kong, Japan, Macao, Malaysia, Singapore, South Korea, and Taiwan. Although these countries and jurisdictions varied widely in size of population, educational provision and economic strength, separate chapters of roughly equal length were devoted to each. A comparative study designed in this way could not achieve the depth of the book which focused only on Hong Kong and Macao, but achieved greater breadth and thus a wider vision. Figure 15.3 is a simplified diagrammatic representation of this type of study (only showing arrows between pairs of locations, though of course many other arrows could be shown to indicate multiple comparisons within the group).

Figure 15.3: Diagrammatic Representation of an Eight-Location Comparative Study

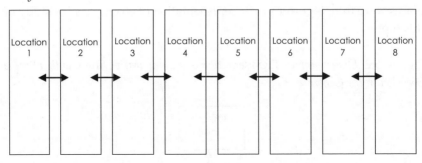

Continuing along the scale would be a study of many more locations, such as the Trends in International Mathematics and Science Study (TIMSS) mentioned in Chapter 14. TIMSS 2003 focused on Grade 4 mathematics achievement in 25 countries or systems, and on Grade 8 mathematics achievement in 46 countries or systems (Mullis et al. 2005). Figure 15.4 is a diagrammatic representation of the Grade 4 study (with arrows omitted), and begins to resemble a forest rather than a group of trees. This impression would be even stronger in a diagram of the 46 countries and systems in the Grade 8 study; and TIMSS 2011 took the pattern further still with 63 countries and systems (Mullis et al. 2012).

Figure 15.4: Diagrammatic Representation of a 25-Location Comparative Study

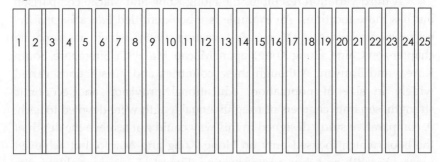

With so many units for analysis, the data on individual countries and systems in TIMSS and similar studies are inevitably shallow. However, the large number of cases has methodological advantages. The TIMSS studies were conducted under the auspices of the International Association for the Evaluation of Educational Achievement (IEA), which, in addition to the discussion in Chapter 14, has been mentioned in several chapters of this book. Thus, Fairbrother in Chapter 3 highlights the IEA studies of literacy achievement; and Lee and Manzon in Chapter 9 focus on the IEA studies of civic education. Parallel work has been conducted by the Organisation for Economic Co-operation and Development (OECD) in its Programme for International Student Assessment (PISA). Such studies can amass a systematic body of evidence through standardised questionnaires, and thus can permit directly comparable judgements about countries and groups of countries. They can also permit comparisons at many other levels, including classroom, school, district and province. The collection of data from multiple settings provides benchmarks for policy makers.

On the other side, the weaknesses of the studies included the difficulty of ensuring comparable samples, negotiating questions that fit different cultures, and achieving adequate translations across languages. Also, the analyses are commonly reduced to numerical scores and correlations, losing much of the qualitative flavour that helps to explain patterns. With such factors in mind, the PISA team have also prepared reports on single countries that draw on the large-scale comparative data but also have much qualitative material (see e.g. OECD 2011a, 2011b, 2012). OECD videos of education have enhanced the qualitative dimension. Some of these videos have a country-level focus, e.g. for Brazil, Germany, Japan, Netherlands, and Poland, while others have had a sub-national focus, e.g. on Flanders (Belgium), Ontario (Canada) and Shanghai (China).

Further questions for researchers when deciding on the number of units for comparison concern the capacity to undertake the work. Large international surveys are usually undertaken by teams rather than by individual scholars, since such surveys require considerable labour and commonly demand knowledge of many cultures and languages. Individual researchers can of course undertake valuable secondary analysis of the data generated by large teams; but original research cannot usually be undertaken by individual researchers when it demands data collection in many countries. Thus, the choice of model for comparative study may be shaped by the availability of human, financial and other resources as well as by considerations of breadth and depth.

Finally, when researchers are designing projects they need to consider access to information. The TIMSS and PISA surveys are in most cases undertaken either directly by the governments in the countries concerned or by teams working in collaboration with the governments. This assists in gaining access to the schools controlled by those governments. However, other researchers many feel unable or unwilling to operate with and through governments. Indeed certain types of research would be more difficult if the persons to whom the researchers wished to talk perceived a link with governments. This would especially be the case if the research focused on activities which are not consistent with government regulations and ideologies. In such cases, researchers would have to find alternative means of access. Cross-national work may be assisted by NGOs and other bodies that work across national boundaries, but researchers can also find other channels including personal contacts.

Revisiting the Bray and Thomas cube
The multilevel model devised by Bray and Thomas in the mid-1990s noted that much research in comparative education focused primarily on cross-national comparisons, and pointed out the benefits of also considering intranational comparisons. The model has been widely cited, and has helped to develop the field in new directions. It is thus worth evaluating two decades later, to see what refinements and extensions can usefully be made.

At the core of the model is the cube reproduced as Figure 0.1 in the Introduction. The face of the cube presented a set of geographical/locational levels: from world regions or continents through countries, provinces, districts and schools to classrooms and individuals. A second axis located the dimensions of comparison in terms of nonlocational demographic groups, such as ethnicity, age, religion and gender; and the third axis incorporated substantive educational issues such as curriculum, teaching methods, finance, management structures, political change, and the labour market.

Within this book, Manzon's chapter explicitly addresses the front face of the cube. Manzon notes that the geographic classification could be expanded to include clusters of countries based on colonial history, economic alliances, and religion. With respect to colonial history, for example, territories in Sub-Saharan Africa may be categorised as former British, French or Portuguese colonies; and regional economic blocks could include the European Union (EU) and members of the North American Free Trade Agreement (NAFTA). Religious groupings could include countries dominated by Islam compared with countries dominated by Christianity, Buddhism and/or other beliefs. Geographic entities on the cube could also include cities and/or villages. These aspects could easily be included in the cube through addition of categories on the front face.

Presentation on the cube of units which do not occupy contiguous geographic space might seem more problematic; but even this can be conceptualised within the cube. Thus, in line with Chapter 5 and taking the system rather than the country as the unit of analysis, Flemish-speaking schools in Belgium could be compared with French-speaking schools because those individual schools occupy physical space and the systems can be conceived geographically as the sum of the physical spaces occupied by the schools even if the spaces are not contiguous. A similar remark would apply to institutions and systems serving families of different classes, races, genders and cultures, as discussed in Chapters 7 and 8. Perhaps more challenging would be conceptualisation of education which is conducted over the internet and which therefore exists in cyber space rather than physical space; but even in those lessons the learners and the teachers occupy physical spaces, which means that the geographic territory could be taken as the aggregate of these physical spaces.

Thus, perhaps the only chapter in Part II of this book which represents a unit of analysis which cannot be covered in the cube is Chapter 6 on comparing times. Comparisons across time were in fact considered by Bray and Thomas (1995, p.474), though in order to permit focus on the main thrusts of the article were relegated to a footnote. An early draft of the article included a diagram showing the cube three times, for past, present and future, as in Figure 15.5. In this case, the shaded box represents a comparison of curriculum for a single state/province at three points in time. Of course the labels could easily be changed, e.g. to refer to three points in the past.

Figure 15.5: Comparisons across Time using the Bray & Thomas Cube

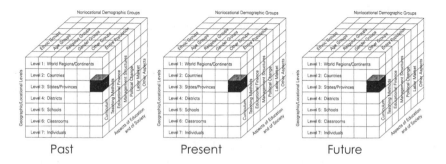

424 Mark Bray, Bob Adamson & Mark Mason

The categories listed on the cube could be broken down into sub-categories for comparison. For example, the study of Hong Kong's education system outlined in Chapter 5 focuses on the state and private providers of education, the different media of instruction, and the diverse curricula. However, a decision to map these sub-categories on the cube in advance would run the risk of prescription. Certainly researchers may sometimes benefit from fixing the points for comparison at the outset – for instance, if the study is an evaluative comparison designed to address specific issues. Researchers using a hermeneutic or an inductive approach would probably prefer the sub-categories to emerge from the data.

Nevertheless, while these remarks seem to leave the cube intact and to demonstrate that it is robust in a conceptual sense, it must be recognised that, especially in quantitative research, the cube is best employed conceptually since, especially at the upper levels, the number of units is insufficient for random selection and statistical analysis.

Further, one important point in the earlier chapters of the present book concerns the nature of the categories. In a number of cases, remarks have been made about the 'slipperiness' of some units of comparison when a clear definition is attempted. For example, as noted in Chapter 11 curriculum can be viewed as embracing the whole learning experience or simply a body of knowledge to be studied. This problem of sharp definition is most clearly explained by Manzon in Chapter 4. She suggests that the levels on the front face of the cube, and by implication perhaps also the categories on the other two faces, should in many circumstances be seen as having blurred and perhaps permeable boundaries. In Manzon's words (pp.129-130):

> The different levels of geographic units, while distinct are not disjointed, hermetically sealed spaces. Rather, they are like ecological environments, conceived as a set of nested structures, each inside the next.... The higher and lower geographic levels mutually influence and shape each other as in a 'dialectic of the global and the local'.... A recognition and understanding of the mutual relationships across each of the spatial levels is indispensable for a holistic comprehension of the essence of educational phenomena.

With this in mind, perhaps even better than blurred boundaries would be ones that are in continuous dynamic flux. Sobe and Kowalczyk (2014) would want to "explode the cube" in order to pre-empt the deployment of pre-existing categories of context. An alternative approach adopted by

Wiseman and Huang (2011), at least for understanding education re-search on policy reform in a particular country, is replacement of the faces of the cube by themes, topics and methods of change. This, they have asserted (pp.13-14) permits:

> amorphous sets of sociocultural factors, empirical quantitative and qualitative evidence, and intangible relationships and cultures [to] work through cube-like clouds carving out a space across these fac-tors, forces, and issues, which are both defined by these strata within our framework but also uninhibited by them.

Other researchers may find such frameworks difficult to grasp; but they do at least bring new ideas and consideration of alternative possibilities.

Epistemological approaches

Of course consideration of models goes far beyond mere counting of units for comparison and identification of geographic levels on the face of a cube – or even working through cube-like clouds. Models in a broader sense include more fundamental epistemological approaches. As ob-served in Chapter 2, the field of comparative education embraces a wide range of paradigms, some of which were mapped by Paulston as repro-duced in Figure 2.2. Some researchers who favour particular paradigms barely communicate with researchers who favour other paradigms. In-stead they live in separate academic worlds dominated by different con-ceptual models which are commonly incompatible.

As such, continuing the remarks about the Bray and Thomas cube, it may be noted that the cube is in itself more a descriptive model for clas-sifying (existing) comparative studies than an instrument for recom-mending researchers to investigate particular types of comparison. The model does encourage researchers to consider multilevel analyses, but even that is not always essential. Nevertheless, good comparative educa-tion researchers may usefully consider factors along each of the axes be-fore they isolate the variables pertinent to their hypotheses. In order to do this, researchers need to relate methods to the appropriateness of the epistemological approach selected, i.e. to ask whether the epistemological framework and its methodological correlate are likely to generate the desired type of investigation. This in turn requires researchers to consider the purposes and contexts of their studies. Such considerations relate to the normative questions that are always associated with research in the social sciences. The questions arise from the discourses that inform specific studies, and thus the values that inform or drive those studies.

Researchers will stand more chance of identifying sources of variance if they design their studies after they have formulated hypotheses about what might cause the variance. It may seem a trivial example, but the designers of the IEA studies of reading literacy would be unlikely to seek variance in levels of ability by comparing the eye colours of pupils. This is because they would probably have a theory, before they even began the study, about what factors might or might not influence reading ability. However, they could well have found that shoe size or the numbers of light bulbs in the home were both quite strongly correlated with reading ability. This is because each of these variables may be a proxy for other more pertinent factors, like age, and therefore level of individual development (in the case of shoe size), or socioeconomic status (in the case of light bulbs). The point is that apparently irrelevant or trivial factors might or might not be relevant, and that researchers cannot begin their research designs until they have formulated hypotheses about the relevance or otherwise of these factors.

A further dimension concerns the ways in which researchers themselves interact with and interpret their data. Social sciences refer to perspectives which are emic (culture-bound, based on intrinsic, indigenous definition and distinction of values) or etic (cross-cultural, based on extrinsic, outsider definition and distinction of values). At first glance, it would appear that the etic perspective has more to offer comparative studies. The Bereday model implied that researchers could and should remain detached and objective. Yet as noted by Arthur (2004, p.1), this could only be achieved by researchers who investigate countries in which they have not had any previous experience – and this would commonly be considered disadvantageous in the field of comparative education since so much depends on contextual understanding. Arthur observed (p.4) that in practice most comparative research requires construction of understanding and building of bridges (see also Crossley 2000, 2006), and that this in turn requires interaction and personalisation of research.

From these remarks it will be evident that the number of cases considered in parallel, or the number of levels considered in a cube, cannot themselves provide appropriate hypotheses. Researchers should therefore set out epistemological issues alongside whatever model they select for their studies, so that method and approach inform each other. Researchers need theoretically-informed perspectives both on what they are looking at and on what they are looking for, and they need hypotheses about the axes along which various elements for investigation might be differentially distributed. These hypotheses then lead to choices of the appropriate domains to assess and, if appropriate, measure.

Emphases in Comparative Education Research

The above discussion leads to further consideration of emphases within the broad field of comparative education. The Introduction to this book noted that different decades have brought evolution and shifts. Kazamias and Schwartz (1977, p.151) suggested that despite uncertainties during the 1950s when the foundations were consolidated for comparative education as a respected field of studies, it was possible to identify both authoritative spokesmen and texts which defined the contours and subject matter of the field. By the mid-1970s, Kazamias and Schwartz felt, the coherence had been lost: there was "no internally consistent body of knowledge, no set of principles or canons or research that are generally agreed upon by people who associate themselves with the field". A similar view was presented a decade later by Altbach and Kelly (1986, p.1).

However, many commentators have subsequently presented much more optimistic appraisals, commonly viewing diversity as an asset as much as a weakness (e.g. Kubow & Fossum 2007, pp.18-24; Rust et al. 2009, p.133). Ninnes and Mehta (2004, p.1) viewed positively the eclecticism which "incorporates a range of theories and methods from the social sciences and intersects a range of subfields, including sociology of education, educational planning, anthropology of education, economics of education and education and development". In related vein, Arnove (2013, p.12) has noted the "continued vitality and growth" of the field, adding (p.14) that this vitality "depends on strengthening dialogue with one another and welcoming diverse approaches to gathering and analyzing data on education-society relations".

Chapter 2 in this book considered a survey by Foster et al. (2012), who had analysed articles published in four major English-language journals. They highlighted the tendency of scholars in the field to address macro issues much more than micro ones, and also to neglect themes such as information and communication technology, education leadership, examinations, and textbooks. The analysis built on those by Rust et al. (1999) and Wolhuter (2008), who found that a large proportion of articles were based on literature review and qualitative methods. Nevertheless, both studies observed a diversification of paradigms. Rust et al. noted (p.106) that "comparative educators would tend to see reality as somewhat subjective and multiple, rather than objective and singular"; and that "comparative educators would tend not to see research as value free and unbiased; rather, they would accept the notion that their research is value laden and includes the biases of the researcher". The chapters in this book fit with these statements. The chapters themselves are based mostly on literature review, though the literature which the authors cover is both quantitative and qualitative; and all chapters either implicitly or explicitly recognise the role of the researcher in selection and interpretation of data.

Also important to note is that the surveys by Rust et al. (1999), Wolhuter (2008) and Foster et al. (2012) were based on journals that were published only in English and only in two countries. Those journals did attract authors who were competent in other languages and based in other countries; but again the processes of self-selection are likely to have generated biases. Survey of journals and other activities of the 39 professional societies which are members of the World Council of Comparative Education Societies (WCCES) would indicate that each has its own characteristics and emphases not only in theoretical or applied orientation but also in the choice of topics for investigation.

Elaborating on the matter of topics, even cursory analysis would show for example that gender issues are a much stronger feature of conference presentations and other outputs of the US-based Comparative and International Education Society (CIES) than in the Japan Comparative Education Society (JCES). On another dimension, a much greater proportion of scholars in the British Association for International and Comparative Education (BAICE) is interested in Africa than is the case among the members of the Korean Comparative Education Society (KCES); and issues of postcolonial identity are much more likely to be discussed in the conferences of the Australian and New Zealand Comparative and International Education Society (ANZCIES) than in the Ukraine Comparative Education Society (UCES). These differences partly reflect leadership in the societies concerned, but also reflect differences in international links among particular countries as a result of languages, governments' foreign policies, and historical ties through colonialism or other forces. Also, major differences exist in the paradigmatic emphases of academic literatures written for example in Chinese, English, Korean, Russian and Spanish. For these and other reasons, it is often more appropriate, as observed by Cowen and Kazamias (2009, p.1295) quoted in the Introduction to this book, to note the co-existence of multiple comparative educations than to suppose that the field is unified and homogeneous (see also Cowen 1990, p.322; Cowen 2000, p.333; Manzon 2010, p.83; Wiseman & Anderson 2013, pp.221-226).

At the same time, many people who undertake comparative studies of education are not members of these professional bodies and perhaps do not even identify with the field. Chapter 1 noted that categories of people who undertake comparative studies include policy makers and employees of international agencies as well as academics. Policy makers are usually interested only in experiences elsewhere from which they think that practical lessons might be learned. International agencies are also expected to be practical, so that they might give appropriate advice to their clients. As such, policy makers and international agencies are much less likely than academics to be concerned with theories; and even among academics, some groups build their careers more strongly on consultancies and other practical work than on theoretical conceptualisation. With the advent of globalisation, government policy making and consultancy work are much more likely than before to have international dimensions; but, perhaps regrettably, such practitioners are relatively unlikely to identify with the field of comparative education or to use the tools associated with the field.

Finally, it is instructive to note continuities and changes as reflected in the contents of the present book. The themes in Parts I and III of the book, which include quantitative and qualitative approaches and issues of paradigmatic identity, echo much existing literature; and the units of analysis in Part II also all have antecedents. However, each chapter also brings a contemporary flavour and new insights; and the book brings some conceptual advance in the field. The juxtaposition of units of analysis in the 11 chapters in Part II was much welcomed by readers of the first edition of this book, and has been retained in the second edition. Certainly many scholars have undertaken comparisons in education across places, systems, times, cultures, etc., as is evident in the bibliographic references of each chapter. However, no previous book had undertaken commentary on units of analysis in quite the way that has been presented here.

In addition, new themes in the book arise from the sorts of geomorphic shifts identified in Chapter 2. Political and economic realignments have impacted on comparative education as much as on other fields, and have determined the choices of countries on which external scholars have focused. Chapter 2 contrasted the visibility of China in international comparative education conferences and literature during the 1970s and the opening years of the present century. The growth of attention to China reflects not only that country's open-door policy but also its increased economic strength. With Shanghai appearing as a distinct entity in PISA studies – and ranking at the top on important indicators – much attention has focused on a specific part of China as well as on the country as a whole.

Further, scholars have explored new combinations for analyses. Chapter 4 described a study which juxtaposed scores on school tests in individual states of the USA with scores in a range of countries elsewhere in the world. It also noted a study which took sub-national regions within different countries as the unit of analysis, comparing education and development in Northeast Brazil with patterns in Northeast Thailand. On different dimensions, Chapter 12 has compared pedagogical innovations, and Chapter 13 has compared ways of learning. Such studies have taken the field a long way beyond the straightforward comparisons of patterns in whole countries which dominated for many years.

Enduring Threads

Despite these remarks, many conceptual dimensions of the field of comparative education remain as valid as they have always been. For example, Chapter 1 cited the well-known phrase of Sadler, who wrote in 1900 (reprinted 1964, p.310) about the value of studying foreign systems of education in order to become "better fitted to study and understand our own". This can be related to an equally well-known statement by Johann Wolfgang Goethe who wrote (quoted by Rust 2002, p.54): "He who knows nothing of foreign languages, knows nothing about his own".

In turn, this perspective can be related to the role of comparative enquiry in "making strange patterns familiar, and familiar patterns strange". The first part of this clause is about looking outwards, i.e. learning about patterns, usually in other places, that are unfamiliar. The second part of the clause is about reflection, challenging taken-for-granted assumptions about familiar patterns which may need to be called into question (see Spindler & Spindler 1982, p.43; Choksi & Dyer 2011, p.271).

Nearly a century after Sadler, Watson (1996, p.387) recognised ambiguity and plurality within the field of comparative education, but added that:

> there is little doubt that comparative education research has led to a substantial increase in our understanding of, and awareness of, educational systems and processes in different parts of the world; of the infinite variety of aims, purposes, philosophies and structures; and of the growing similarities of the issues facing educational policy-makers across the world.

Watson highlighted the wealth of statistical and other data available around the world – and since that time the volume and quality of data have increased substantially. Moreover, the access to such data has also greatly increased, in particular through the internet. Watson rightly added, however, that such data, information and knowledge are "not easily understood or analysed". In this he perceived a role for comparative education:

> Perhaps more significant than anything else ... is the realisation that education and development, education and social change and the impact of educational reform on society are far more complex than was originally thought.

This remark deserves underlining and elaboration. Many observers consider that one of the most important uses of comparative education research is the identification of models that are employed elsewhere and that can be imported for use in other settings. This is indeed a major practical reason for comparative study; but dangers exist in shallow treatment with methodological approaches that are not sound. Within the field of comparative education, this has long been recognised. Again to cite Sadler, writing in 1900 (reprinted 1964, p.310):

> We cannot wander at pleasure among the educational systems of the world, like a child strolling through a garden, and pick off a flower from one bush and some leaves from another, and then expect that if we stick what we have gathered into the soil at home, we shall have a living plant.

Yet this lesson needs repeating in multiple settings and on multiple occasions, since the temptations are strong to make simplistic analyses and to copy models that are perceived to have worked well in other settings.

Thus, while comparative education research can indeed help politicians and others to identify practice elsewhere that could have domestic application, such research should also indicate the complexities involved.

In order to do this well, comparative education researchers need to pay close attention to both the choice and the application of methods. Care needs to be taken with the complexities of educational comparison and transfer discussed above, and sloppy research can be betrayed by linguistic and cultural pitfalls. Comparative studies of middle schools, for example, need to acknowledge that in the United Kingdom a 'middle school' bridges primary and secondary education. This is very different from China, where the term (*zhongxue* 中学) refers to an institution between primary and higher education, i.e. a secondary school. Again, in Hong Kong, the nature, roles and purposes of the secondary school History curricula (there are two) are very unlike those of the History curricula of the USA, for instance. The greater access to data afforded by the internet does not mean that the researcher's guard can slip in ensuring the accuracy of the information thus obtained, even if the source is purportedly reliable. Academic rigour is of paramount importance. Some parts of the field of comparative education are regrettably amateurish and, because of that, possibly even dangerous.

This book has not provided, and has not sought to provide, a manual on specific ways to use particular tools; but it has presented an overview of the types of tools in the toolbox and of major contextual considerations which should influence the choices of tools. If the book has encouraged its readers to think more carefully about the field and about its strengths, challenges and potential, then it will have achieved its purpose.

References

Altbach, Philip G. & Kelly, Gail P. (1986): 'Introduction: Perspectives on Comparative Education', in Altbach, Philip G. & Kelly, Gail P. (eds.), *New Approaches to Comparative Education*. Chicago: The University of Chicago Press, pp.1-10.

Andere, Eduardo (2008): *The Lending Power of PISA: League Tables and Best Practice in International Education*. CERC Monographs in Comparative & International Education & Development 6, Hong Kong: Comparative Education Research Centre, The University of Hong Kong.

Arnove, Robert F. (2013): 'Introduction: Reframing Comparative Education: The Dialectic of the Global and the Local', in Arnove, Robert F.; Torres, Carlos Alberto & Franz, Stephen (eds.), *Comparative Education: The Dialectic of the Global and the Local*. 4th edition, Lanham: Rowman & Littlefield, pp.1-25.

Arthur, Lore (2004): 'Bridging Gaps and Clearing Pathways: Towards the Construction of Intercultural Meaning'. Paper presented at the 12th World Congress of Comparative Education Societies, Havana, Cuba, 25-29 October.

Bereday, George Z.F. (1964): *Comparative Method in Education*. New York: Holt, Rinehart & Winston.

Bray, Mark & Koo, Ramsey (eds.) (2004): *Education and Society in Hong Kong and Macao: Comparative Perspectives on Continuity and Change.* CERC Studies in Comparative Education 7, 2nd edition, Hong Kong: Comparative Education Research Centre, The University of Hong Kong.

Bray, Mark & Lee, W.O. (eds.) (1997): *Education and Political Transition: Implications of Hong Kong's Change of Sovereignty.* Special issue of *Comparative Education*, Vol.33, No.2, pp.157-169; reprinted as CERC Studies in Comparative Education 2, Hong Kong: Comparative Education Research Centre, The University of Hong Kong.

Bray, Mark & Thomas, R. Murray (1995): 'Levels of Comparison in Educational Studies: Different Insights from Different Literatures and the Value of Multilevel Analyses'. *Harvard Educational Review*, Vol.65, No.3, pp.472-490.

Choksi, Archana & Dyer, Caroline (2011): 'North-South Collaboration in Educational Research: Reflections on Indian Experience', in Crossley, Michael & Vulliamy, Graham (eds.), *Qualitative Educational Research in Developing Countries: Current Perspectives*. New York: Garland, pp. 265-299.

Cowen, Robert (1990): 'The National and International Impact of Comparative Education Infrastructures', in Halls, W.D. (ed.), *Comparative Education: Contemporary Issues and Trends*. Paris: UNESCO, and London: Jessica Kingsley, pp.321-352.

Cowen, Robert (2000): 'Comparing Futures or Comparing Pasts?'. *Comparative Education*, Vol.36, No.3, pp.333-342.

Cowen, Robert & Kazamias, Andreas M. (2009): 'Conclusion', in Cowen, Robert & Kazamias, Andreas M. (eds.), *International Handbook of Comparative Education*. Dordrecht: Springer, pp.1295-1296.

Crossley, Michael (2000): 'Bridging Cultures and Traditions in the Reconceptualisation of Comparative and International Education'. *Comparative Education*, Vol.36, No.3, pp.319-332.

Crossley, Michael (2006): 'Bridging Cultures and Traditions: Perspectives from Comparative and International Research in Education'. Inaugural Professorial Lecture, University of Bristol, 9 February.

Crossley, Michael & Jarvis, Peter (2000): 'Introduction: Continuity and Change in Comparative and International Education'. *Comparative Education*, Vol.36, No.3, pp.261-265.

Foster, Jesse; Addy, Nii Antiaye & Samoff, Joel (2012): 'Crossing Borders: Research in Comparative and International Education'. *International Journal of Educational Development*, Vol.32, No.6, pp.711-732.

Kazamias, Andreas M. & Schwartz, Karl A. (1977): 'Introduction'. *Comparative Education Review*, special issue on 'The State of the Art', Vol.21, Nos.2 & 3, pp.151-152.

Kubow, Patricia K. & Fossum, Paul R. (2007): *Comparative Education: Exploring Issues in International Context*. 2nd edition, Upper Saddle River: Pearson Merrill Prentice Hall.

Manzon, Maria (2010): 'Shape-shifting of Comparative Education: Towards a Comparative History of the Field', in Larsen, Marianne A. (ed.), *New Thinking in Comparative Education: Honouring Robert Cowen*. Rotterdam: Sense, pp.83-101.

Meyer, Heinz-Dieter & Benavot, Aaron (eds.) (2013): *PISA, Power and Policy: The Emergence of Global Educational Governance*. Oxford: Symposium.

Morris, Paul & Sweeting, Anthony (eds.) (1996): *Education and Development in East Asia*. New York: Garland.

Mullis, Ina V.C.; Martin, Michael O. & Foy, Pierre (2005): *IEA's TIMSS 2003 International Report on Achievement in the Mathematics Cognitive Domains: Findings from a Developmental Project*. Chestnut Hill: TIMSS & PIRLS International Study Center, Boston College.

Mullis, Ina V.C.; Martin, Michael O.; Foy, Pierre & Alka, Arora (2012): *TIMSS 2011 International Results in Mathematics*. Chestnut Hill: TIMSS & PIRLS International Study Center, Boston College.

Ninnes, Peter & Mehta, Sonia (2004): 'A Meander through the Maze: Comparative Education and Postfoundational Studies', in Ninnes, Peter & Mehta, Sonia (eds.), *Re-imagining Comparative Education: Postfoundational Ideas and Applications for Critical Times*. New York: RoutledgeFalmer, pp.1-18.

OECD (2011a): *Strong Performers and Successful Reformers in Education: Lessons from PISA for the United States*. Paris: Organisation for Economic Co-operation and Development (OECD).

OECD (2011b): *Strong Performers and Successful Reformers in Education: Education Policy Advice for Greece*. Paris: Organisation for Economic Co-operation and Development (OECD).

OECD (2012): *Strong Performers and Successful Reformers in Education: Lessons from PISA for Japan States*. Paris: Organisation for Economic Co-operation and Development (OECD).

Pereyra, Miguel A.; Kotthof, Hans-Georg & Cowen, Robert (eds.) (2011): *PISA Under Examination: Changing Knowledge, Changing Tests, and Changing Schools*. Rotterdam: Sense.

Phillips, David & Schweisfurth, Michele (2008): *Comparative and International Education: An Introduction to Theory, Method and Practice*. London: Continuum.

Rust, Val D. (2002): 'The Meanings of the Term Comparative in Comparative Education'. *World Studies in Education*, Vol.3, No.1, pp.53-67.

Rust, Val D.; Johnstone, Brian & Allaf, Carine (2009): 'Reflections on the Development of Comparative Education', in Cowen, Robert & Kazamias, Andreas M. (eds.), *International Handbook of Comparative Education*. Dordrecht: Springer, pp.121-139.

Rust, Val D.; Soumaré, Aminata; Pescador, Octavio & Shibuya, Megumi (1999): 'Research Strategies in Comparative Education'. *Comparative Education Review*, Vol.43, No.1, pp.86-109.

Sadler, Sir Michael (1900): 'How Far can we Learn Anything of Practical Value from the Study of Foreign Systems of Education?'. Reprinted 1964 in *Comparative Education Review*, Vol.7, No.3, pp.307-314.

Sobe, Noah W. & Kowalczyk, Jamie (2014): 'Exploding the Cube: Revisioning "Context" in the Field of Comparative Education'. *Current Issues in Comparative Education*, Vol.17, No.1.

Spindler, George & Spindler, Louise (1982): 'Roger Harker and Schönhausen: From Familiar to Strange and Back Again', in Spindler, George (ed.), *Doing the Ethnography of Schooling: Educational Anthropology in Action*. New York: Holt, Rinehart & Winston, pp.20-46.

Watson, Keith (1996): 'Comparative Education', in Gordon, Peter (ed.), *A Guide to Educational Research*. London: Woburn Press, pp.360-397.

Wolhuter, C.C. (2008): 'Review of the Review: Constructing the Identity of Comparative Education'. *Research in Comparative and International Education*, Vol.3, No.4, pp.323-344.

Wiseman, Alexander W. & Anderson, Emily (2013): 'Diversification of the Field', in Wiseman, Alexander W. & Anderson, Emily (eds.), *Annual Review of Comparative and International Education 2013*. Bingley: Emerald, pp.221-226.

Wiseman, Alexander W. & Huang, Tiedan (2011): 'The Development of Comparative Education Research on Chinese Educational Policy Reform: An Introduction', in Huang, Tiedan & Wiseman, Alexander W. (eds.), *The Impact and Transformation of Education Policy in China*. Bingley: Emerald, pp.1-18.

Contributors

Bob ADAMSON is a Professor at the Hong Kong Institute of Education, and was formerly Director of the Comparative Education Research Centre at the University of Hong Kong. He is also a Past President of the Comparative Education Society of Hong Kong. He has taught in schools and colleges in mainland China and in Hong Kong, at the Queensland University of Technology, Australia, and at Liverpool Hope University, UK. He teaches and publishes in the fields of English language teaching, applied linguistics, curriculum studies and comparative education. *Correspondence*: Department of International Education and Lifelong Learning, Hong Kong Institute of Education, 10 Lo Ping Road, Tai Po, Hong Kong, China. E-mail: badamson@ied.edu.hk.

Mark BRAY is Director of the Comparative Education Research Centre and UNESCO Chair Professor in Comparative Education at the University of Hong Kong. He has taught at that University since 1986. Between 2006 and 2010 he took leave to work in Paris as Director of UNESCO's International Institute for Educational Planning (IIEP). He is also a Past President of the Comparative Education Society of Hong Kong, and a Past President and Past Secretary General of the World Council of Comparative Education Societies (WCCES). He previously taught in secondary schools in Kenya and Nigeria, and at the Universities of Edinburgh, Papua New Guinea and London. *Correspondence*: Comparative Education Research Centre, Faculty of Education, The University of Hong Kong, Pokfulam Road, Hong Kong, China. E-mail: mbray@hku.hk.

Gregory P. FAIRBROTHER is Associate Professor in the Department of Social Sciences at the Hong Kong Institute of Education. He completed his doctoral studies at the University of Hong Kong, and has been engaged in research on citizenship (moral, political, ideological, national) education in China and Hong Kong for over 15 years. Among his research foci is how the Chinese state develops and promotes its legitimacy claims by "demonstrating paternalism" in citizenship education. Another project explores how citizens in Hong Kong, where a stronger individualism characterizes the state-citizen-education relationship, have resisted perceived state attempts to import a paternalistic approach to national education by activating an institutionalized myth of indoctrination. *Correspondence*: Department of Social Sciences, Hong Kong Institute of Education, 10 Lo Ping Road, Tai Po, Hong Kong, China. E-mail: gfairbro@ied.edu.hk.

Liz JACKSON is an Assistant Professor and member of the Comparative Education Research Centre at the University of Hong Kong. Prior to joining this university, she managed policy for the Higher Colleges of Technology, with 17 campuses across the United Arab Emirates, and served as a policy consultant to regional offices of the South African Department of Education (North-West Province and KwaZulu-Natal). Her primary areas of research include philosophy of education, multicultural education, and civic education, with a focus on curricular representation of ethnic and religious minorities. She is the author of *Muslims and Islam in U.S. Education: Reconsidering Multiculturalism* (2014). *Correspondence*: Comparative Education Research Centre, Faculty of Education, The University of Hong Kong, Pokfulam Road, Hong Kong, China. E-mail: lizjackson@hku.hk

JIANG Kai is an Associate Professor and an Assistant Dean in the Graduate School of Education of Peking University. He is also the Coordinator of the UNESCO Chair in Higher Education for the Asia-Pacific Region. He has worked as a post-doctoral fellow at the Comparative Education Research Centre at the University of Hong Kong. He is the former Managing Editor of the *Peking University Education Review*. His doctoral thesis for Peking University focused on higher education in the USA; and he has also written extensively on aspects of methodology in educational research. *Correspondence*: Graduate School of Education, Peking University, Beijing 100871, China. E-mail: kjiang@pku.edu.cn.

Nancy LAW is a Professor at the University of Hong Kong. She is currently Deputy Director of the Centre for Information Technology in Education (CITE), after serving as its Founding Director for 15 years from 1998. She is also the corresponding co-convenor of the Sciences of Learning Strategic Research Theme. She has served on the

Editorial and Publication Committee of the International Associa-
tion for the Evaluation of Educational Achievement (IEA), the
Technology Working Group of the Cisco-Intel-Microsoft Project on
Assessment and Teaching of 21st Century Skills, and the Board of
Directors of the International Society of the Learning Sciences.
Correspondence: Centre for Information Technology in Education,
Faculty of Education, The University of Hong Kong, Pokfulam
Road, Hong Kong, China. E-mail: nlaw@hku.hk.

Lee Wing On is Dean of Education Research at the National Institute of
Education, Singapore. He was the founding Director of the Com-
parative Education Research Centre at the University of Hong
Kong, and is a Past President of the World Council of Comparative
Education Societies. He has served at the Hong Kong Institute of
Education as Vice President (Academic), Deputy to the President,
Chair Professor of Comparative Education, Founding Dean of the
School of Foundations in Education, Head of two Departments,
and founding Head of the Citizenship Education Centre. In 2005,
he was invited by the University of Sydney to be Professor of Ed-
ucation at the Faculty of Education and Social Work and Director
(International) at the College of Humanities and Social Sciences.
Correspondence: Office of Education Research, National Institute of
Education, 1 Nanyang Walk, Singapore 637616. E-mail: wingon.lee@
nie.edu.sg.

Frederick K.S. Leung is a Professor in the Faculty of Education of the
University of Hong Kong and was Dean of the Faculty between
1996 and 2002. His major research interests are in the comparison of
mathematics education in different countries, and in the influence
of culture on teaching and learning. He is principal investigator of
the Hong Kong component of the Trends in International Mathematics and Science Study (TIMSS). He is one of the editors of the
second and third International Handbooks on Mathematics Education. He was also a member of the Executive Committee of the International Commission on Mathematical Instruction (ICMI) and
the Standing Committee of the International Association for the
Evaluation of Academic Achievement (IEA). He was awarded the
Freudenthal Medal 2013, and a Fulbright Scholarship in 2003. *Correspondence*: Faculty of Education, The University of Hong Kong,
Pokfulam Road, Hong Kong, China. E-mail: frederickleung@
hku.hk.

Maria MANZON is a Research Scientist at the National Institute of Education, Singapore. She is Chair of the Admissions and New Societies Standing Committee of the World Council of Comparative Education Societies (WCCES). She was previously a Research Associate of the Comparative Education Research Centre at the University of Hong Kong. She was co-editor of a volume of histories of comparative education societies (2007), and of another volume about comparative education in universities worldwide (2008). Her 2011 book entitled *Comparative Education: The Construction of a Field* has been acclaimed for its comprehensive approach and path-breaking conceptualisation. *Correspondence*: Office of Education Research, National Institute of Education, 1 Nanyang Walk, Singapore 637616. Email: maria.manzon@nie.edu.sg.

Mark MASON is a Senior Programme Specialist at UNESCO's International Bureau of Education (IBE) in Geneva, and Professor at the Hong Kong Institute of Education. He is the former Editor of the *International Journal of Educational Development*. He is also a Past President of the Comparative Education Society of Hong Kong and a former Director of the Comparative Education Research Centre at the University of Hong Kong. He works in the field of comparative and international education and development, from a disciplinary background in philosophy, social theory and education studies. Prior to his current positions, he taught at the University of Hong Kong for 10 years, and before that at the University of Cape Town and at a secondary school in Cape Town. *Correspondence*: Hong Kong Institute of Education, 10 Lo Ping Road, Tai Po, Hong Kong, China. E-mail: mmason@ied.edu.hk.

Paul MORRIS worked at the University of Hong Kong from 1976 until 2002. During this time he was an elected Dean of Faculty for six years, and became a full professor in 1997. He also served on the Hong Kong Government's Education Commission and Advisory Committee on Teacher Education and Qualifications. He was President of the Hong Kong Institute of Education until 2007. He then joined the Institute of Education, University of London, where he currently works as a Professor of Education. *Correspondence*: Faculty of Policy and Society, Institute of Education, University of London, 20 Bedford Way, London WC1H 0AL, UK. E-mail: p.morris@ioe.ac.uk.

Kyungmee PARK is a Professor at Hongik University in the Republic of Korea, teaching pre-service teachers. She was a member of the PISA

Mathematics Expert Group from 1998 to 2004, and worked as a researcher at the Korean Institute of Curriculum and Evaluation, responsible for PISA in Korea. She has been involved in mathematics curriculum and textbook developments for two decades. She writes columns about mathematics and education in major daily newspapers, and has contributed to the popularisation of mathematics for the general public. *Correspondence*: Department of Mathematics Education, Hongik University, Sangsu-dong, Mapo-gul, Seoul, Republic of Korea. E-mail: kpark@hongik.ac.kr.

Anthony SWEETING taught for several decades at the University of Hong Kong, where he was also a member of the Comparative Education Research Centre. He passed away in 2008, leaving a rich legacy of scholarship in the domains of history and comparative education. Much of this work focused on Hong Kong, while other parts had international and cross-cultural components.

Jan VAN AALST is an Associate Professor and Assistant Dean (Research Proposals and Centres) in the Faculty of Education of the University of Hong Kong. He is an Associate Editor of *Journal of the Learning Sciences*, and serves on the editorial boards of several journals in science education and computer-supported learning. His research focuses on classroom studies of knowledge building. It has involved computer-mediated discourse by means of which students collaboratively work on their communities' ideas. His recent research has examined this approach in the contexts of recent curriculum reforms in Hong Kong. He has taught many courses on research methodology, science education, and learning with computers. *Correspondence*: Faculty of Education, The University of Hong Kong, Pokfulam Road, Hong Kong, China. E-mail: vanaalst@ hku.hk.

David A. WATKINS was a Professor in the Faculty of Education at the University of Hong Kong, and retired in 2009. He has formerly taught or been a full-time researcher in four universities in Australia and New Zealand. He has also been an Executive Committee member of the International Association of Applied Psychology and the International Association of Cross-Cultural Psychology. He is a cross-cultural researcher and has published widely in areas such as self-concept, student learning, and conceptions of teaching. *Correspondence*: E-mail: drdawatkins@gmail.com.

YANG Rui is a Professor at the University of Hong Kong and a former Director of the Comparative Education Research Centre. He has also taught at the University of Western Australia, Monash University (Australia) and Shantou University (China). He has undertaken many projects in the field of comparative education, and is the editor of the journal *Frontiers of Education in China*. *Correspondence*: Comparative Education Research Centre, Faculty of Education, The University of Hong Kong, Pokfulam Road, Hong Kong, China. E-mail: yangrui@hku.hk.

Index

A

achievement (educational), 4-5, 11, 25, 76, 78, 110, 115, 200-2, 205, 207-8, 213, 223-4, 260, 334, 387-412, 420
approach to learning, 369, 372
Advanced (A) Level examinations, 155
Africa, 26, 29
    Africanists, 65
aided schools, 148
Alabama, 113-4
Algeria, 107
America *See: United States of America*
Anglo-Chinese,
    Schools, 148-9
    System, 149, 151
anthropological approaches, 225, 228
anthropologist(s), 65, 224, 238-9, 244, 247
anthropology, 49, 227-9, 241, 369, 427
Approaches to Studying Inventory, 367
Arabic, 21, 30-1, 79, 82
Aristotle, 172
Arkansas, 113-4
Armenia, 408-9
Asia, 7, 24-5, 38, 55, 104, 178, 259, 261, 267, 334, 345-7,
Asia-Pacific Economic Cooperation, 105
assessment practices, 340, 345
Australia, 23-4, 33, 36, 62, 112, 121, 128, 148, 159, 262, 265, 271, 299-301, 327, 353, 367-8

Australian and New Zealand Comparative and International Education Society, 59, 428
Australian Curriculum Studies Association, 315
Austria, 36, 111

B

Bahrain, 107
Balkan States, 104
Bangladesh, 28, 79, 86
Bantu, 101, 221
Belgium, 34, 36, 111, 140
    Belgium (Flemish), 33-4, 144, 421, 423
    Belgium (French), 111, 144, 158
belief systems, 260, 313-4
Bereday, George, 1-2, 99, 106, 108, 143, 170, 387, 417-8, 426
Bhutan, 28, 234
biological trait, 196
Bologna Process, 141, 159
Book Flood Project, 83
Bosnia, 233
Botswana, 84-5
Bray and Thomas
    cube/framework/model, 8-10, 97, 102-4, 124-5, 127-8, 422-5
Brazil, 35-6, 84, 101, 109-10, 116-7, 128, 421, 430
Britain, 154
    British, 23, 101, 103, 118, 221-2, 299-300, 378, 422 *see also: England, Scotland, United Kingdom, Wales*

essentialist, 196, 199
   institutional, 197-8, 200
   postmodern, 198
rational,
   approach, 291
   perspective, 289-292
reading literacy, 78, 83, 374, 389, 391,
   408, 426
reliability, 74, 182, 225, 266, 274, 355,
   366-7, 369-70, 380
Republic of Korea, 23-4, 28, 64, 113,
   267, 349, 419
Research Assessment Exercises, 50
Rhodesia, 419
Roman Catholic church, 141, 147
Romania, 36, 273
Romansh, 115-6
Rosselló, Pedro, 2
rote learning, 374-7
Rousseau, Jean-Jacques, 172
Russia, 26, 35, 142, 242, 262, 319, 337,
   353
Russian-speaking countries, 3

S

Sadler, Sir Michael, 2, 39-40, 295, 430
Scholastic Aptitude Test (SAT), 199-
   200
school subjects, 315
Scotland, 24, 34, 110, 154-8
Senegal, 210, 353
Serbian nationalism, 233
Shanghai, 23-4, 36-7, 118, 145-6, 249,
   375, 408, 421, 430
Sigma Survey, 269
simultaneous comparison, 99, 106,
   117
Singapore, 23, 36, 121, 128, 148, 199,
   349, 353, 374, 411, 419
Sinologists, 65
Slovak Republic, 36
Slovenian, 36, 233
social construction, 197

Social Darwinism, 196
socioeconomic status (SES), 200, 203-4,
   206-7, 211, 426
sociologists (of education), 204, 206
sociology, 3, 38, 51-2, 66, 98, 241, 252,
   289, 427
South Africa, 35, 101, 196, 200, 221,
   223, 300
   Apartheid South Africa, 196, 200
   black South African, 200
South America, 103-4
South Korea *see Republic of Korea*
South Pacific, 104, 369
Southeast Asian Moralists, 270
Southern Africa, 85
Southern and Eastern African
   Consortium for Monitoring
   Educational Quality, 390, 398
Soviet Union, 61, 233
Spain, 36, 114
Special Administrative Region, 112,
   118, 147, 150, 418
specialisms, 49-50, 65
stakeholders in education, 309
stereotyping, 222-3
structuralism, 229
   structuralist, 181, 237
student practices, 342
Study Process Questionnaire, 367-71,
   376
Sub-Saharan Africa, 29, 103, 107, 422
survey research, 55, 73
Sweden, 4, 36, 223, 409
Switzerland, 2, 4, 22, 26, 30, 36, 112-7
Sydney, 64
syllogism, 374
symbolic interactionism, 253
synchronism, 168

T

Taiwan, 7, 23, 151, 153, 212, 271, 374,
   411, 419
   Taipei, 23-4, 36

CERC Studies in Comparative Education (ctd)

14. W.O. Lee, David L. Grossman, Kerry J. Kennedy & Gregory P. Fairbrother (eds.) (2004): *Citizenship Education in Asia and the Pacific: Concepts and Issues*. ISBN 978-962-8093-59-5. 313pp. HK$200/US$32.

13. Mok Ka-Ho (ed.) (2003): *Centralization and Decentralization: Educational Reforms and Changing Governance in Chinese Societies*. ISBN 978-962-8093-58-8. 230pp. HK$200/US$32.

12. Robert A. LeVine (2003, reprinted 2010): *Childhood Socialization: Comparative Studies of Parenting, Learning and Educational Change*. ISBN 978-962-8093-61-8. 299pp. HK$200/US$32.

11. Ruth Hayhoe & Julia Pan (eds.) (2001): *Knowledge Across Cultures: A Contribution to Dialogue Among Civilizations*. ISBN 978-962-8093-73-1. 391pp. [Out of print]

10. William K. Cummings, Maria Teresa Tatto & John Hawkins (eds.) (2001): *Values Education for Dynamic Societies: Individualism or Collectivism*. ISBN 978-962-8093-71-7. 312pp. HK$200/US$32.

9. Gu Mingyuan (2001): *Education in China and Abroad: Perspectives from a Lifetime in Comparative Education*. ISBN 978-962-8093-70-0. 252pp. HK$200/US$32.

8. Thomas Clayton (2000): *Education and the Politics of Language: Hegemony and Pragmatism in Cambodia, 1979-1989*. ISBN 978-962-8093-83-0. 243pp. HK$200/US$32.

7. Mark Bray & Ramsey Koo (eds.) (2004): *Education and Society in Hong Kong and Macao: Comparative Perspectives on Continuity and Change*. Second edition. ISBN 978-962-8093-34-2. 323pp. HK$200/US$32.

6. T. Neville Postlethwaite (1999): *International Studies of Educational Achievement: Methodological Issues*. ISBN 978-962-8093-86-1. 86pp. HK$100/US$20.

5. Harold Noah & Max A. Eckstein (1998): *Doing Comparative Education: Three Decades of Collaboration*. ISBN 978-962-8093-87-8. 356pp. HK$250/US$38.

4. Zhang Weiyuan (1998): *Young People and Careers: A Comparative Study of Careers Guidance in Hong Kong, Shanghai and Edinburgh*. ISBN 978-962-8093-89-2. 160pp. HK$180/US$30.

3. Philip G. Altbach (1998): *Comparative Higher Education: Knowledge, the University, and Development*. ISBN 978-962-8093-88-5. 312pp. HK$180/US$30.

2. Mark Bray & W.O. Lee (eds.) (1997): *Education and Political Transition: Implications of Hong Kong's Change of Sovereignty*. ISBN 978-962-8093-90-8. 169pp. [Out of print]

1. Mark Bray & W.O. Lee (eds.) (2001): *Education and Political Transition: Themes and Experiences in East Asia*. Second edition. ISBN 978-962-8093-84-7. 228pp. HK$200/US$32.

Order through bookstores or from:

Comparative Education Research Centre
Faculty of Education, The University of Hong Kong, Pokfulam Road, Hong Kong, China.
Fax: (852) 2517 4737   E-mail: cerc@hku.hk   Website: http://cerc.edu.hku.hk

The list prices above are applicable for order from CERC, and include sea mail postage. For air mail postage costs, please contact CERC.

No. 7 in the series and Nos. 13-15 are co-published with Kluwer Academic Publishers and the Comparative Education Research Centre of the University of Hong Kong. Books from No. 16 onwards are co-published with Springer. Springer publishes hardback and electronic versions.

CERC Studies in Comparative Education 29

Comparative Education:
The Construction
of a Field

Maria Manzon

Publishers: Comparative Education Research
Centre and Springer
ISBN 978-988-17852-6-8
2011; 295 pages
Price: HK$200 / US$32

This book is a remarkable feat of scholarship — so remarkable in fact that I put it in the same league as the great classics of the field that had so much to do with setting the direction of Comparative Education. Indeed, this volume goes further than earlier classics to reveal, through textual analysis and interviews with key figures, how the epistemological foundations of the field and crucial professional developments combined to, as the title indicates, construct Comparative Education.

Manzon's work is indispensable — a word I do not use lightly — for scholars who seek a genuine grasp of the field: how it was formed and by whom, its major theoreticians, its professional foundations, and so on. Clearly too, this book marks the rise of a young star, Maria Manzon, who shows promise of joining the ranks of our field's most illustrious thinkers.

Erwin H. Epstein
Director, Center for Comparative Education
Loyola University, Chicago, USA

Maria Manzon is a Research Associate of the Comparative Education Research Centre (CERC) at the University of Hong Kong. She was Editor of CIEclopedia in 2009 and 2010, and Assistant Secretary General of the World Council of Comparative Education Societies (WCCES) in 2005.

More details:
http://cerc.edu.hku.hk/publications/cerc-studies-in-comparative-education/

CERC Monograph Series in Comparative and International Education and Development No.9

Shadow Education:
Private Supplementary Tutoring and Its Implications for Policy Makers in Asia

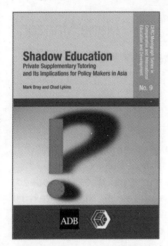

Mark Bray and Chad Lykins

Publishers:
Comparative Education Research Centre (CERC) in collaboration with Asian Development Bank (ADB)

ISBN 978-92-9092-658-0 (Print)
ISBN 978-92-9092-659-7 (PDF)

May 2012; 100 pages
This book is downloadable for free

In all parts of Asia, households devote considerable expenditures to private supplementary tutoring. This tutoring may contribute to students' achievement, but it also maintains and exacerbates social inequalities, diverts resources from other uses, and can contribute to inefficiencies in education systems.

Such tutoring is widely called shadow education, because it mimics school systems. As the curriculum in the school system changes, so does the shadow.

This study documents the scale and nature of shadow education in different parts of the region. For many decades, shadow education has been a major phenomenon in East Asia. Now it has spread throughout the region, and it has far-reaching economic and social implications.

More details:
http://cerc.edu.hku.hk/publications/cerc-monograph-series/